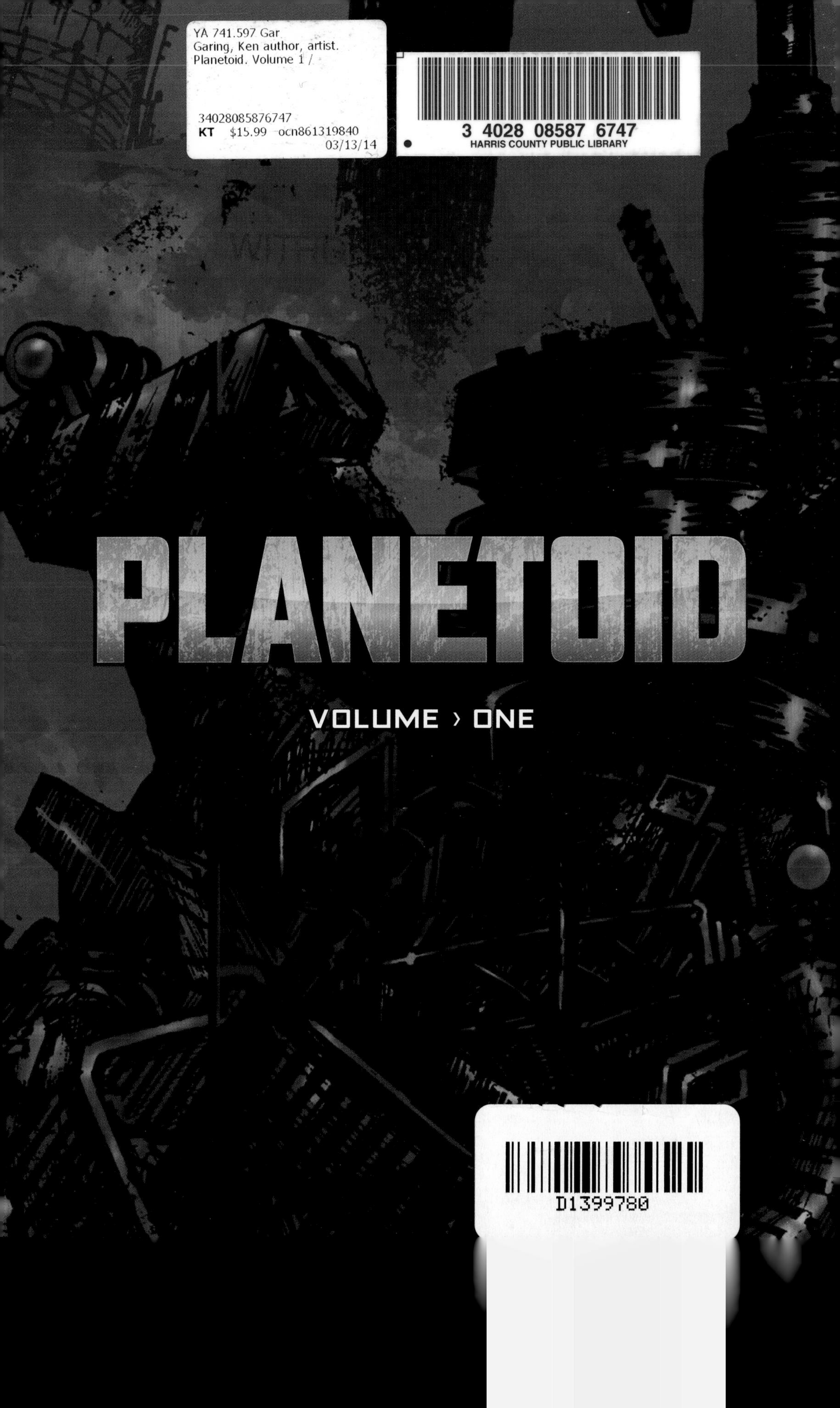
PLANETOID
VOLUME › ONE

STORY › ART › LETTERING
KEN GARING

GRAPHIC DESIGN › LOGO
DREW GILL

IMAGE COMICS, INC.
Robert Kirkman - chief operating officer
Erik Larsen - chief financial officer
Todd McFarlane - president
Marc Silvestri - chief executive officer
Jim Valentino - vice-president

Eric Stephenson - publisher
Ron Richards - director of business development
Jennifer de Guzman - pr & marketing director
Branwyn Bigglestone - accounts manager
Emily Miller - accounting assistant
Jamie Parreno - marketing assistant
Emilio Bautista - sales assistant
Jaemie Dudas - administrative assistant
Kevin Yuen - digital rights coordinator
Tyler Shainline - events coordinator
David Brothers - content manager
Jonathan Chan - production manager
Drew Gill - art director
Jana Cook - print manager
Monica Garcia - senior production artist
Vincent Kukua - production artist
Jenna Savage - production artist
Addison Duke - production artist
www.imagecomics.com

This book is dedicated with love to
my parents, Tom and Linda.

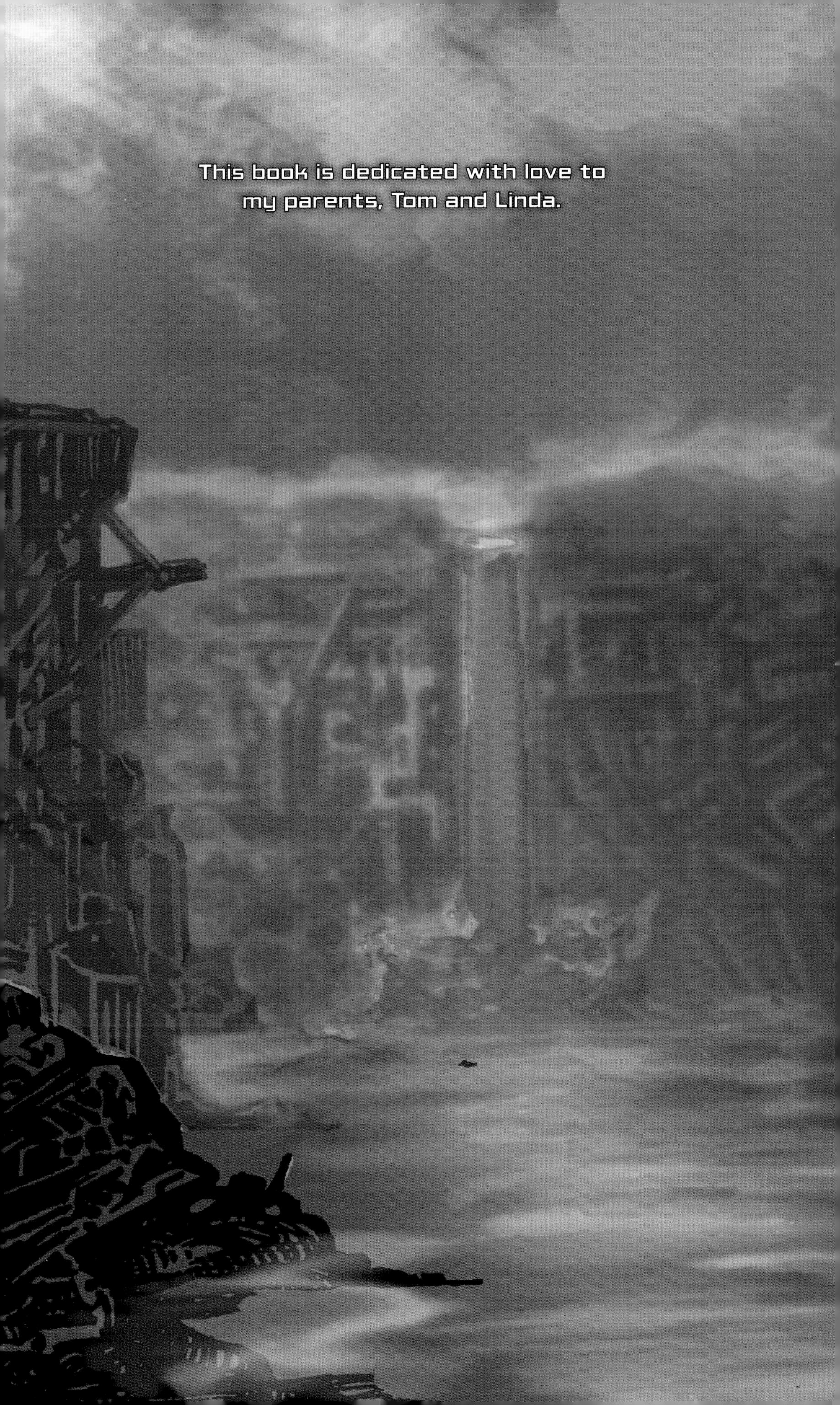

CHAPTER › ONE

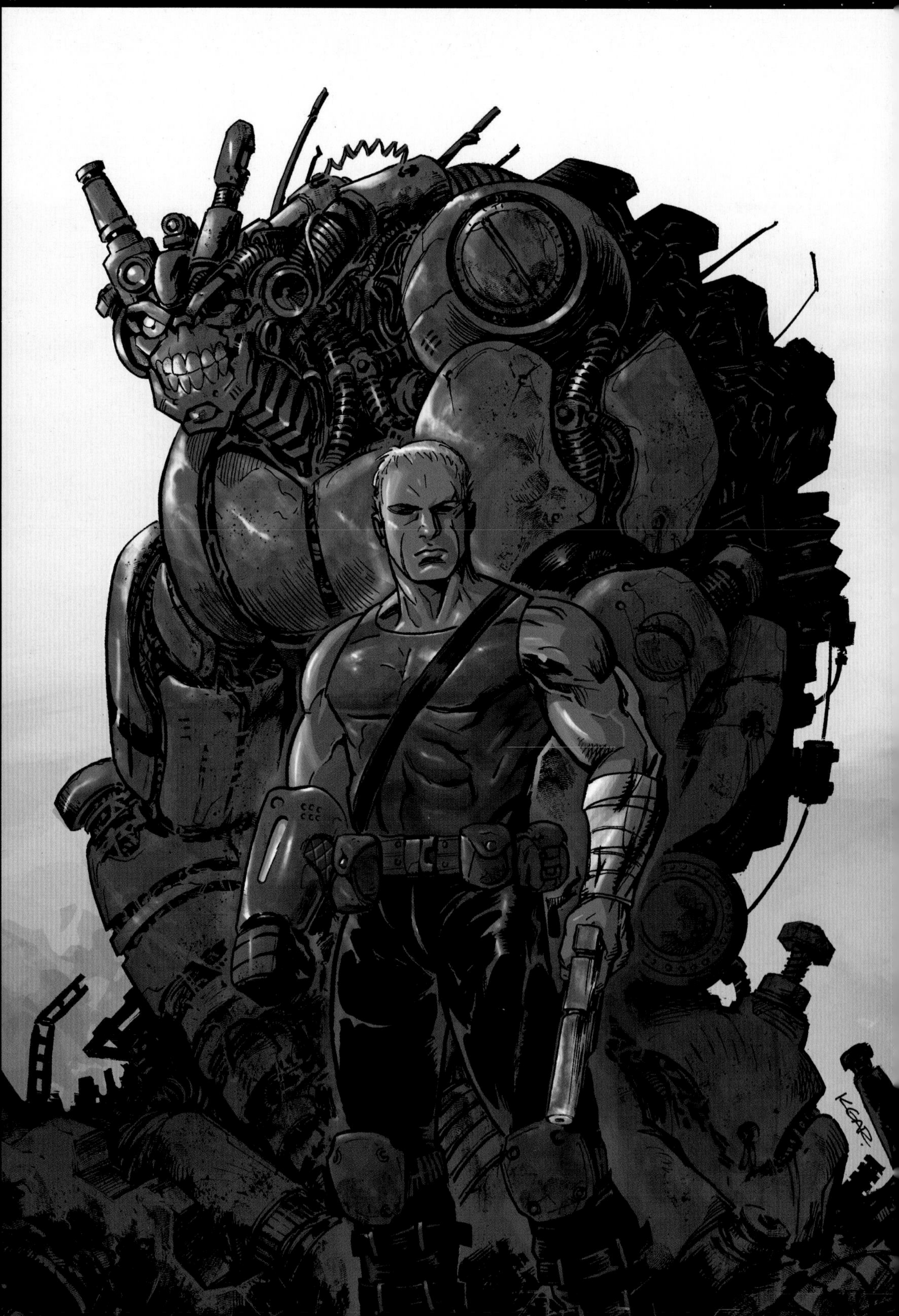

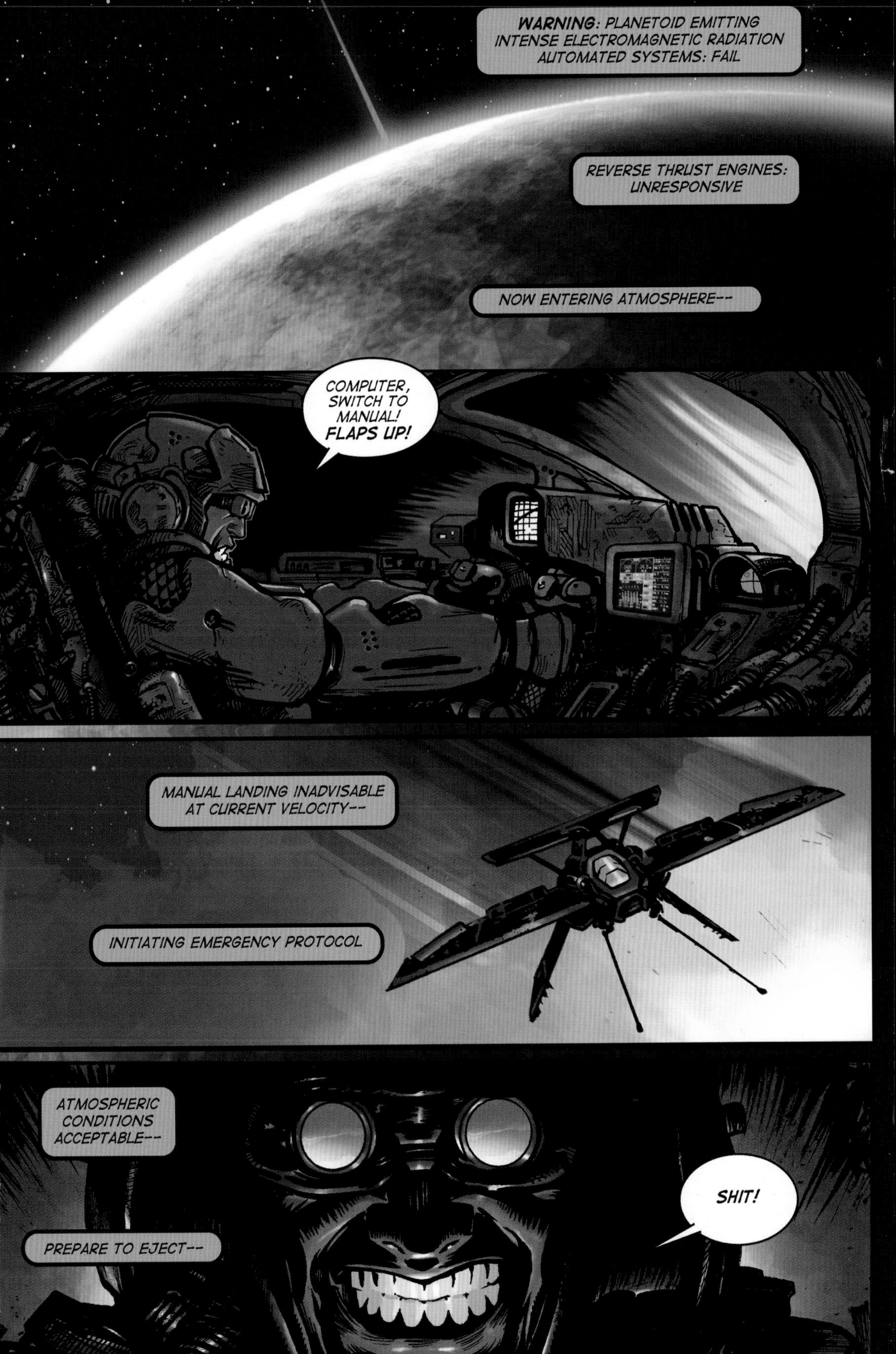
WARNING: PLANETOID EMITTING INTENSE ELECTROMAGNETIC RADIATION AUTOMATED SYSTEMS: FAIL
REVERSE THRUST ENGINES: UNRESPONSIVE
NOW ENTERING ATMOSPHERE--
COMPUTER, SWITCH TO MANUAL! FLAPS UP!
MANUAL LANDING INADVISABLE AT CURRENT VELOCITY--
INITIATING EMERGENCY PROTOCOL
ATMOSPHERIC CONDITIONS ACCEPTABLE--
PREPARE TO EJECT--
SHIT!

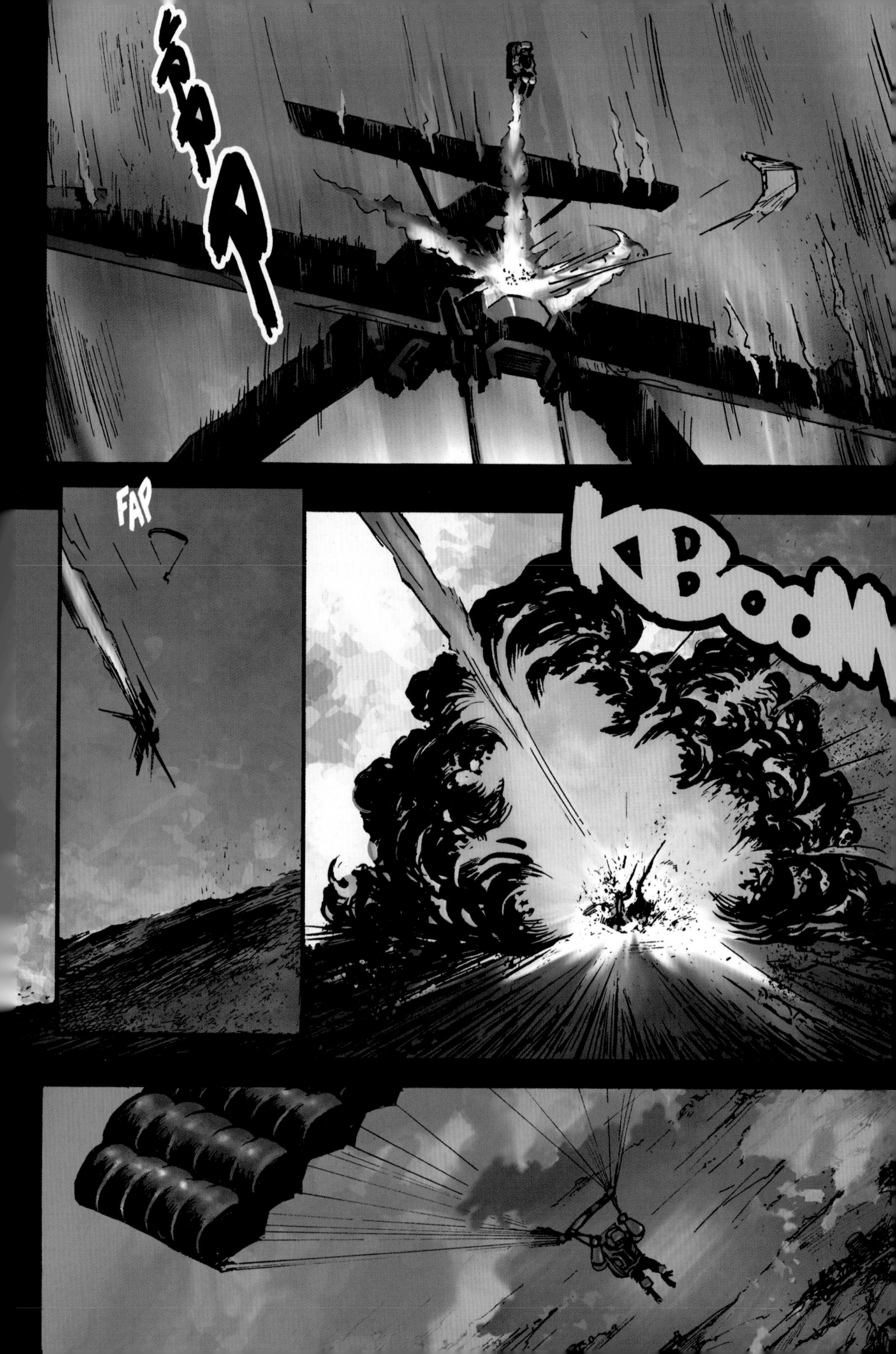
FAP
KBOOM

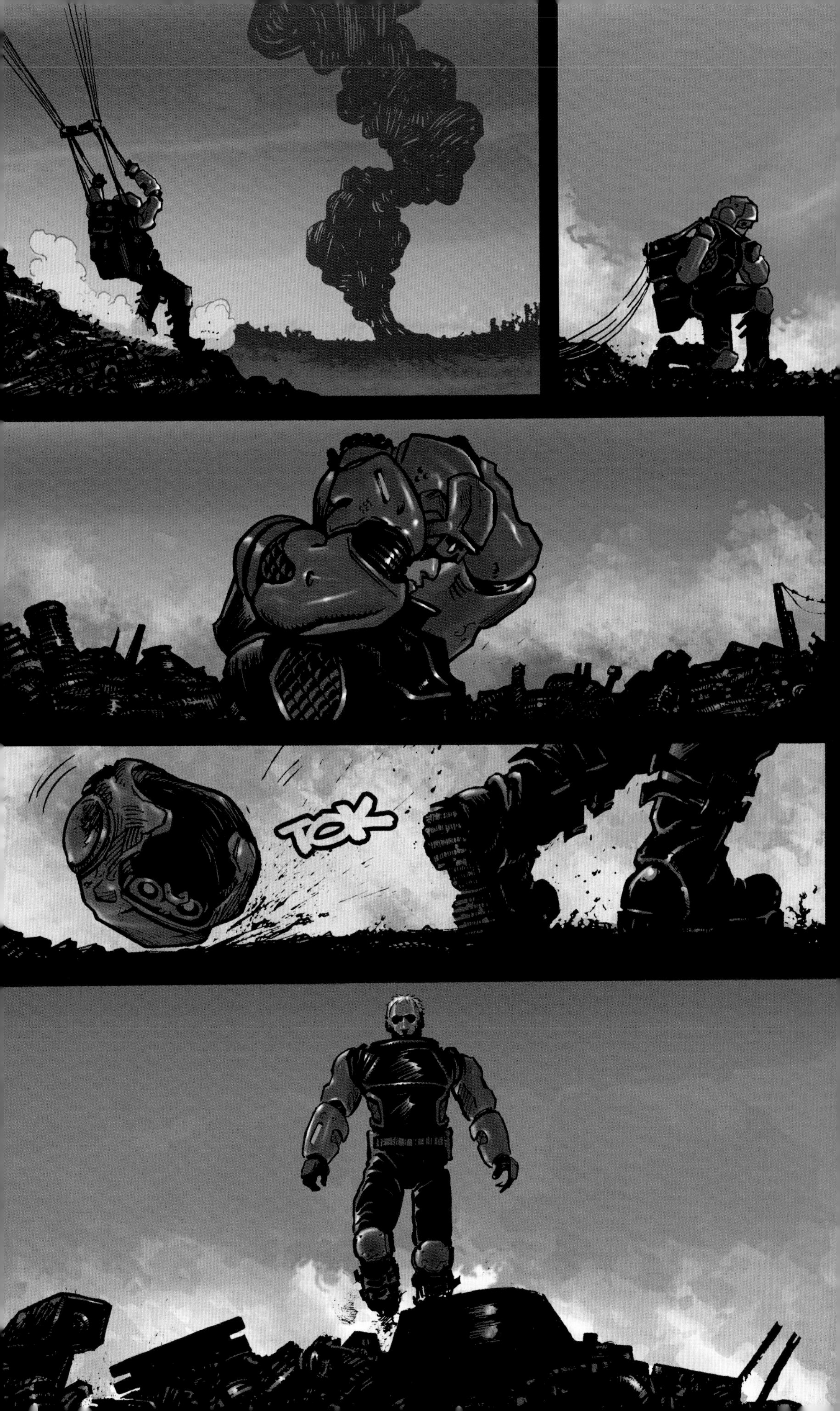
TOK

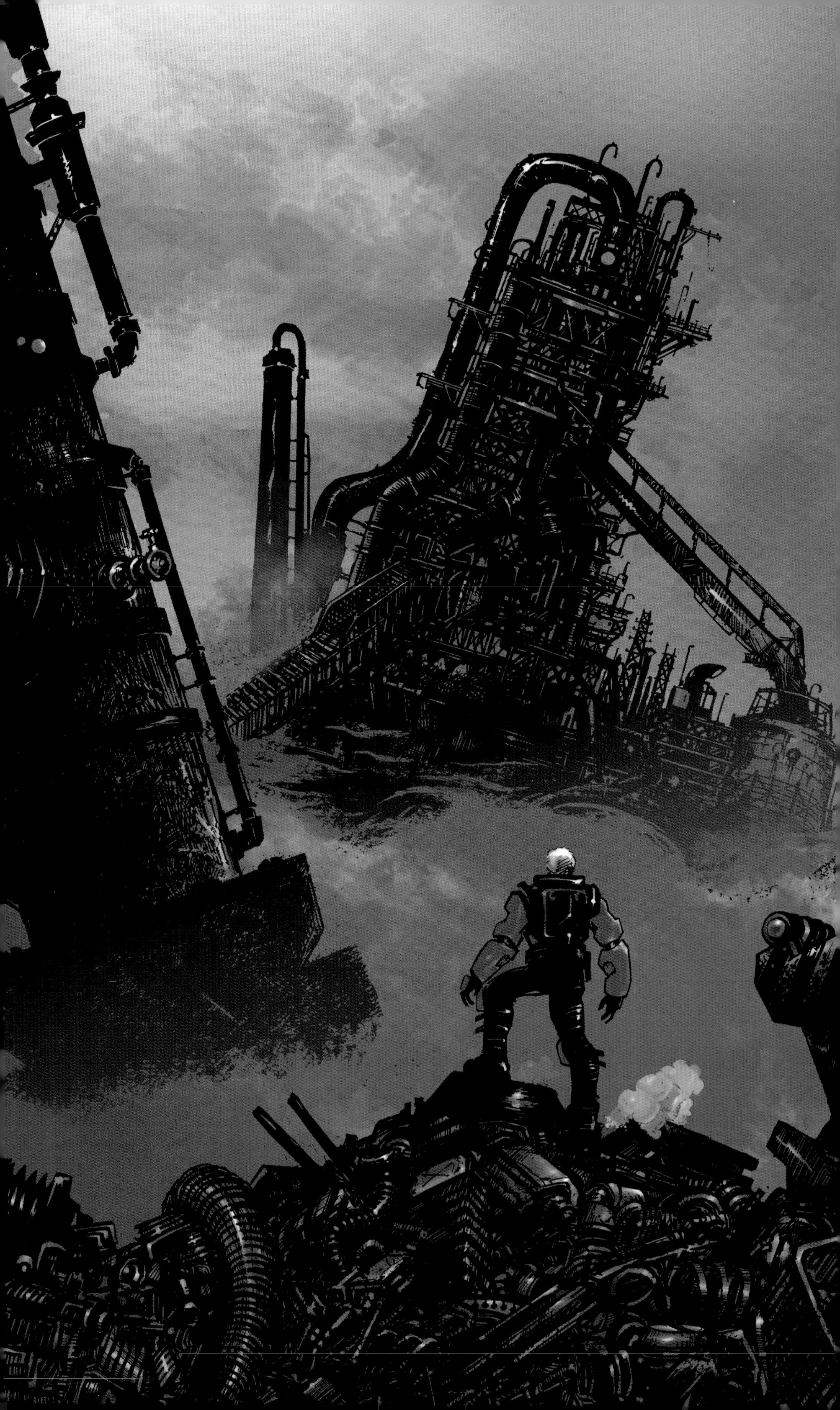

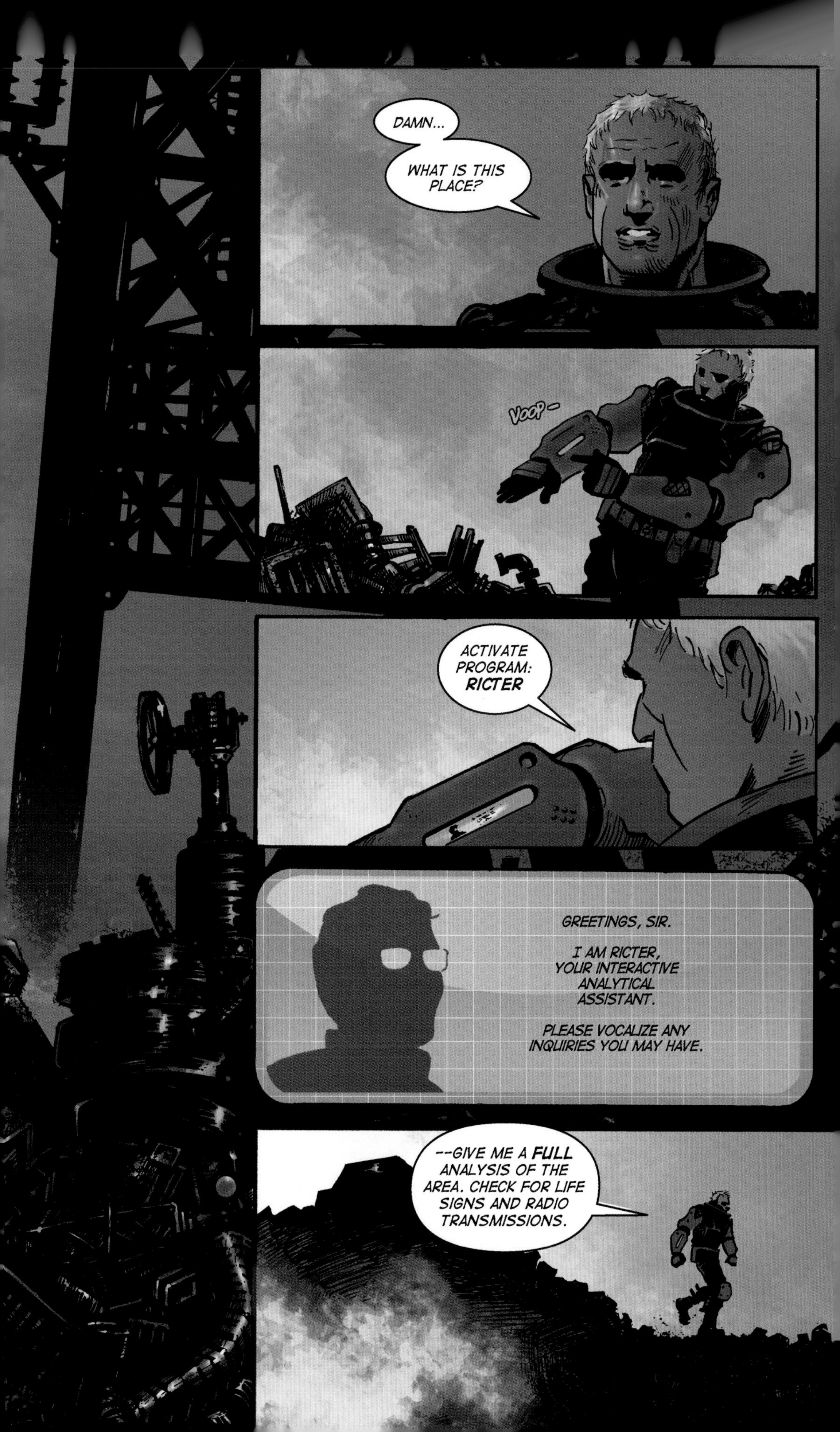
DAMN...
WHAT IS THIS PLACE?
VOOP—
ACTIVATE PROGRAM: RICTER
GREETINGS, SIR.
I AM RICTER, YOUR INTERACTIVE ANALYTICAL ASSISTANT.
PLEASE VOCALIZE ANY INQUIRIES YOU MAY HAVE.
--GIVE ME A FULL ANALYSIS OF THE AREA. CHECK FOR LIFE SIGNS AND RADIO TRANSMISSIONS.

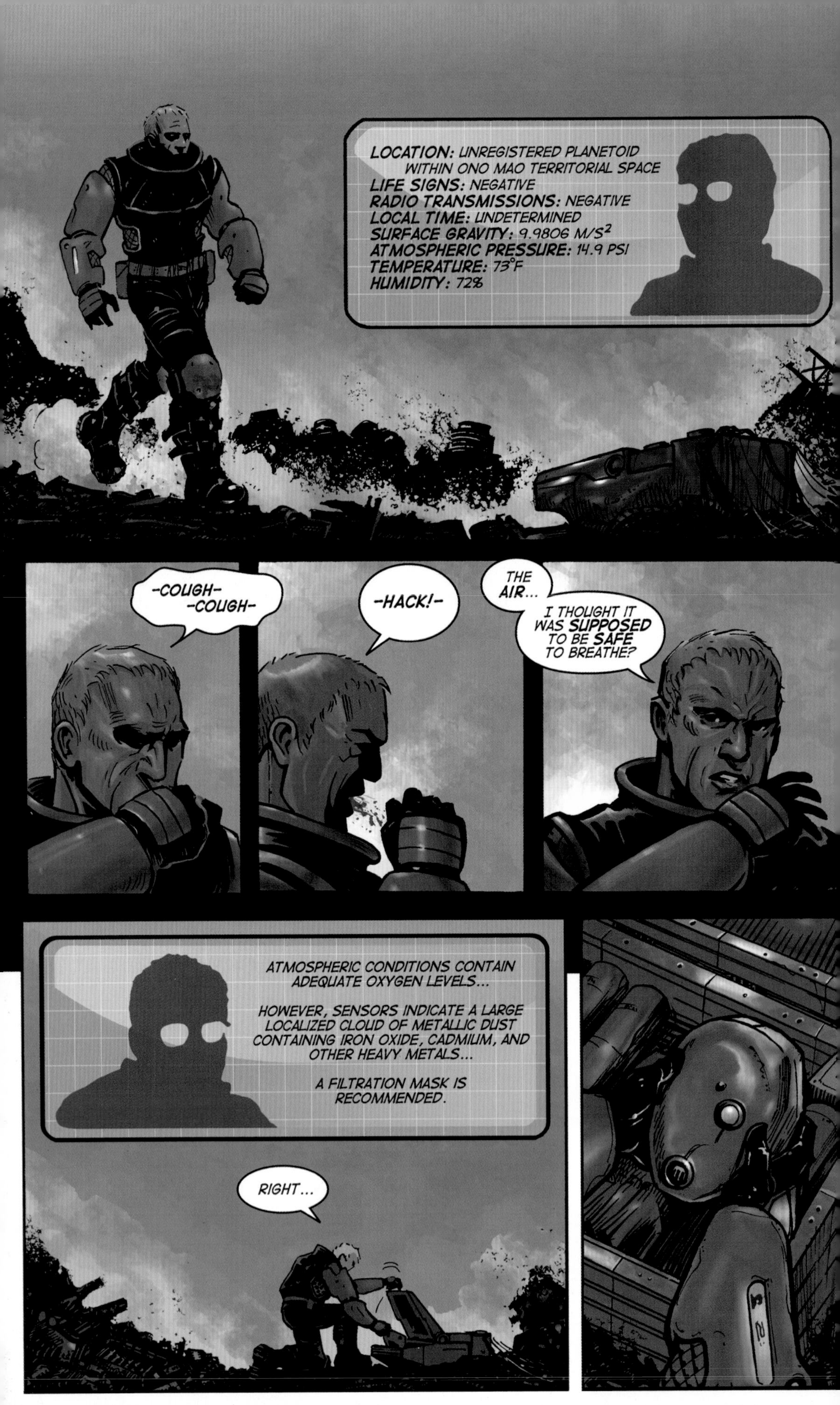
LOCATION: UNREGISTERED PLANETOID WITHIN ONO MAO TERRITORIAL SPACE
LIFE SIGNS: NEGATIVE
RADIO TRANSMISSIONS: NEGATIVE
LOCAL TIME: UNDETERMINED
SURFACE GRAVITY: 9.9806 M/S^2
ATMOSPHERIC PRESSURE: 14.9 PSI
TEMPERATURE: 73°F
HUMIDITY: 72%
-COUGH- -COUGH-
-HACK!-
THE AIR...
I THOUGHT IT WAS SUPPOSED TO BE SAFE TO BREATHE?
ATMOSPHERIC CONDITIONS CONTAIN ADEQUATE OXYGEN LEVELS...
HOWEVER, SENSORS INDICATE A LARGE LOCALIZED CLOUD OF METALLIC DUST CONTAINING IRON OXIDE, CADMIUM, AND OTHER HEAVY METALS...
A FILTRATION MASK IS RECOMMENDED.
RIGHT...

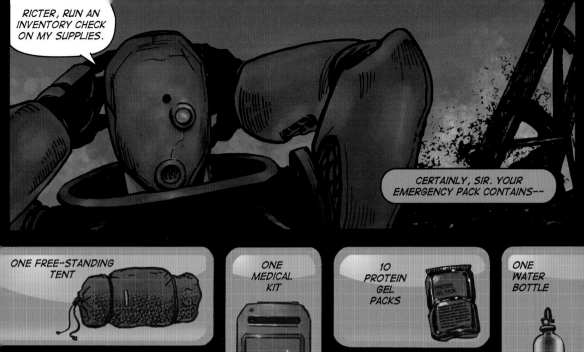

RICTER, RUN AN INVENTORY CHECK ON MY SUPPLIES.

CERTAINLY, SIR. YOUR EMERGENCY PACK CONTAINS--

ONE FREE-STANDING TENT

ONE MEDICAL KIT

10 PROTEIN GEL PACKS

ONE WATER BOTTLE

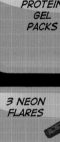

ONE CANVAS PONCHO

ONE CARRY ALL BAG

3 NEON FLARES

ONE TOOL KIT

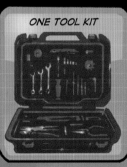

...YOUR PACK ALSO CONTAINS AN UNIDENTIFIED FIREARM.

WOULD YOU LIKE TO CATALOG THIS ITEM?

NEVERMIND THAT...

GIVE ME A COMPASS READING.

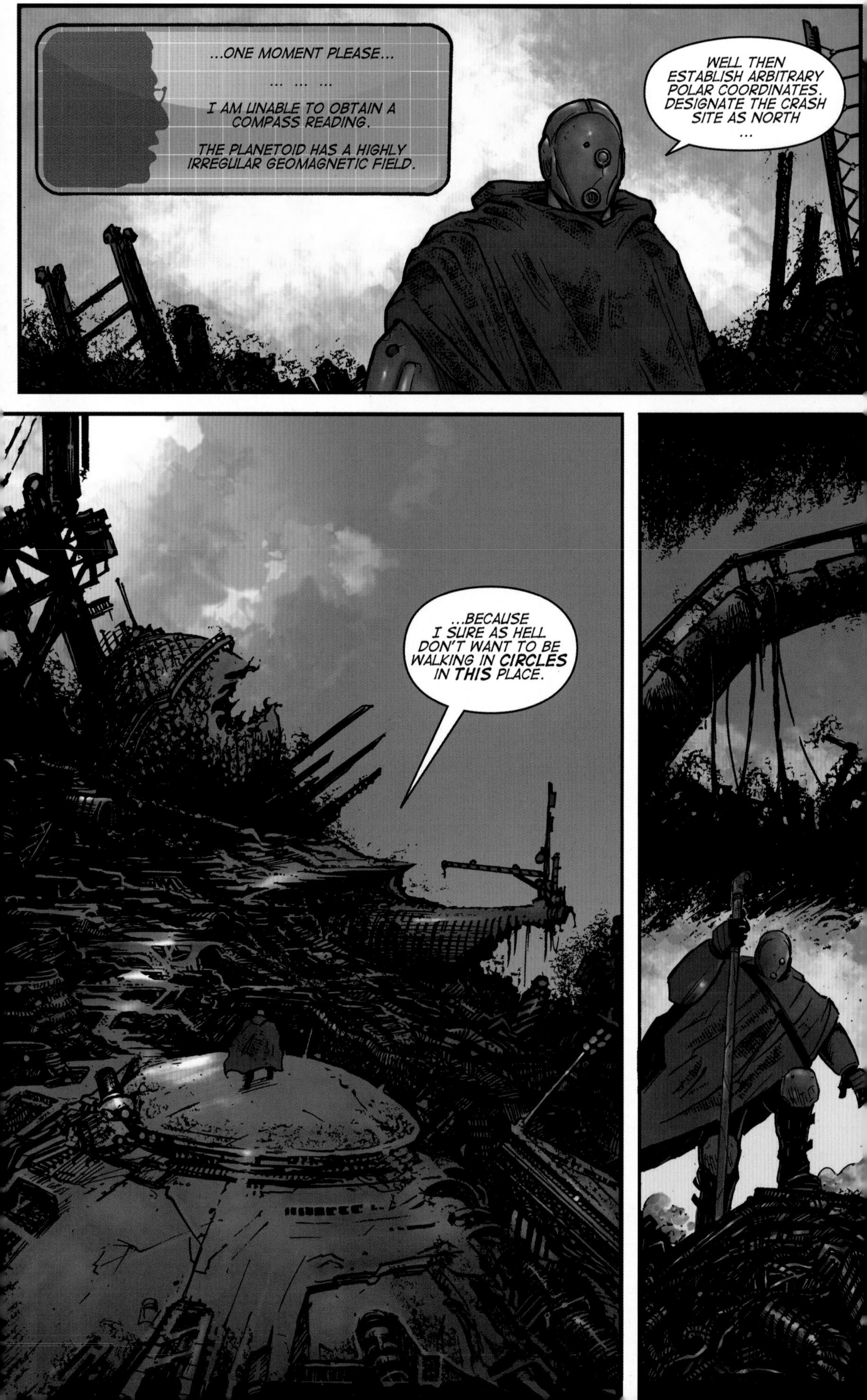
...ONE MOMENT PLEASE...
... ...
I AM UNABLE TO OBTAIN A COMPASS READING.
THE PLANETOID HAS A HIGHLY IRREGULAR GEOMAGNETIC FIELD.
WELL THEN ESTABLISH ARBITRARY POLAR COORDINATES. DESIGNATE THE CRASH SITE AS NORTH ...
...BECAUSE I SURE AS HELL DON'T WANT TO BE WALKING IN CIRCLES IN THIS PLACE.

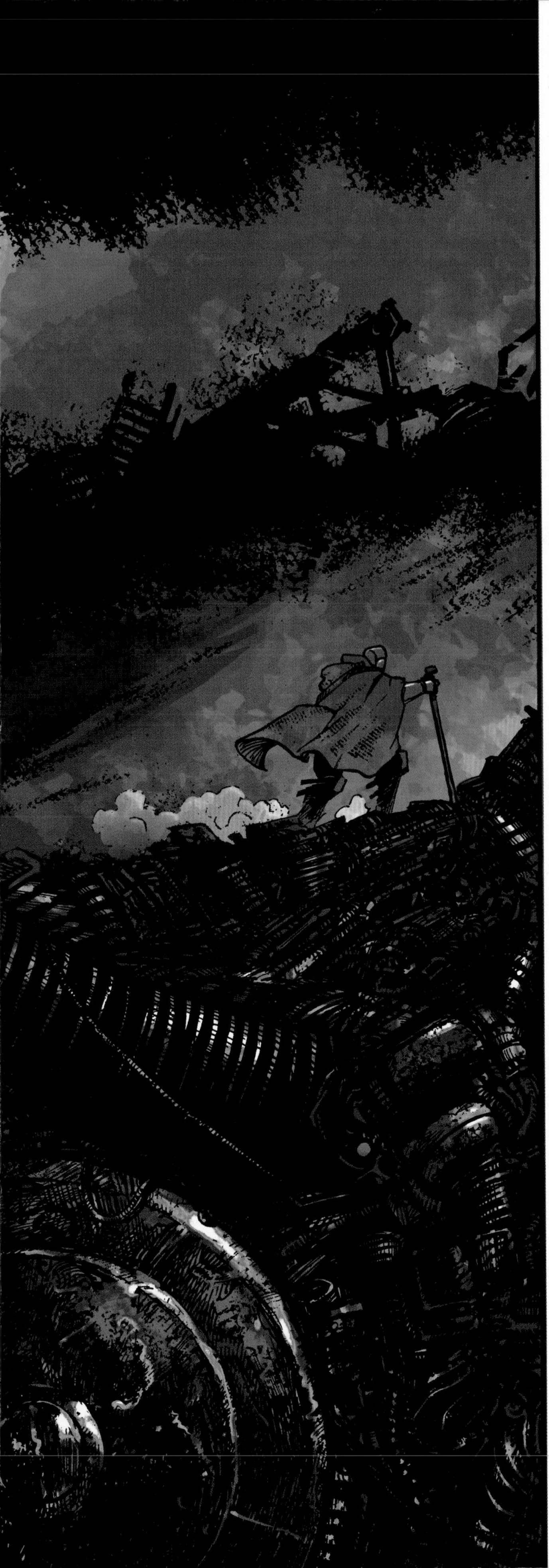
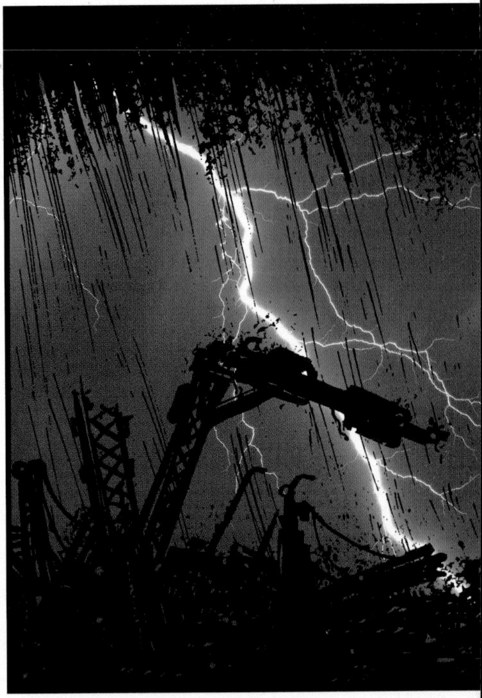
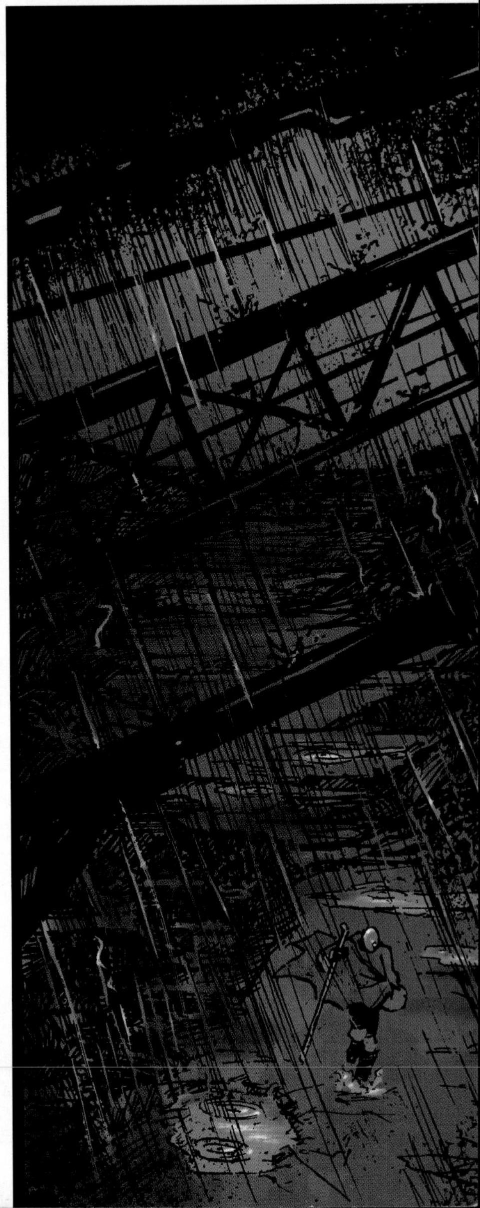

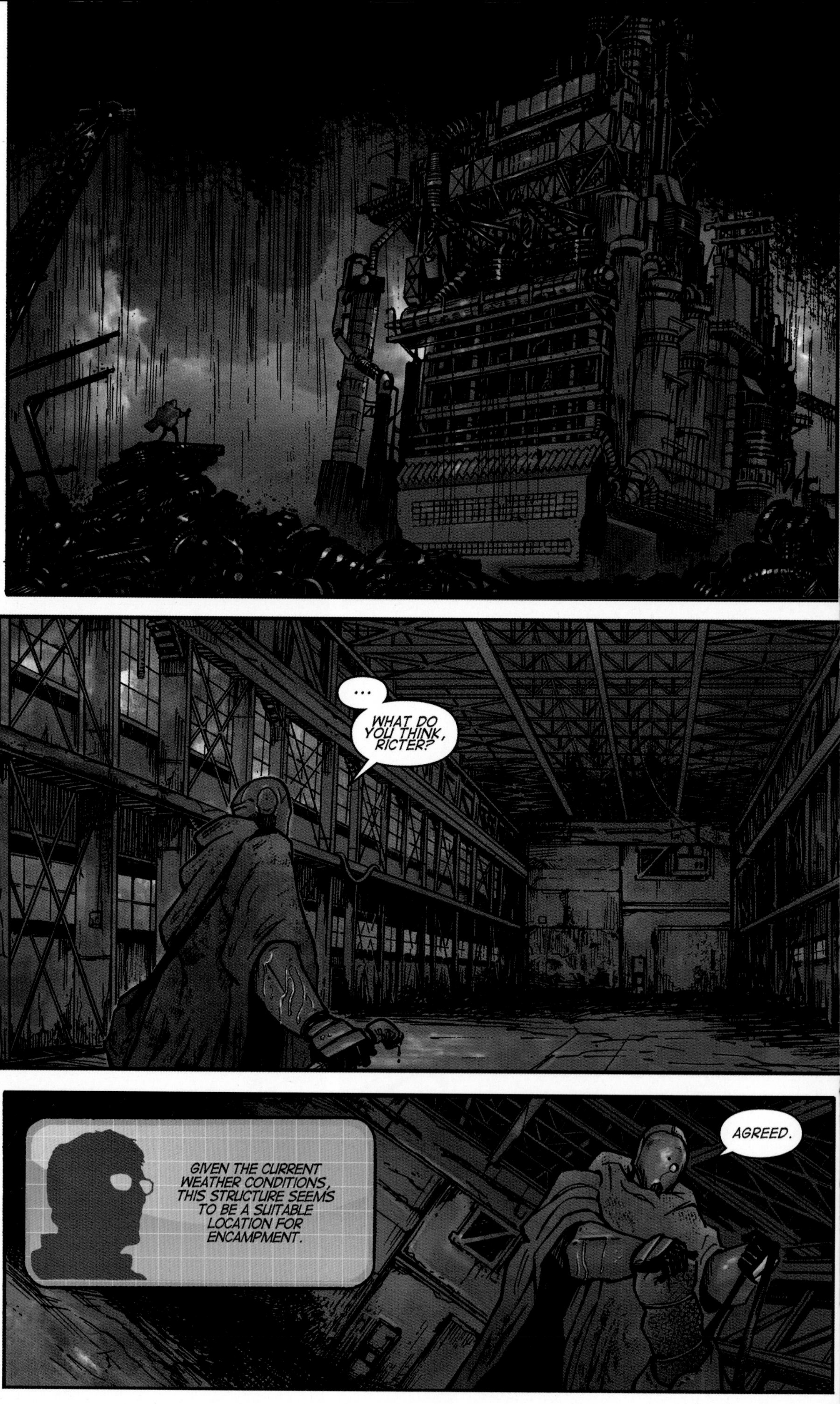
...
WHAT DO YOU THINK, RICTER?
GIVEN THE CURRENT WEATHER CONDITIONS, THIS STRUCTURE SEEMS TO BE A SUITABLE LOCATION FOR ENCAMPMENT.
AGREED.

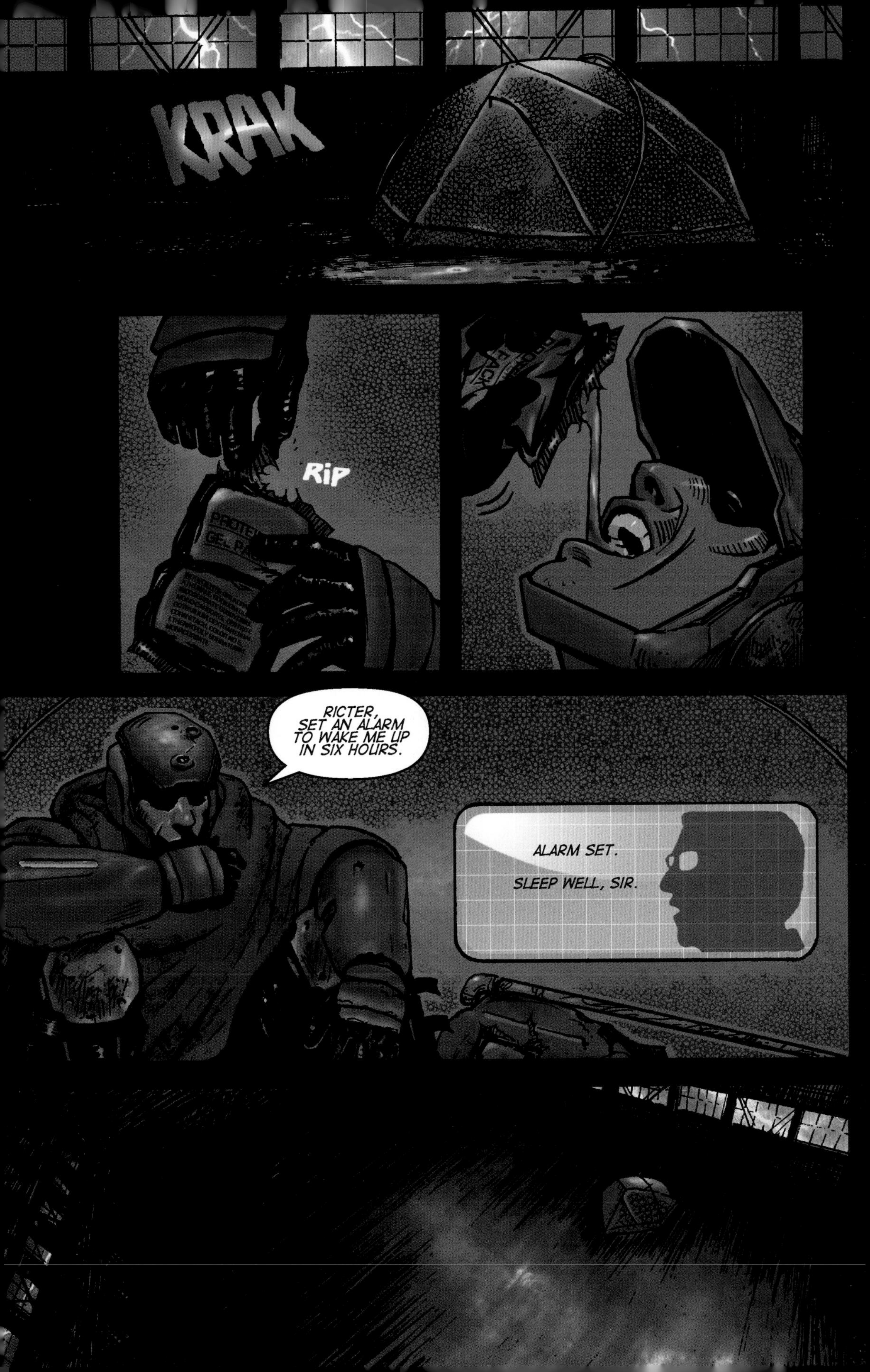
KRAK
RIP
RICTER, SET AN ALARM TO WAKE ME UP IN SIX HOURS.
ALARM SET.
SLEEP WELL, SIR.

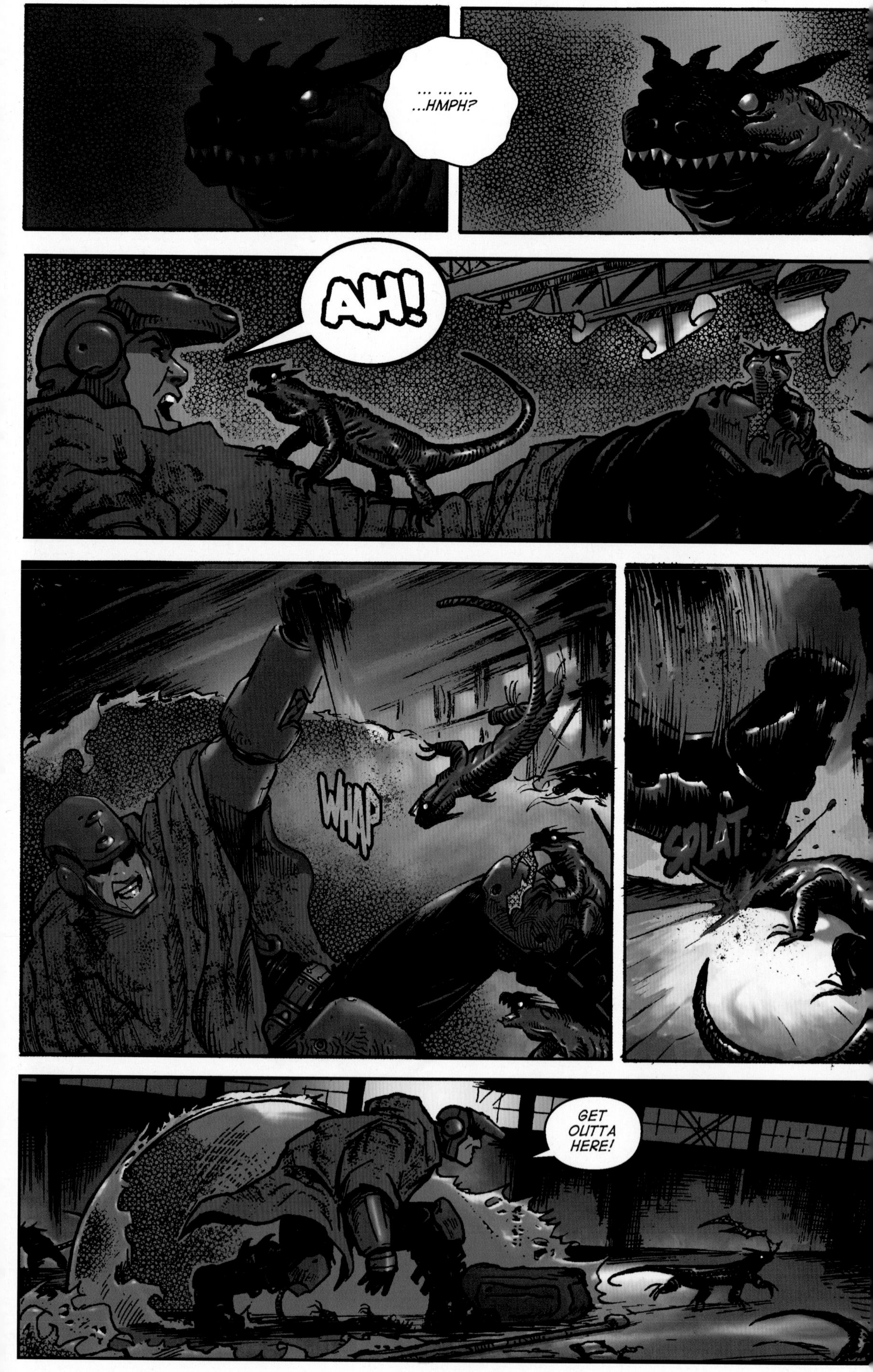

... ...
...HMPH?
AH!
WHAP
SPLAT
GET OUTTA HERE!

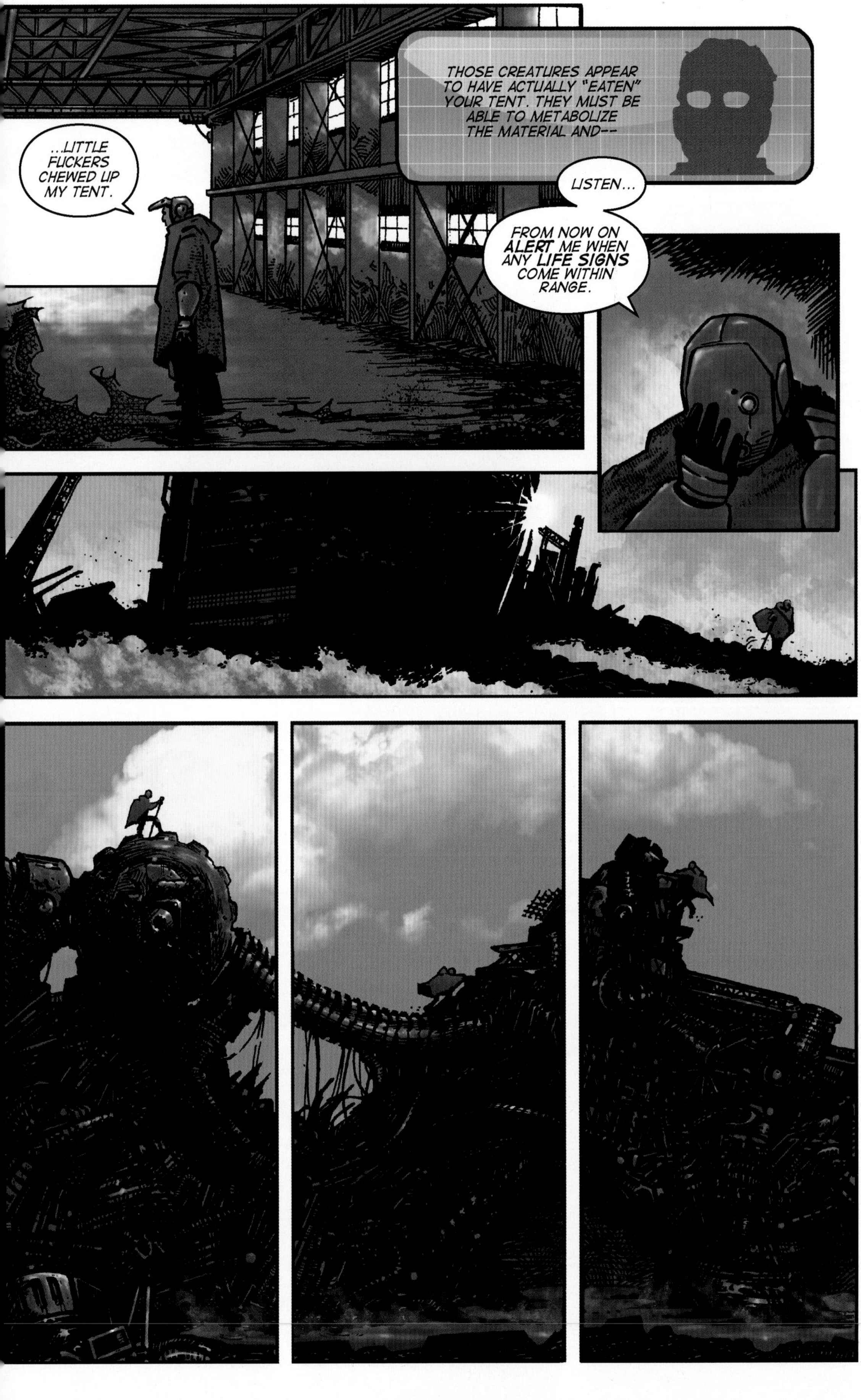

...LITTLE FUCKERS CHEWED UP MY TENT.
THOSE CREATURES APPEAR TO HAVE ACTUALLY "EATEN" YOUR TENT. THEY MUST BE ABLE TO METABOLIZE THE MATERIAL AND--
LISTEN...
FROM NOW ON ALERT ME WHEN ANY LIFE SIGNS COME WITHIN RANGE.

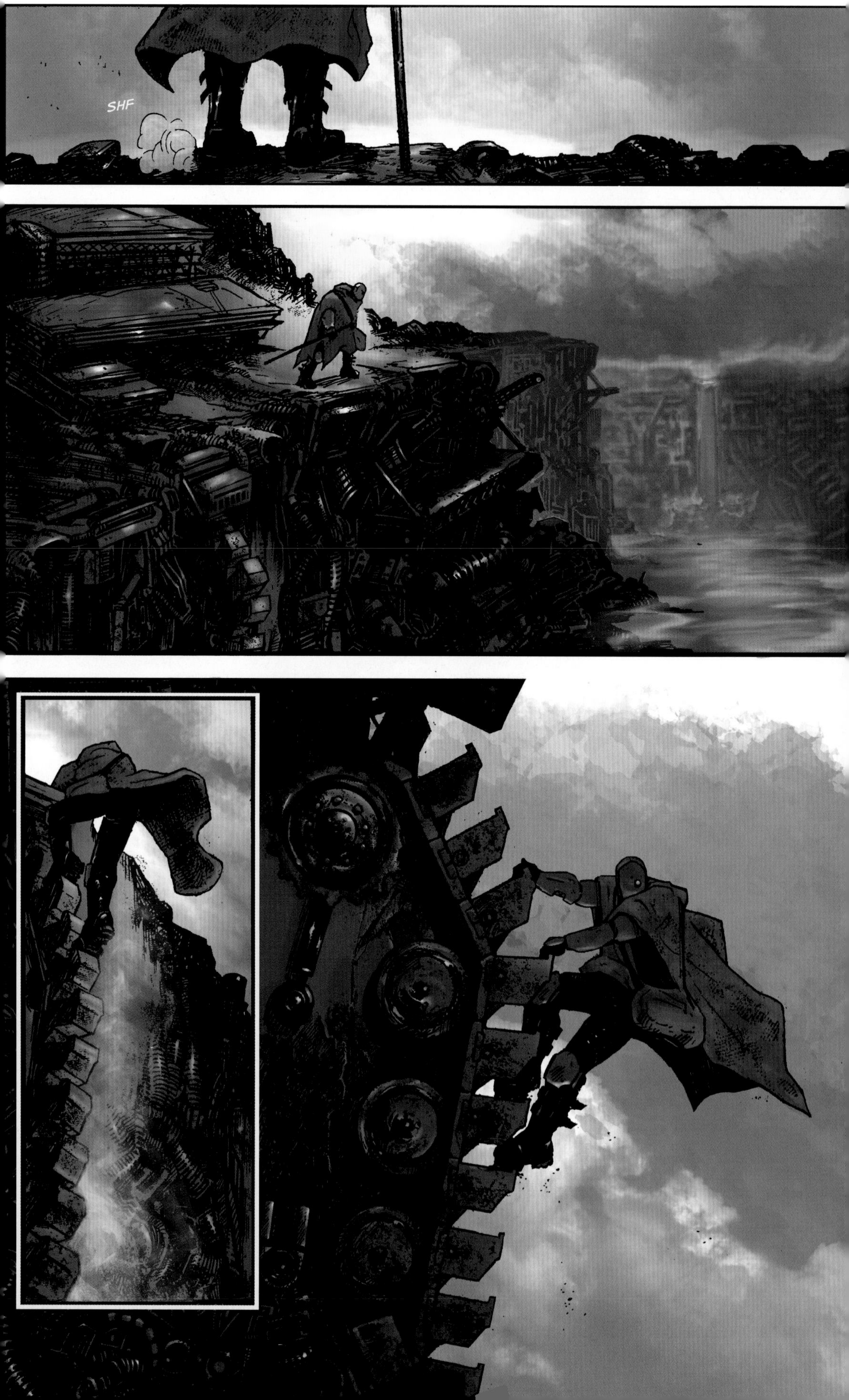
SHF

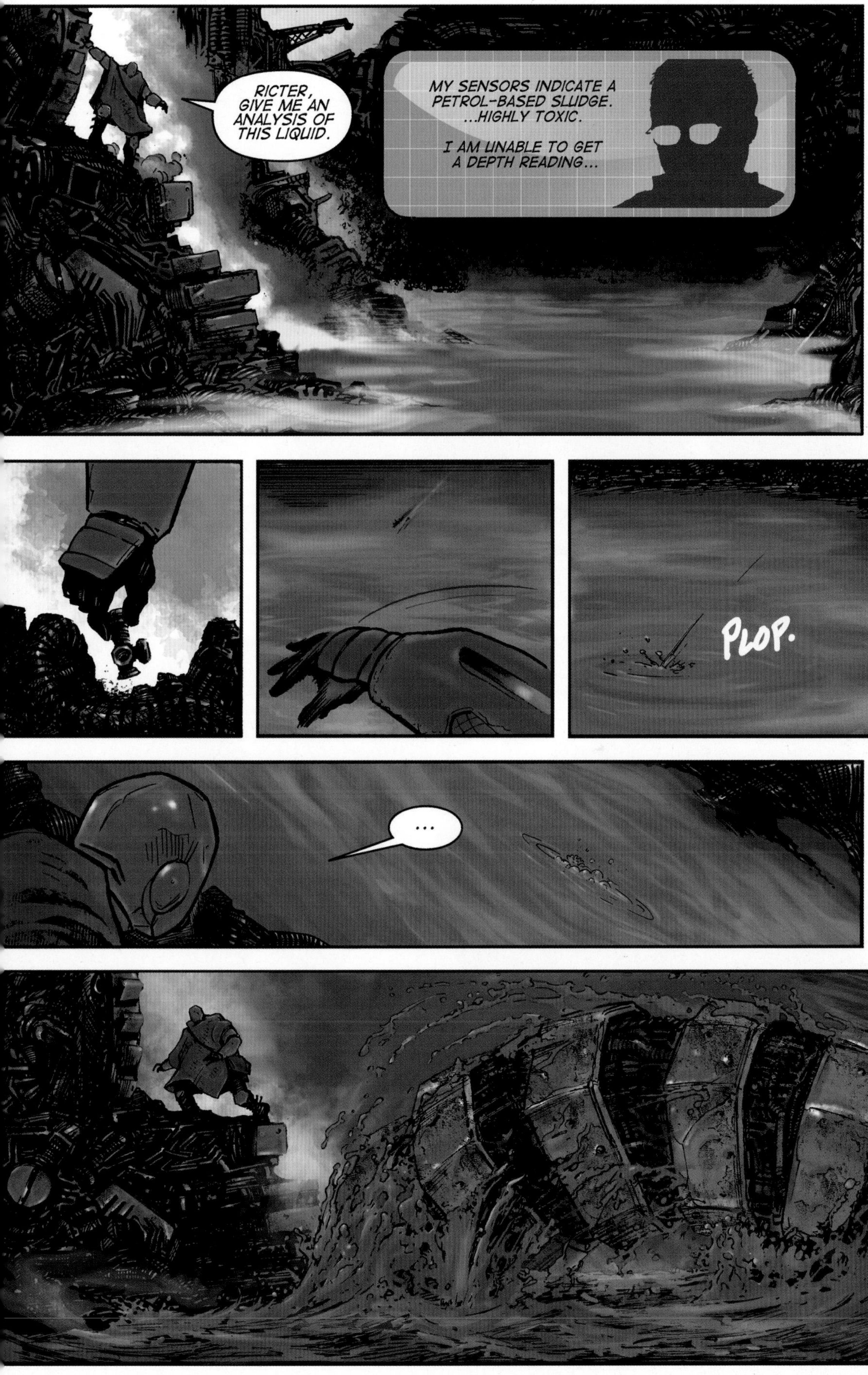
RICTER, GIVE ME AN ANALYSIS OF THIS LIQUID.
MY SENSORS INDICATE A PETROL-BASED SLUDGE. ...HIGHLY TOXIC.
I AM UNABLE TO GET A DEPTH READING...
PLOP.
...

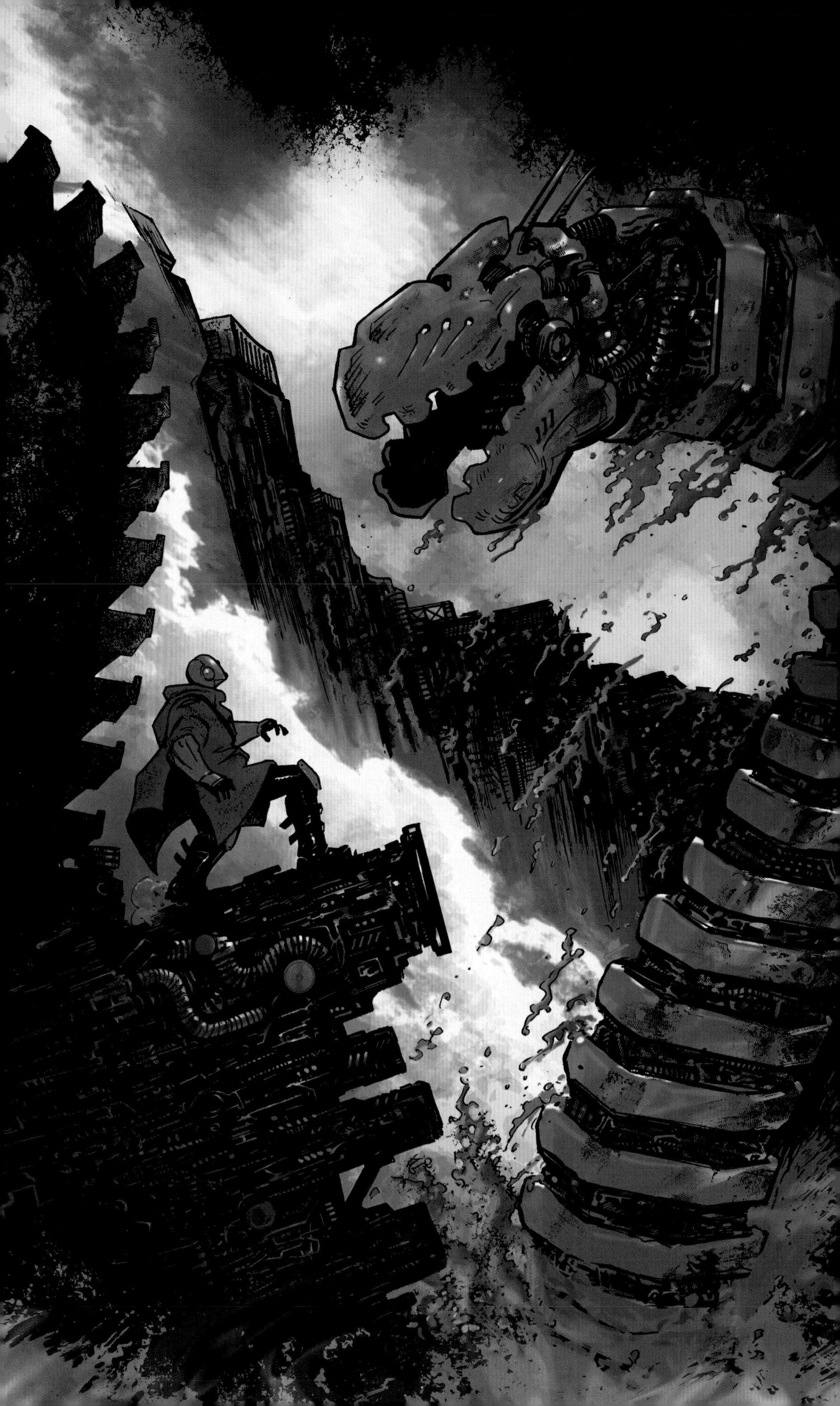

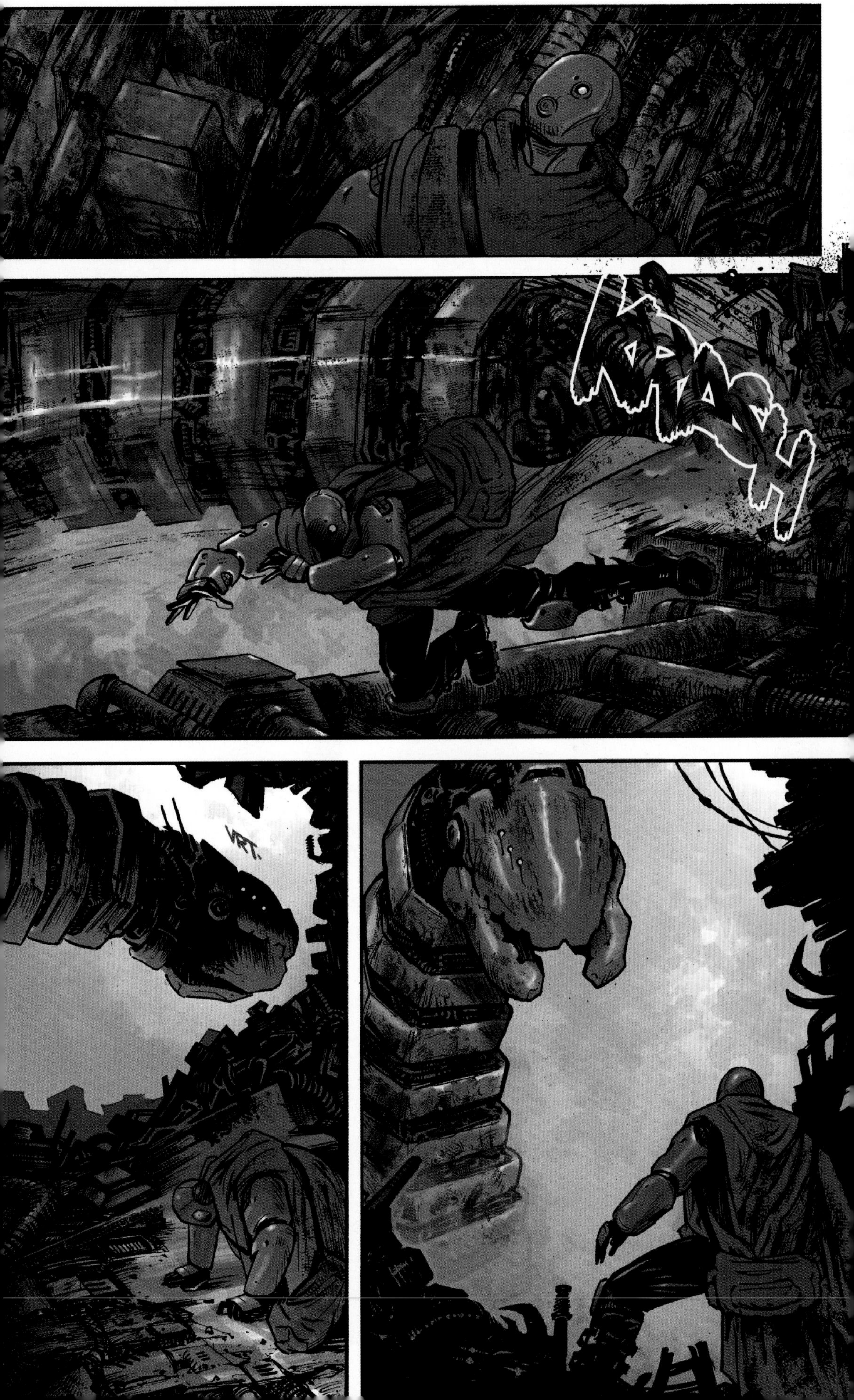
KRAASH
VRT.

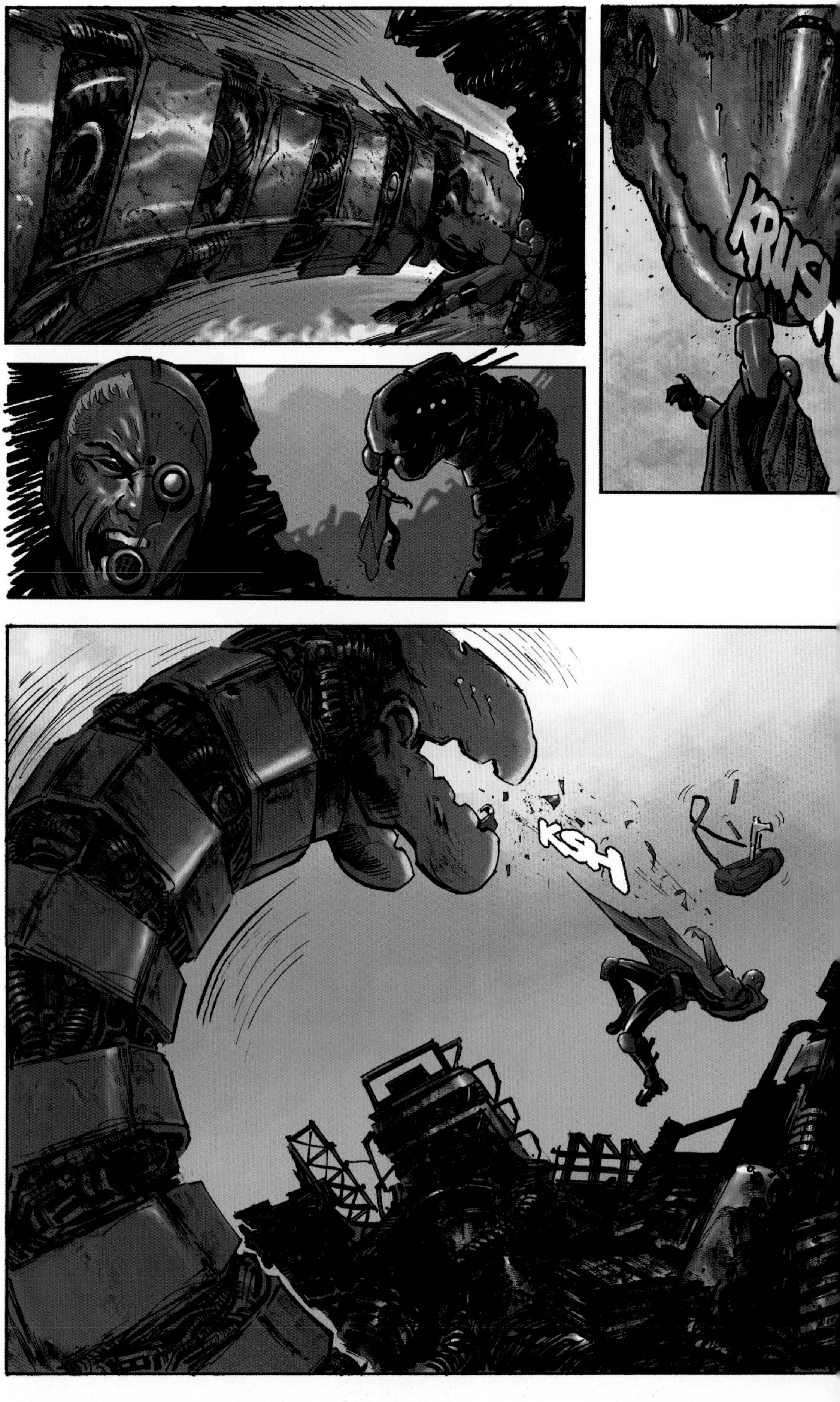

KRUS
KSH

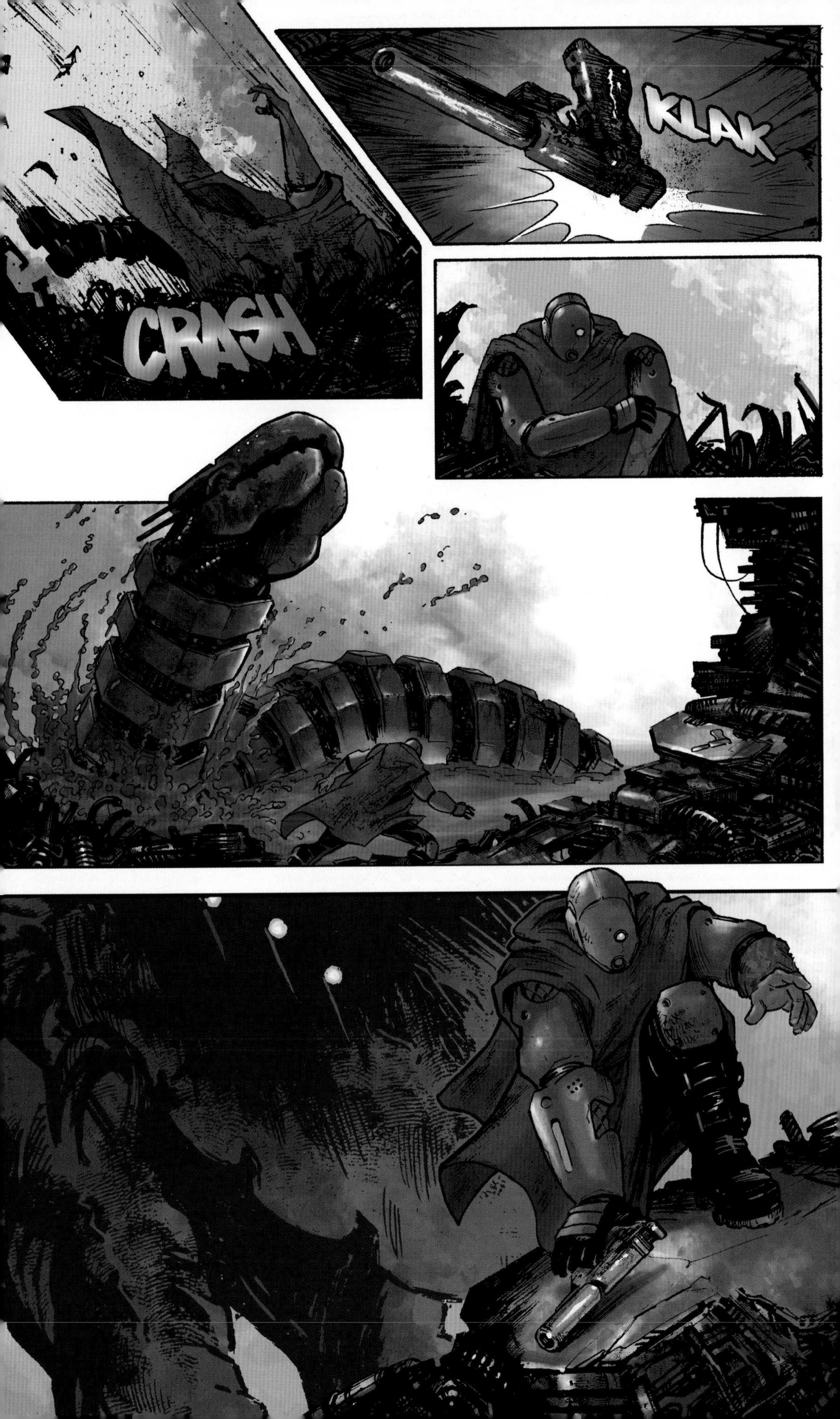
CRASH
KLAK

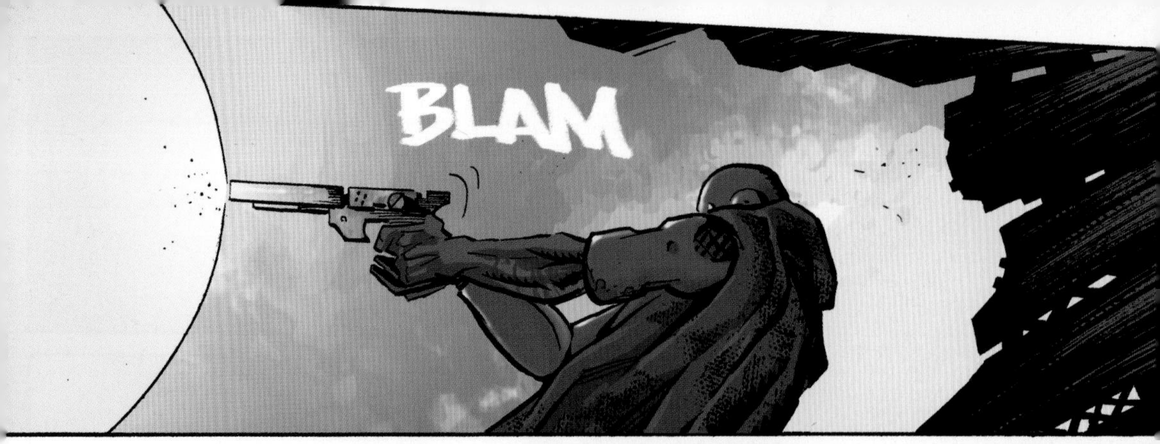
BLAM
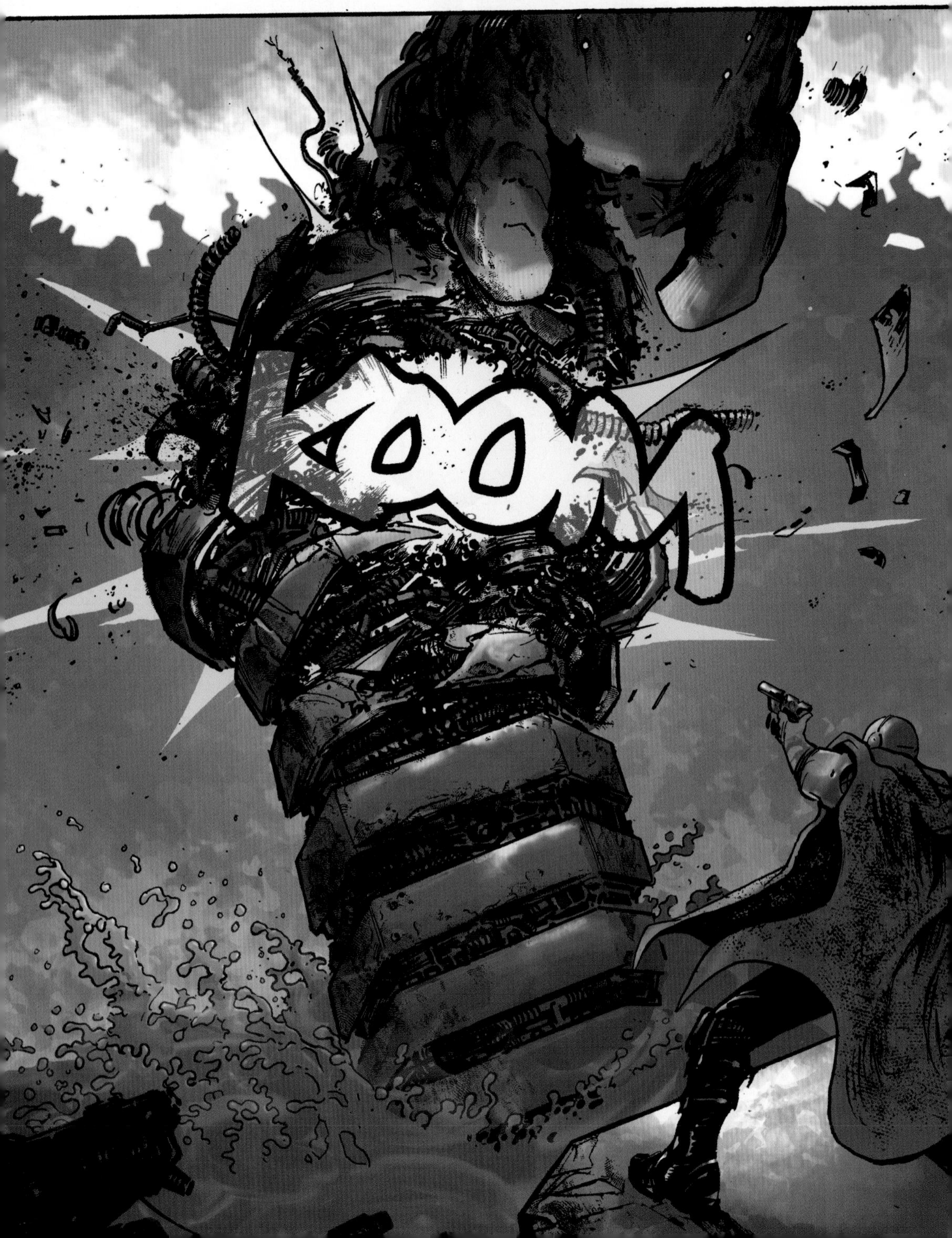
KOOM

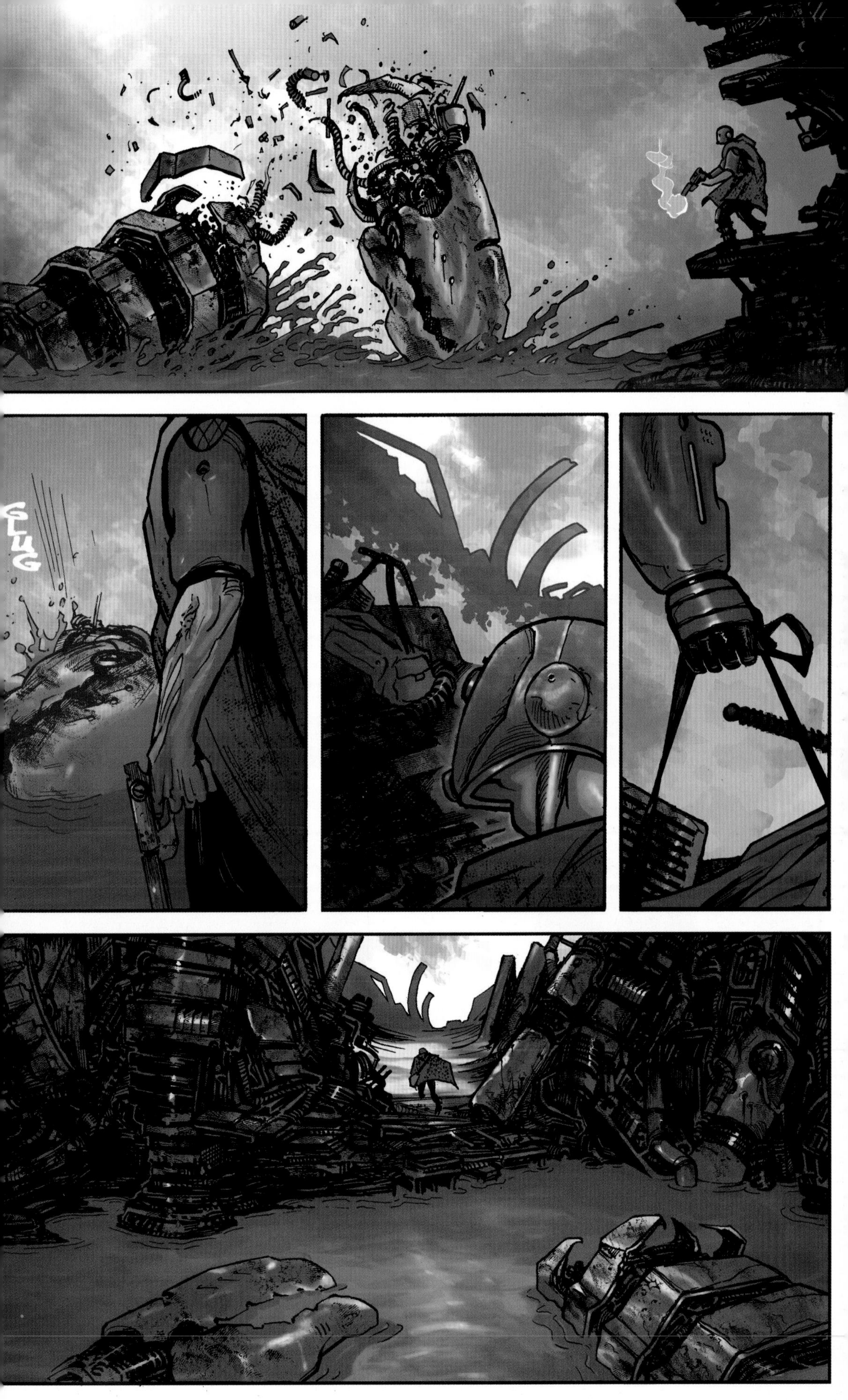
SLUG

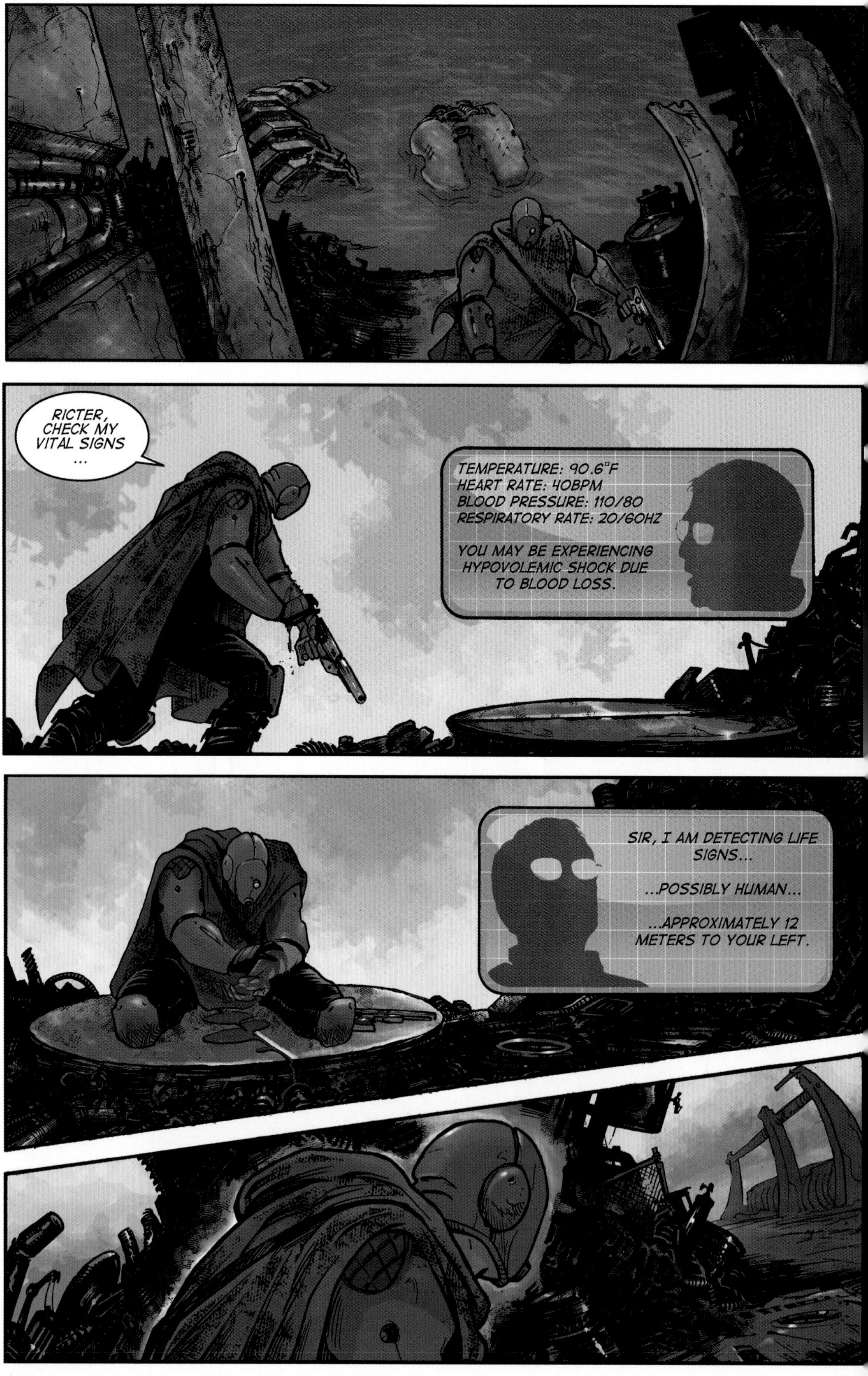
RICTER, CHECK MY VITAL SIGNS ...
TEMPERATURE: 90.6°F
HEART RATE: 40BPM
BLOOD PRESSURE: 110/80
RESPIRATORY RATE: 20/60HZ
YOU MAY BE EXPERIENCING HYPOVOLEMIC SHOCK DUE TO BLOOD LOSS.
SIR, I AM DETECTING LIFE SIGNS...
...POSSIBLY HUMAN...
...APPROXIMATELY 12 METERS TO YOUR LEFT.

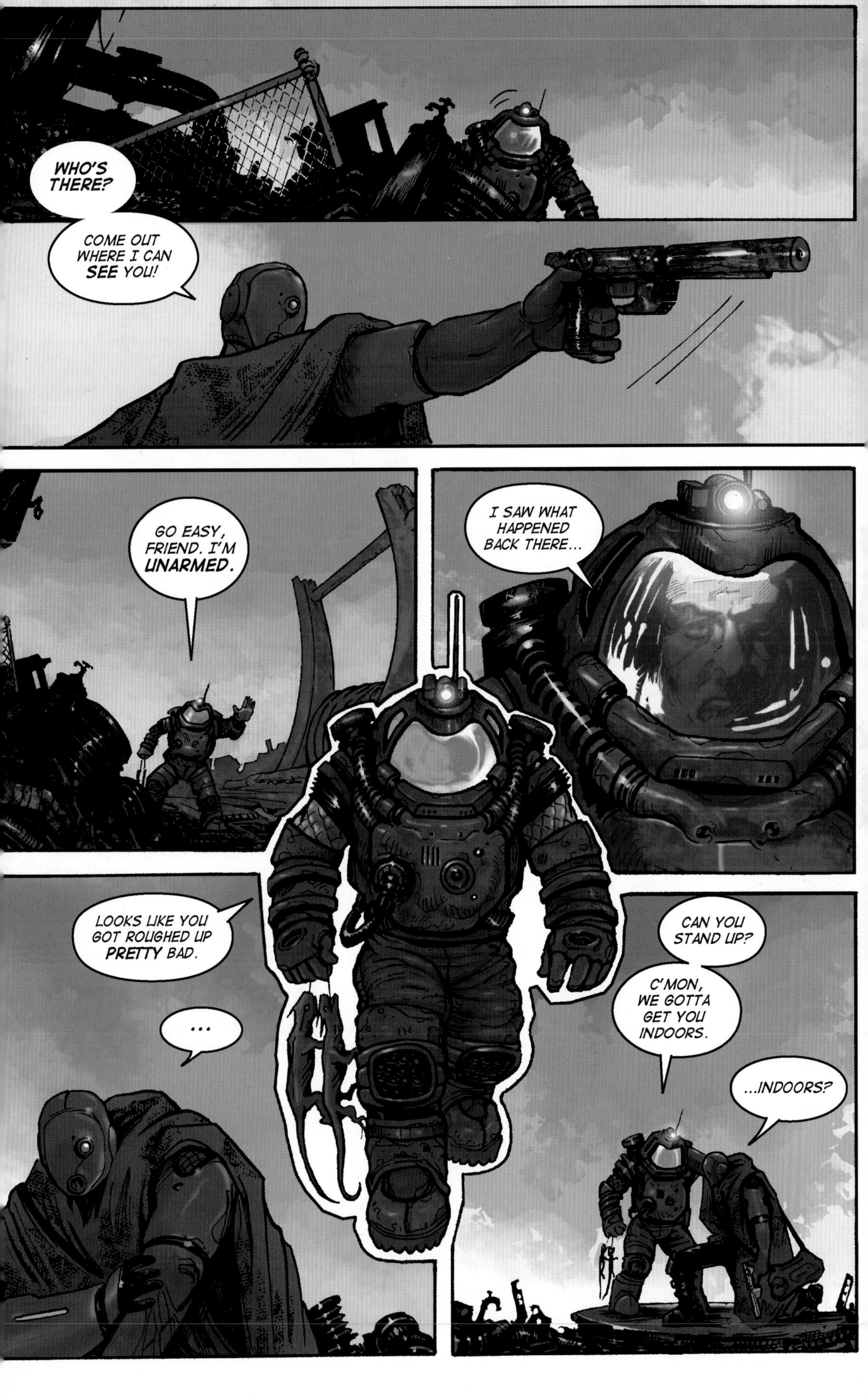
WHO'S THERE?
COME OUT WHERE I CAN SEE YOU!
GO EASY, FRIEND. I'M UNARMED.
I SAW WHAT HAPPENED BACK THERE...
LOOKS LIKE YOU GOT ROUGHED UP PRETTY BAD.
...
CAN YOU STAND UP?
C'MON, WE GOTTA GET YOU INDOORS.
...INDOORS?

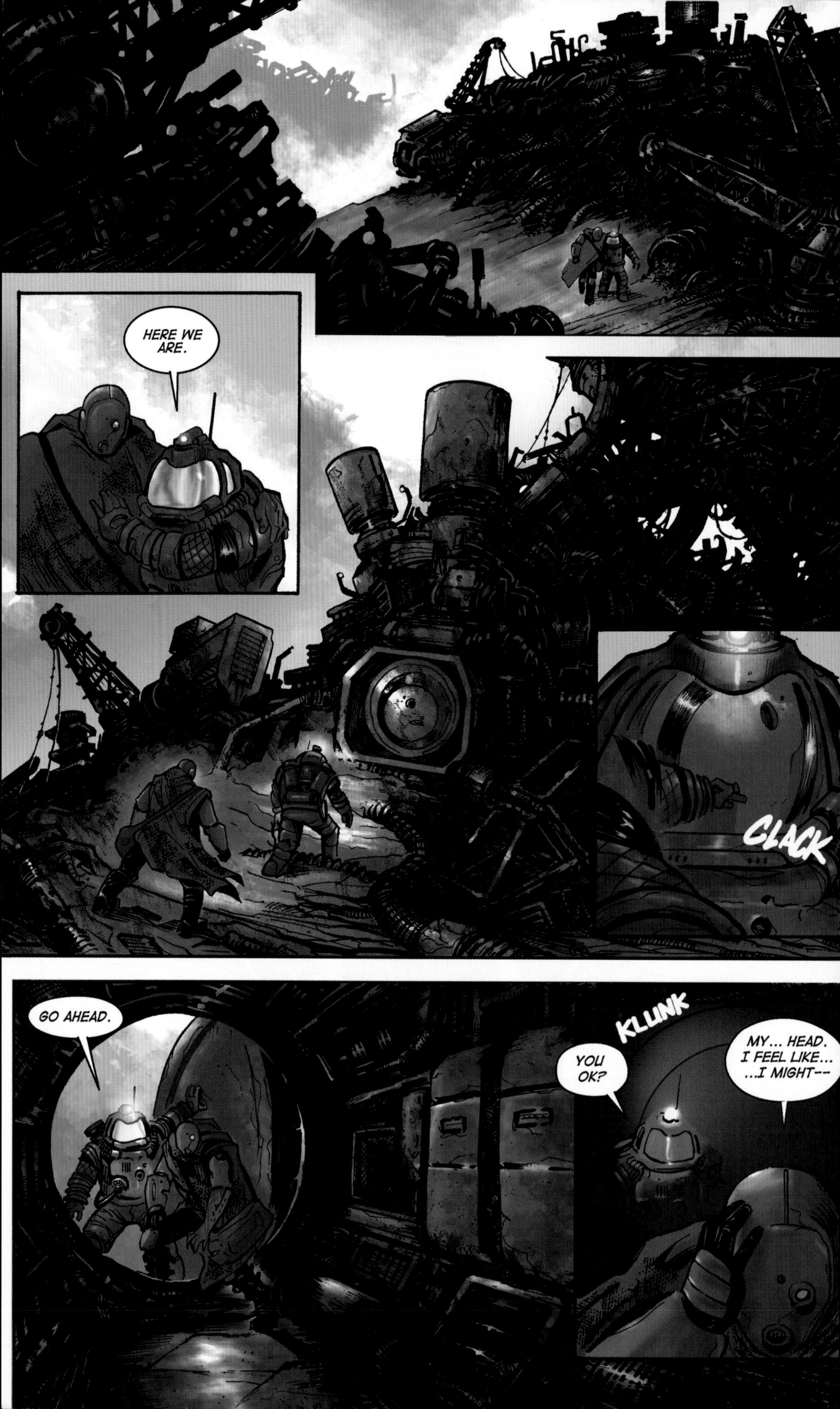
HERE WE ARE.
CLACK
GO AHEAD.
KLUNK
YOU OK?
MY... HEAD. I FEEL LIKE... ...I MIGHT--

?

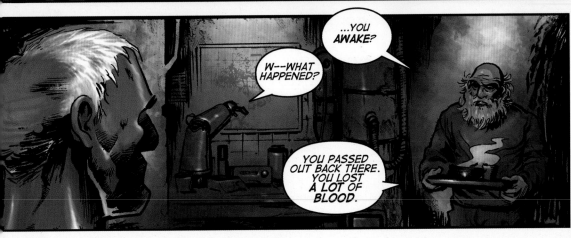

...YOU AWAKE?

W--WHAT HAPPENED?

YOU PASSED OUT BACK THERE. YOU LOST A LOT OF BLOOD.

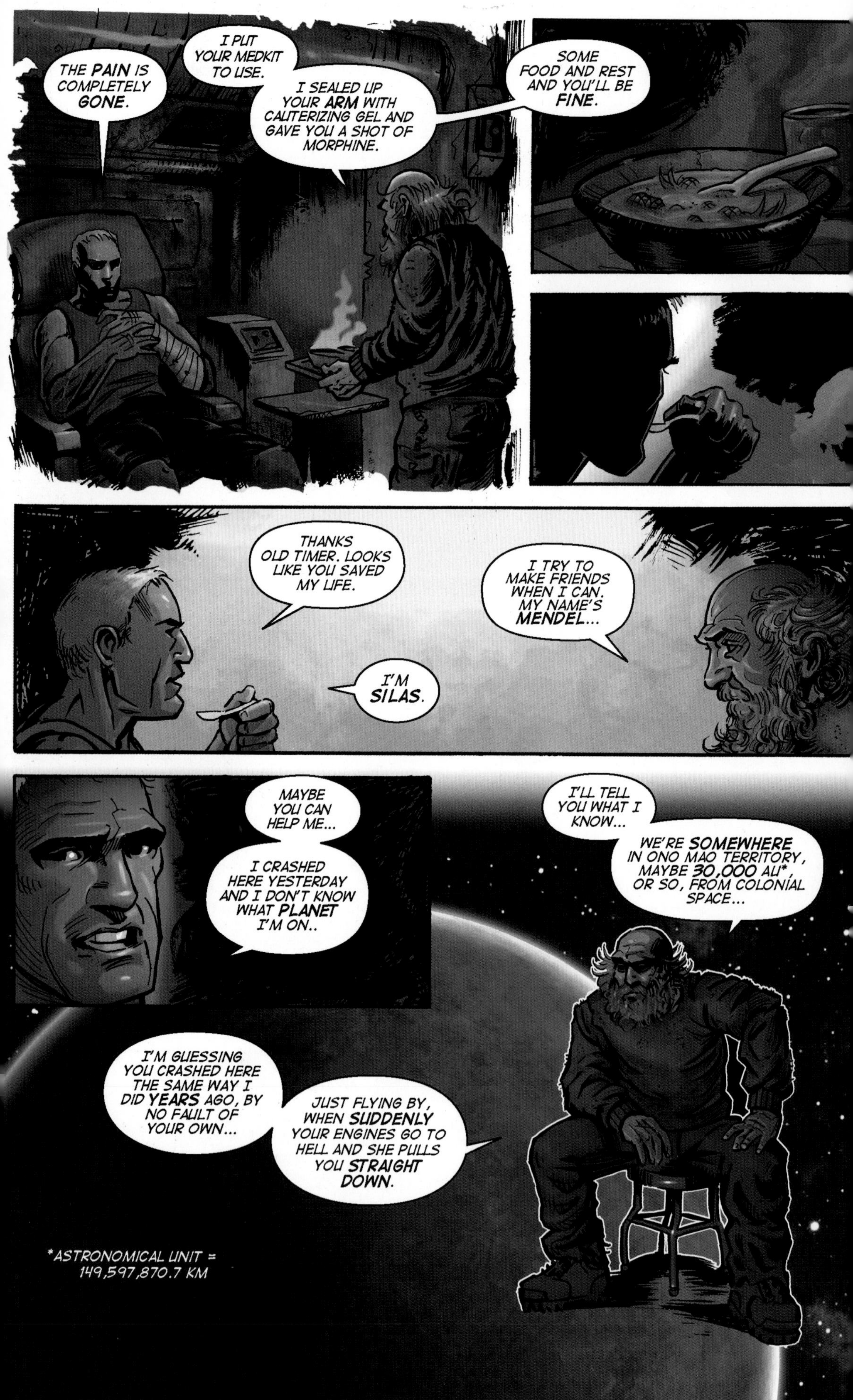
THE PAIN IS COMPLETELY GONE.
I PUT YOUR MEDKIT TO USE.
I SEALED UP YOUR ARM WITH CAUTERIZING GEL AND GAVE YOU A SHOT OF MORPHINE.
SOME FOOD AND REST AND YOU'LL BE FINE.
THANKS OLD TIMER. LOOKS LIKE YOU SAVED MY LIFE.
I TRY TO MAKE FRIENDS WHEN I CAN. MY NAME'S MENDEL...
I'M SILAS.
MAYBE YOU CAN HELP ME...
I CRASHED HERE YESTERDAY AND I DON'T KNOW WHAT PLANET I'M ON..
I'LL TELL YOU WHAT I KNOW...
WE'RE SOMEWHERE IN ONO MAO TERRITORY, MAYBE 30,000 AU*, OR SO, FROM COLONIAL SPACE...
I'M GUESSING YOU CRASHED HERE THE SAME WAY I DID YEARS AGO, BY NO FAULT OF YOUR OWN...
JUST FLYING BY, WHEN SUDDENLY YOUR ENGINES GO TO HELL AND SHE PULLS YOU STRAIGHT DOWN.
*ASTRONOMICAL UNIT = 149,597,870.7 KM

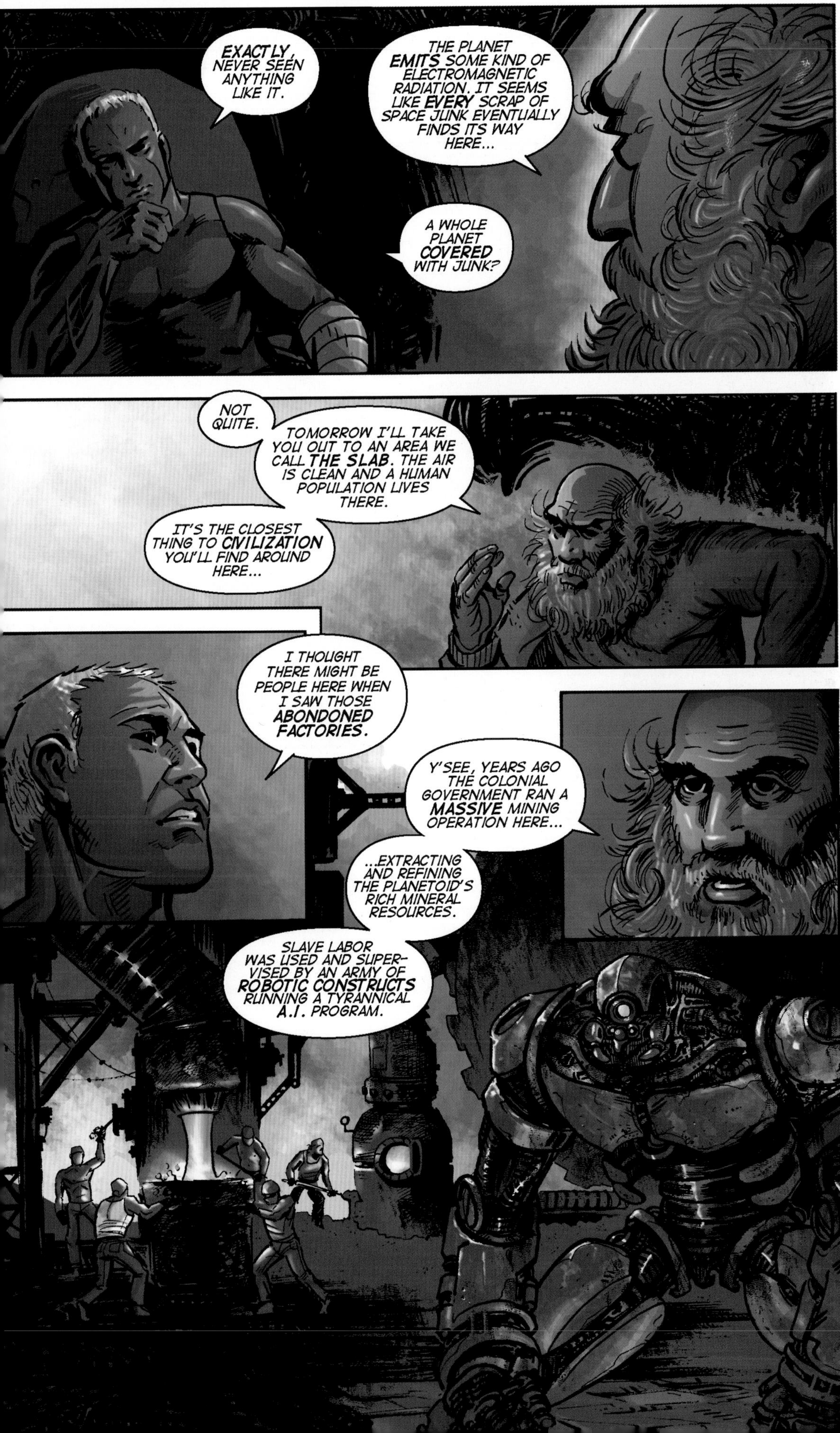
EXACTLY, NEVER SEEN ANYTHING LIKE IT.
THE PLANET EMITS SOME KIND OF ELECTROMAGNETIC RADIATION. IT SEEMS LIKE EVERY SCRAP OF SPACE JUNK EVENTUALLY FINDS ITS WAY HERE...
A WHOLE PLANET COVERED WITH JUNK?
NOT QUITE.
TOMORROW I'LL TAKE YOU OUT TO AN AREA WE CALL THE SLAB. THE AIR IS CLEAN AND A HUMAN POPULATION LIVES THERE.
IT'S THE CLOSEST THING TO CIVILIZATION YOU'LL FIND AROUND HERE...
I THOUGHT THERE MIGHT BE PEOPLE HERE WHEN I SAW THOSE ABONDONED FACTORIES.
Y'SEE, YEARS AGO THE COLONIAL GOVERNMENT RAN A MASSIVE MINING OPERATION HERE...
...EXTRACTING AND REFINING THE PLANETOID'S RICH MINERAL RESOURCES.
SLAVE LABOR WAS USED AND SUPER-VISED BY AN ARMY OF ROBOTIC CONSTRUCTS RUNNING A TYRANNICAL A.I. PROGRAM.

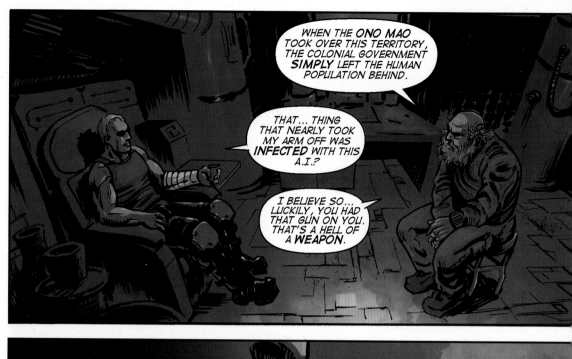

WHEN THE **ONO MAO** TOOK OVER THIS TERRITORY, THE COLONIAL GOVERNMENT **SIMPLY** LEFT THE HUMAN POPULATION BEHIND.

THAT... THING THAT NEARLY TOOK MY ARM OFF WAS **INFECTED** WITH THIS A.I.?

I BELIEVE SO... LUCKILY, YOU HAD THAT GUN ON YOU. THAT'S A HELL OF A **WEAPON**.

SO... WHAT'S YOUR STORY? HOW DID YOU WIND UP ALL THE WAY OUT **HERE**?

I **TOLD** YOU, I CRASHED HERE THE OTHER DAY.

I WAS THINKING MAYBE YOU COULD START A **LITTLE** FURTHER BACK THAN THAT.

YEAH, WELL...
...

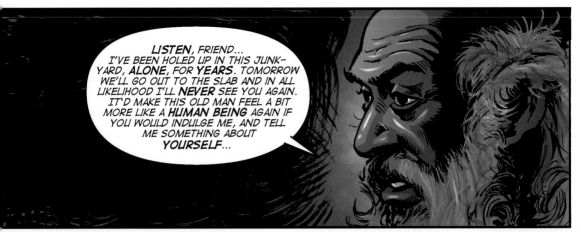

LISTEN, FRIEND... I'VE BEEN HOLED UP IN THIS JUNK-YARD, **ALONE**, FOR **YEARS**. TOMORROW WE'LL GO OUT TO THE SLAB AND IN ALL LIKELIHOOD I'LL **NEVER** SEE YOU AGAIN. IT'D MAKE THIS OLD MAN FEEL A BIT MORE LIKE A **HUMAN BEING** AGAIN IF YOU WOULD INDULGE ME, AND TELL ME SOMETHING ABOUT **YOURSELF**...

FAIR ENOUGH.

I GREW UP AN ORPHAN IN A REFUGEE CAMP ON EREBUS MINOR. I SPENT MY DAYS SCAVENGING FOR **FOOD** AND **SHELTER**.

THE ONLY WAY OUT OF THERE WAS THROUGH THE MILITARY. SO, AS SOON AS I COULD, I ENLISTED IN THE **COLONIAL INFANTRY**. I WAS SENT OFF ON **MULTIPLE** TOURS OF DUTY IN THE **OUTER TERRITORIES**...

AFTER YEARS OF **WAR** AND **STRUGGLE** I WANTED OUT. ONCE ON LEAVE I MET UP WITH A FEW OTHER GUYS WHO FELT THE SAME WAY. TOGETHER WE DEVISED A PLAN TO GO AWOL AND ENTER THE SMUGGLING BUISINESS...

--I KNOW A GUY WHO CAN GET US A DEAL ON A SHIP.

WE POOLED OUR RESOURCES TOGETHER AND BOUGHT A RIG.

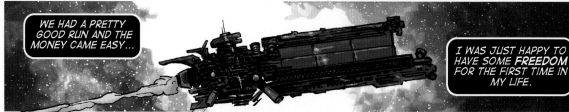

WE HAD A PRETTY GOOD RUN AND THE MONEY CAME EASY...

I WAS JUST HAPPY TO HAVE SOME **FREEDOM** FOR THE FIRST TIME IN MY LIFE.

THEN, JUST A FEW DAYS AGO, WE TOOK A SHORTCUT THROUGH ONO MAO TERRITORY, IN ORDER TO **AVOID** THE COLONIAL PATROLS, WHEN WE NOTICED--

-- AN **ONO MAO** RESEARCH VESSEL. LOOKS LIKE IT'S IN **DISTRESS**.

I BET THEY'VE GOT SOME HEAVY GEAR ONBOARD!

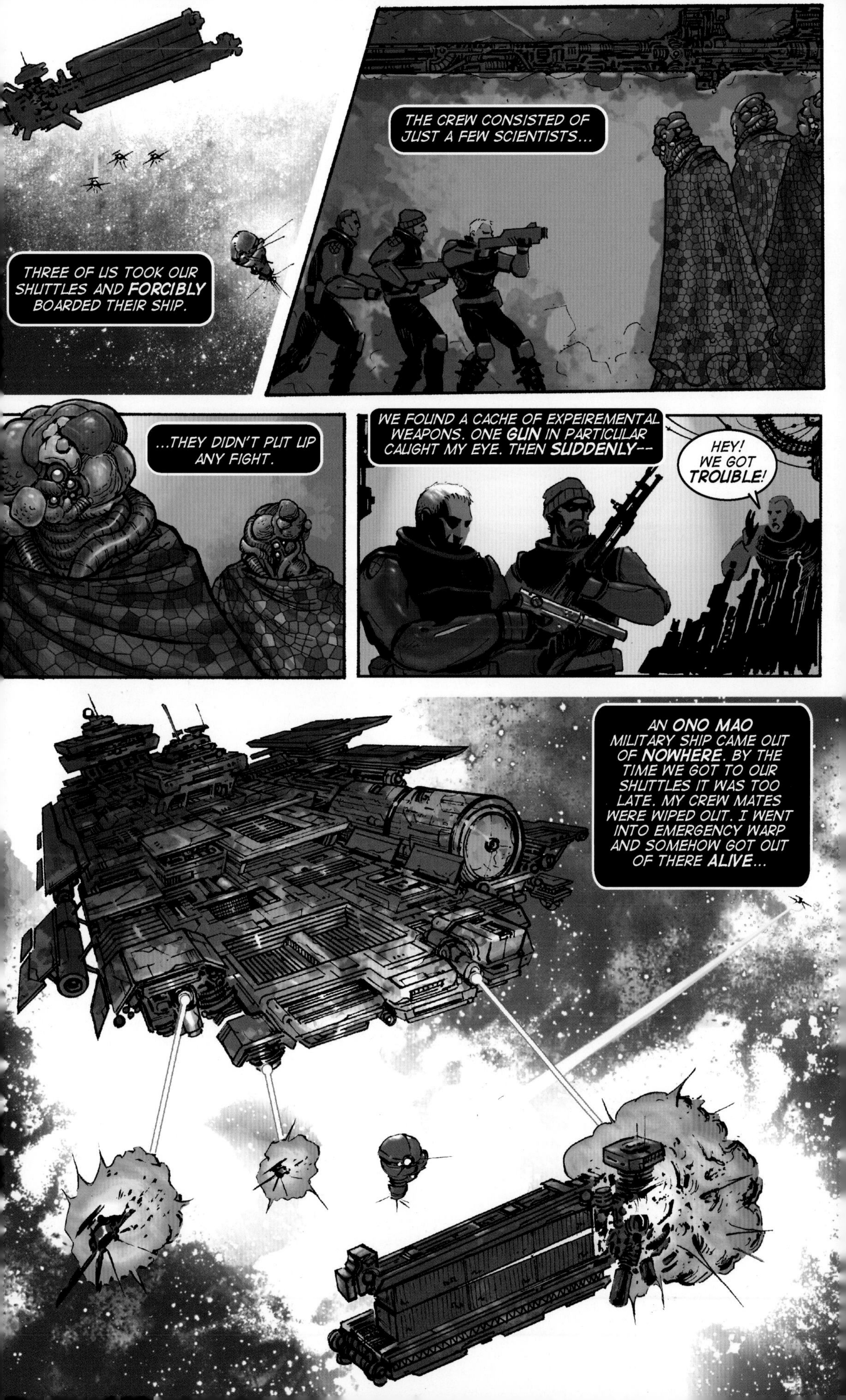
THREE OF US TOOK OUR SHUTTLES AND FORCIBLY BOARDED THEIR SHIP.
THE CREW CONSISTED OF JUST A FEW SCIENTISTS...
...THEY DIDN'T PUT UP ANY FIGHT.
WE FOUND A CACHE OF EXPEIREMENTAL WEAPONS. ONE GUN IN PARTICULAR CAUGHT MY EYE. THEN SUDDENLY--
HEY! WE GOT TROUBLE!
AN ONO MAO MILITARY SHIP CAME OUT OF NOWHERE. BY THE TIME WE GOT TO OUR SHUTTLES IT WAS TOO LATE. MY CREW MATES WERE WIPED OUT. I WENT INTO EMERGENCY WARP AND SOMEHOW GOT OUT OF THERE ALIVE...

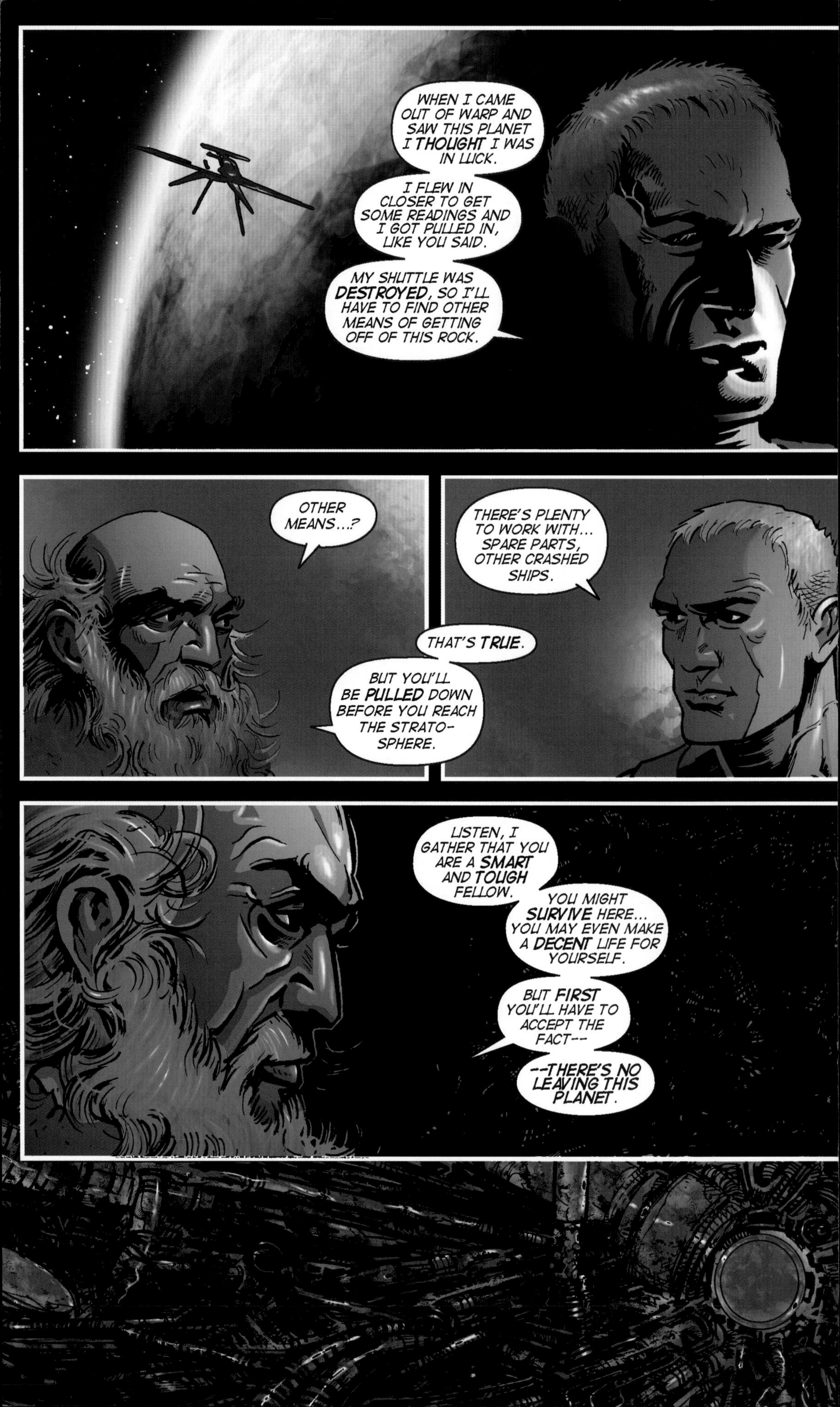

WHEN I CAME OUT OF WARP AND SAW THIS PLANET I THOUGHT I WAS IN LUCK.
I FLEW IN CLOSER TO GET SOME READINGS AND I GOT PULLED IN, LIKE YOU SAID.
MY SHUTTLE WAS DESTROYED, SO I'LL HAVE TO FIND OTHER MEANS OF GETTING OFF OF THIS ROCK.
OTHER MEANS...?
THERE'S PLENTY TO WORK WITH... SPARE PARTS, OTHER CRASHED SHIPS.
THAT'S TRUE.
BUT YOU'LL BE PULLED DOWN BEFORE YOU REACH THE STRATO-SPHERE.
LISTEN, I GATHER THAT YOU ARE A SMART AND TOUGH FELLOW.
YOU MIGHT SURVIVE HERE... YOU MAY EVEN MAKE A DECENT LIFE FOR YOURSELF.
BUT FIRST YOU'LL HAVE TO ACCEPT THE FACT--
--THERE'S NO LEAVING THIS PLANET.

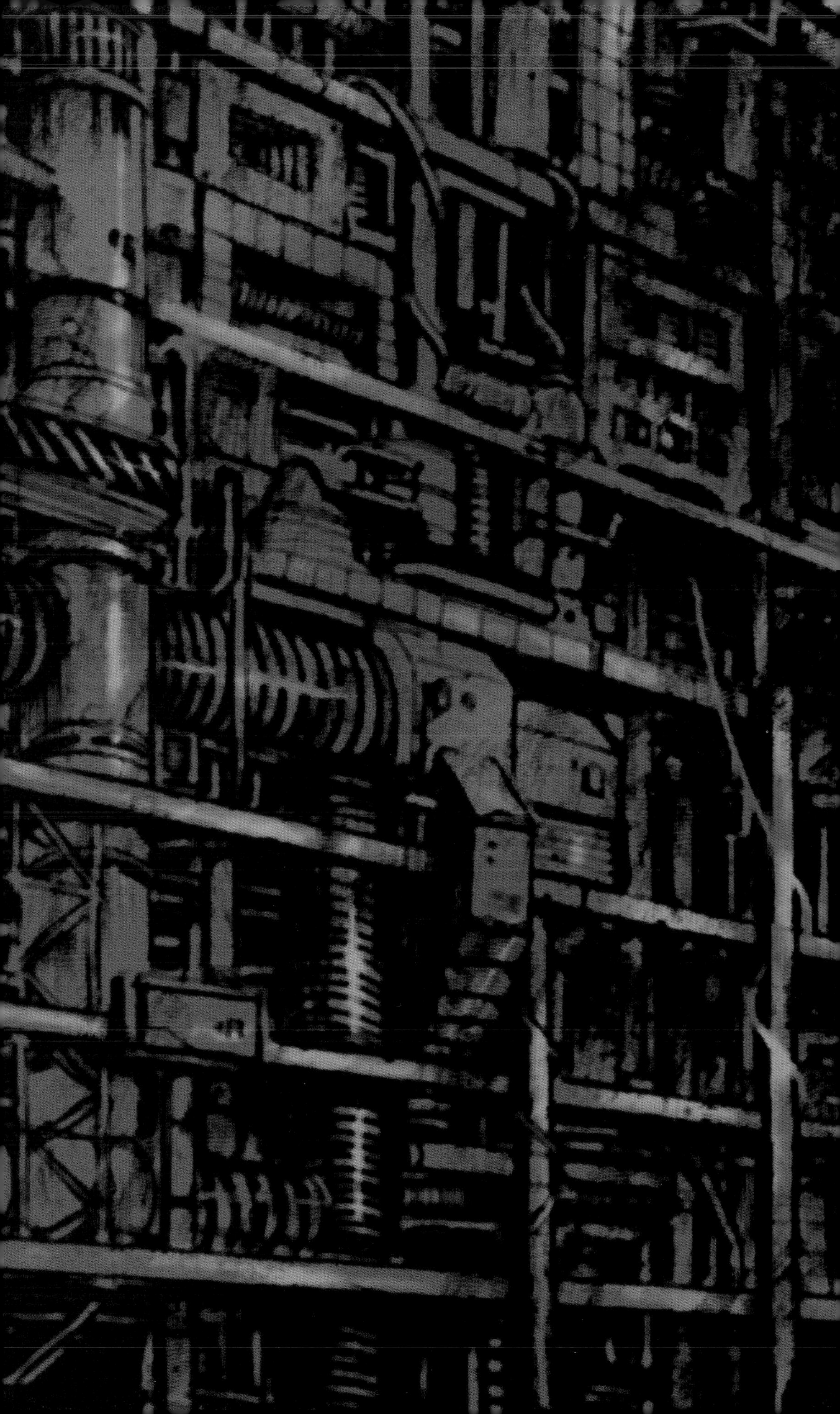

CHAPTER › TWO

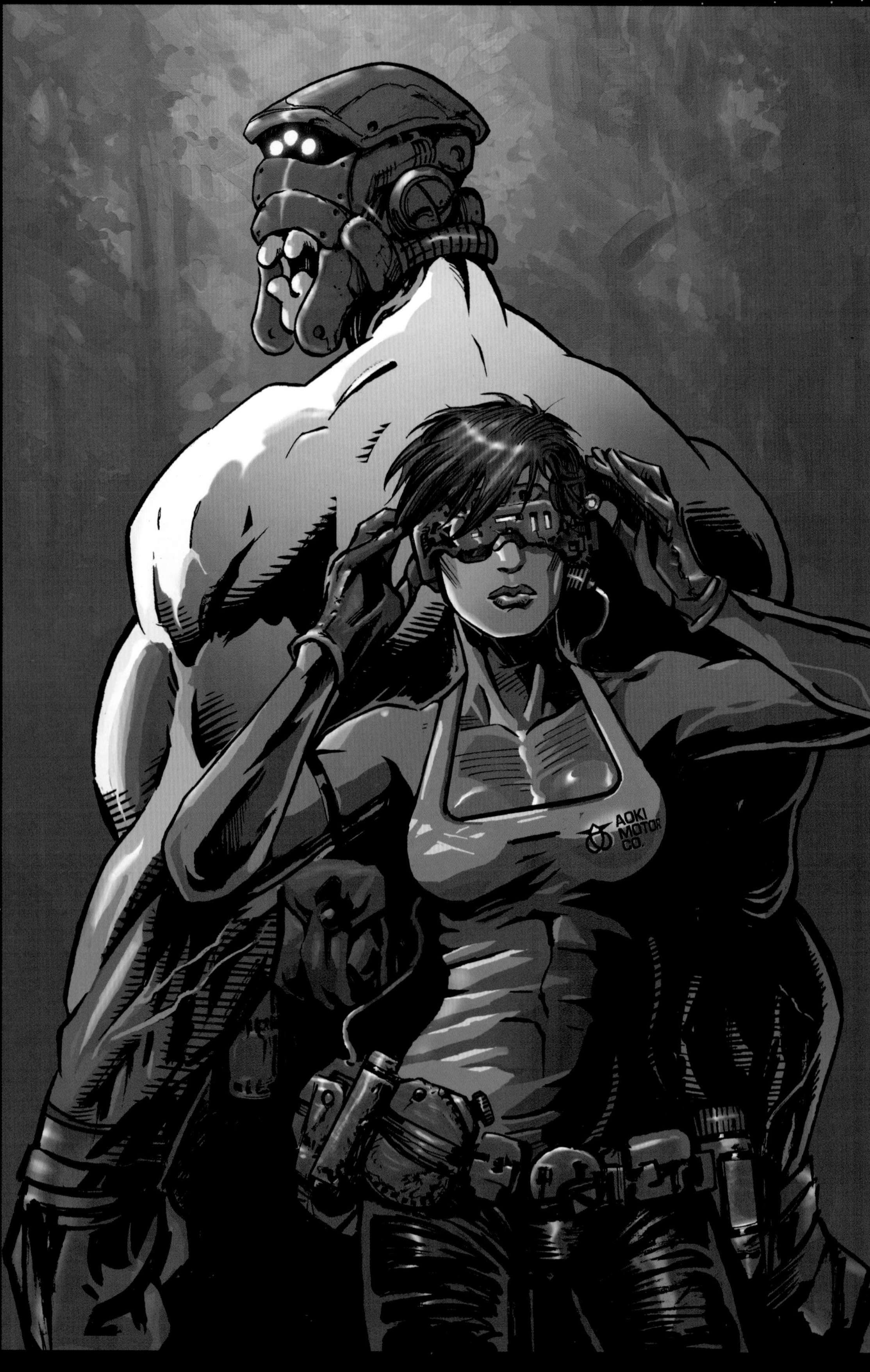
AOKI MOTOR CO.

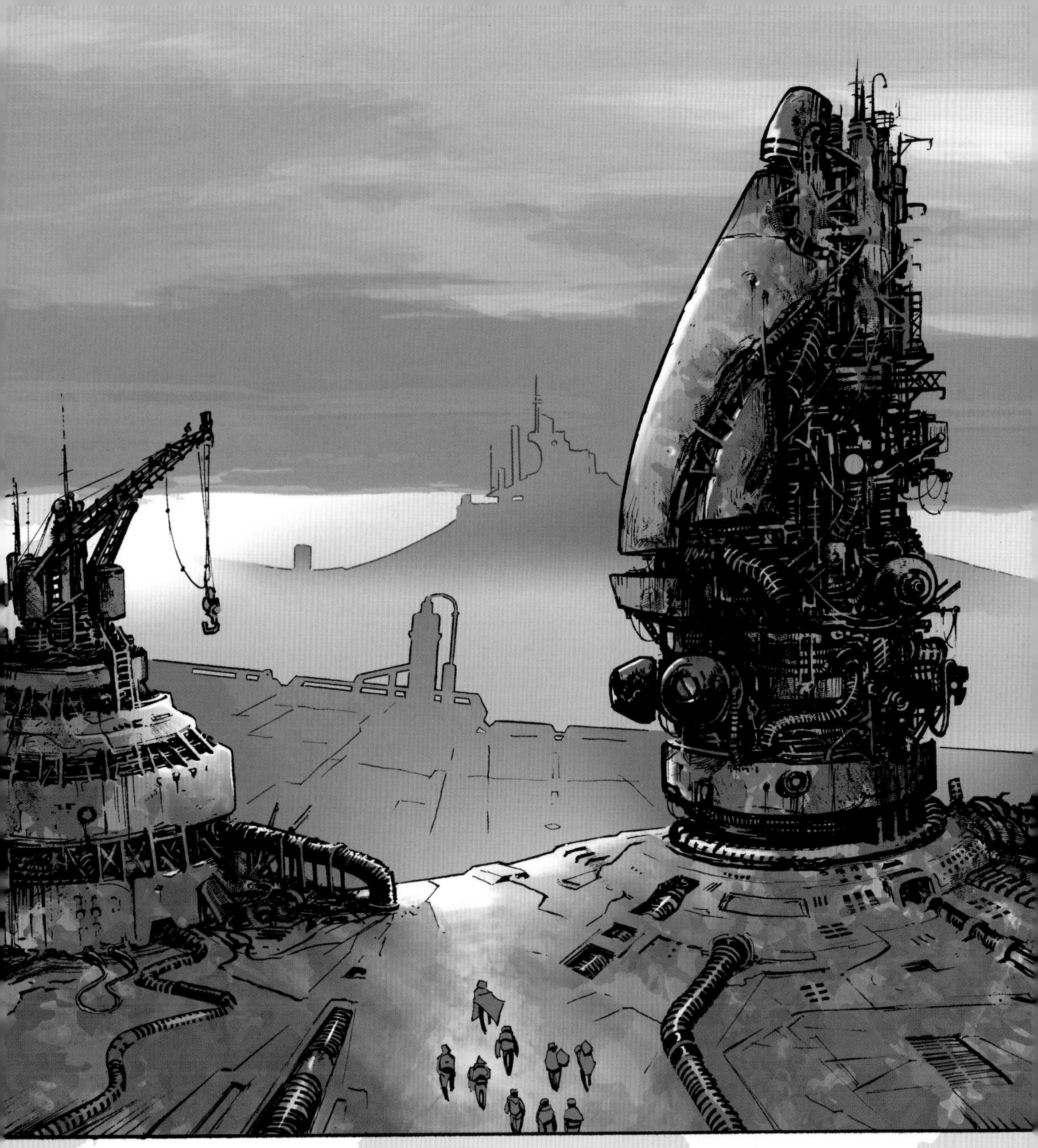
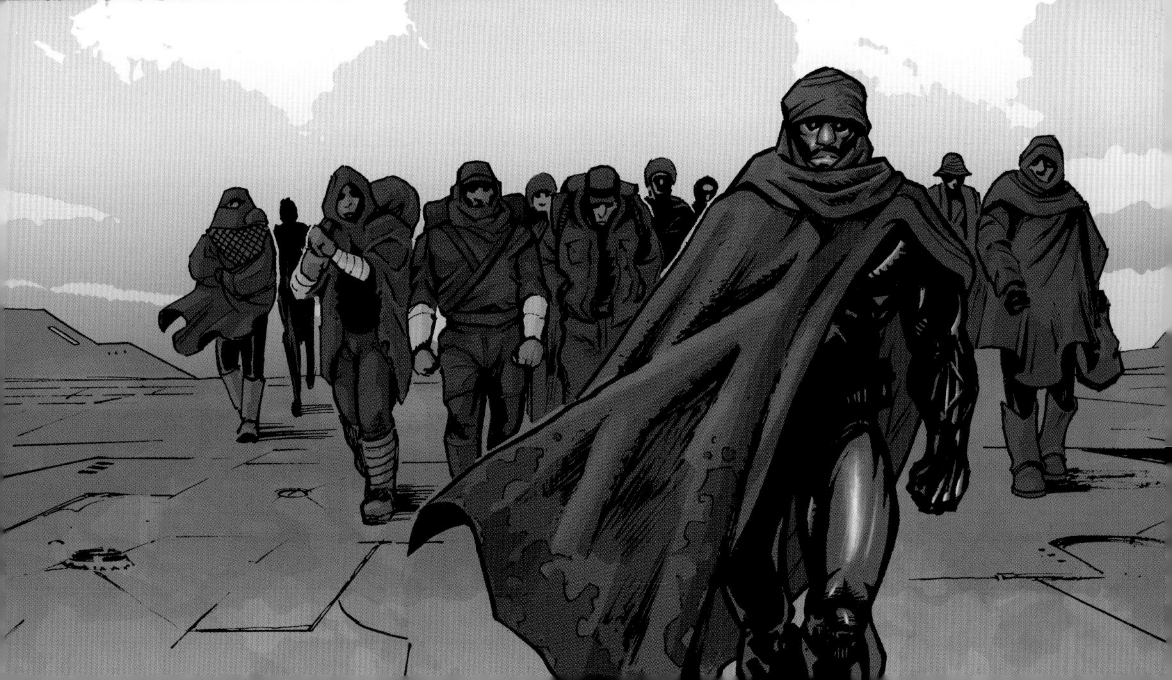

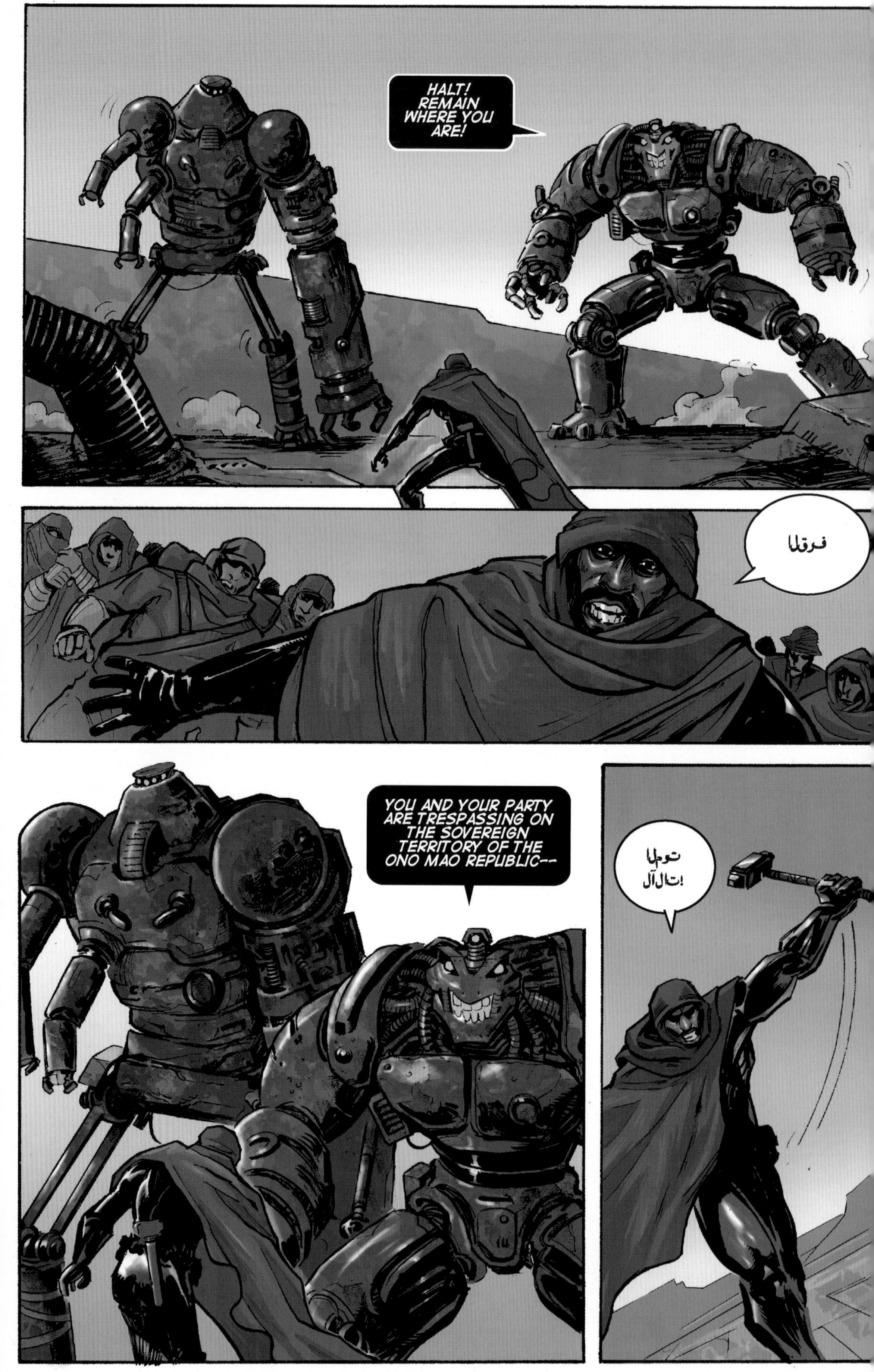
HALT! REMAIN WHERE YOU ARE!
فرقلا
YOU AND YOUR PARTY ARE TRESPASSING ON THE SOVEREIGN TERRITORY OF THE ONO MAO REPUBLIC--
تولما
!تاالآل

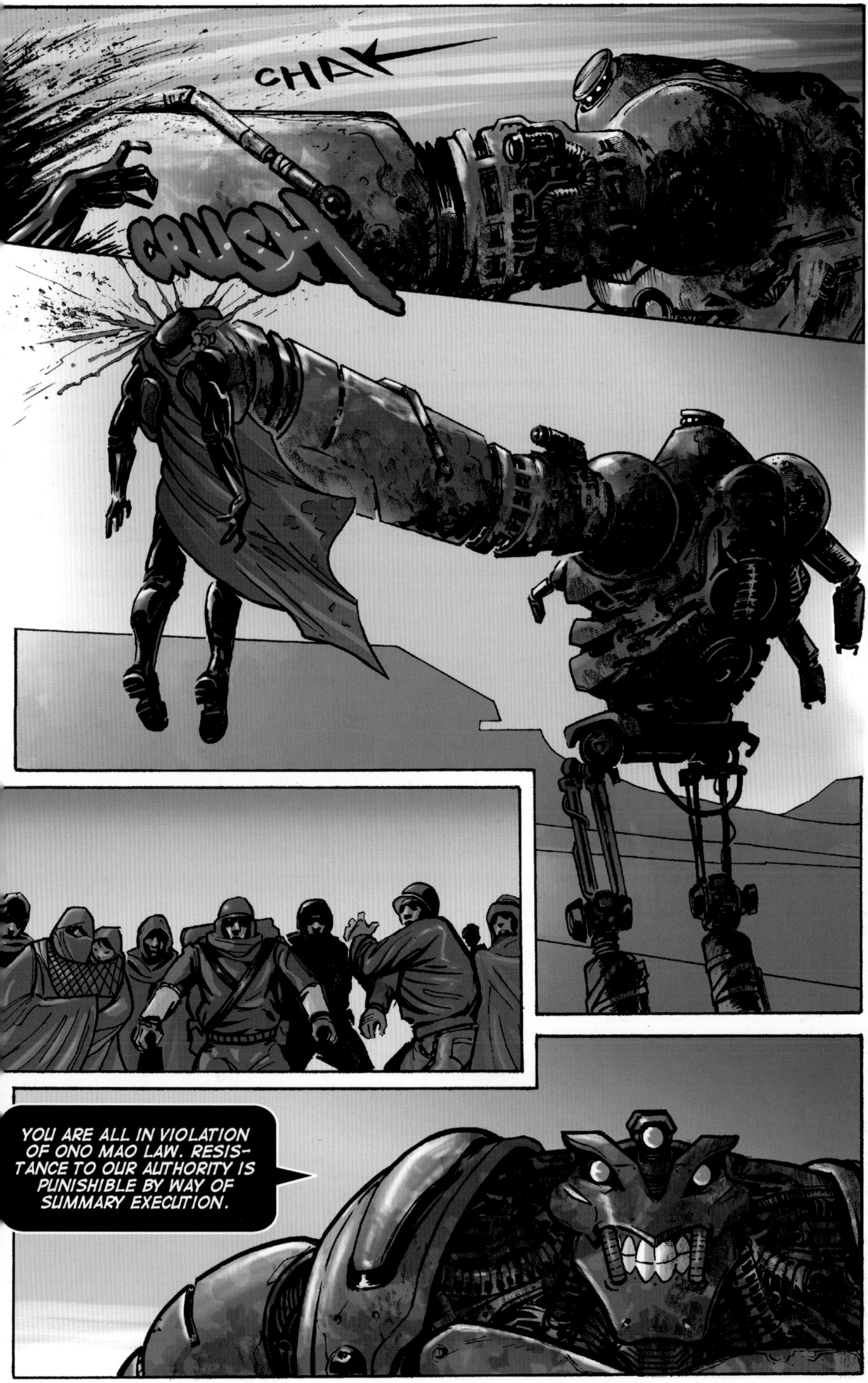
CHAK
CRUSH
YOU ARE ALL IN VIOLATION OF ONO MAO LAW. RESISTANCE TO OUR AUTHORITY IS PUNISHIBLE BY WAY OF SUMMARY EXECUTION.

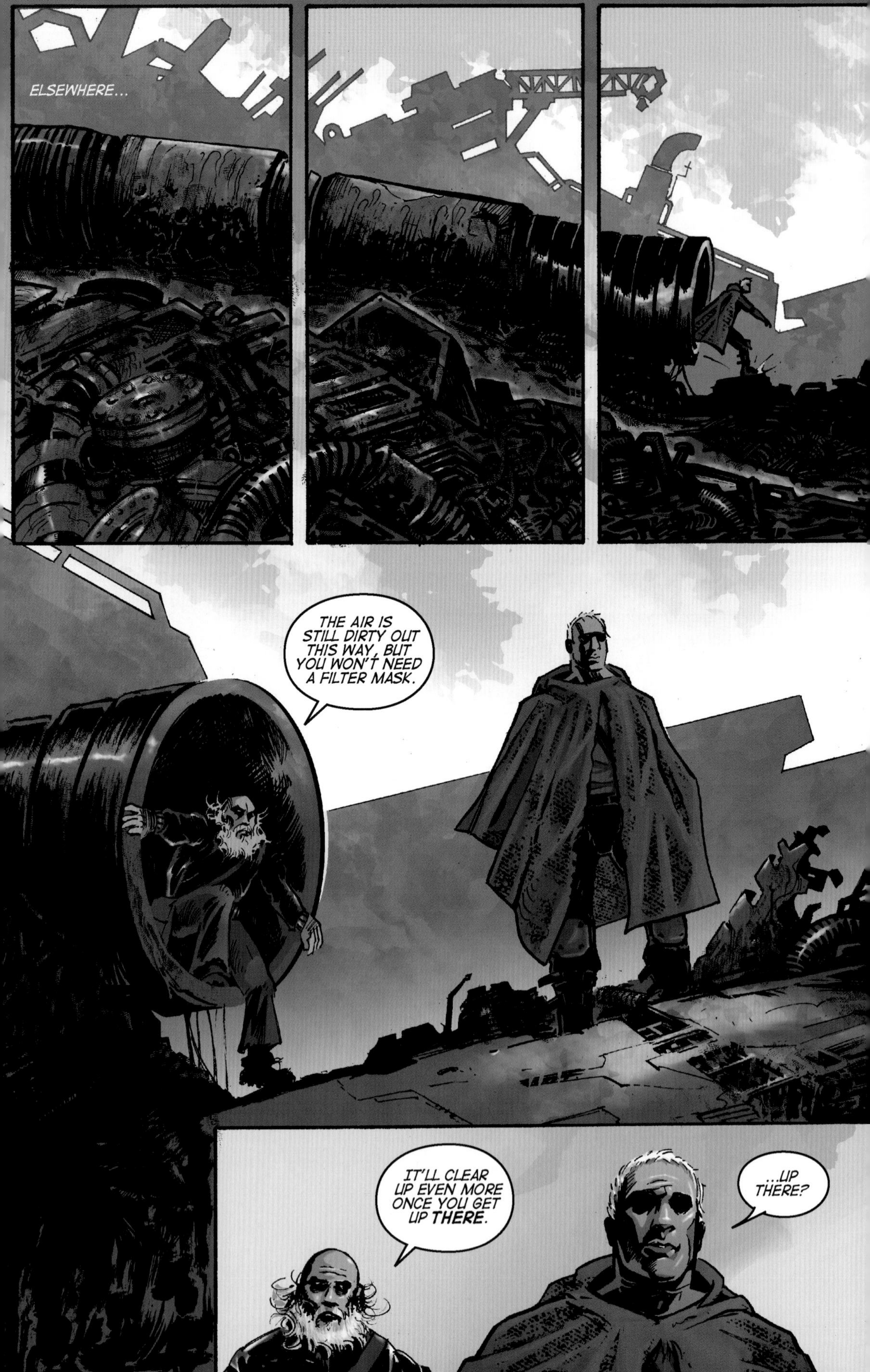
ELSEWHERE...
THE AIR IS STILL DIRTY OUT THIS WAY, BUT YOU WON'T NEED A FILTER MASK.
IT'LL CLEAR UP EVEN MORE ONCE YOU GET UP THERE.
...UP THERE?

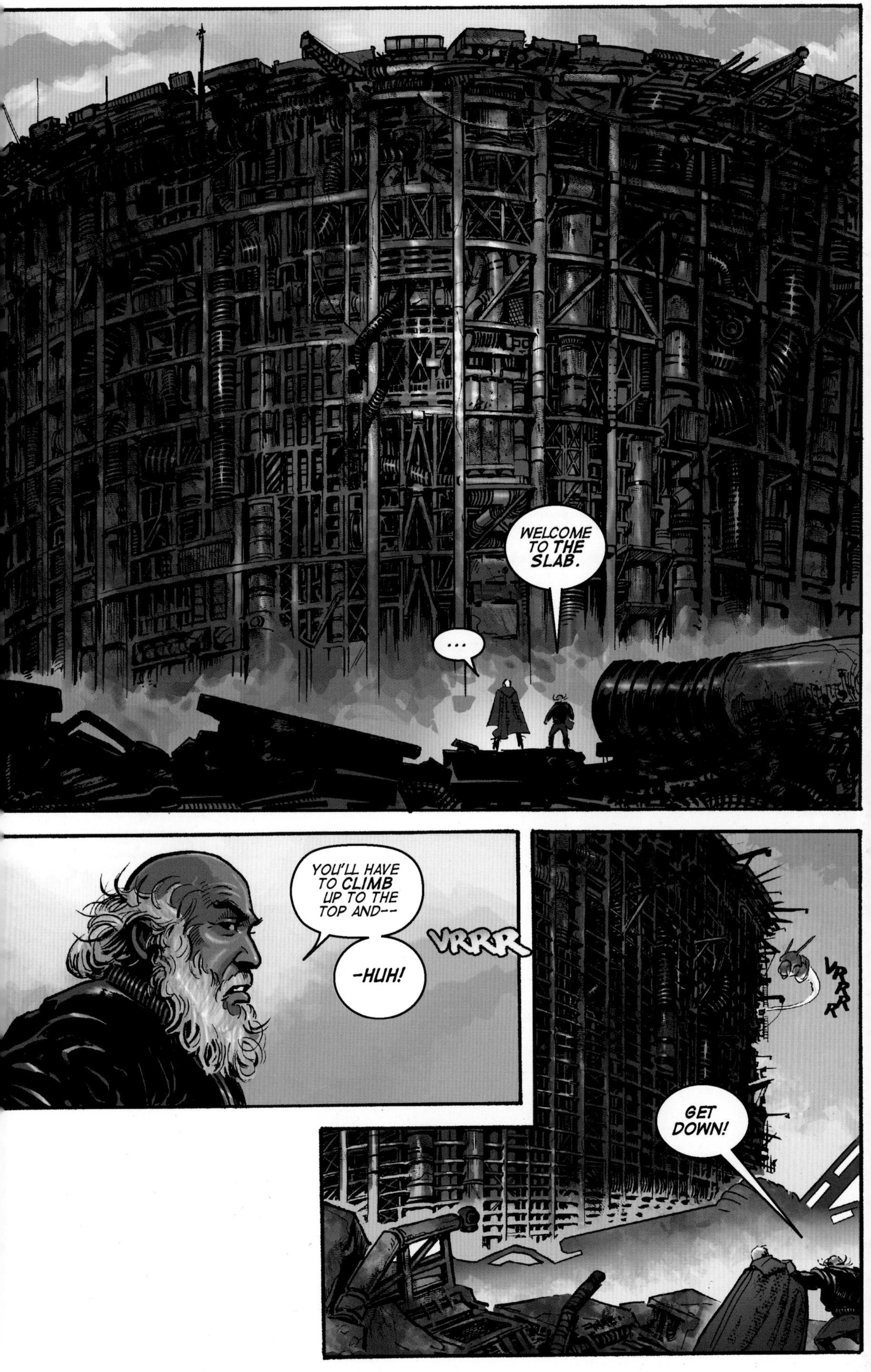
WELCOME TO THE SLAB.
...
YOU'LL HAVE TO CLIMB UP TO THE TOP AND--
VRRR
-HUH!
VRRRR
GET DOWN!

VRRRR

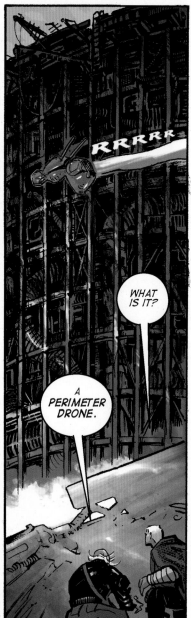

RRRRR

WHAT IS IT?

A PERIMETER DRONE.

VRR

YOU'LL HAVE TO BE **CAREFUL** FROM **NOW** ON...

IT **DIDN'T** DETECT US...?

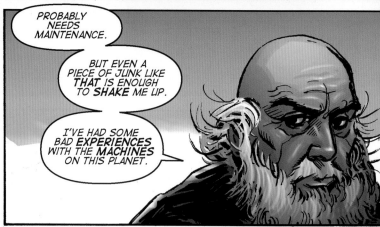

PROBABLY NEEDS MAINTENANCE.

BUT EVEN A PIECE OF JUNK LIKE **THAT** IS ENOUGH TO **SHAKE** ME UP.

I'VE HAD SOME BAD **EXPERIENCES** WITH THE **MACHINES** ON THIS PLANET.

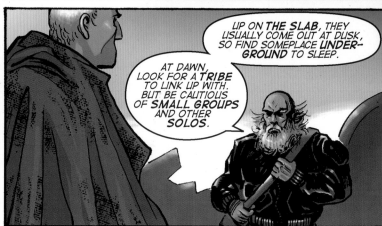

UP ON **THE SLAB**, THEY USUALLY COME OUT AT DUSK, SO FIND SOMEPLACE **UNDERGROUND** TO SLEEP.

AT DAWN, LOOK FOR A **TRIBE** TO LINK UP WITH. BUT BE CAUTIOUS OF **SMALL GROUPS** AND OTHER **SOLOS**.

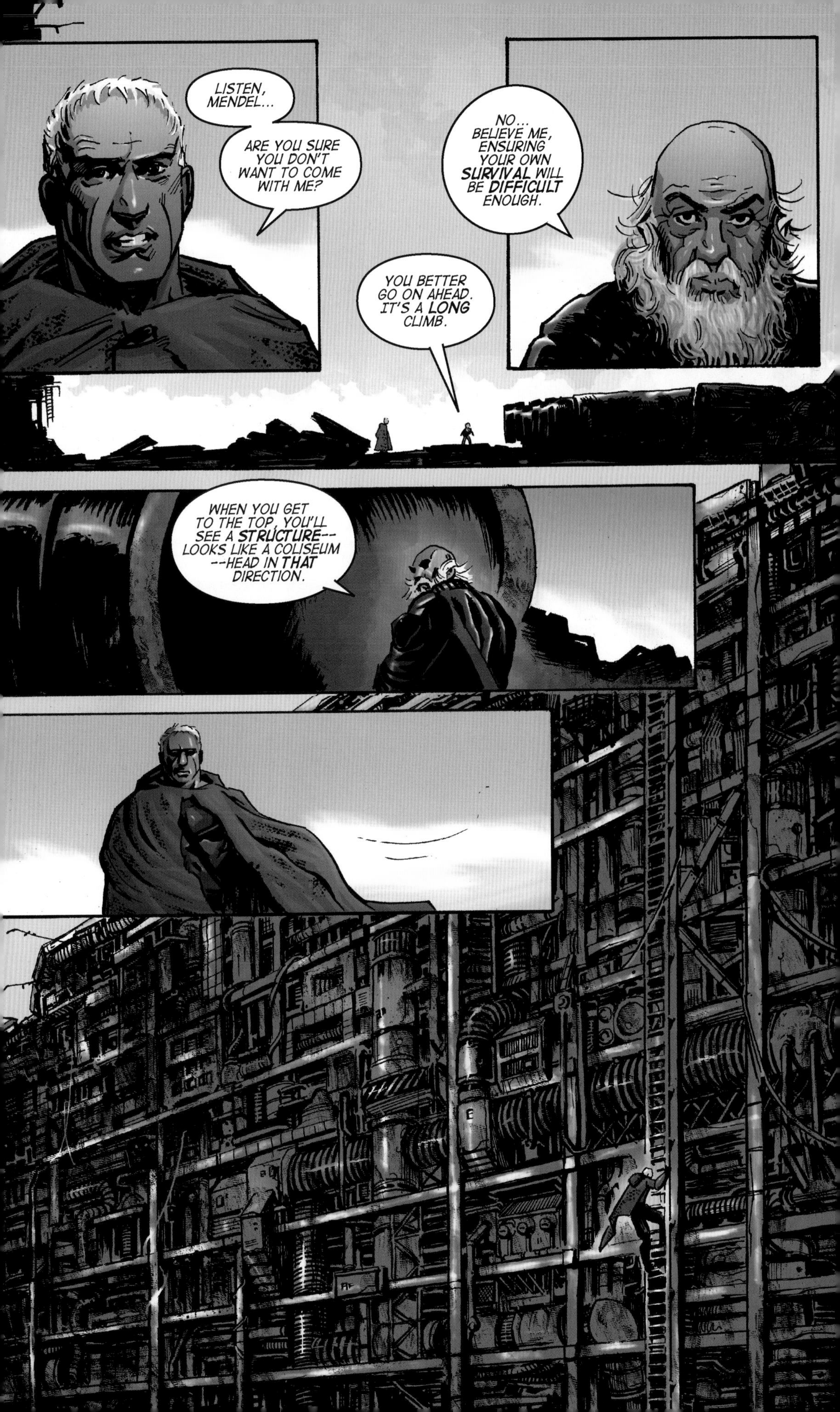
LISTEN, MENDEL...
ARE YOU SURE YOU DON'T WANT TO COME WITH ME?
NO... BELIEVE ME, ENSURING YOUR OWN SURVIVAL WILL BE DIFFICULT ENOUGH.
YOU BETTER GO ON AHEAD. IT'S A LONG CLIMB.
WHEN YOU GET TO THE TOP, YOU'LL SEE A STRUCTURE-- LOOKS LIKE A COLISEUM --HEAD IN THAT DIRECTION.

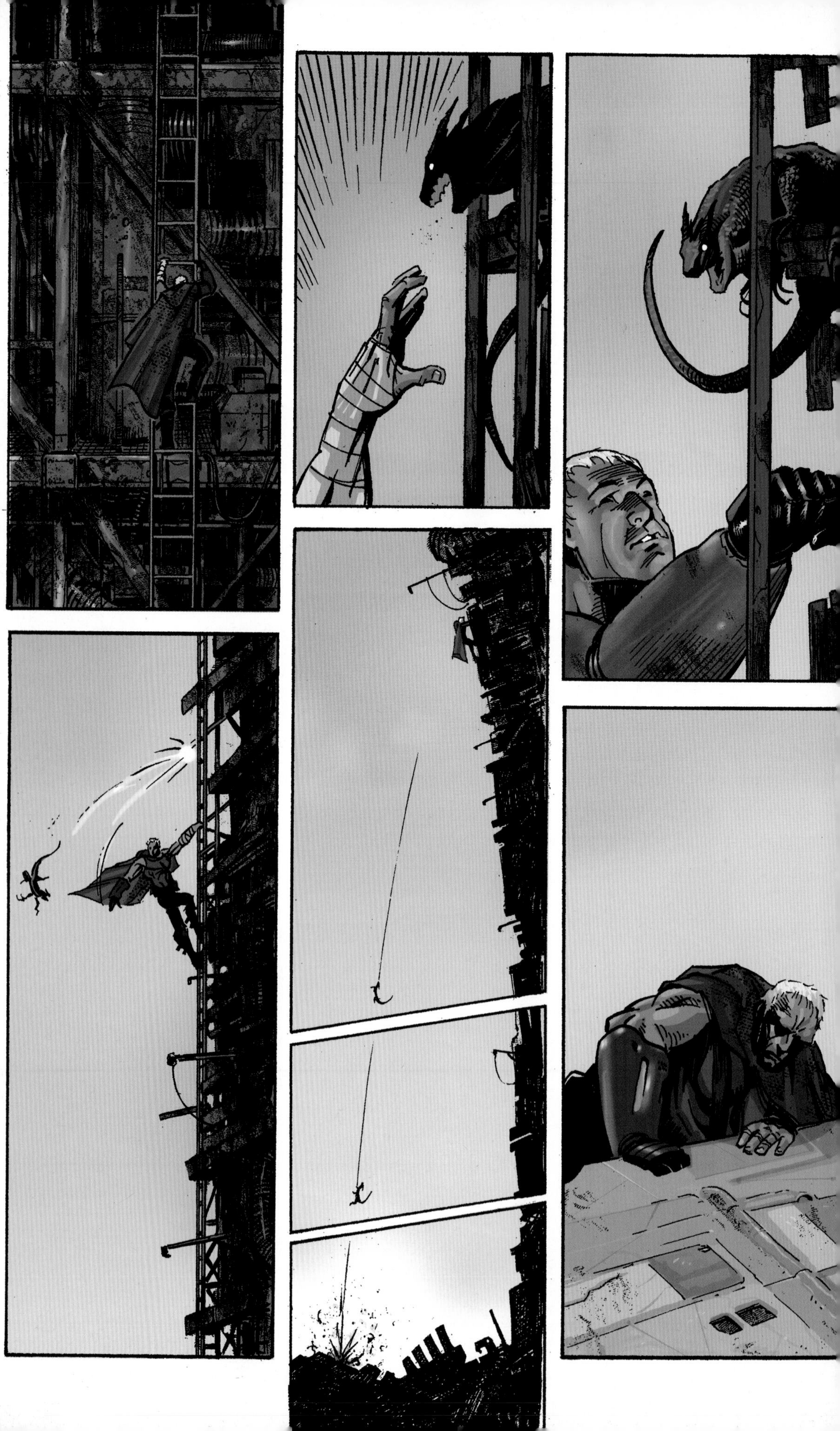

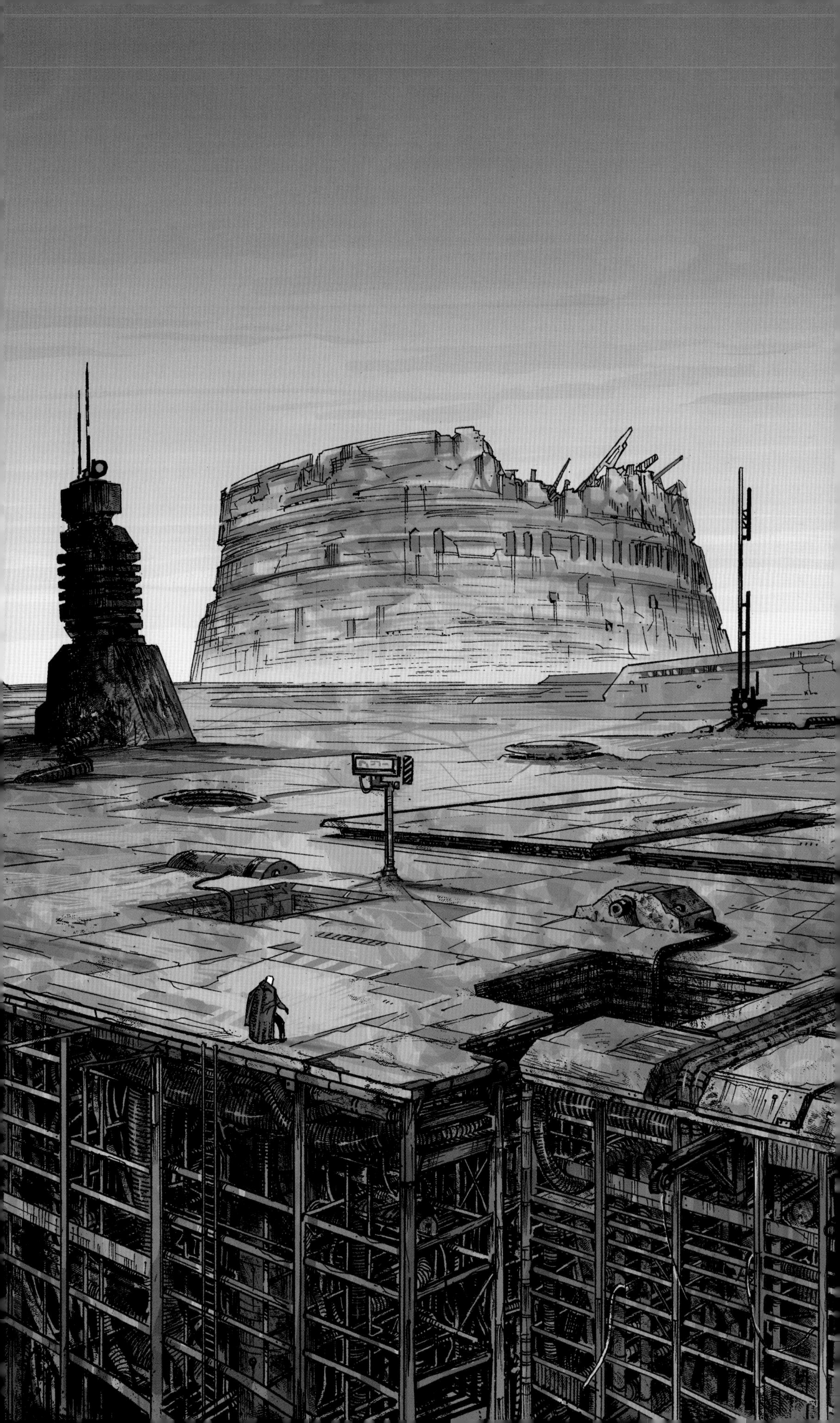

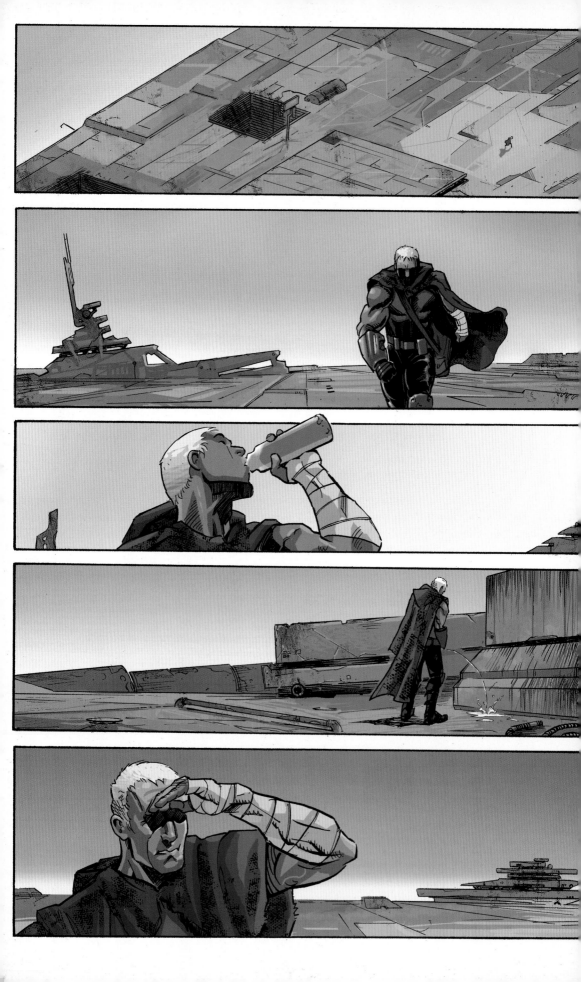

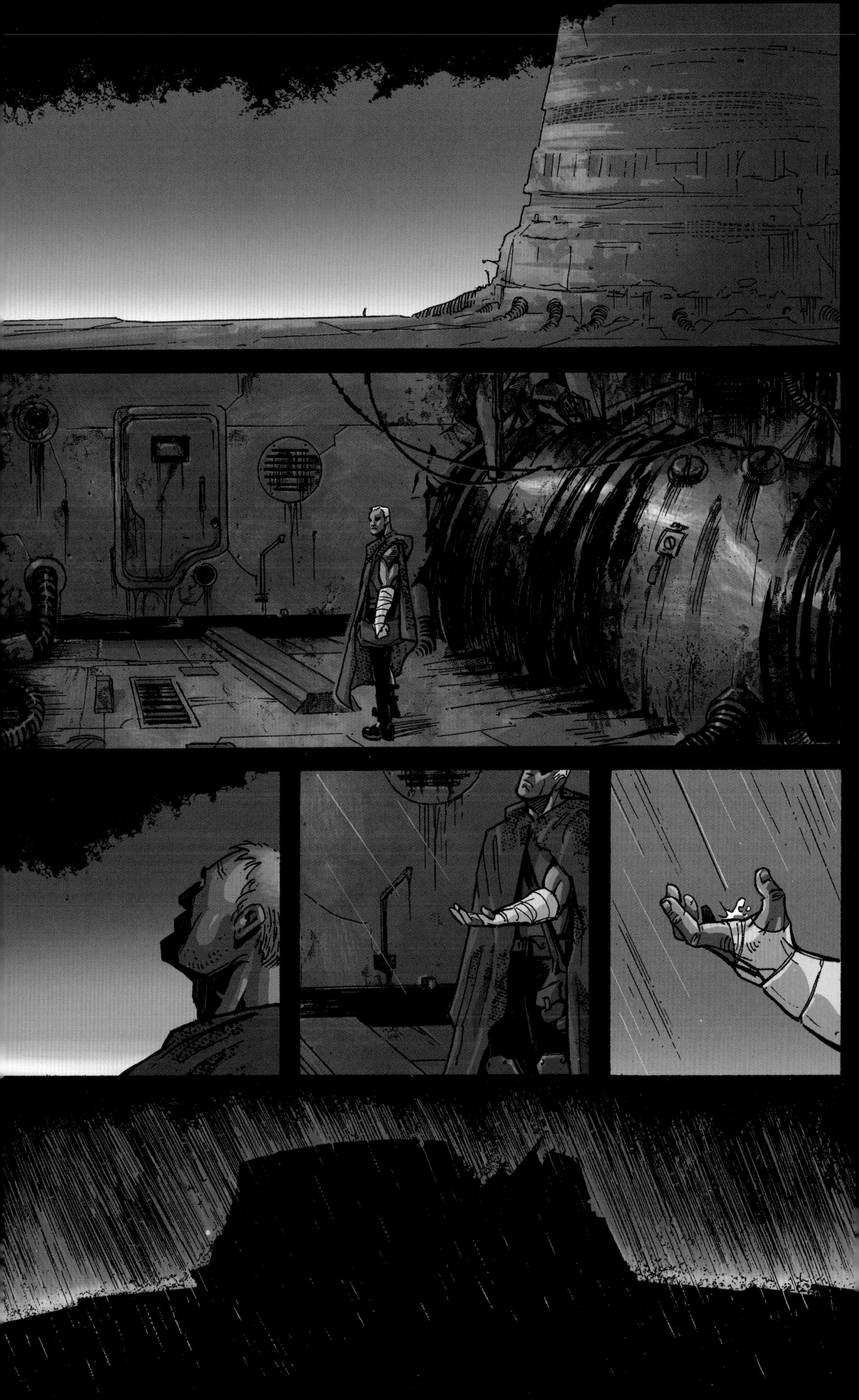

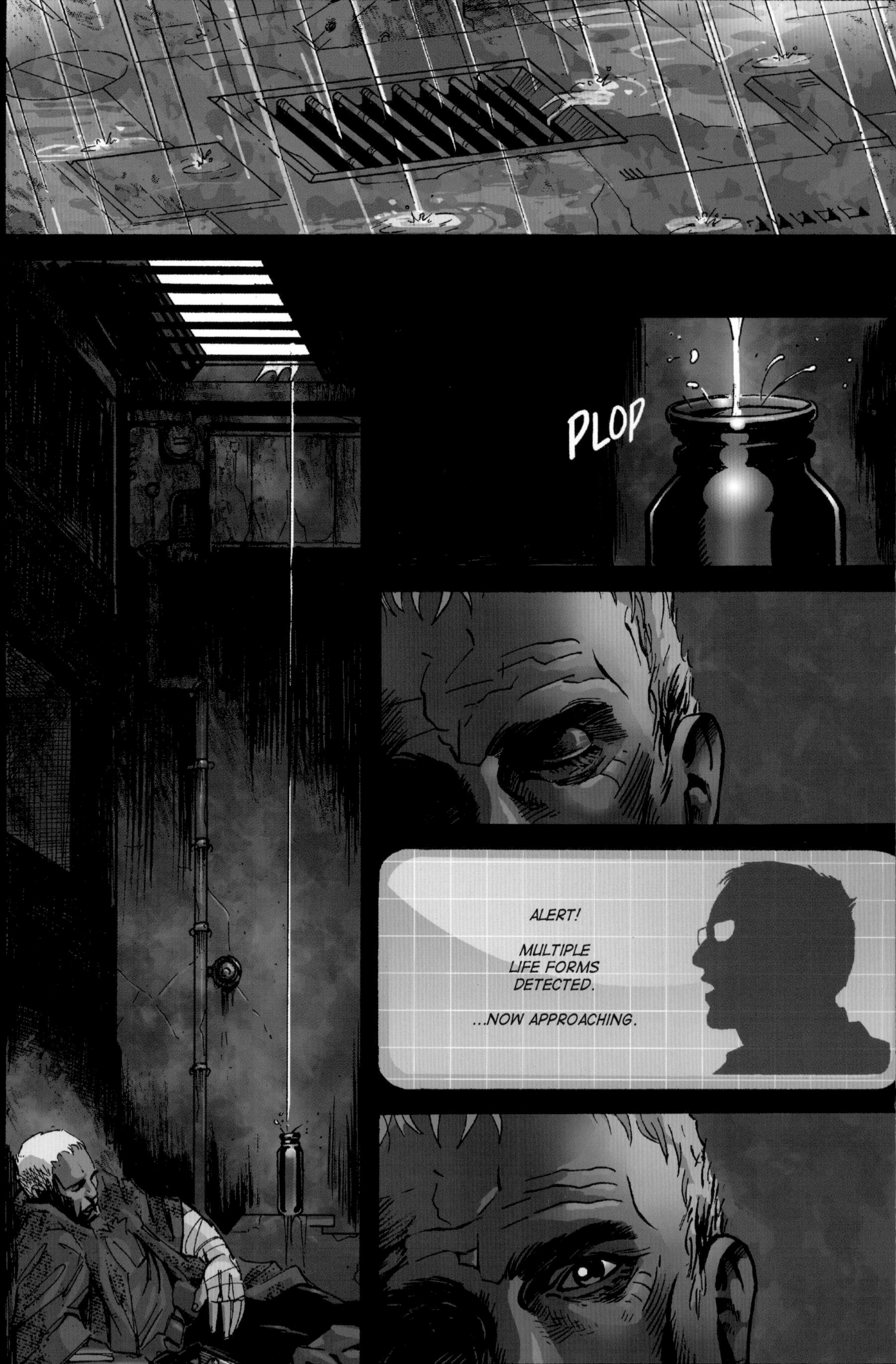
PLOP
ALERT!
MULTIPLE LIFE FORMS DETECTED.
...NOW APPROACHING.

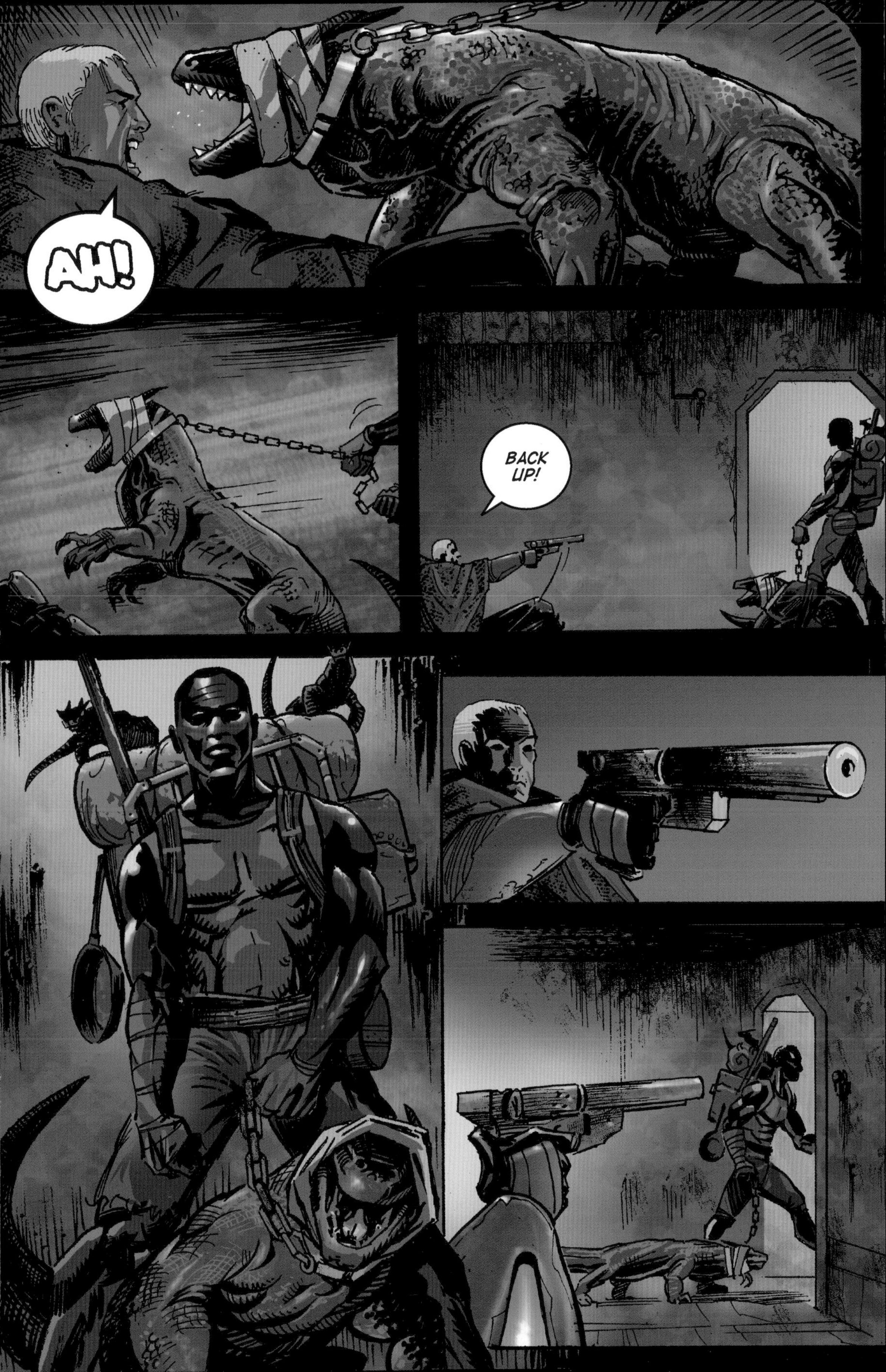
AH!
BACK UP!

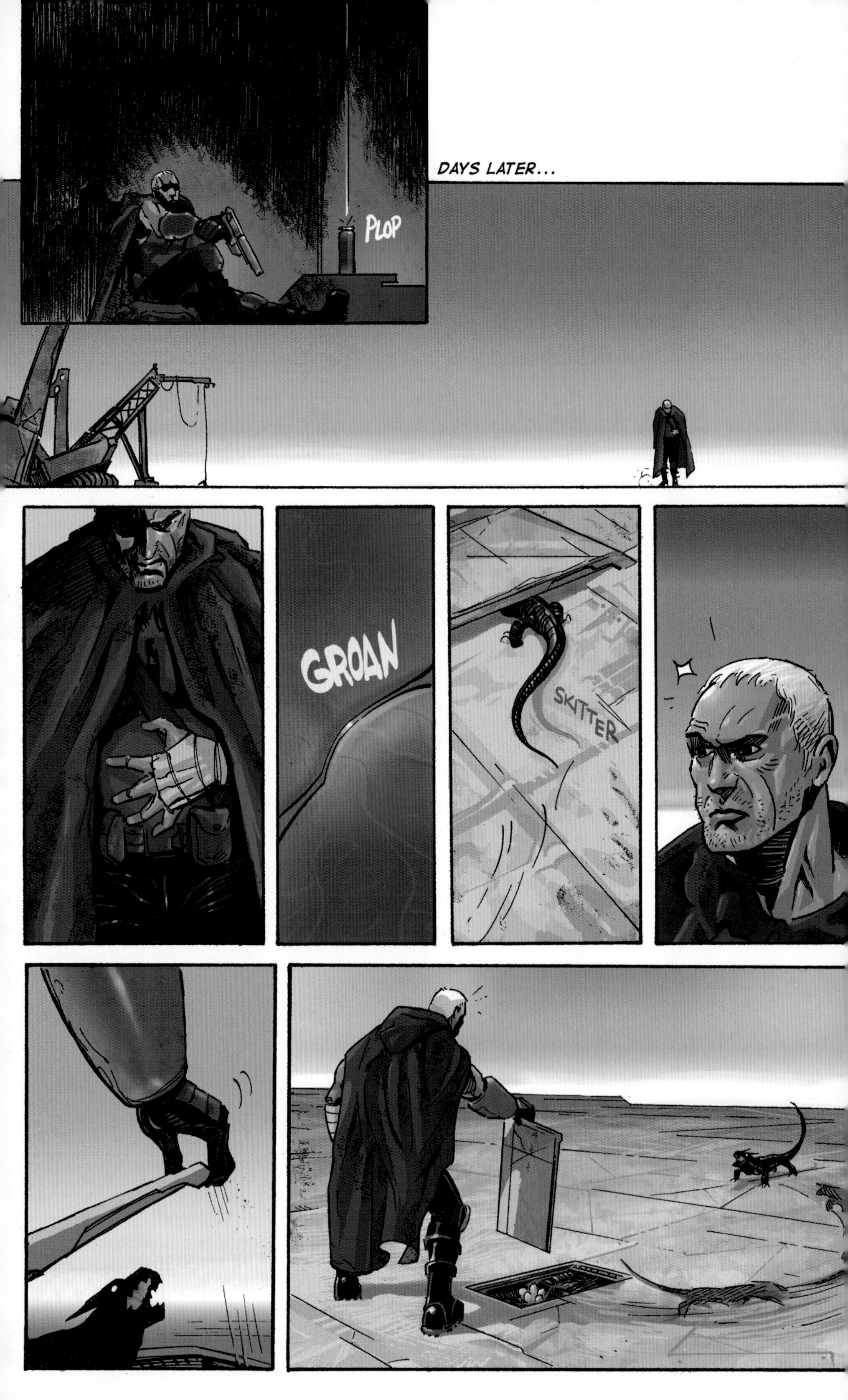
PLOP
DAYS LATER...
GROAN
SKITTER

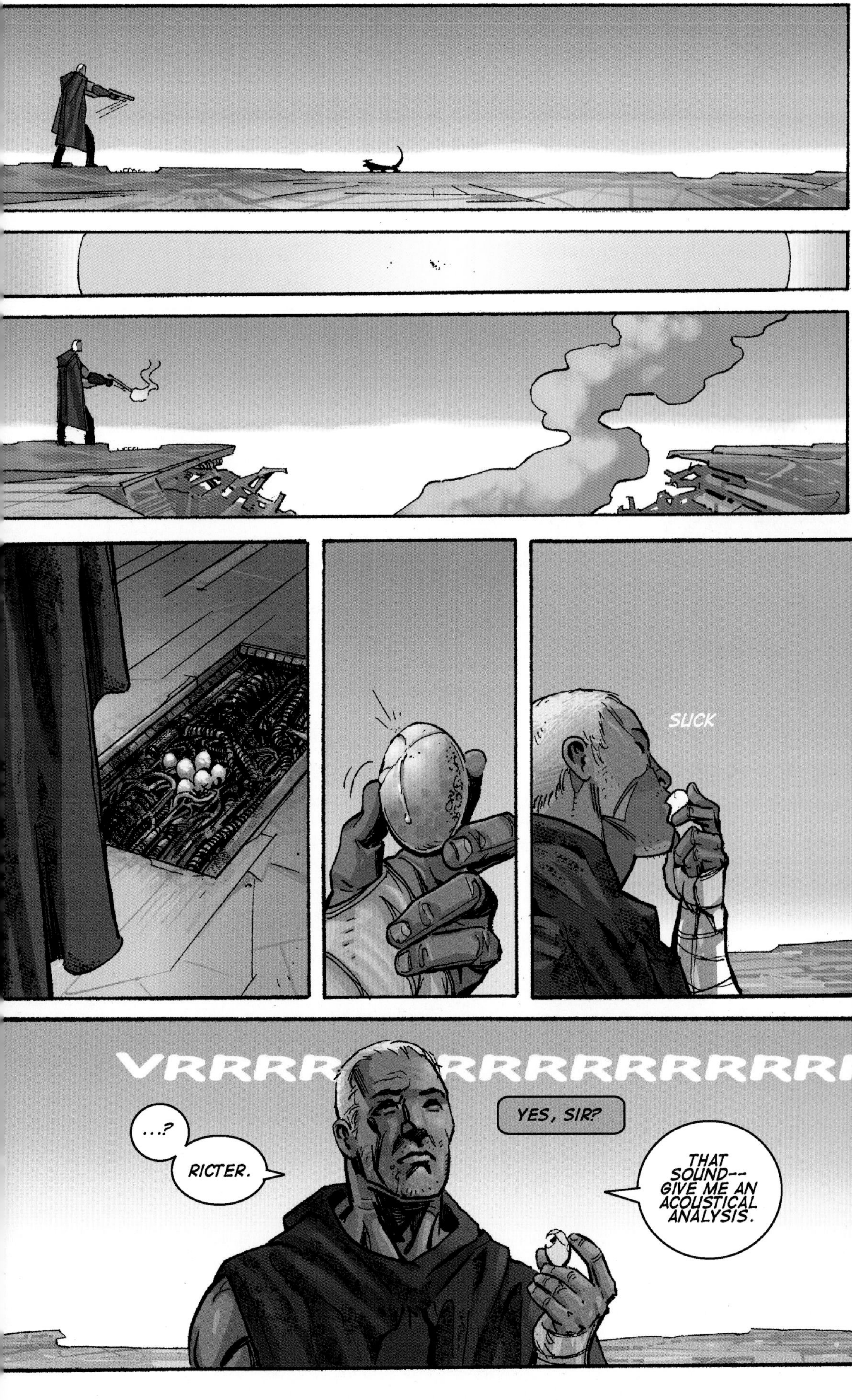
SLICK
VRRRRRRRRRRRRRRRRR
...?
RICTER.
YES, SIR?
THAT SOUND-- GIVE ME AN ACOUSTICAL ANALYSIS.

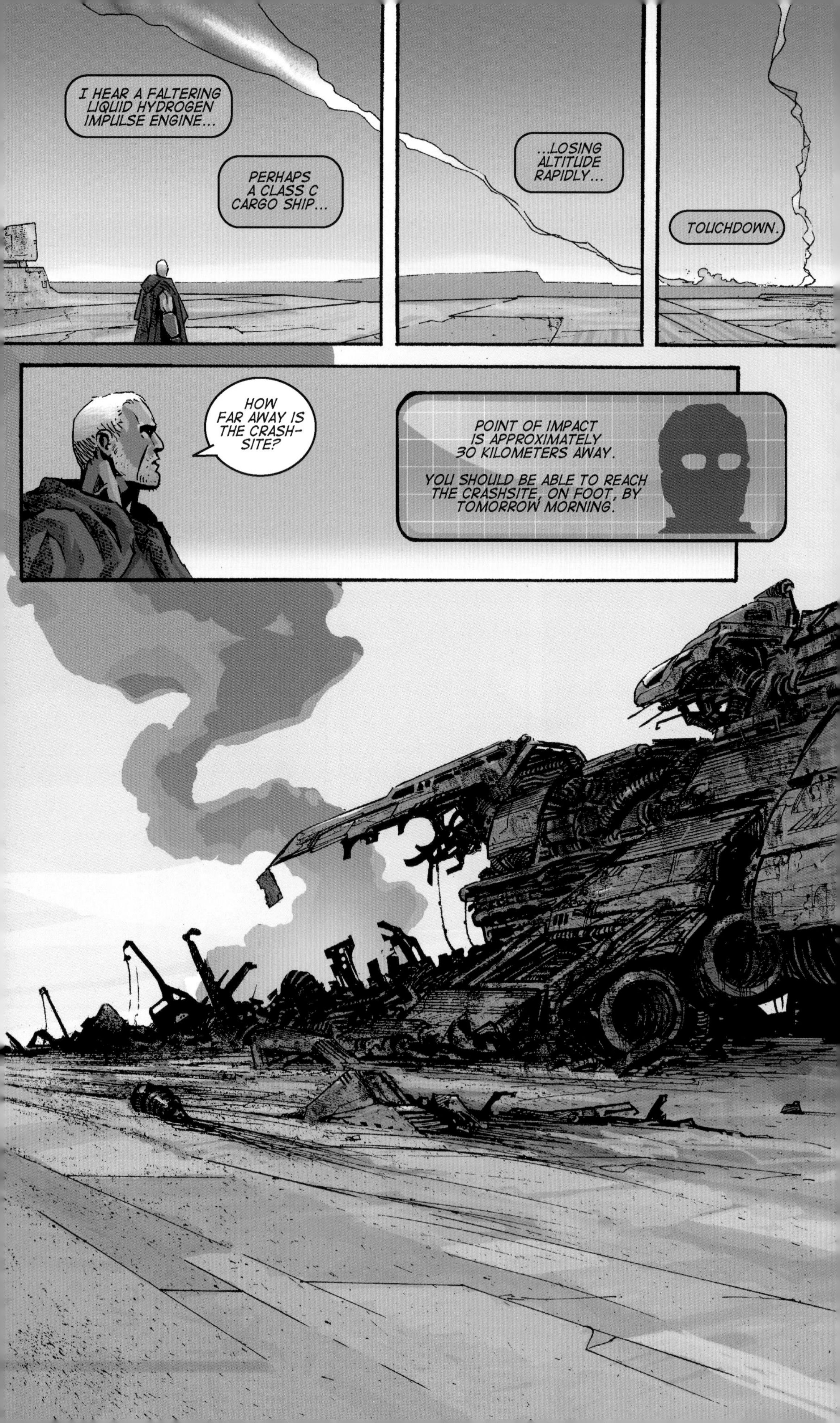
I HEAR A FALTERING LIQUID HYDROGEN IMPULSE ENGINE...
PERHAPS A CLASS C CARGO SHIP...
...LOSING ALTITUDE RAPIDLY...
TOUCHDOWN.
HOW FAR AWAY IS THE CRASH-SITE?
POINT OF IMPACT IS APPROXIMATELY 30 KILOMETERS AWAY.
YOU SHOULD BE ABLE TO REACH THE CRASHSITE, ON FOOT, BY TOMORROW MORNING.

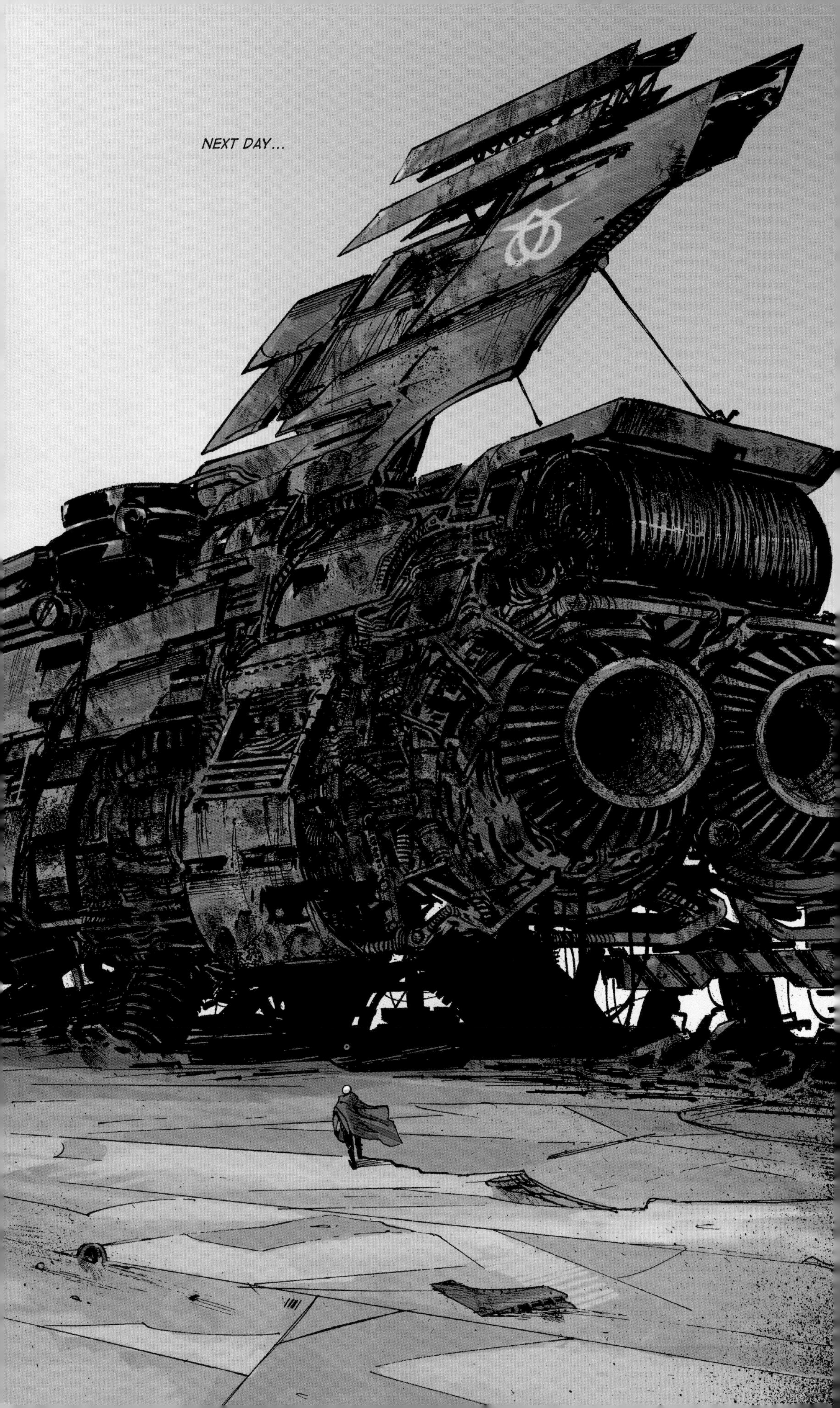
NEXT DAY...

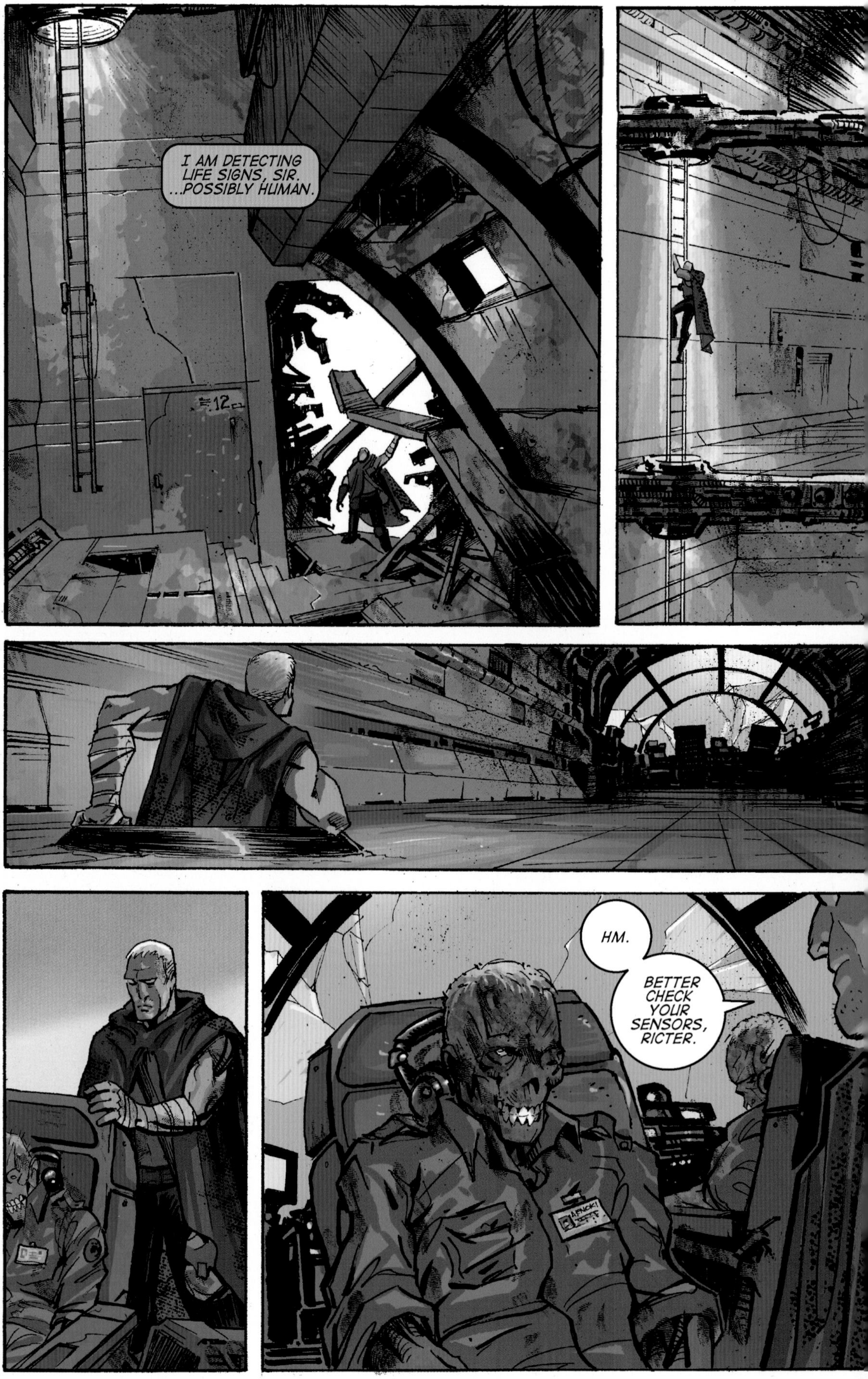
I AM DETECTING LIFE SIGNS, SIR. ...POSSIBLY HUMAN.
HM.
BETTER CHECK YOUR SENSORS, RICTER.

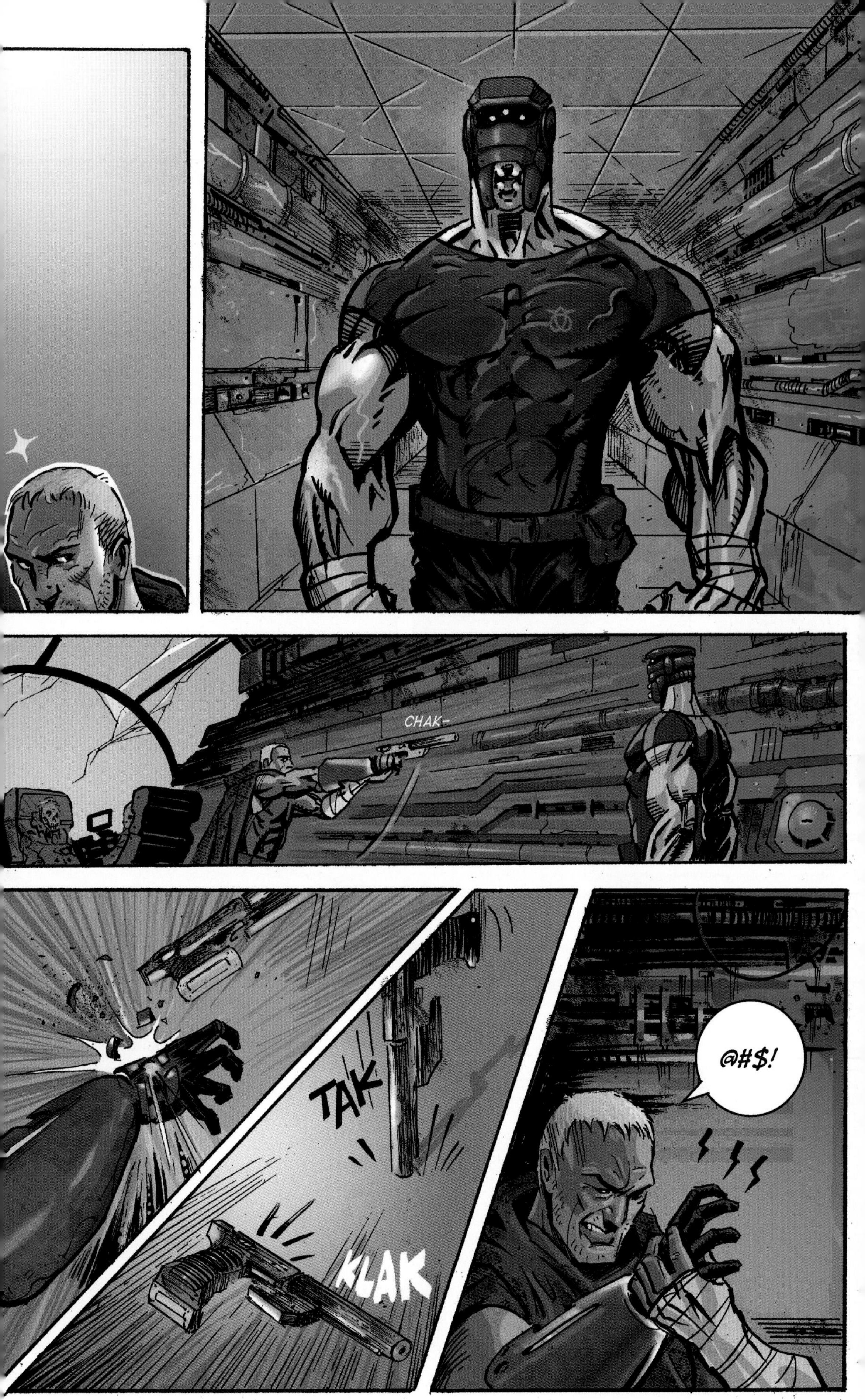
CHAK-
TAK
KLAK
@#$!

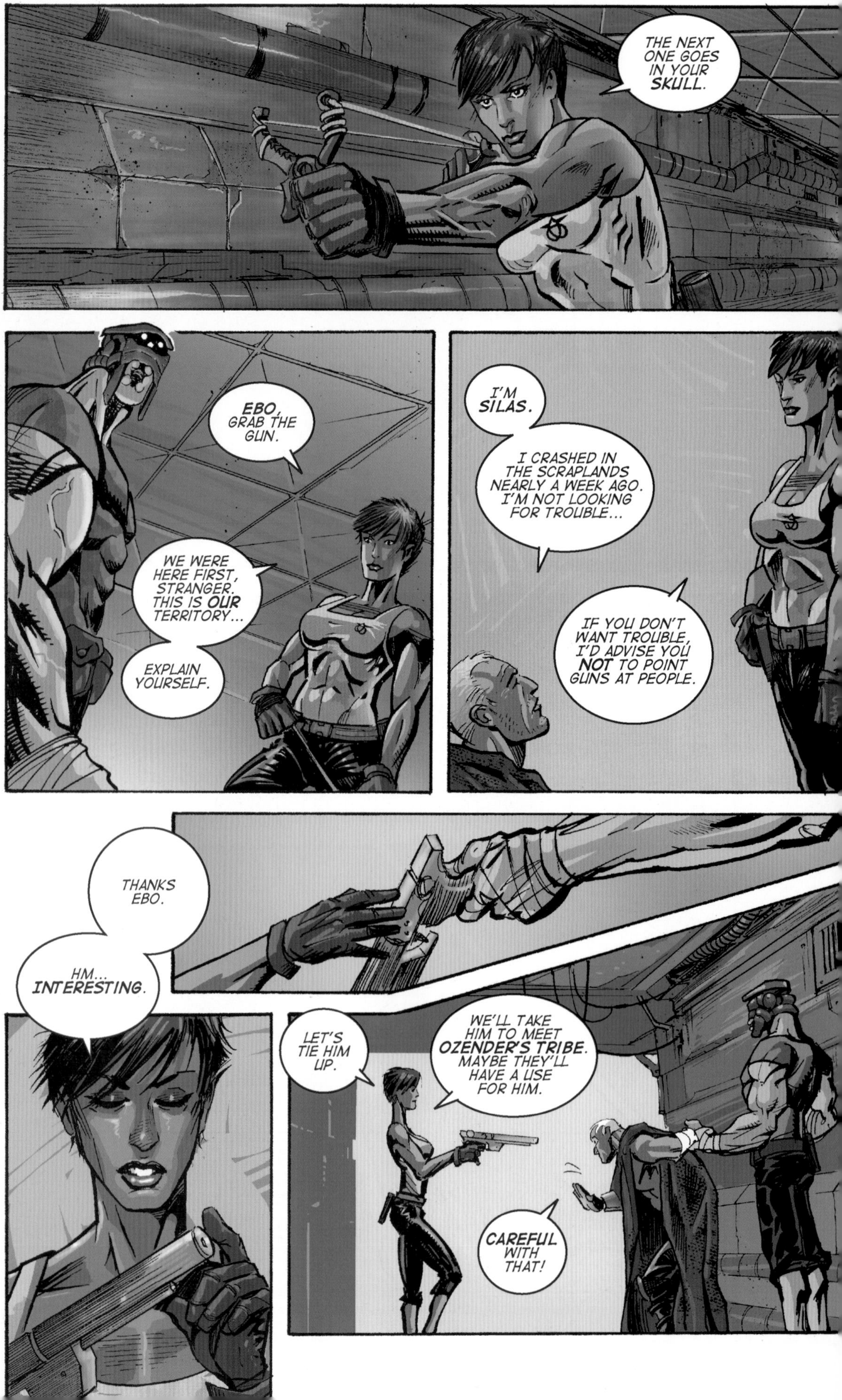

THE NEXT ONE GOES IN YOUR **SKULL**.
EBO, GRAB THE GUN.
WE WERE HERE FIRST, STRANGER. THIS IS **OUR** TERRITORY...
EXPLAIN YOURSELF.
I'M **SILAS**.
I CRASHED IN THE SCRAPLANDS NEARLY A WEEK AGO. I'M NOT LOOKING FOR TROUBLE...
IF YOU DON'T WANT TROUBLE, I'D ADVISE YOU **NOT** TO POINT GUNS AT PEOPLE.
THANKS EBO.
HM... **INTERESTING**.
LET'S TIE HIM UP.
WE'LL TAKE HIM TO MEET **OZENDER'S TRIBE**. MAYBE THEY'LL HAVE A USE FOR HIM.
CAREFUL WITH THAT!

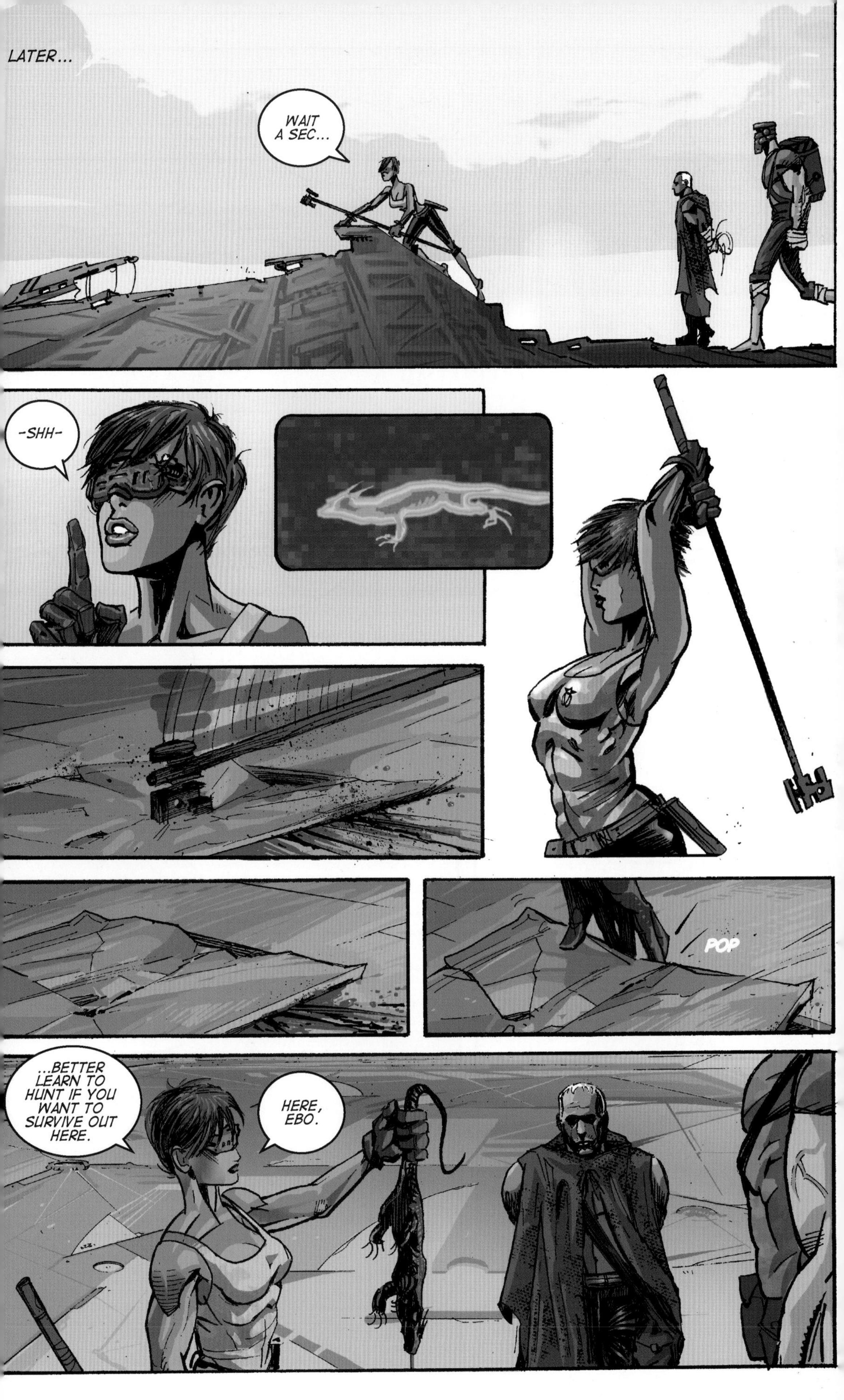
LATER...
WAIT A SEC...
-SHH-
POP
...BETTER LEARN TO HUNT IF YOU WANT TO SURVIVE OUT HERE.
HERE, EBO.

LET ME SHOW YOU SOMETHING ELSE...

COME HERE.

LOOK...

SEE THAT *STRUCTURE* IN THE DISTANCE?

YEAH...

DAMN! IT GOES RIGHT UP INTO THE ATMOSPHERE!

IT'S A *SKY LADDER*--

--A MASSIVE FREIGHT *ELEVATOR* THAT RUNS UP TO AN *ORBITAL* DOCKING PLATFORM.

IT WAS USED TO *EXPORT* RAW MATERIALS OFF-PLANET.

...BUT MORE IMPORTANTLY IT'S THE BASE OF OPERATIONS FOR *THE ROVERS* AND BROADCAST TOWER FOR THEIR *A.I. PROGRAM*.

SO STAY THE HELL *AWAY* FROM IT!

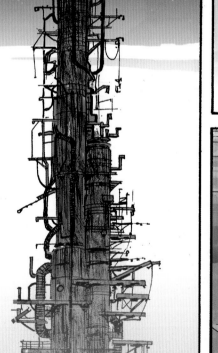

RUH- *ROVERS*?

YEAH, GIANT *ROBOTS* THAT LIKE TO KILL AND TORTURE PEOPLE.

SPEAKING OF WHICH, IT'S TIME TO GO *UNDER-GROUND*.

CAN'T YOU UNTIE ME FOR THIS?

NO, SORRY.

THIS IS *TOO* ENTERTAINING.

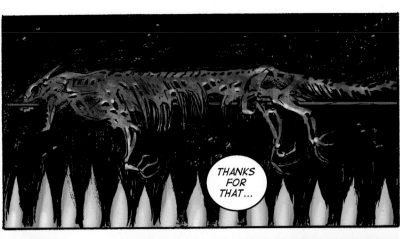

THANKS FOR THAT...

... I WAS *STARVING*.

THERE'S SOME FOOD PROVISIONS ON THAT DOWNED SHIP...

...BUT THAT'S FOR ME AND EBO.

I'M SURPRISED THAT YOU LEFT THAT SHIP *UNATTENDED*.

WE STASHED *SOME* SUPPLIES EARLIER, BUT IT DOESN'T MATTER... THE *ROVERS* WILL SOON COME AND DISMANTLE THE SHIP.

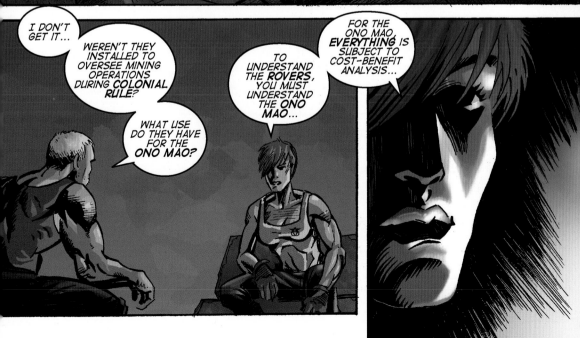

I DON'T GET IT...

WEREN'T THEY INSTALLED TO OVERSEE MINING OPERATIONS DURING *COLONIAL RULE*?

WHAT USE DO THEY HAVE FOR THE *ONO MAO*?

TO UNDERSTAND THE *ROVERS*, YOU MUST UNDERSTAND THE *ONO MAO*...

FOR THE *ONO MAO*, *EVERYTHING* IS SUBJECT TO COST-BENEFIT ANALYSIS...

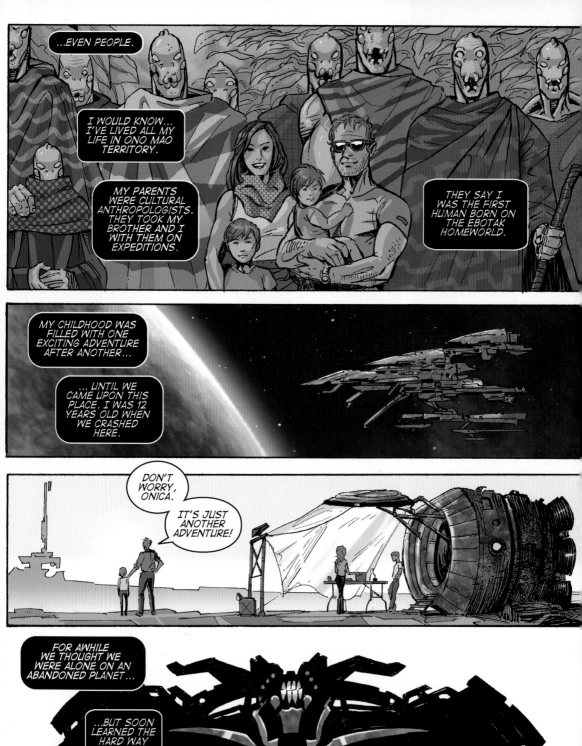

...EVEN PEOPLE.

I WOULD KNOW... I'VE LIVED ALL MY LIFE IN ONO MAO TERRITORY.

MY PARENTS WERE CULTURAL ANTHROPOLOGISTS. THEY TOOK MY BROTHER AND I WITH THEM ON EXPEDITIONS.

THEY SAY I WAS THE FIRST HUMAN BORN ON THE EBOTAK HOMEWORLD.

MY CHILDHOOD WAS FILLED WITH ONE EXCITING ADVENTURE AFTER ANOTHER...

...UNTIL WE CAME UPON THIS PLACE. I WAS 12 YEARS OLD WHEN WE CRASHED HERE.

DON'T WORRY, ONICA.

IT'S JUST ANOTHER ADVENTURE!

FOR AWHILE WE THOUGHT WE WERE ALONE ON AN ABANDONED PLANET...

...BUT SOON LEARNED THE HARD WAY THAT WE WERE NOT.

WE WERE TAKEN TO A CHAMBER AT THE BASE OF THE SKY LADDER.

I WAS SO LITTLE AND SKINNY THAT I MANAGED TO SLIP OUT OF MY BINDINGS...

WHA-- WHAT DO I DO?

-SOB-

FORGET US ONICA! RUN! GO!

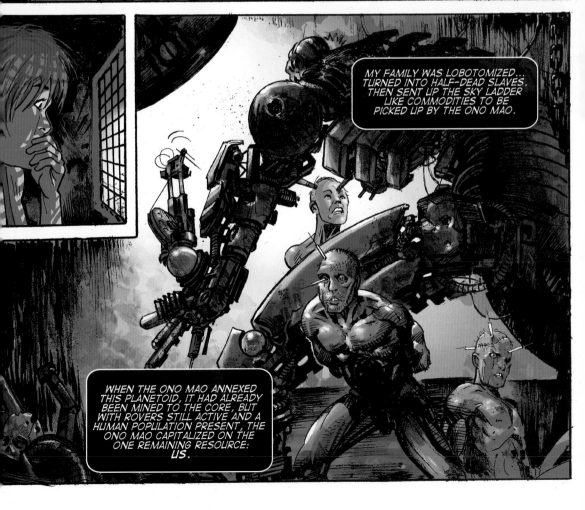

MY FAMILY WAS LOBOTOMIZED... TURNED INTO HALF-DEAD SLAVES. THEN SENT UP THE SKY LADDER LIKE COMMODITIES TO BE PICKED UP BY THE ONO MAO.

WHEN THE ONO MAO ANNEXED THIS PLANETOID, IT HAD ALREADY BEEN MINED TO THE CORE, BUT WITH ROVERS STILL ACTIVE AND A HUMAN POPULATION PRESENT, THE ONO MAO CAPITALIZED ON THE ONE REMAINING RESOURCE: US.

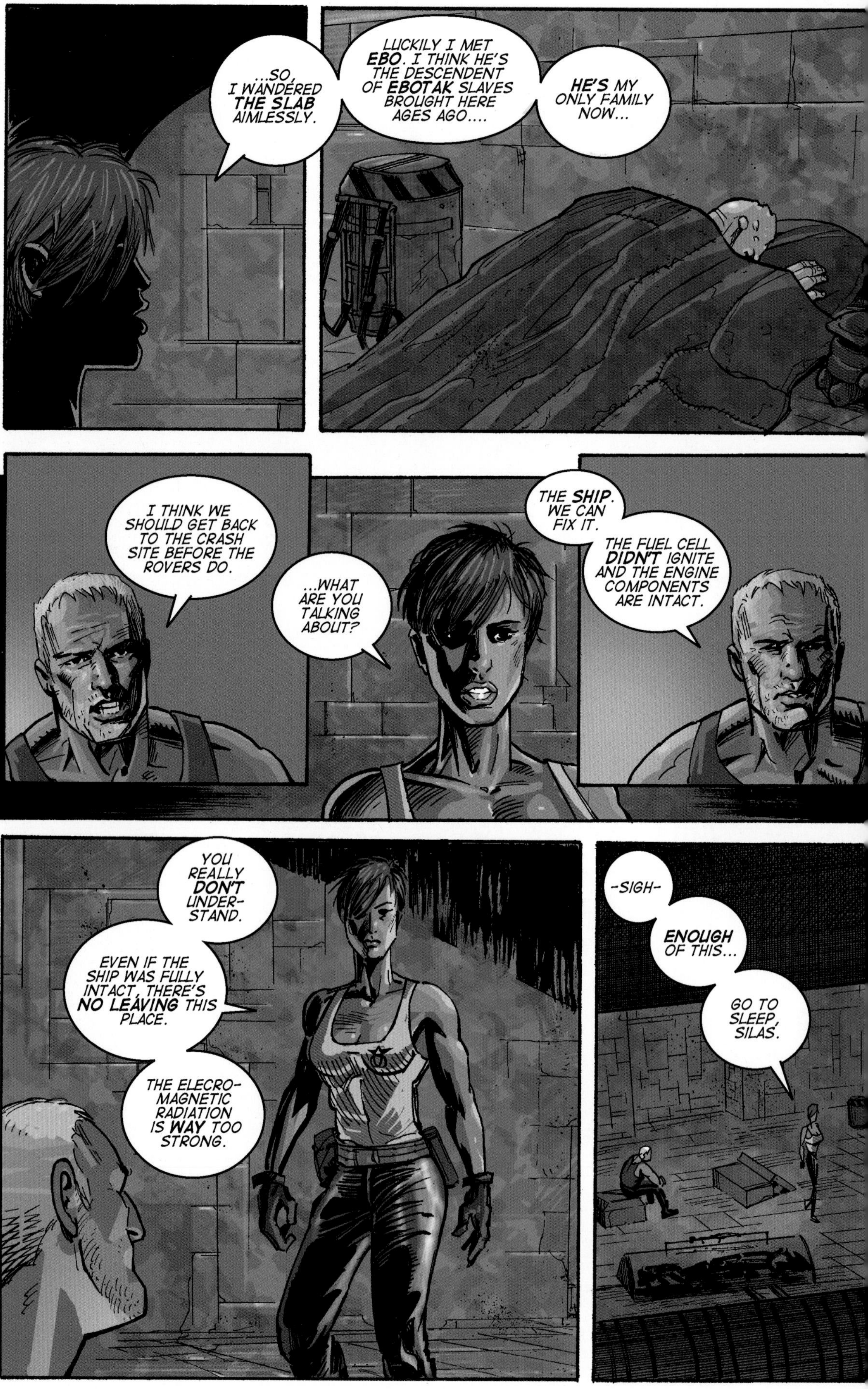
...SO, I WANDERED THE SLAB AIMLESSLY.
LUCKILY I MET EBO. I THINK HE'S THE DESCENDENT OF EBOTAK SLAVES BROUGHT HERE AGES AGO....
HE'S MY ONLY FAMILY NOW...
I THINK WE SHOULD GET BACK TO THE CRASH SITE BEFORE THE ROVERS DO.
...WHAT ARE YOU TALKING ABOUT?
THE SHIP. WE CAN FIX IT.
THE FUEL CELL DIDN'T IGNITE AND THE ENGINE COMPONENTS ARE INTACT.
YOU REALLY DON'T UNDER-STAND.
EVEN IF THE SHIP WAS FULLY INTACT, THERE'S NO LEAVING THIS PLACE.
THE ELECRO-MAGNETIC RADIATION IS WAY TOO STRONG.
-SIGH-
ENOUGH OF THIS...
GO TO SLEEP, SILAS.

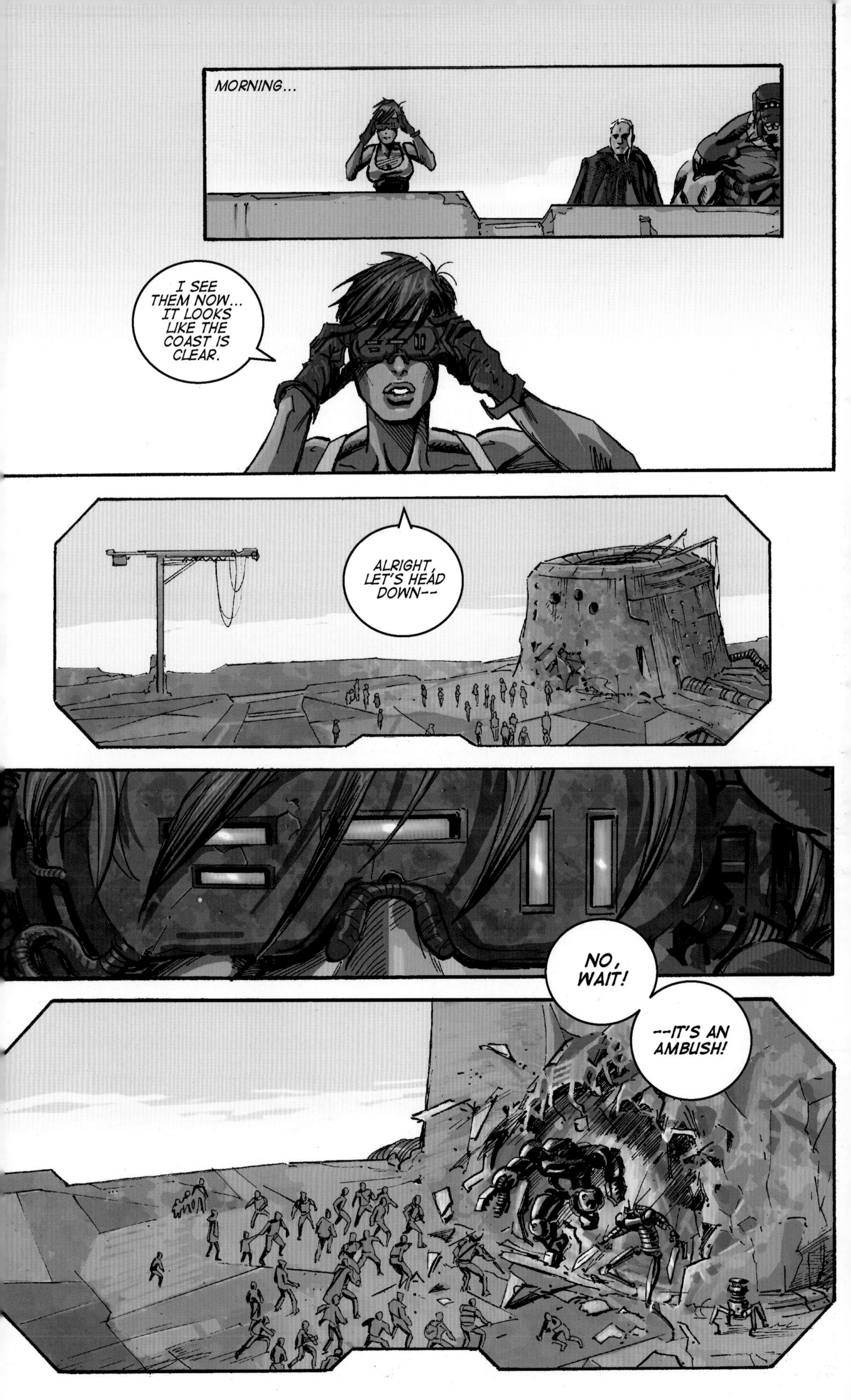
MORNING...
I SEE THEM NOW... IT LOOKS LIKE THE COAST IS CLEAR.
ALRIGHT, LET'S HEAD DOWN--
NO, WAIT!
--IT'S AN AMBUSH!

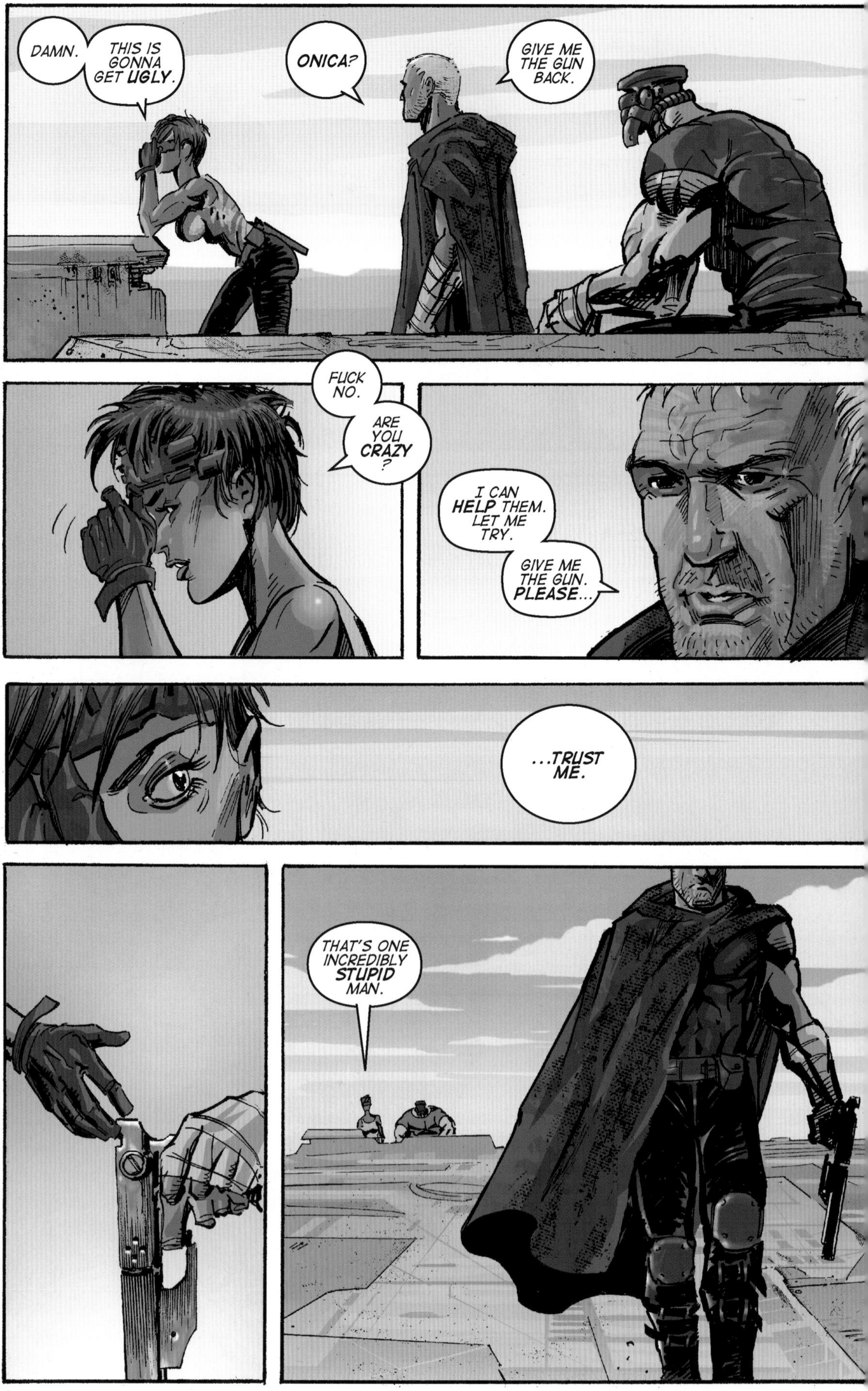
DAMN.
THIS IS GONNA GET UGLY.
ONICA?
GIVE ME THE GUN BACK.
FUCK NO.
ARE YOU CRAZY?
I CAN HELP THEM. LET ME TRY.
GIVE ME THE GUN. PLEASE...
...TRUST ME.
THAT'S ONE INCREDIBLY STUPID MAN.

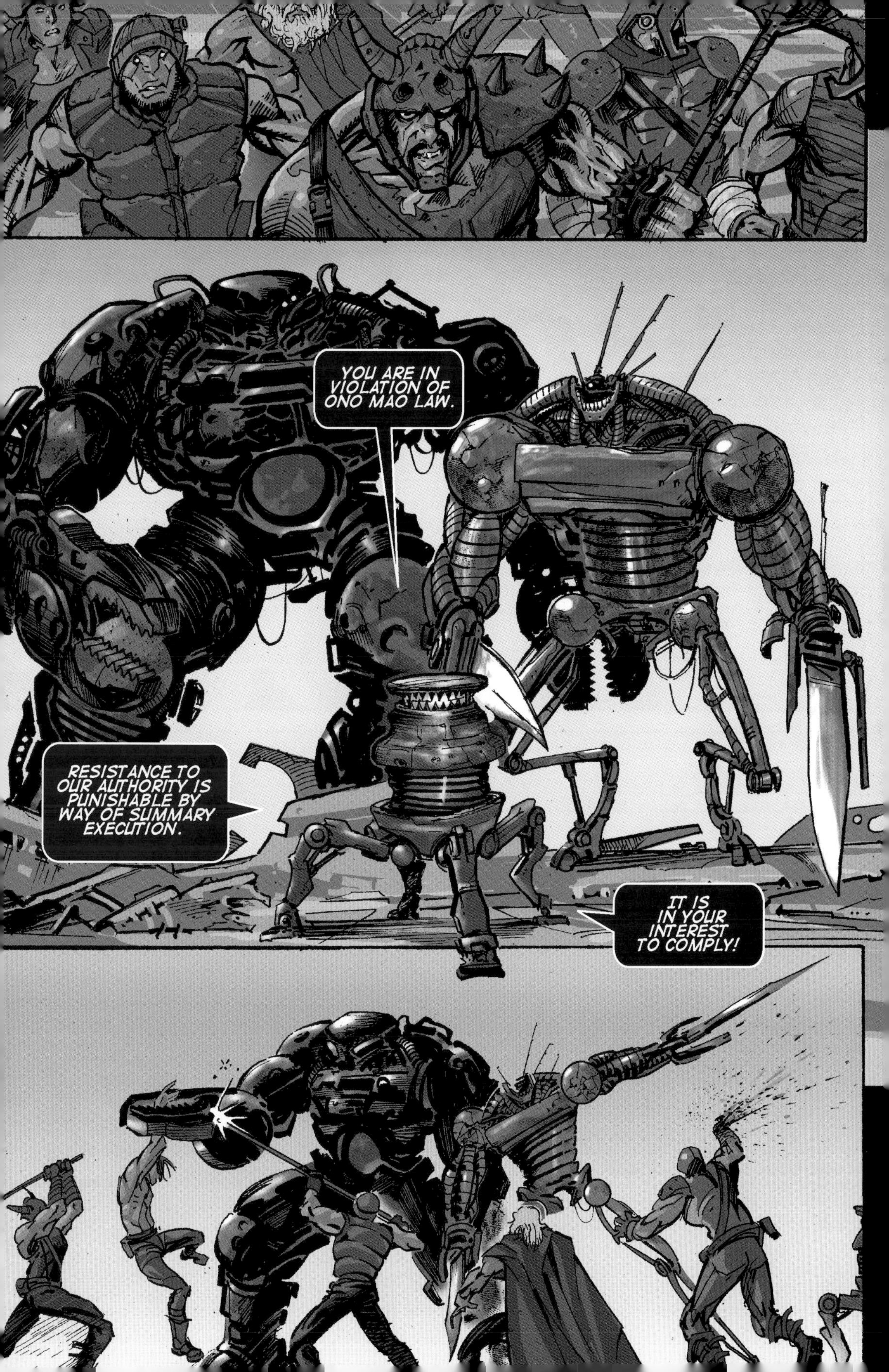
YOU ARE IN VIOLATION OF ONO MAO LAW.
RESISTANCE TO OUR AUTHORITY IS PUNISHABLE BY WAY OF SUMMARY EXECUTION.
IT IS IN YOUR INTEREST TO COMPLY!

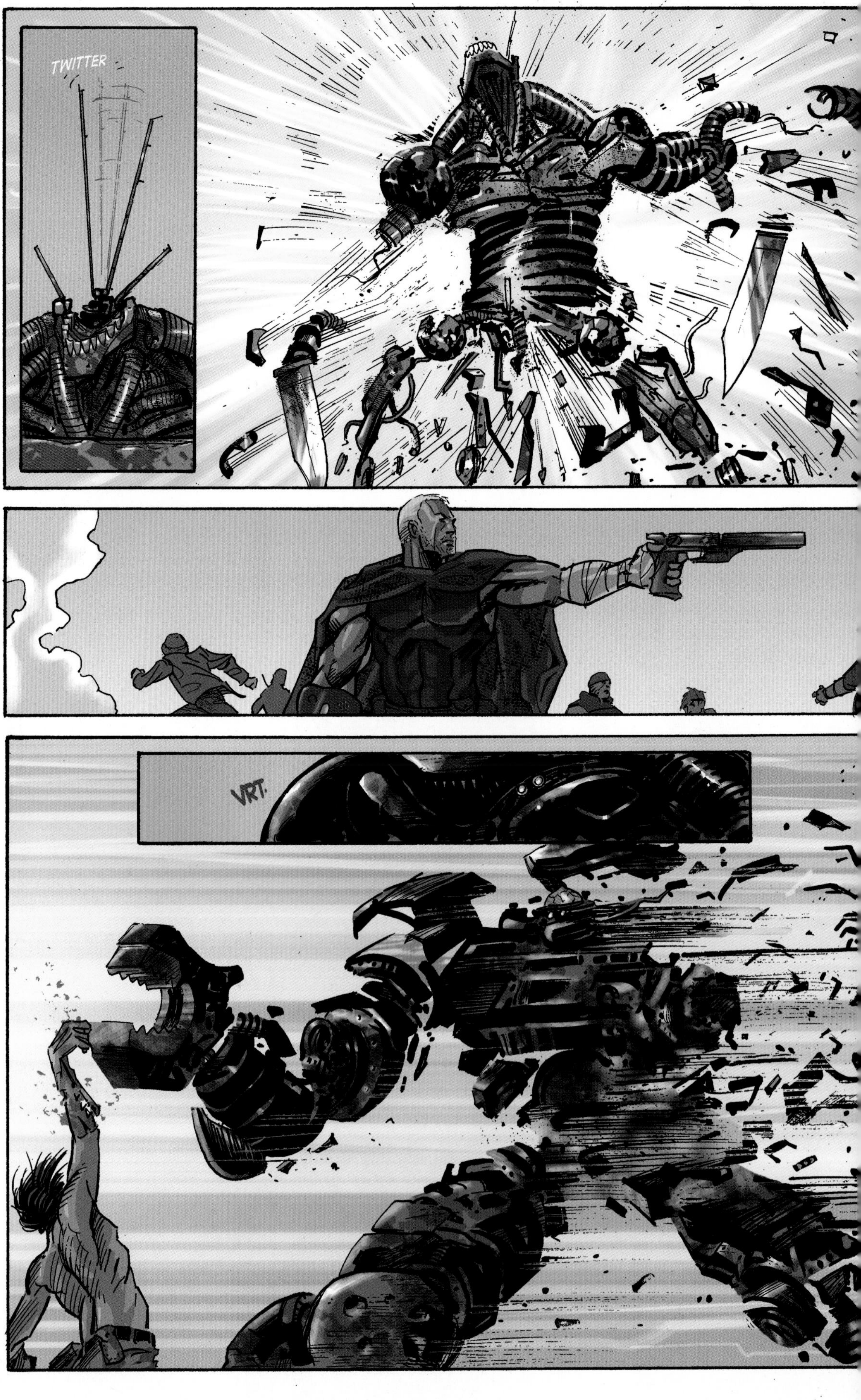
TWITTER
VRT.

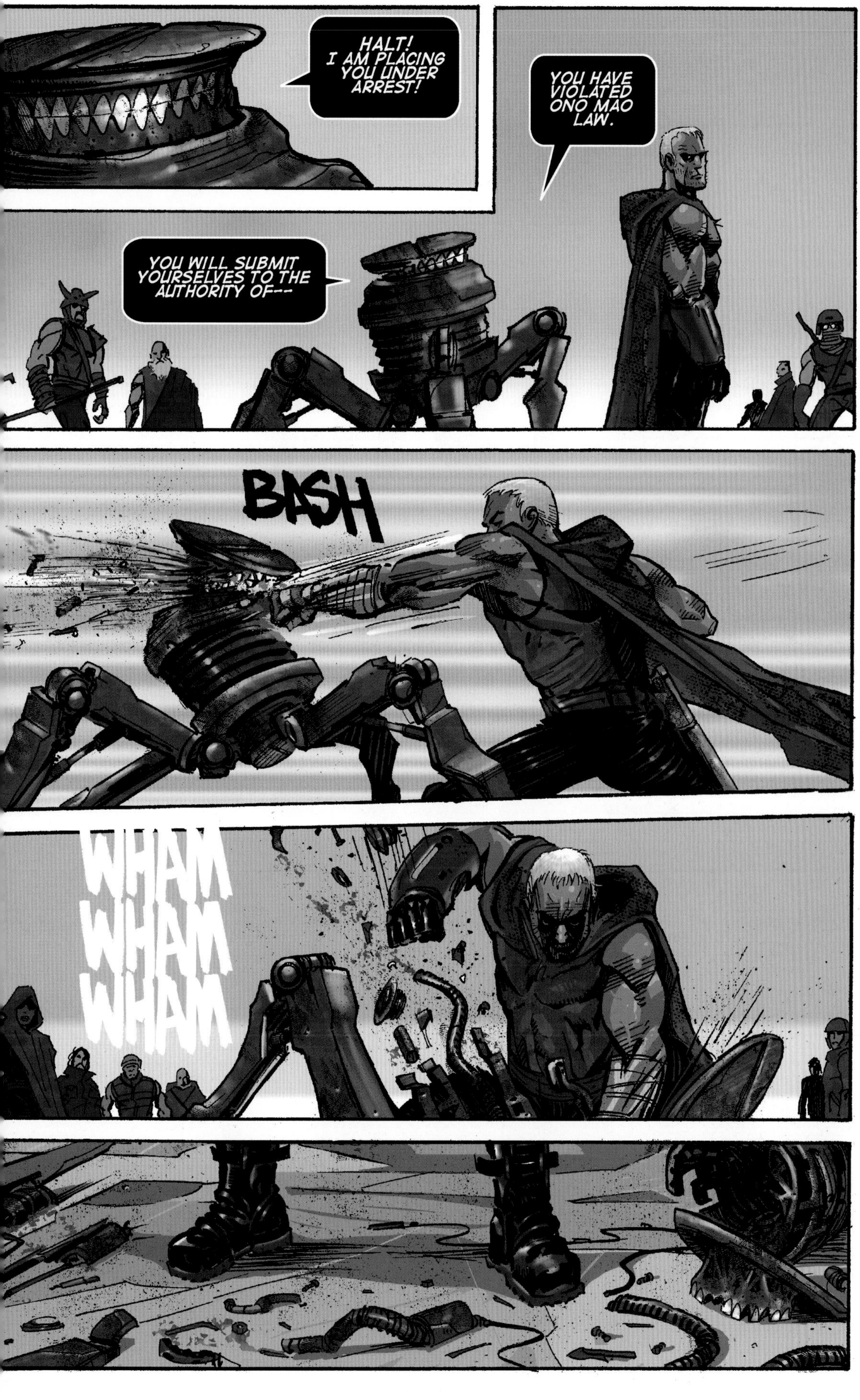
HALT! I AM PLACING YOU UNDER ARREST!
YOU HAVE VIOLATED ONO MAO LAW.
YOU WILL SUBMIT YOURSELVES TO THE AUTHORITY OF--
BASH
WHAM
WHAM
WHAM

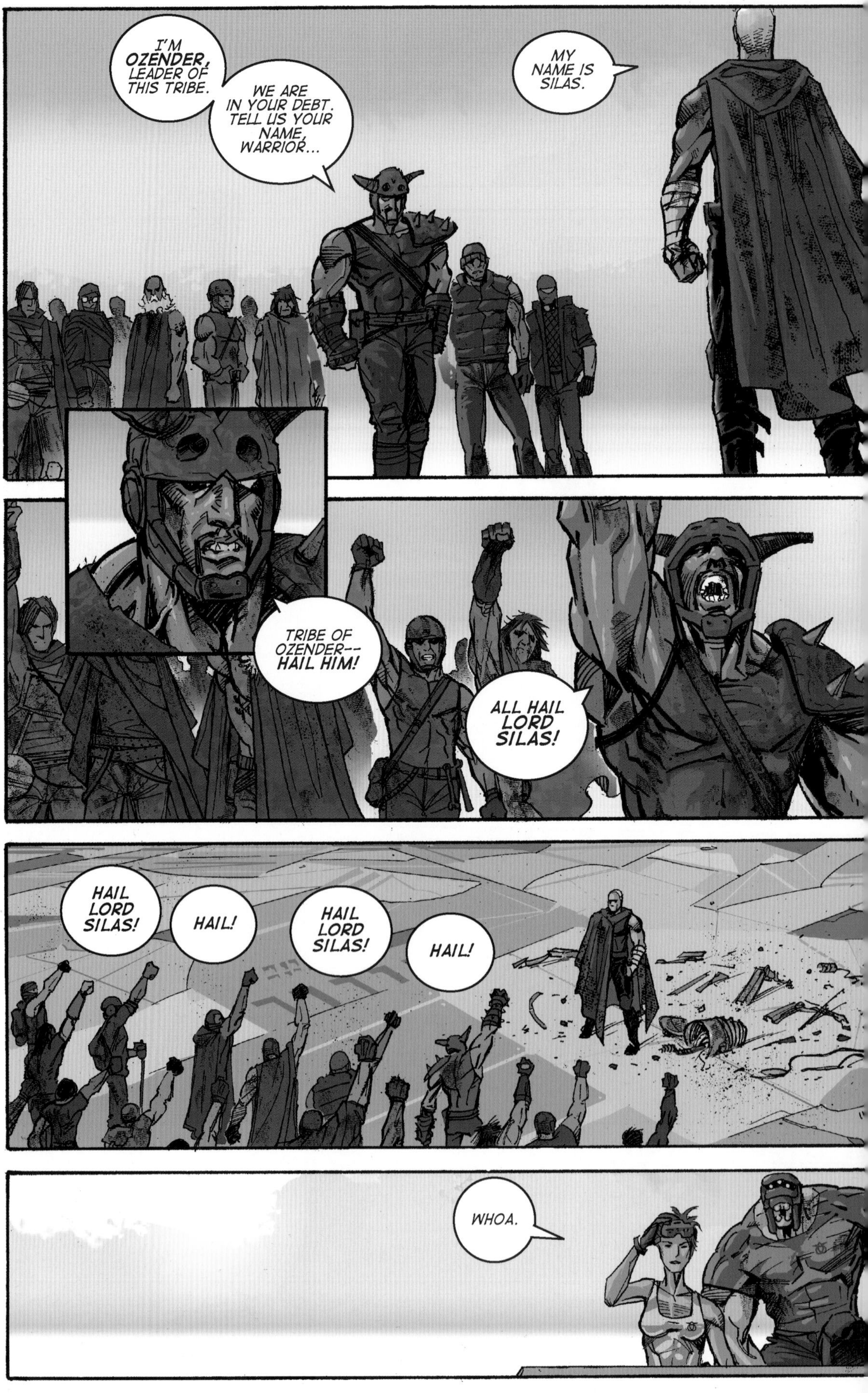
I'M OZENDER, LEADER OF THIS TRIBE.
WE ARE IN YOUR DEBT. TELL US YOUR NAME, WARRIOR...
MY NAME IS SILAS.
TRIBE OF OZENDER-- HAIL HIM!
ALL HAIL LORD SILAS!
HAIL LORD SILAS!
HAIL!
HAIL LORD SILAS!
HAIL!
WHOA.

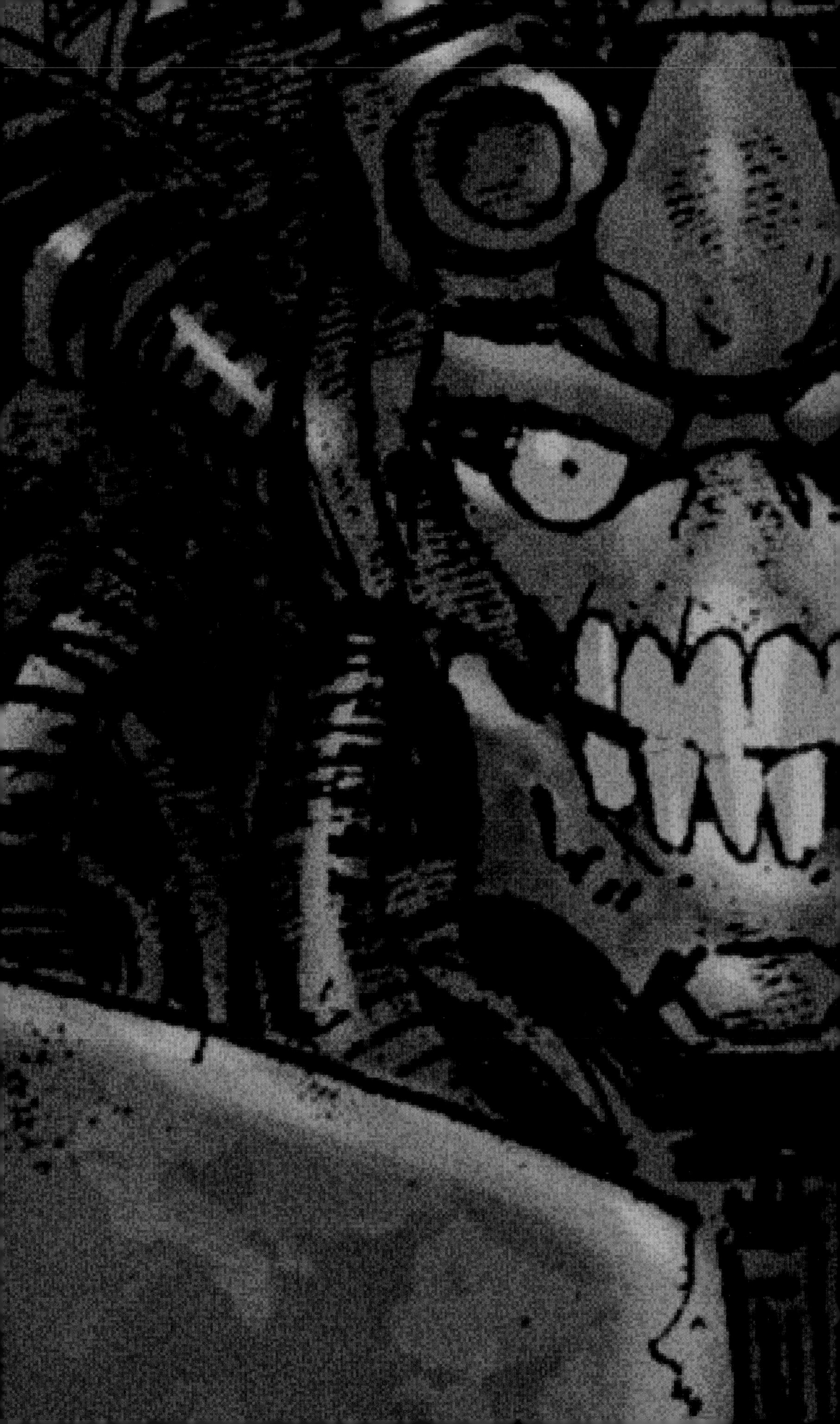

CHAPTER › THREE

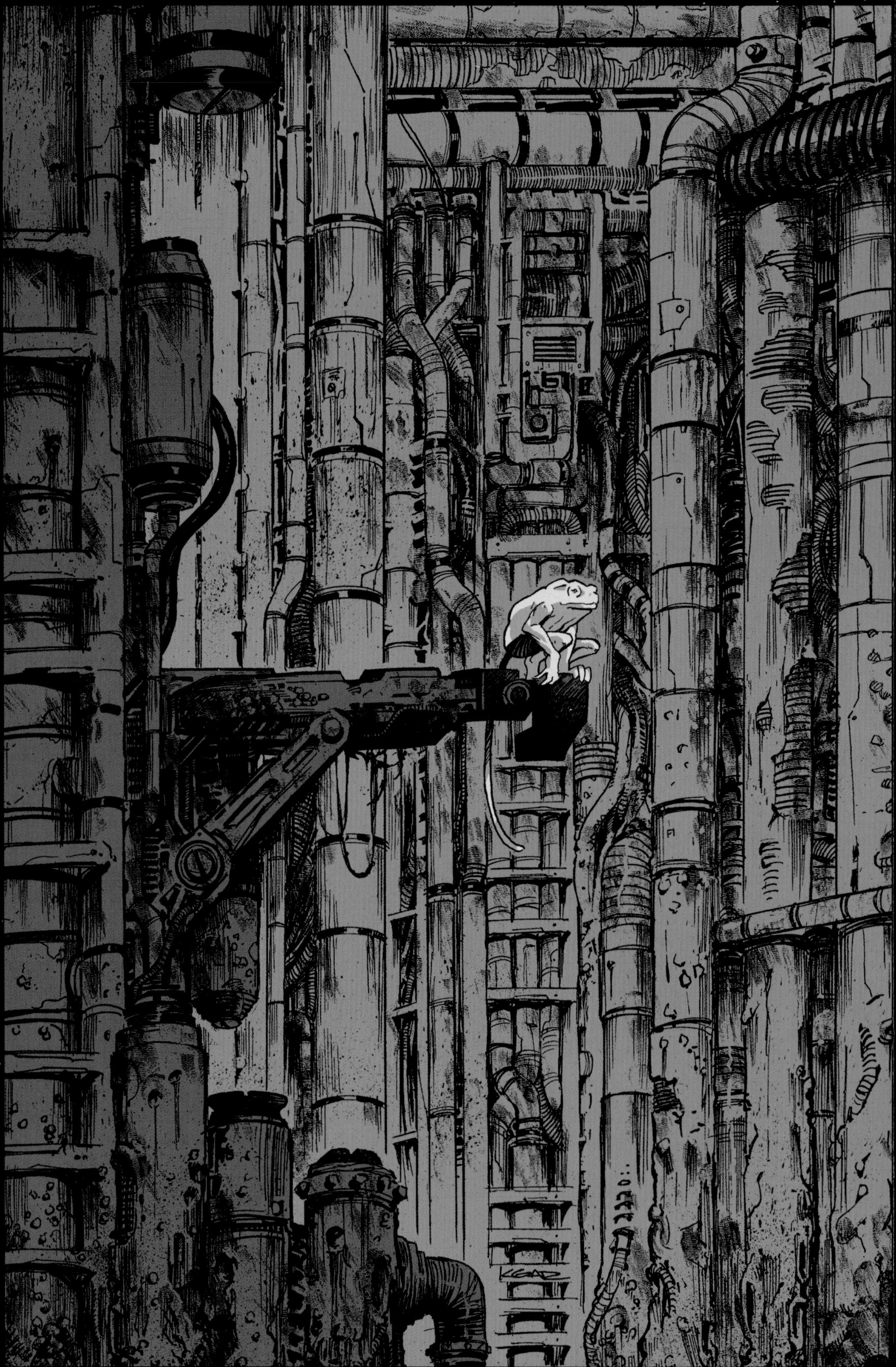

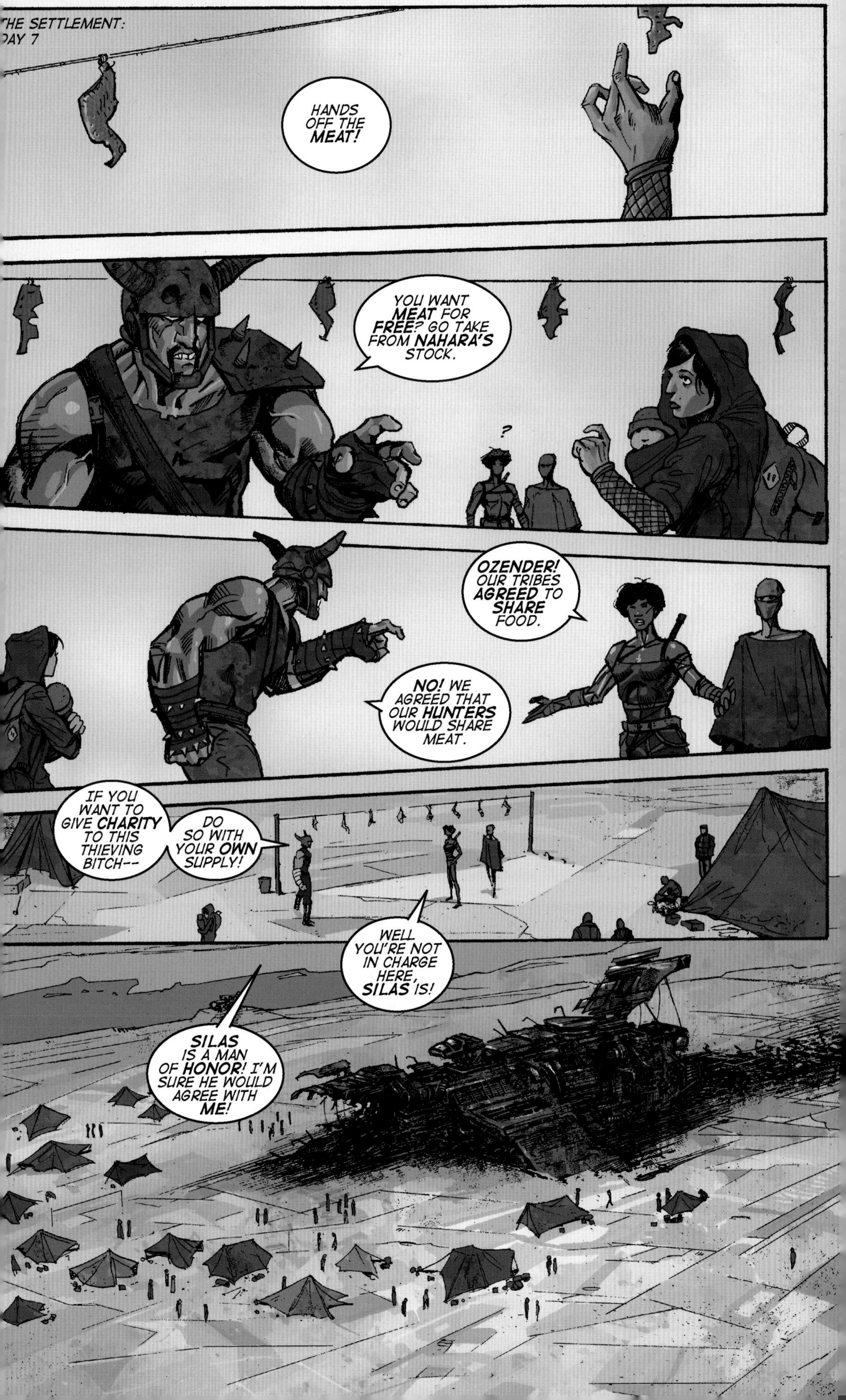

THE SETTLEMENT: DAY 7
HANDS OFF THE MEAT!
YOU WANT MEAT FOR FREE? GO TAKE FROM NAHARA'S STOCK.
?
OZENDER! OUR TRIBES AGREED TO SHARE FOOD.
NO! WE AGREED THAT OUR HUNTERS WOULD SHARE MEAT.
IF YOU WANT TO GIVE CHARITY TO THIS THIEVING BITCH--
DO SO WITH YOUR OWN SUPPLY!
WELL YOU'RE NOT IN CHARGE HERE, SILAS IS!
SILAS IS A MAN OF HONOR! I'M SURE HE WOULD AGREE WITH ME!

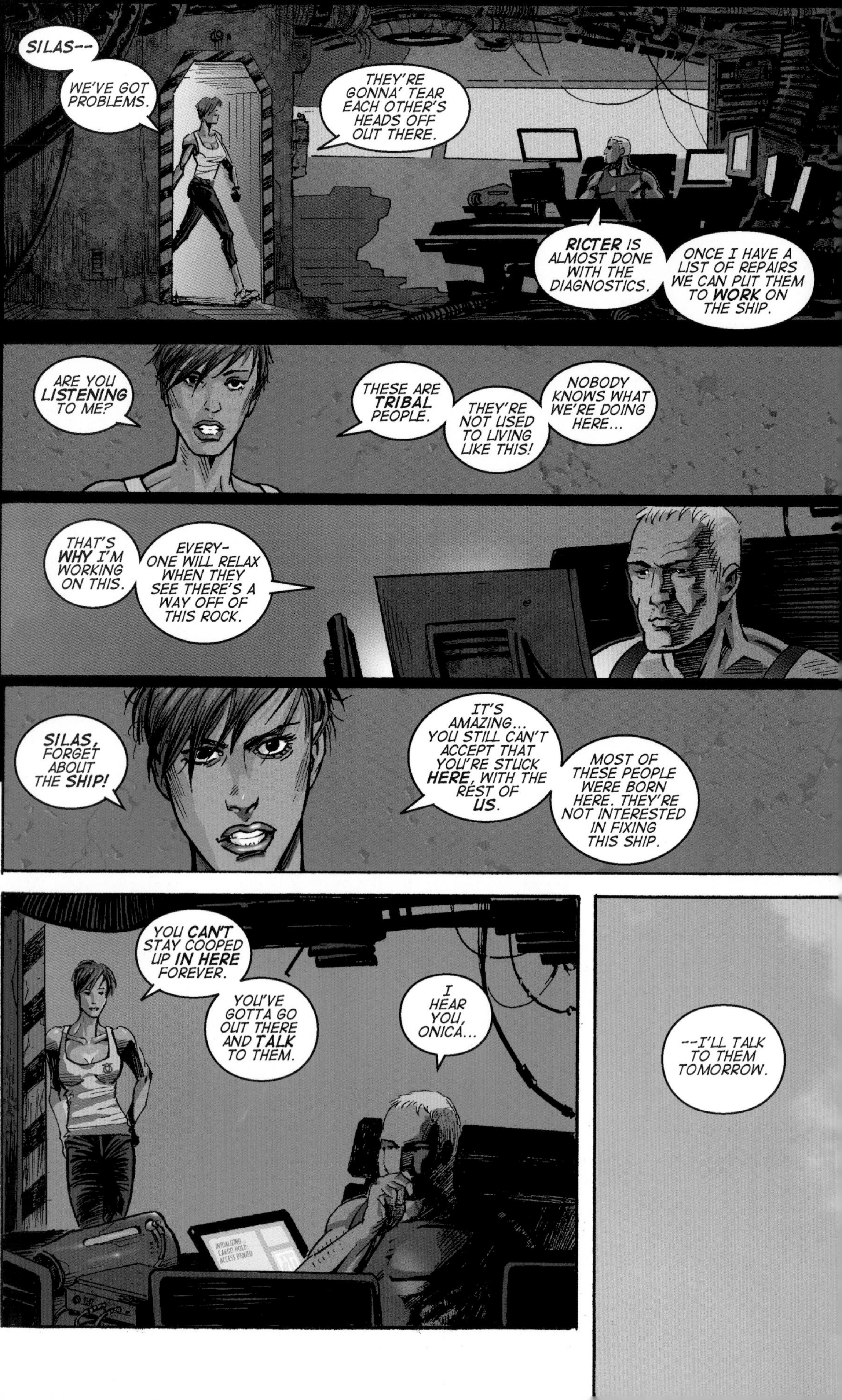
SILAS--
WE'VE GOT PROBLEMS.
THEY'RE GONNA' TEAR EACH OTHER'S HEADS OFF OUT THERE.
RICTER IS ALMOST DONE WITH THE DIAGNOSTICS.
ONCE I HAVE A LIST OF REPAIRS WE CAN PUT THEM TO WORK ON THE SHIP.
ARE YOU LISTENING TO ME?
THESE ARE TRIBAL PEOPLE.
THEY'RE NOT USED TO LIVING LIKE THIS!
NOBODY KNOWS WHAT WE'RE DOING HERE...
THAT'S WHY I'M WORKING ON THIS.
EVERY-ONE WILL RELAX WHEN THEY SEE THERE'S A WAY OFF OF THIS ROCK.
SILAS, FORGET ABOUT THE SHIP!
IT'S AMAZING... YOU STILL CAN'T ACCEPT THAT YOU'RE STUCK HERE, WITH THE REST OF US.
MOST OF THESE PEOPLE WERE BORN HERE. THEY'RE NOT INTERESTED IN FIXING THIS SHIP.
YOU CAN'T STAY COOPED UP IN HERE FOREVER.
YOU'VE GOTTA GO OUT THERE AND TALK TO THEM.
I HEAR YOU, ONICA...
INITIALIZING... CARGO HOLD: ACCESS DENIED
--I'LL TALK TO THEM TOMORROW.

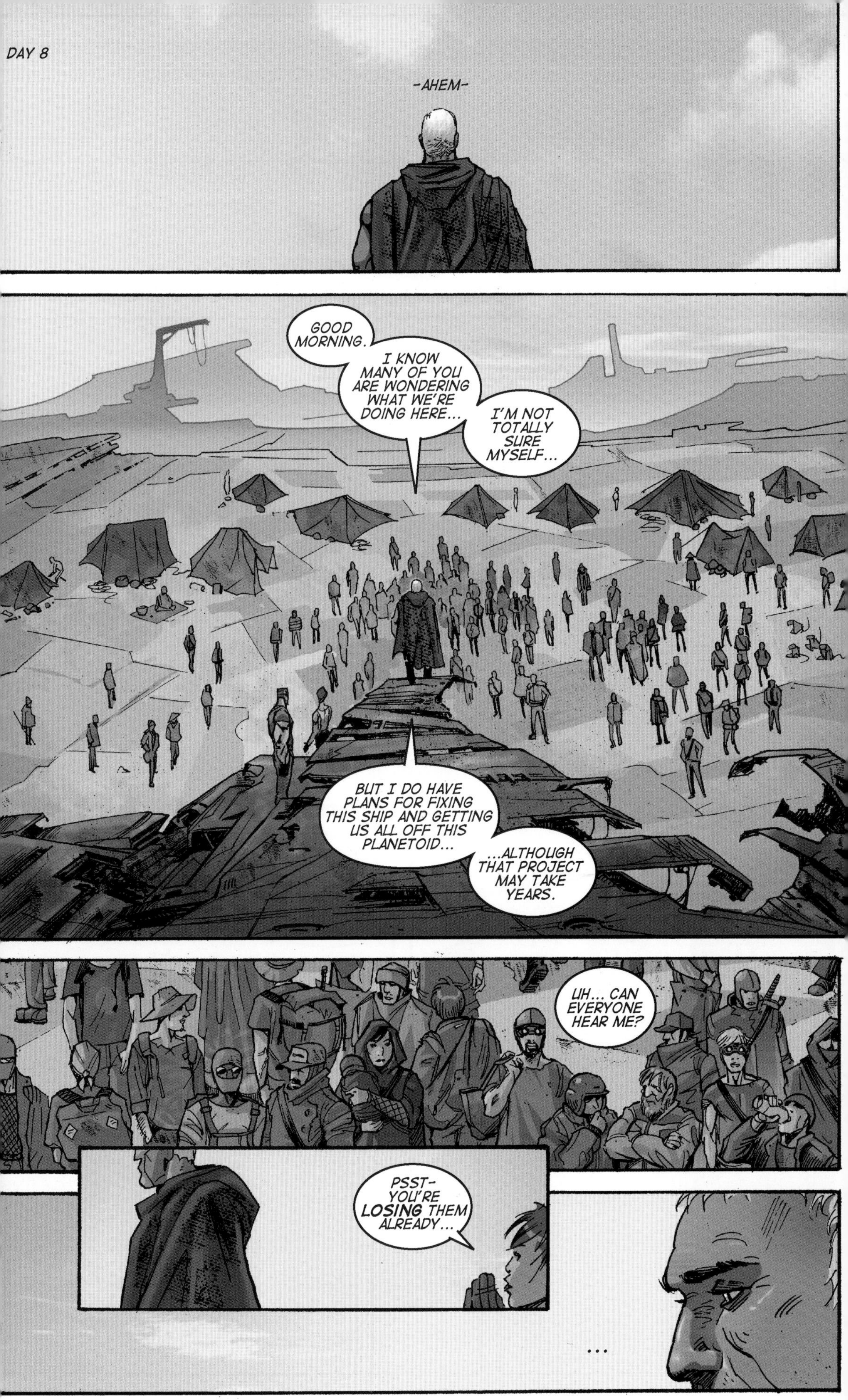
DAY 8
-AHEM-
GOOD MORNING.
I KNOW MANY OF YOU ARE WONDERING WHAT WE'RE DOING HERE...
I'M NOT TOTALLY SURE MYSELF...
BUT I DO HAVE PLANS FOR FIXING THIS SHIP AND GETTING US ALL OFF THIS PLANETOID...
...ALTHOUGH THAT PROJECT MAY TAKE YEARS.
UH... CAN EVERYONE HEAR ME?
PSST- YOU'RE **LOSING** THEM ALREADY...
...

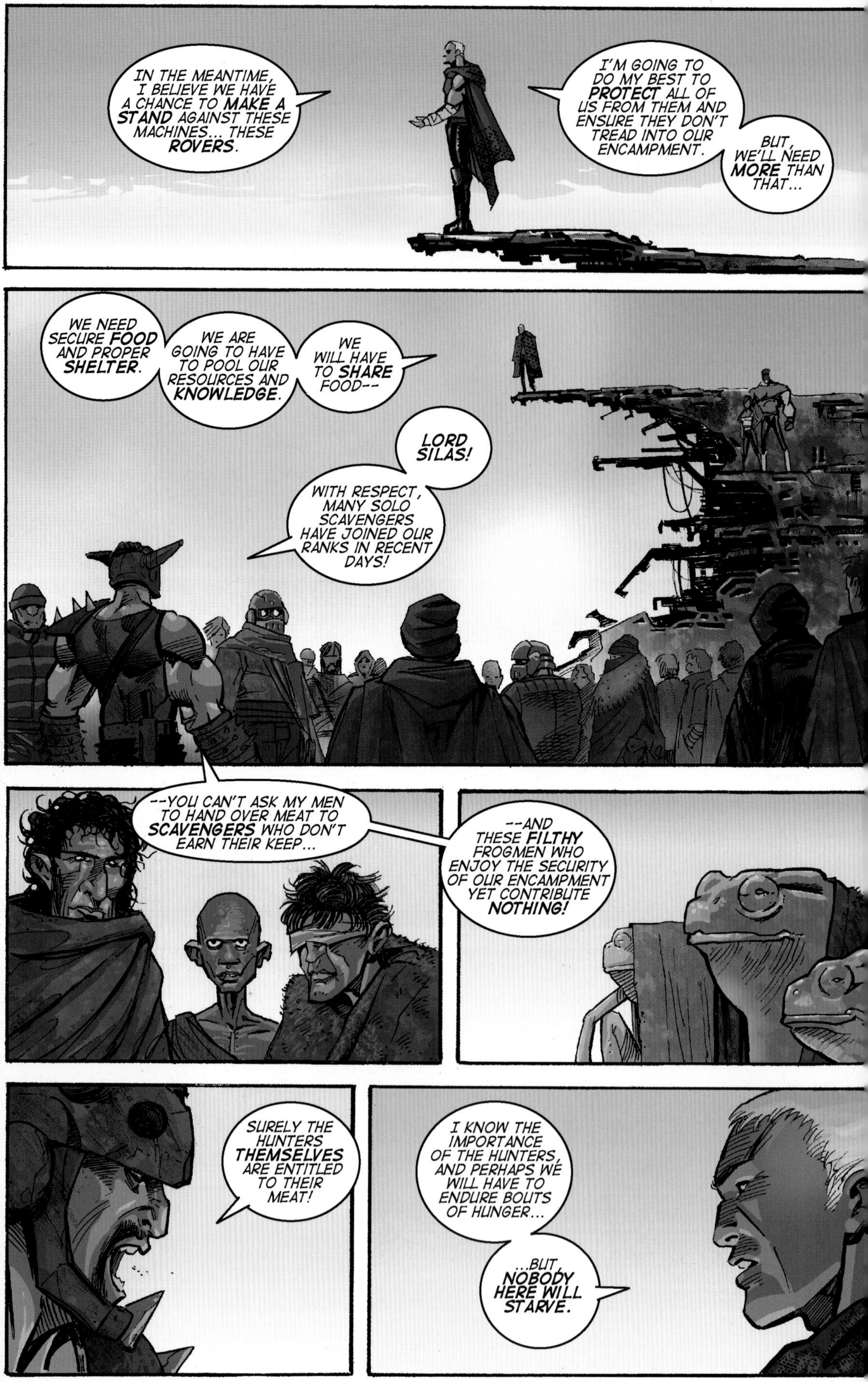
IN THE MEANTIME, I BELIEVE WE HAVE A CHANCE TO MAKE A STAND AGAINST THESE MACHINES... THESE ROVERS.
I'M GOING TO DO MY BEST TO PROTECT ALL OF US FROM THEM AND ENSURE THEY DON'T TREAD INTO OUR ENCAMPMENT.
BUT, WE'LL NEED MORE THAN THAT...
WE NEED SECURE FOOD AND PROPER SHELTER.
WE ARE GOING TO HAVE TO POOL OUR RESOURCES AND KNOWLEDGE.
WE WILL HAVE TO SHARE FOOD--
LORD SILAS!
WITH RESPECT, MANY SOLO SCAVENGERS HAVE JOINED OUR RANKS IN RECENT DAYS!
--YOU CAN'T ASK MY MEN TO HAND OVER MEAT TO SCAVENGERS WHO DON'T EARN THEIR KEEP...
--AND THESE FILTHY FROGMEN WHO ENJOY THE SECURITY OF OUR ENCAMPMENT YET CONTRIBUTE NOTHING!
SURELY THE HUNTERS THEMSELVES ARE ENTITLED TO THEIR MEAT!
I KNOW THE IMPORTANCE OF THE HUNTERS, AND PERHAPS WE WILL HAVE TO ENDURE BOUTS OF HUNGER...
...BUT, NOBODY HERE WILL STARVE.

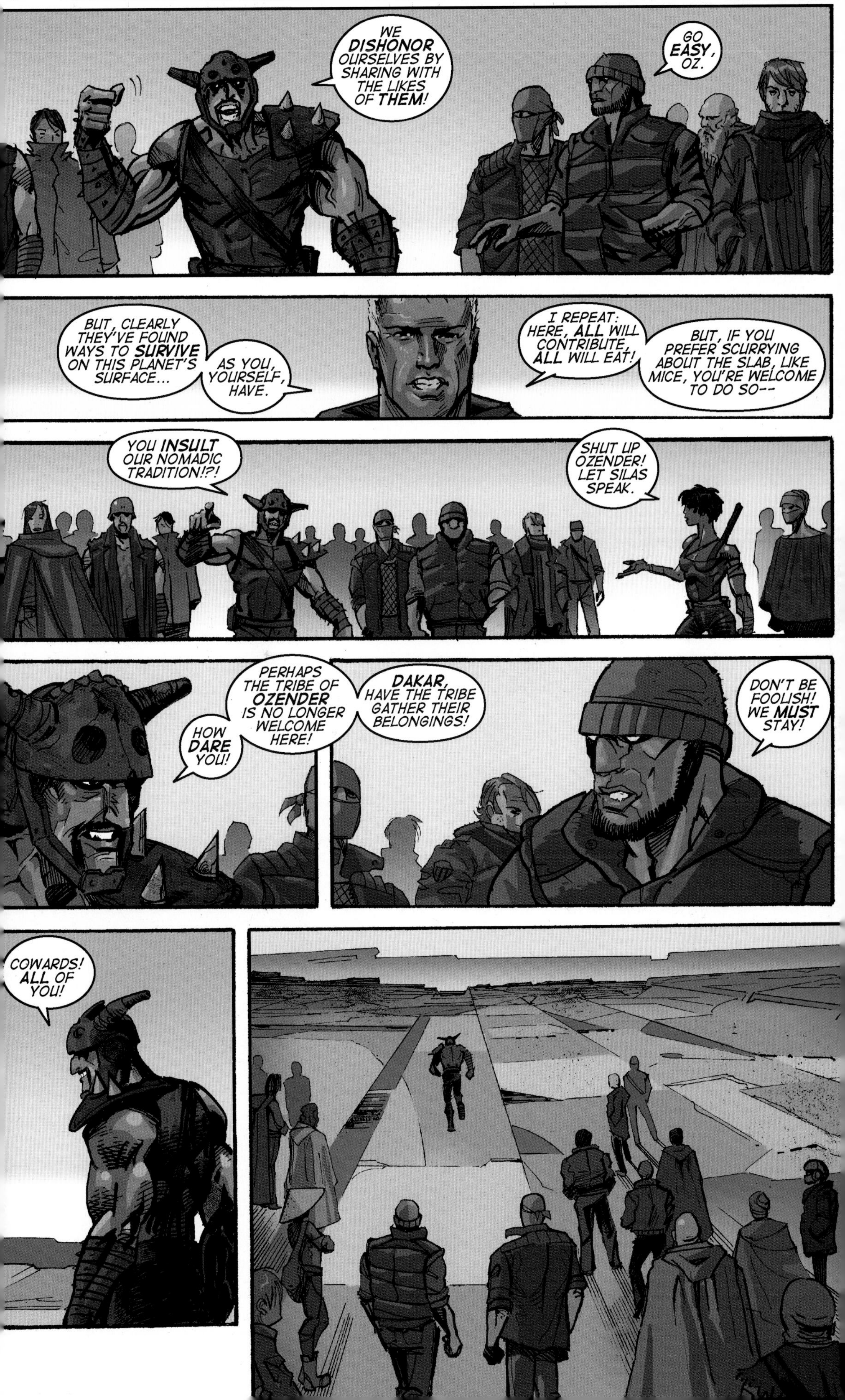

WE DISHONOR OURSELVES BY SHARING WITH THE LIKES OF THEM!
GO EASY, OZ.
BUT, CLEARLY THEY'VE FOUND WAYS TO SURVIVE ON THIS PLANET'S SURFACE...
AS YOU, YOURSELF, HAVE.
I REPEAT: HERE, ALL WILL CONTRIBUTE, ALL WILL EAT!
BUT, IF YOU PREFER SCURRYING ABOUT THE SLAB, LIKE MICE, YOU'RE WELCOME TO DO SO--
YOU INSULT OUR NOMADIC TRADITION!?!
SHUT UP OZENDER! LET SILAS SPEAK.
PERHAPS THE TRIBE OF OZENDER IS NO LONGER WELCOME HERE!
HOW DARE YOU!
DAKAR, HAVE THE TRIBE GATHER THEIR BELONGINGS!
DON'T BE FOOLISH! WE MUST STAY!
COWARDS! ALL OF YOU!

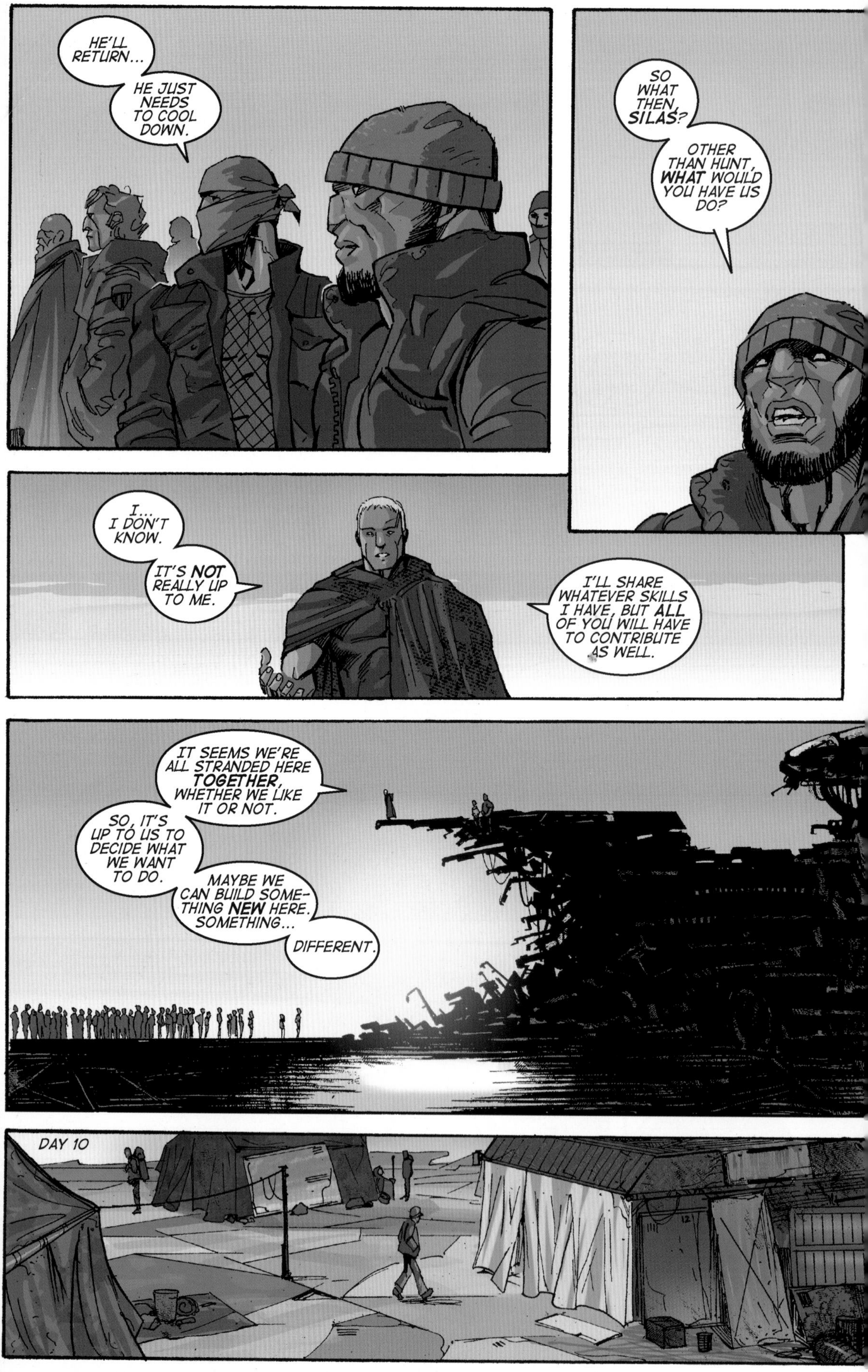
HE'LL RETURN...
HE JUST NEEDS TO COOL DOWN.
SO WHAT THEN, SILAS?
OTHER THAN HUNT, WHAT WOULD YOU HAVE US DO?
I... I DON'T KNOW.
IT'S NOT REALLY UP TO ME.
I'LL SHARE WHATEVER SKILLS I HAVE, BUT ALL OF YOU WILL HAVE TO CONTRIBUTE AS WELL.
IT SEEMS WE'RE ALL STRANDED HERE TOGETHER, WHETHER WE LIKE IT OR NOT.
SO, IT'S UP TO US TO DECIDE WHAT WE WANT TO DO.
MAYBE WE CAN BUILD SOMETHING NEW HERE. SOMETHING...
DIFFERENT.
DAY 10

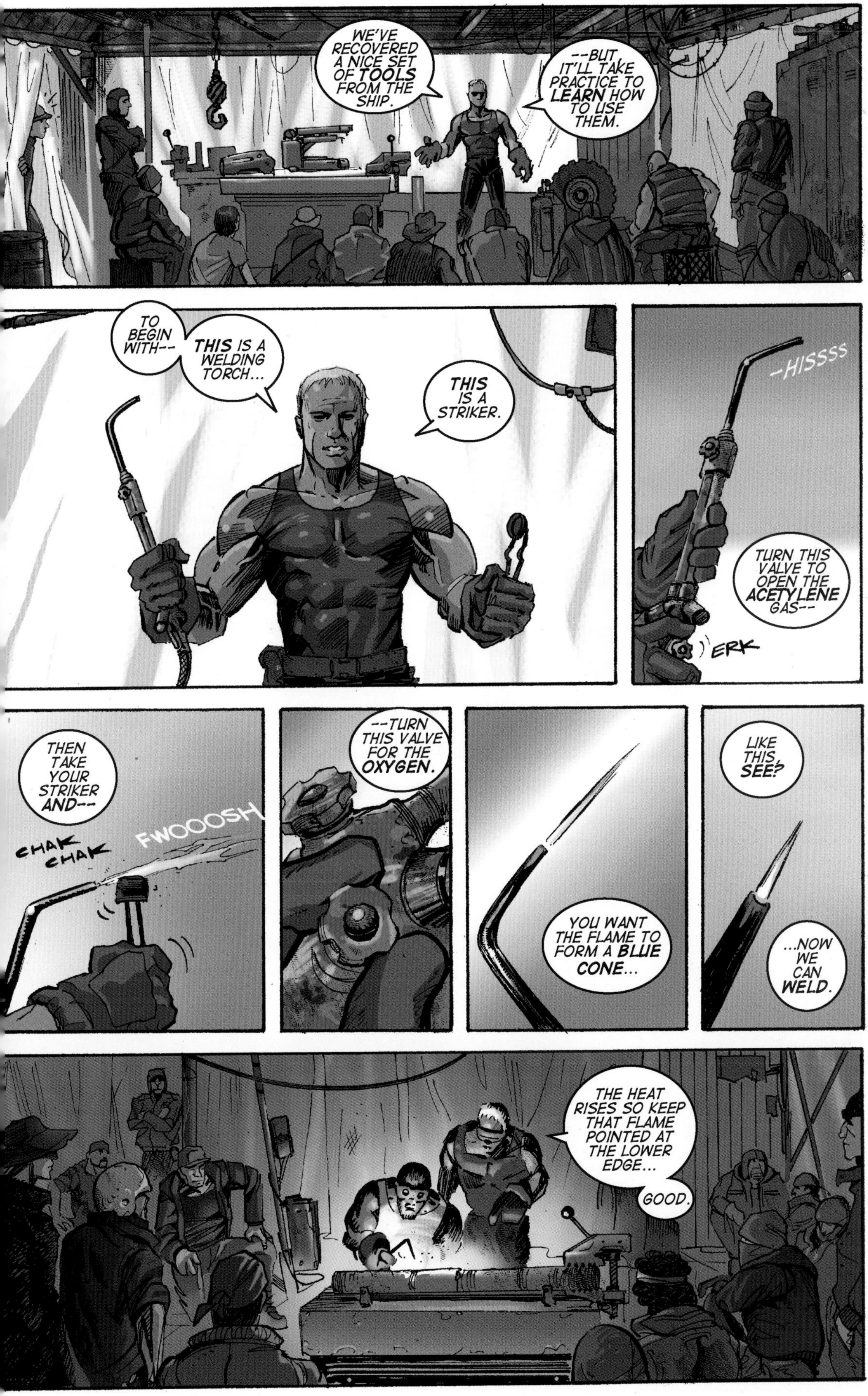
WE'VE RECOVERED A NICE SET OF TOOLS FROM THE SHIP.
--BUT IT'LL TAKE PRACTICE TO LEARN HOW TO USE THEM.
TO BEGIN WITH--
THIS IS A WELDING TORCH...
THIS IS A STRIKER.
-HISSSS
TURN THIS VALVE TO OPEN THE ACETYLENE GAS--
ERK
THEN TAKE YOUR STRIKER AND--
FWOOOSH
CHAK CHAK
--TURN THIS VALVE FOR THE OXYGEN.
YOU WANT THE FLAME TO FORM A BLUE CONE...
LIKE THIS, SEE?
...NOW WE CAN WELD.
THE HEAT RISES SO KEEP THAT FLAME POINTED AT THE LOWER EDGE...
GOOD.

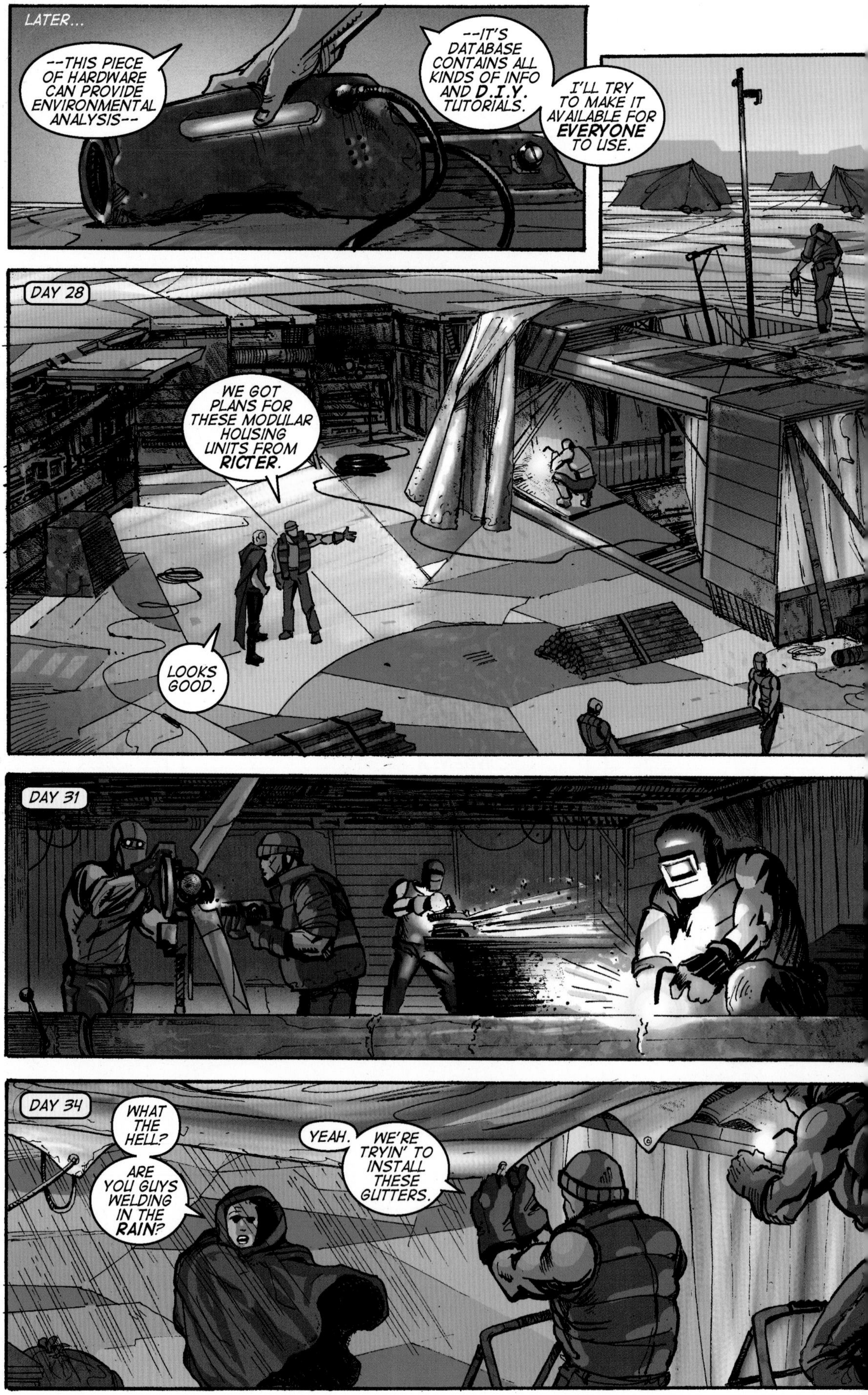
LATER...
--THIS PIECE OF HARDWARE CAN PROVIDE ENVIRONMENTAL ANALYSIS--
--IT'S DATABASE CONTAINS ALL KINDS OF INFO AND D.I.Y. TUTORIALS.
I'LL TRY TO MAKE IT AVAILABLE FOR EVERYONE TO USE.
DAY 28
WE GOT PLANS FOR THESE MODULAR HOUSING UNITS FROM RICTER.
LOOKS GOOD.
DAY 31
DAY 34
WHAT THE HELL?
ARE YOU GUYS WELDING IN THE RAIN?
YEAH.
WE'RE TRYIN' TO INSTALL THESE GUTTERS.

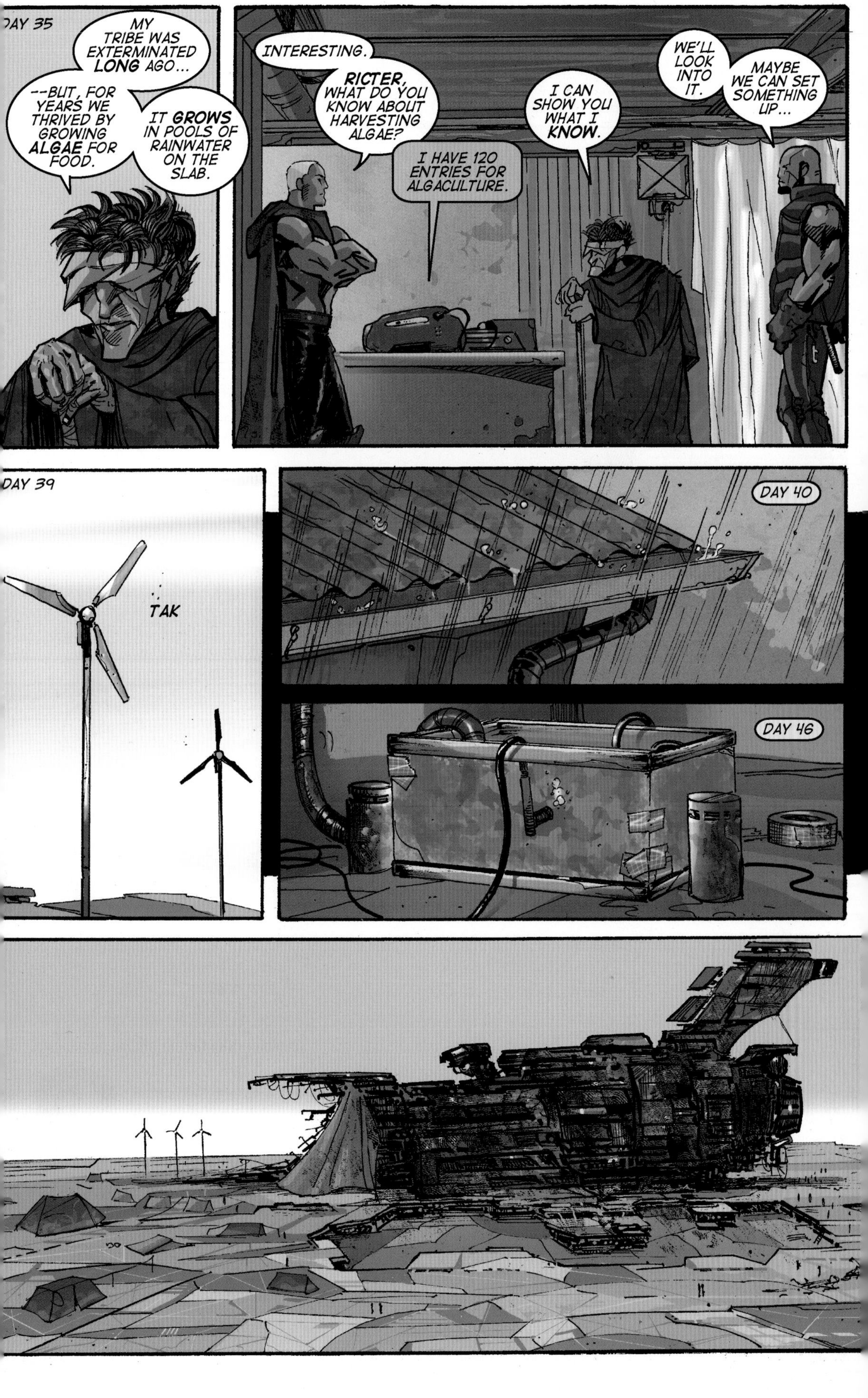
DAY 35
MY TRIBE WAS EXTERMINATED LONG AGO...
--BUT, FOR YEARS WE THRIVED BY GROWING ALGAE FOR FOOD.
IT GROWS IN POOLS OF RAINWATER ON THE SLAB.
INTERESTING.
RICTER, WHAT DO YOU KNOW ABOUT HARVESTING ALGAE?
I HAVE 120 ENTRIES FOR ALGACULTURE.
I CAN SHOW YOU WHAT I KNOW.
WE'LL LOOK INTO IT.
MAYBE WE CAN SET SOMETHING UP...
DAY 39
TAK
DAY 40
DAY 46

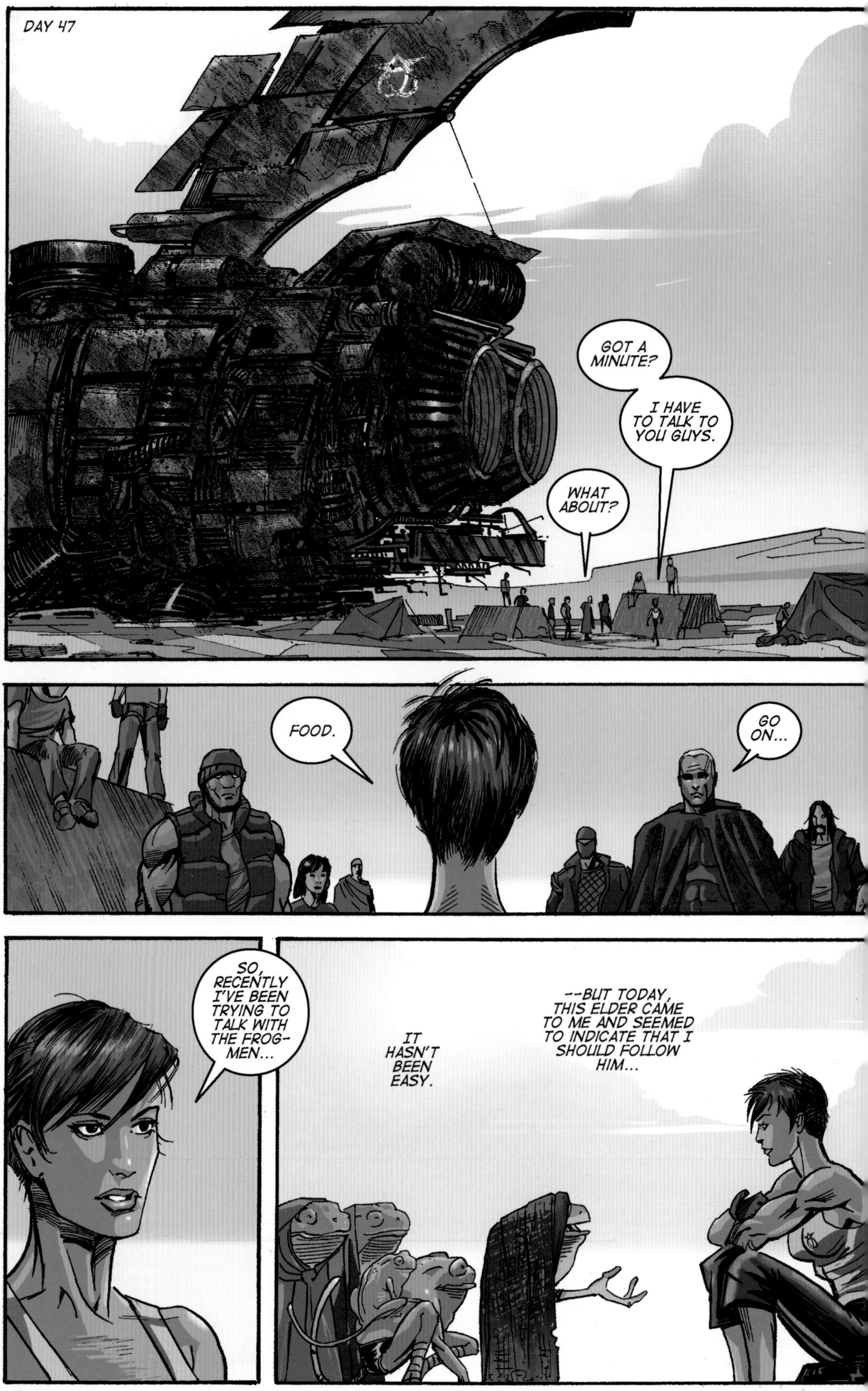

DAY 47
GOT A MINUTE?
I HAVE TO TALK TO YOU GUYS.
WHAT ABOUT?
FOOD.
GO ON...
SO, RECENTLY I'VE BEEN TRYING TO TALK WITH THE FROG-MEN...
IT HASN'T BEEN EASY.
--BUT TODAY, THIS ELDER CAME TO ME AND SEEMED TO INDICATE THAT I SHOULD FOLLOW HIM...

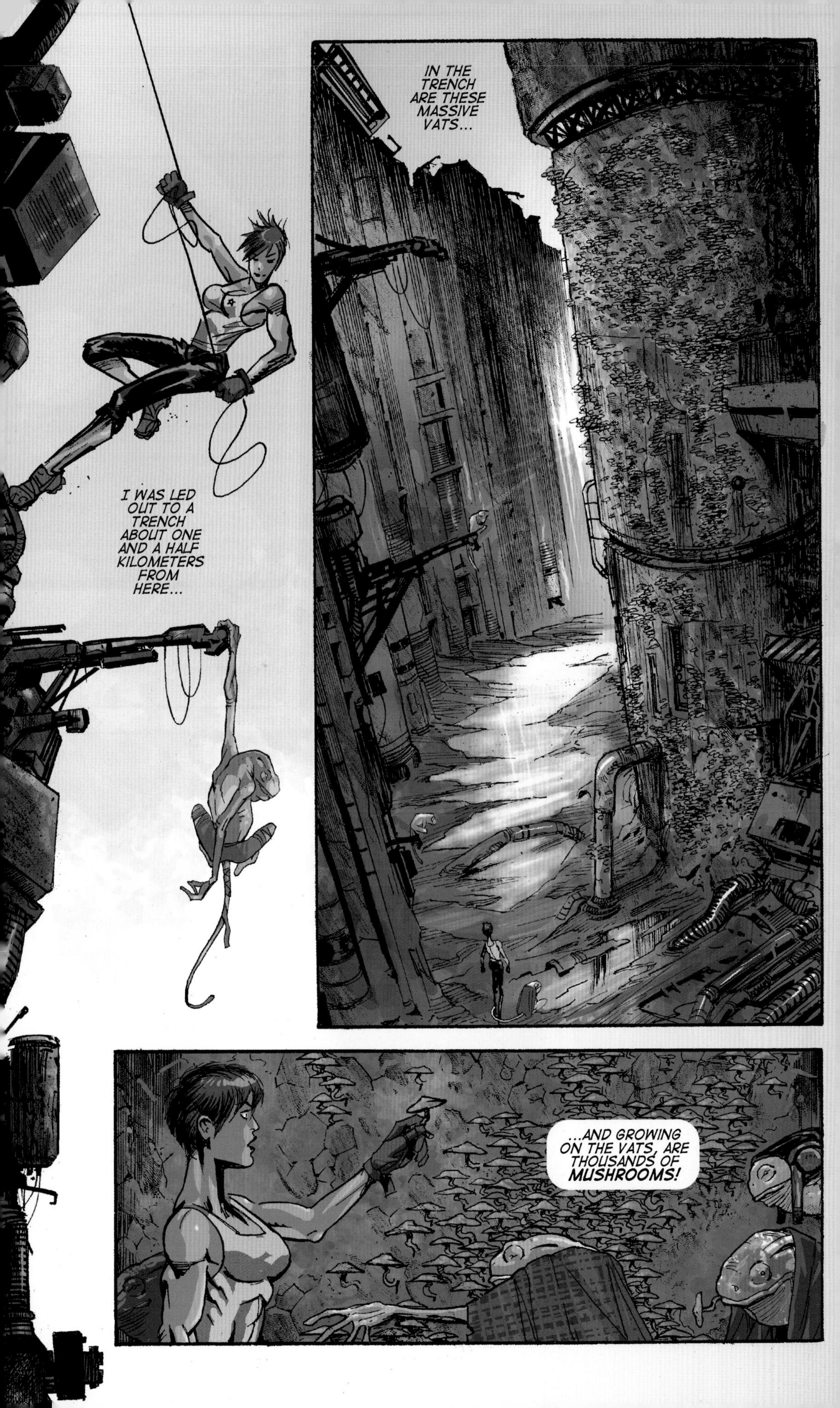
I WAS LED OUT TO A TRENCH ABOUT ONE AND A HALF KILOMETERS FROM HERE...
IN THE TRENCH ARE THESE MASSIVE VATS...
...AND GROWING ON THE VATS, ARE THOUSANDS OF MUSHROOMS!

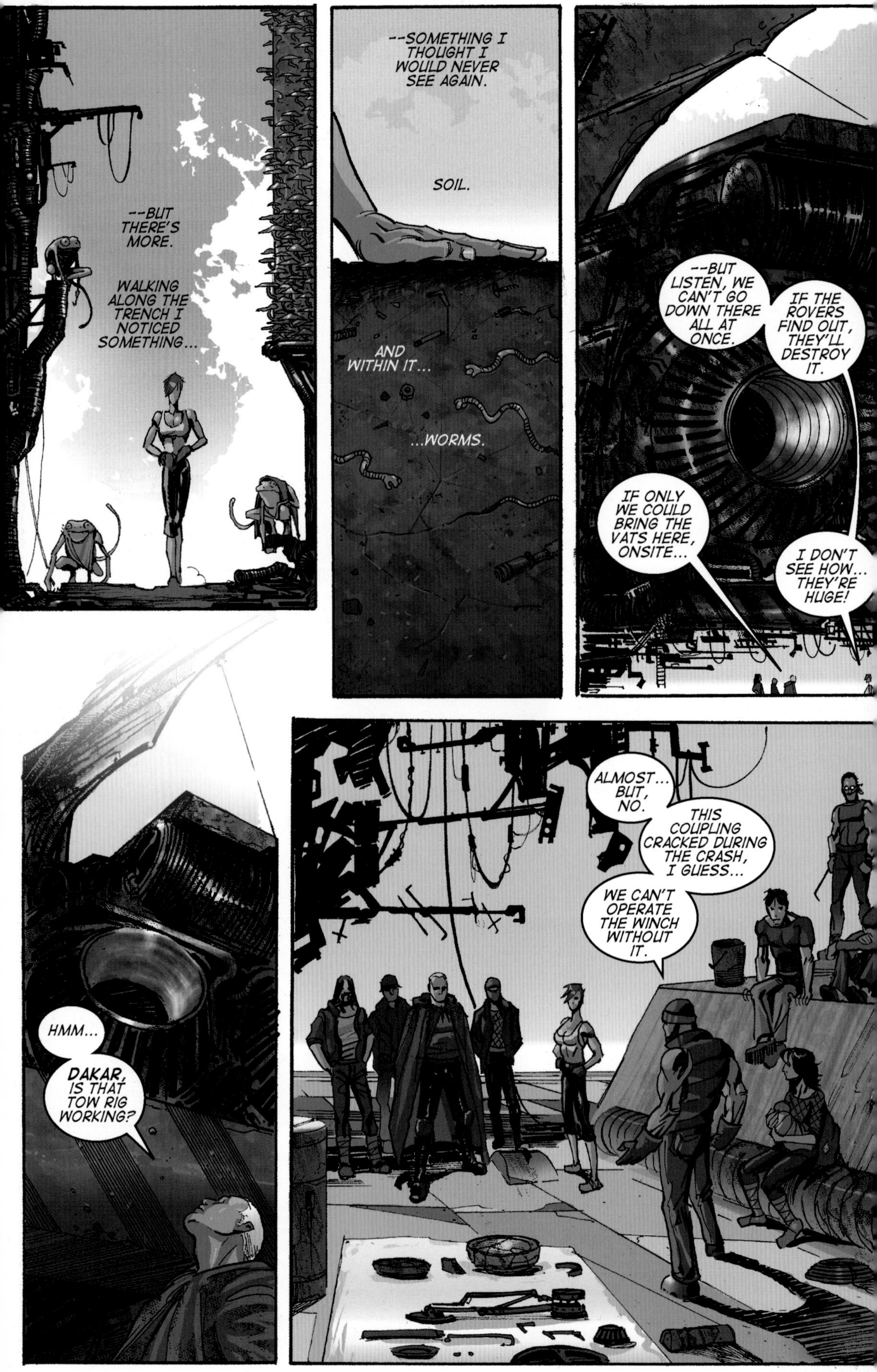
--BUT THERE'S MORE.
WALKING ALONG THE TRENCH I NOTICED SOMETHING...
--SOMETHING I THOUGHT I WOULD NEVER SEE AGAIN.
SOIL.
AND WITHIN IT...
...WORMS.
--BUT LISTEN, WE CAN'T GO DOWN THERE ALL AT ONCE.
IF THE ROVERS FIND OUT, THEY'LL DESTROY IT.
IF ONLY WE COULD BRING THE VATS HERE, ONSITE...
I DON'T SEE HOW... THEY'RE HUGE!
HMM...
DAKAR, IS THAT TOW RIG WORKING?
ALMOST... BUT, NO.
THIS COUPLING CRACKED DURING THE CRASH, I GUESS...
WE CAN'T OPERATE THE WINCH WITHOUT IT.

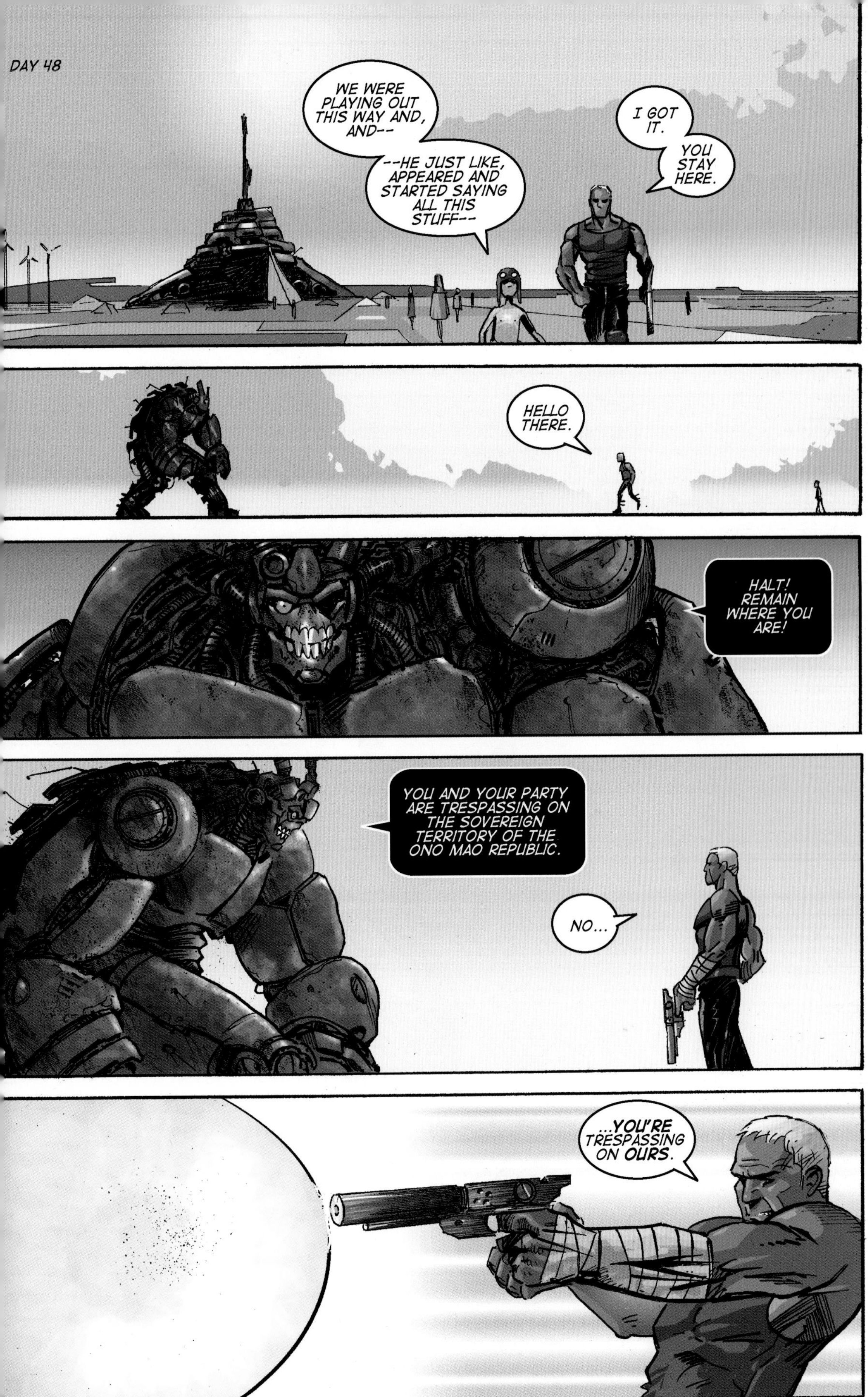
DAY 48
WE WERE PLAYING OUT THIS WAY AND, AND--
--HE JUST LIKE, APPEARED AND STARTED SAYING ALL THIS STUFF--
I GOT IT.
YOU STAY HERE.
HELLO THERE.
HALT! REMAIN WHERE YOU ARE!
YOU AND YOUR PARTY ARE TRESPASSING ON THE SOVEREIGN TERRITORY OF THE ONO MAO REPUBLIC.
NO...
...YOU'RE TRESPASSING ON OURS.

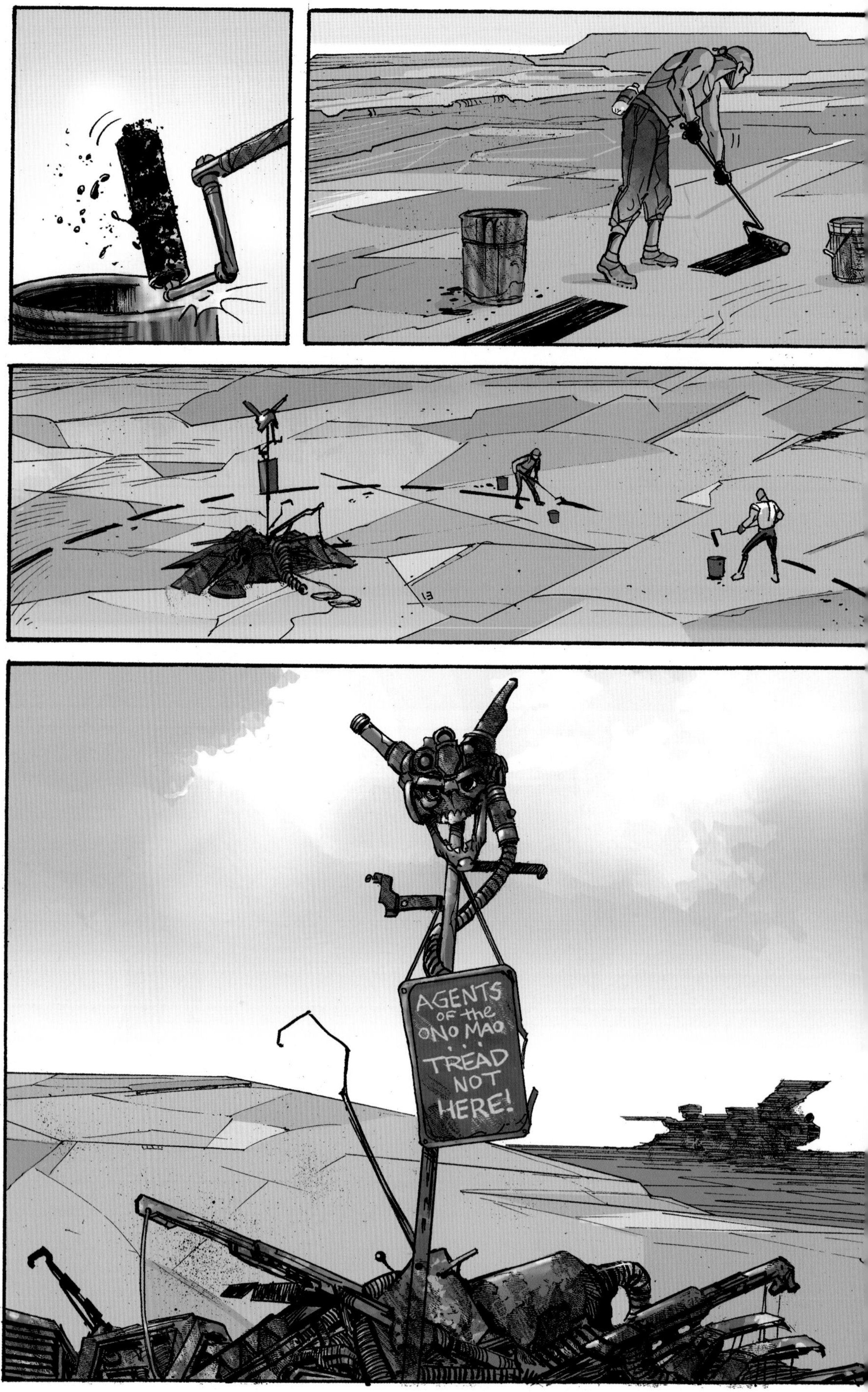
AGENTS of the ONO MAO ... TREAD NOT HERE!

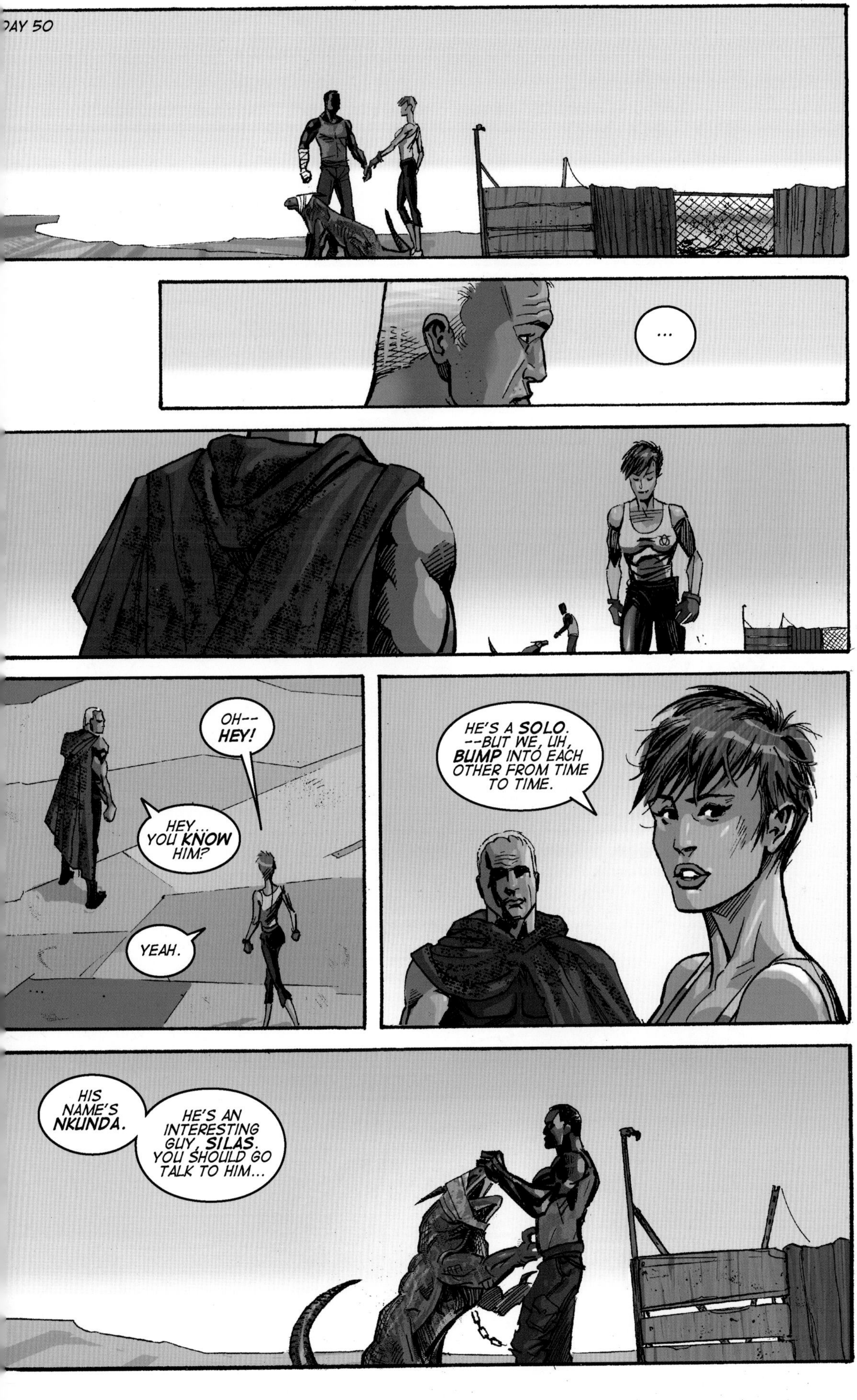
DAY 50
...
OH-- HEY!
HEY... YOU KNOW HIM?
YEAH.
...
HE'S A SOLO. --BUT WE, UH, BUMP INTO EACH OTHER FROM TIME TO TIME.
HIS NAME'S NKUNDA.
HE'S AN INTERESTING GUY, SILAS. YOU SHOULD GO TALK TO HIM...

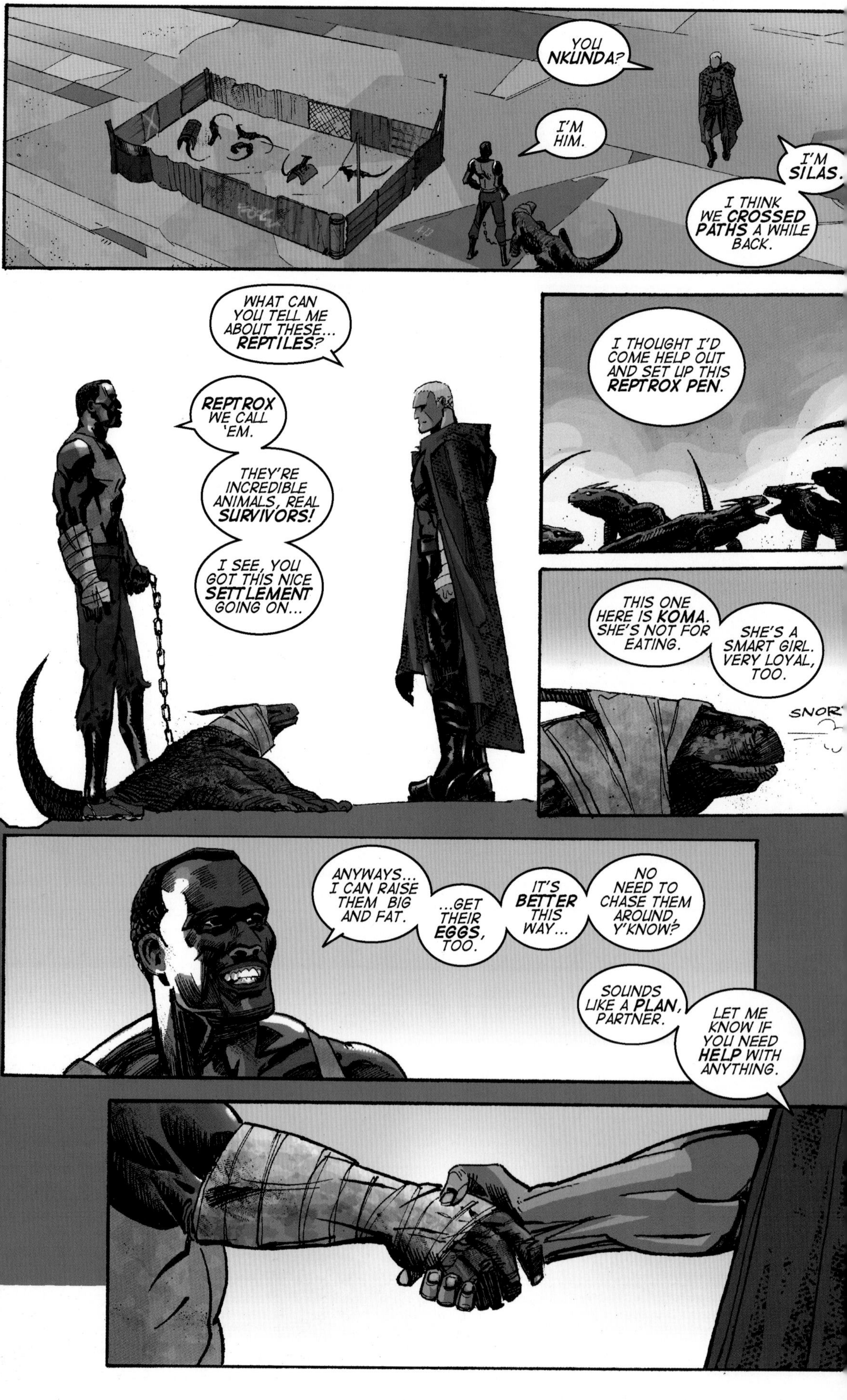
YOU NKUNDA?
I'M HIM.
I'M SILAS.
I THINK WE CROSSED PATHS A WHILE BACK.
WHAT CAN YOU TELL ME ABOUT THESE... REPTILES?
REPTROX WE CALL 'EM.
THEY'RE INCREDIBLE ANIMALS, REAL SURVIVORS!
I SEE, YOU GOT THIS NICE SETTLEMENT GOING ON...
I THOUGHT I'D COME HELP OUT AND SET UP THIS REPTROX PEN.
THIS ONE HERE IS KOMA. SHE'S NOT FOR EATING.
SHE'S A SMART GIRL. VERY LOYAL, TOO.
SNOR
ANYWAYS... I CAN RAISE THEM BIG AND FAT.
...GET THEIR EGGS, TOO.
IT'S BETTER THIS WAY...
NO NEED TO CHASE THEM AROUND, Y'KNOW?
SOUNDS LIKE A PLAN, PARTNER.
LET ME KNOW IF YOU NEED HELP WITH ANYTHING.

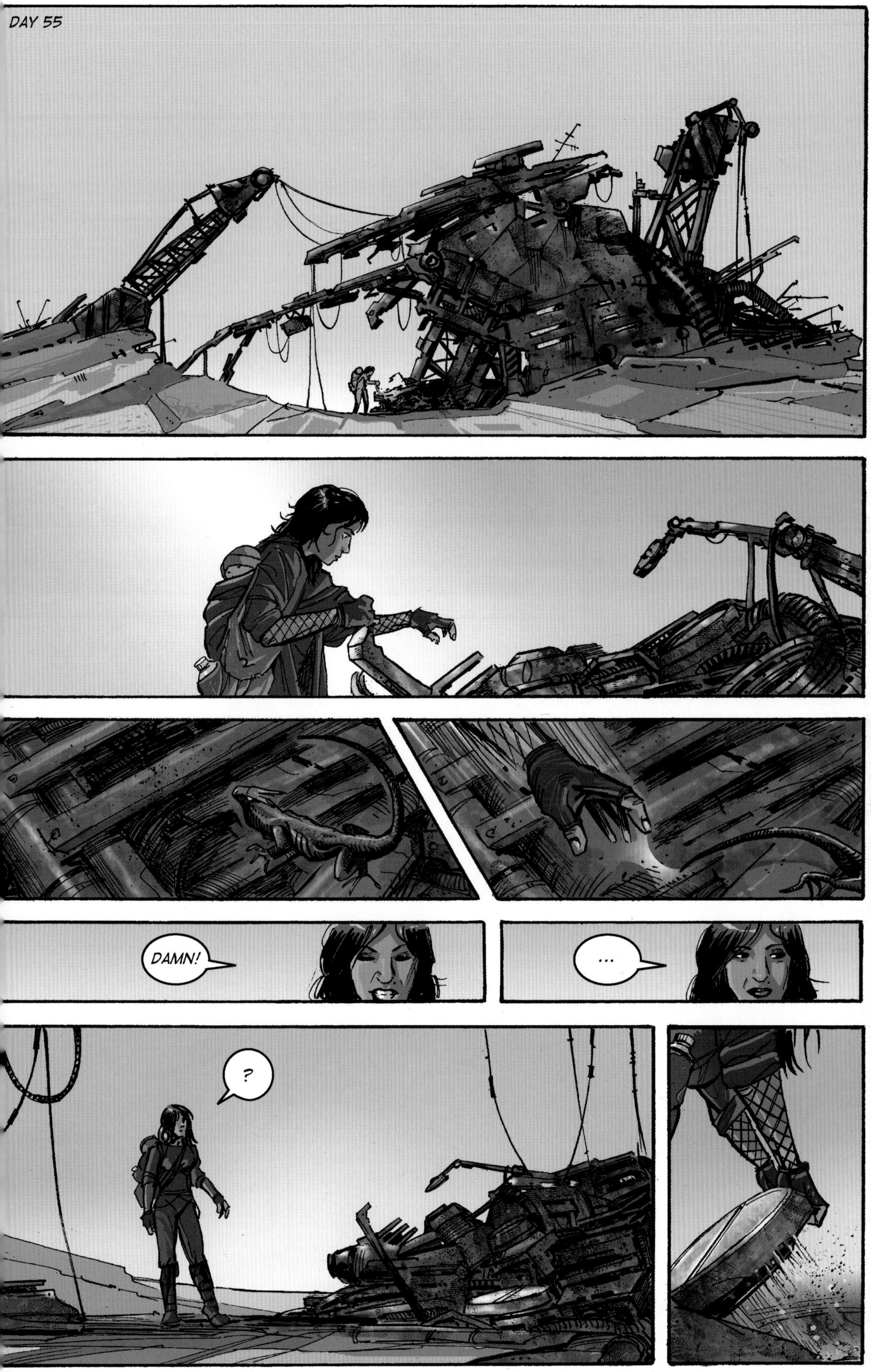
DAY 55
DAMN!
...
?

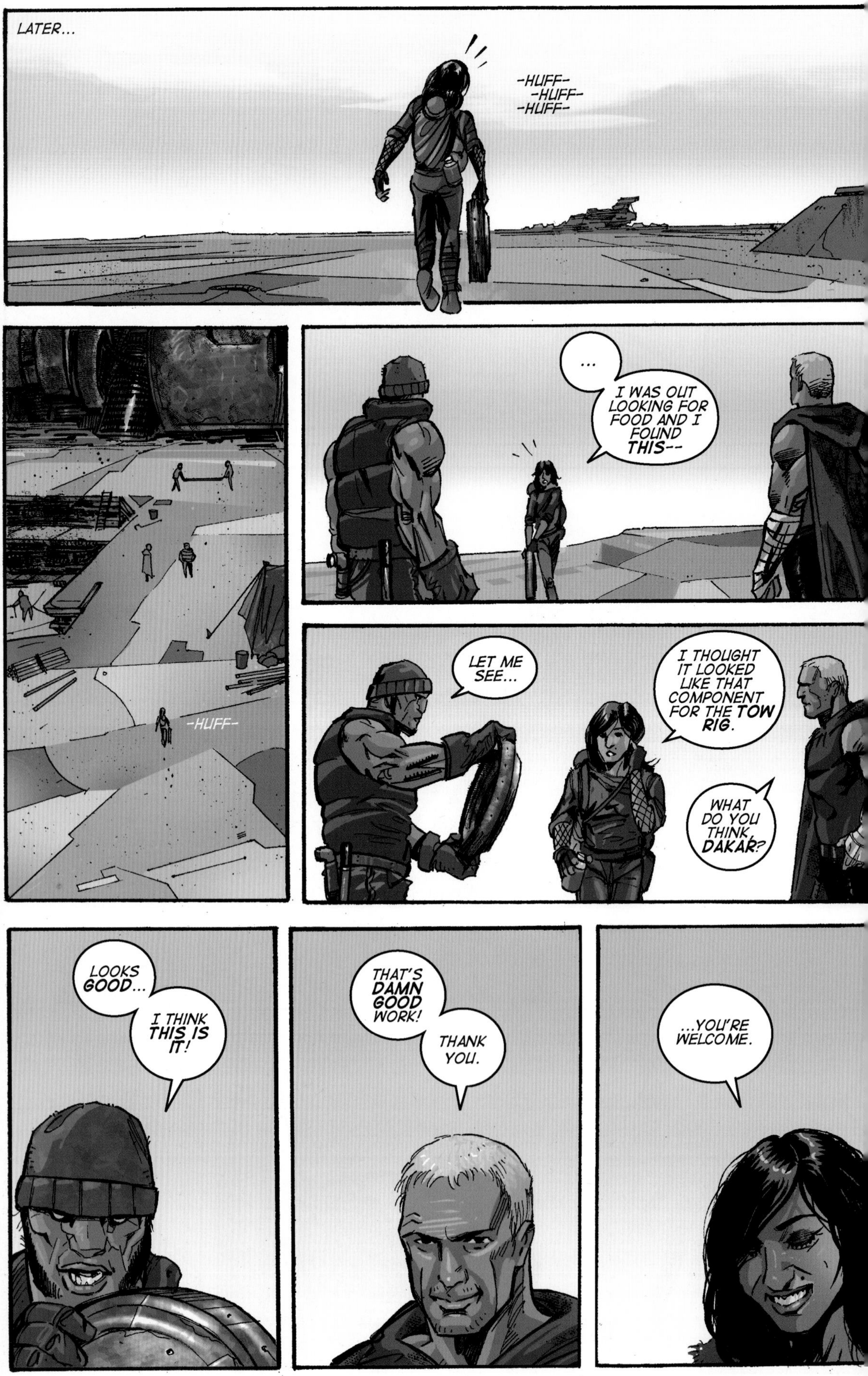
LATER...
-HUFF-
-HUFF-
-HUFF-
-HUFF-
...
I WAS OUT LOOKING FOR FOOD AND I FOUND THIS--
LET ME SEE...
I THOUGHT IT LOOKED LIKE THAT COMPONENT FOR THE TOW RIG.
WHAT DO YOU THINK, DAKAR?
LOOKS GOOD...
I THINK THIS IS IT!
THAT'S DAMN GOOD WORK!
THANK YOU.
...YOU'RE WELCOME.

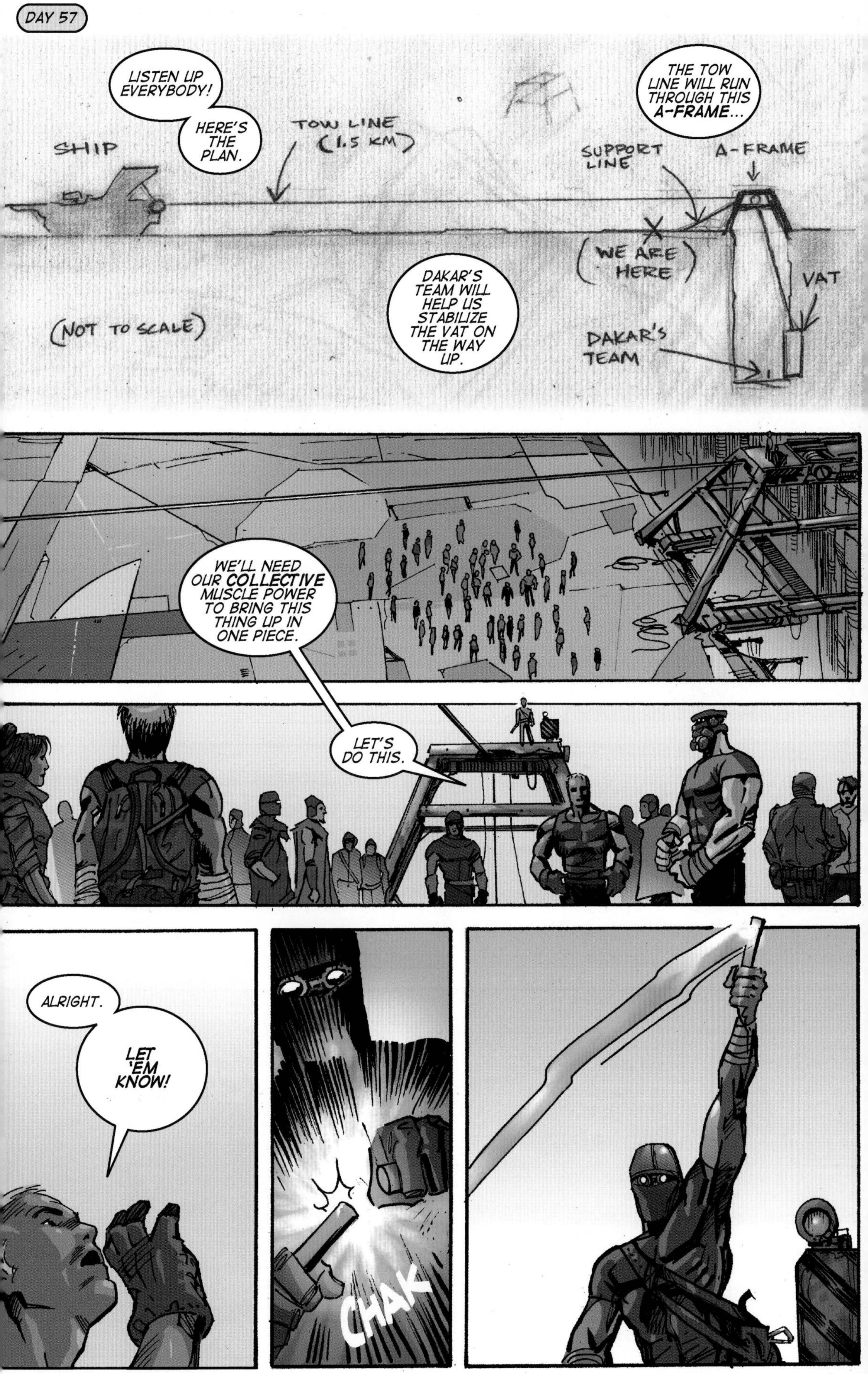
DAY 57
LISTEN UP EVERYBODY!
HERE'S THE PLAN.
THE TOW LINE WILL RUN THROUGH THIS A-FRAME...
SHIP
TOW LINE (1.5 KM)
SUPPORT LINE
A-FRAME
(WE ARE HERE)
VAT
(NOT TO SCALE)
DAKAR'S TEAM WILL HELP US STABILIZE THE VAT ON THE WAY UP.
DAKAR'S TEAM
WE'LL NEED OUR COLLECTIVE MUSCLE POWER TO BRING THIS THING UP IN ONE PIECE.
LET'S DO THIS.
ALRIGHT.
LET 'EM KNOW!
CHAK

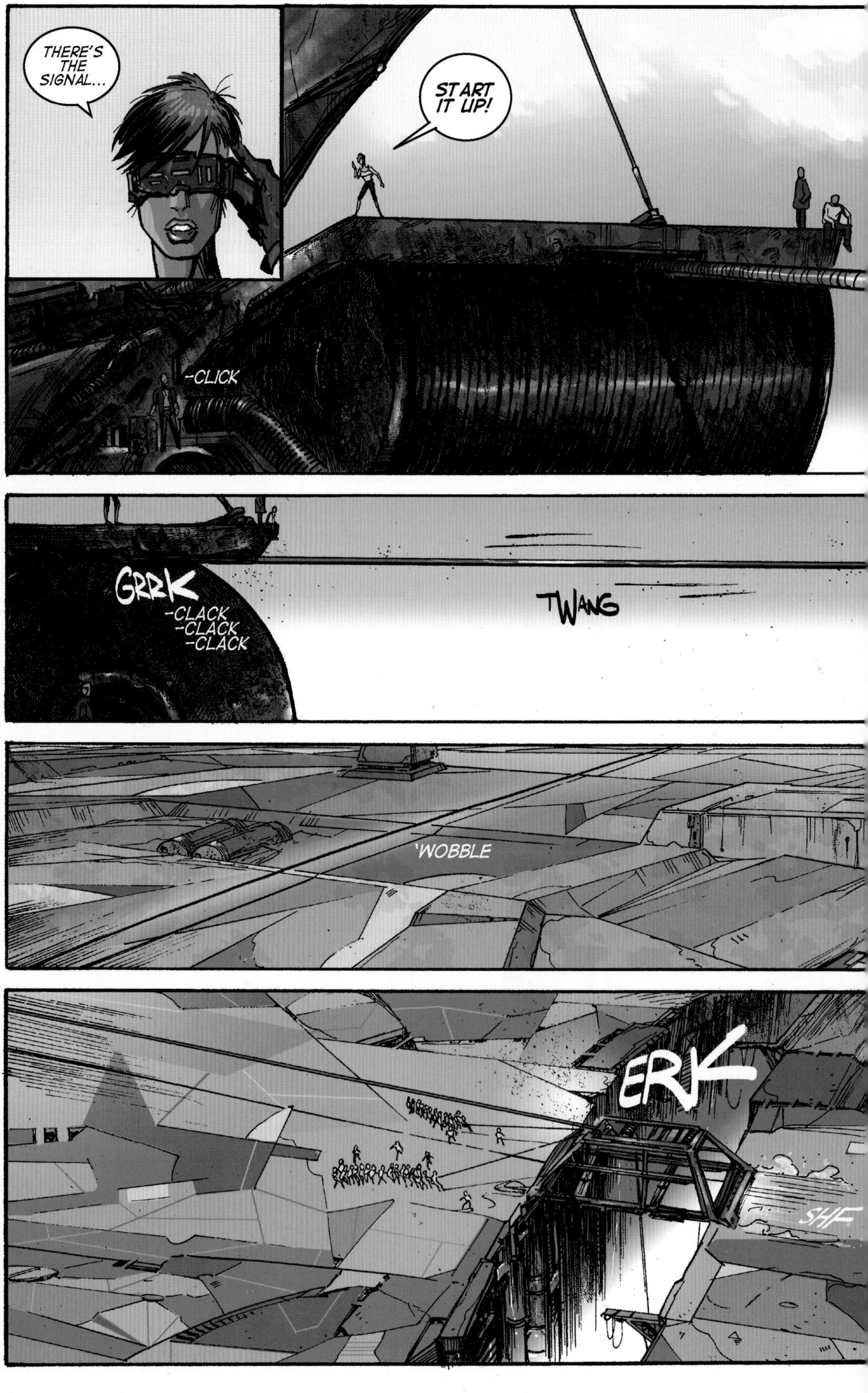
THERE'S THE SIGNAL...
START IT UP!
-CLICK
GRRK
-CLACK
-CLACK
-CLACK
TWANG
'WOBBLE
ERK
SHF

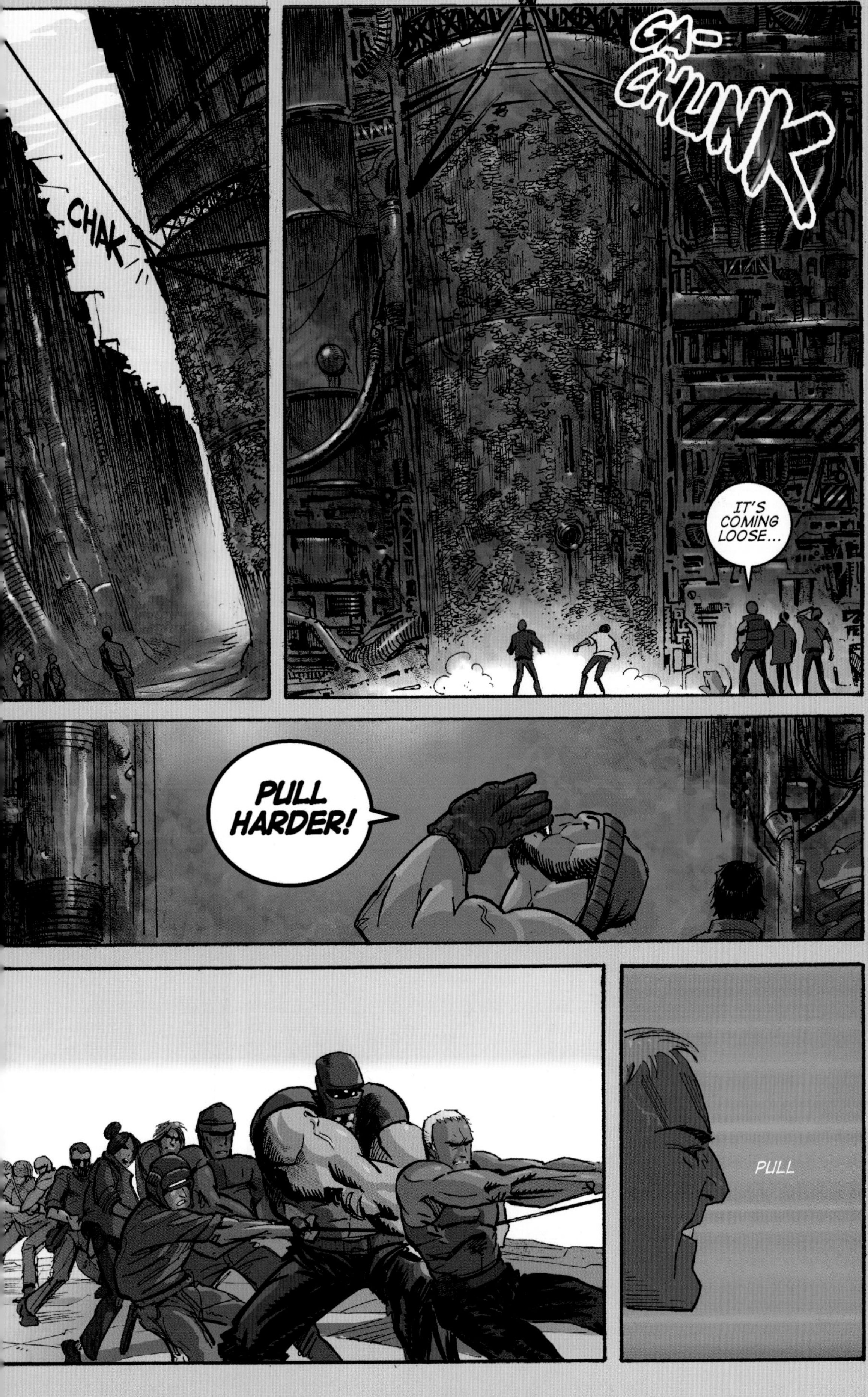
CHAK
GA-CHUNK
IT'S COMING LOOSE...
PULL HARDER!
PULL

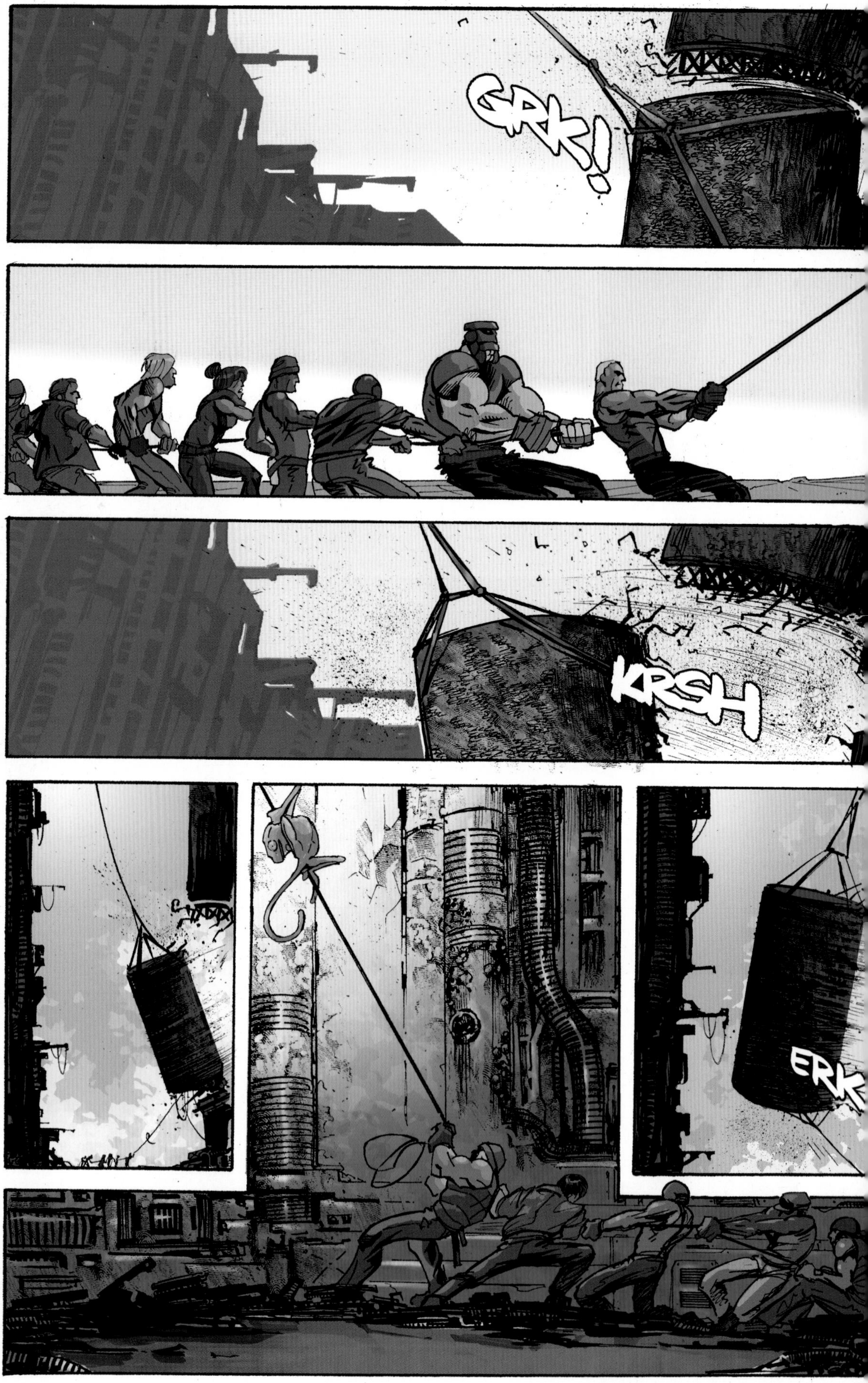
GRK!
KRSH
ERK

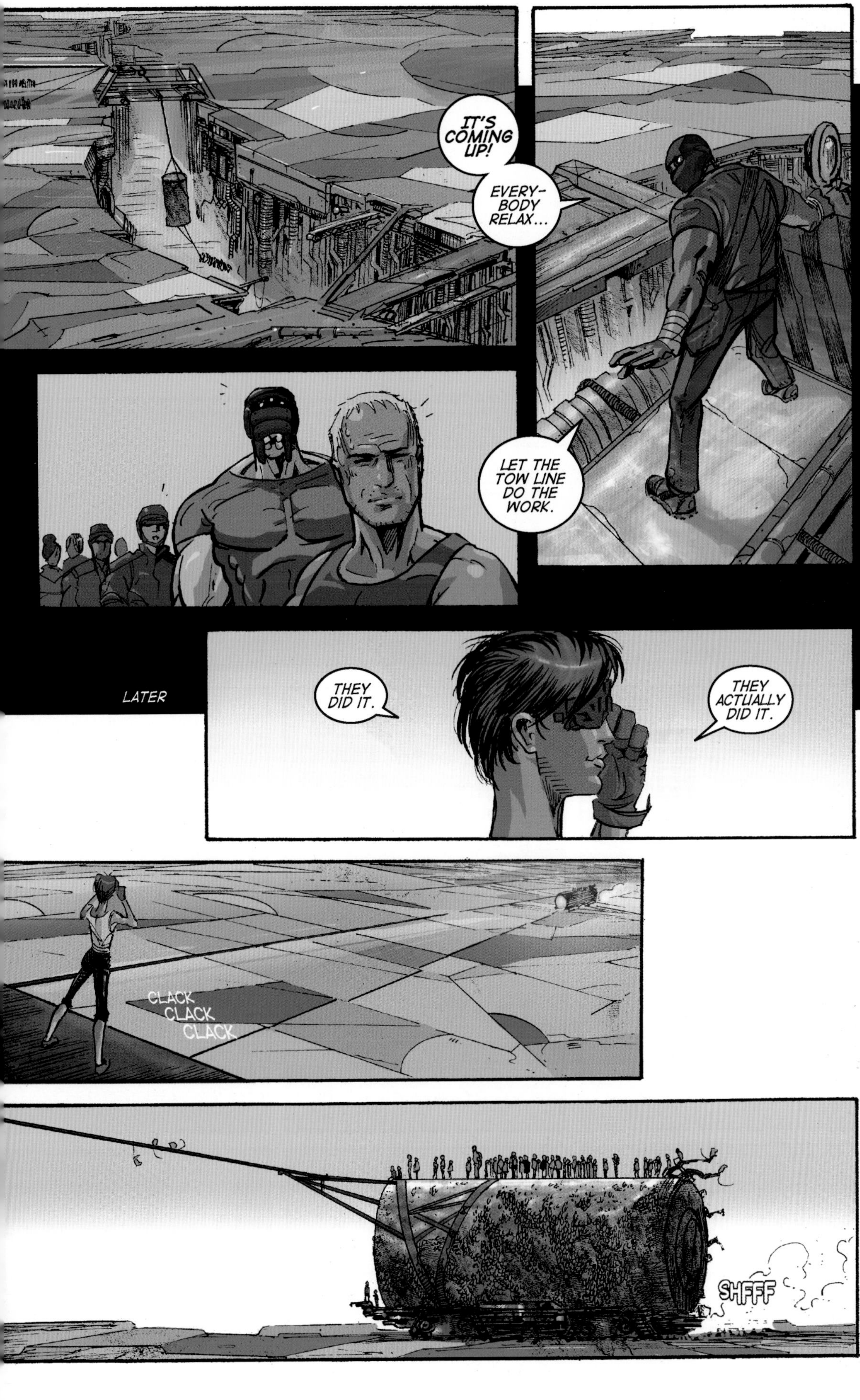
IT'S COMING UP!
EVERY-BODY RELAX...
LET THE TOW LINE DO THE WORK.
LATER
THEY DID IT.
THEY ACTUALLY DID IT.
CLACK CLACK CLACK
SHFFF

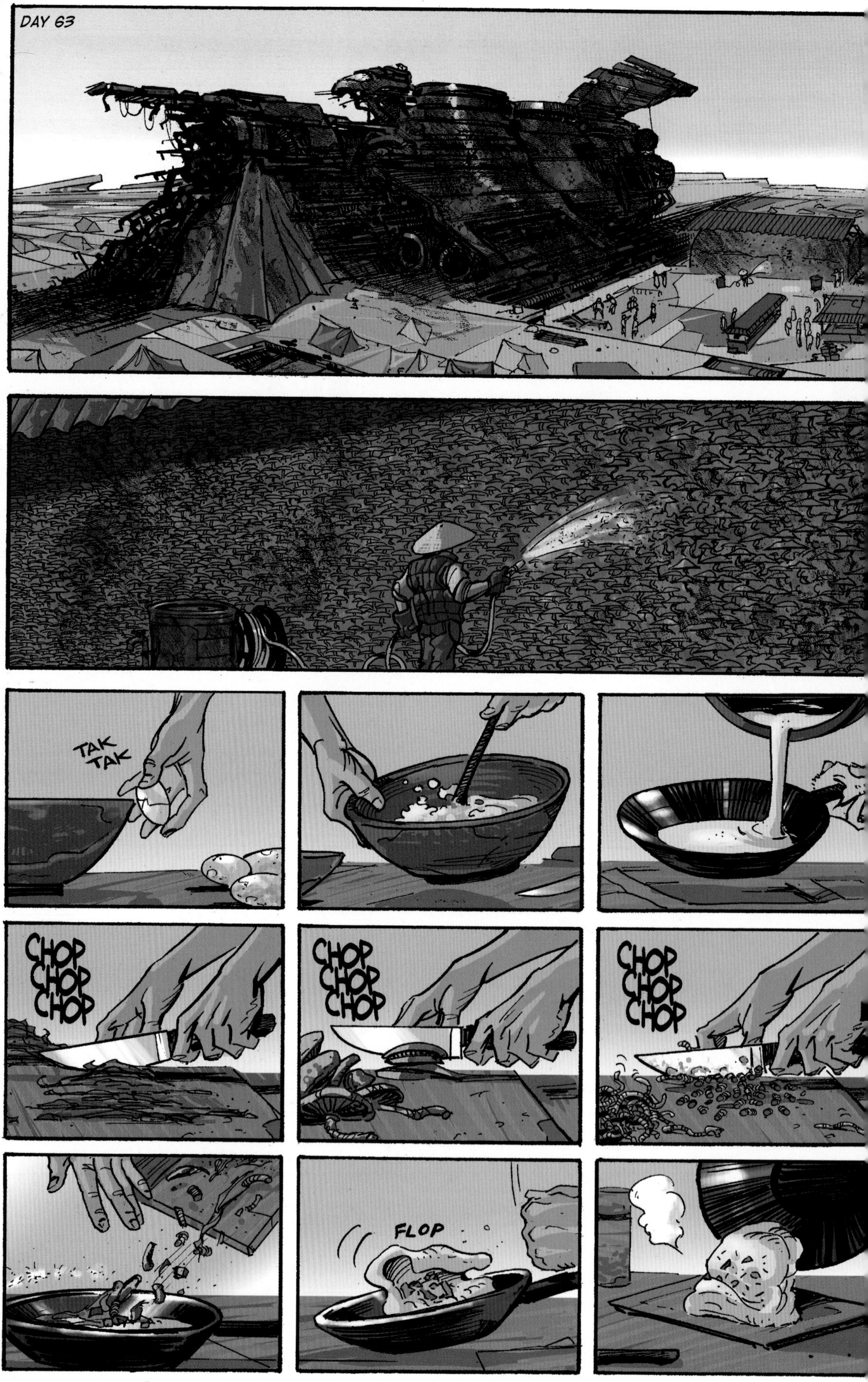
DAY 63
TAK TAK
CHOP CHOP CHOP
CHOP CHOP CHOP
CHOP CHOP CHOP
FLOP

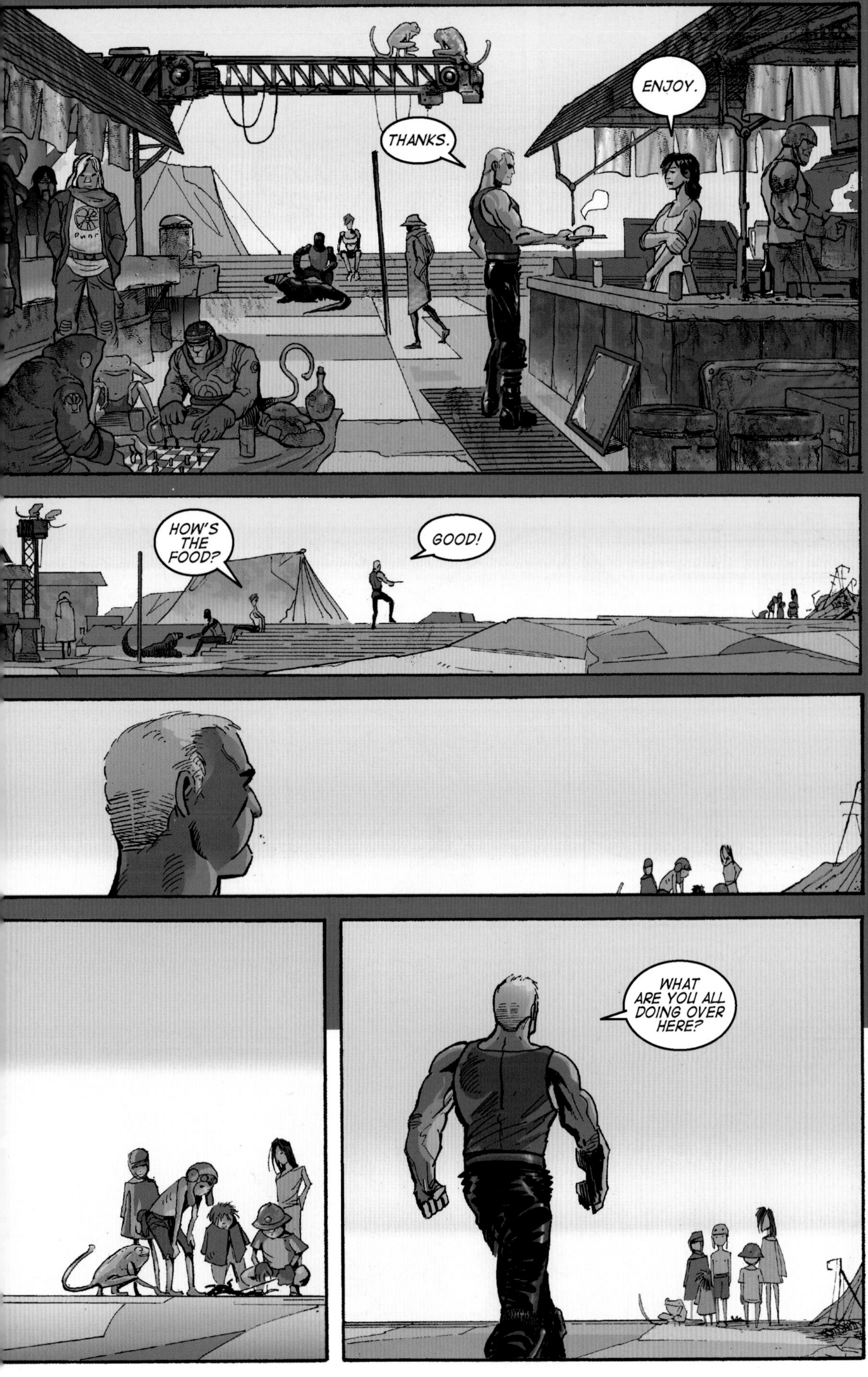
THANKS.
ENJOY.
HOW'S THE FOOD?
GOOD!
WHAT ARE YOU ALL DOING OVER HERE?

NOTHING.

NOTHING, HUH?

THAT SOUNDS REALLY BORING. LET'S SEE HERE...

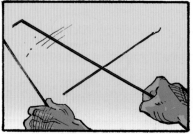

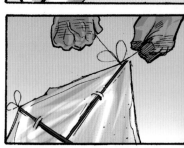

OKAY. YOU TAKE THIS.

--AND YOU TAKE THIS.

NOW SHE'S GOING TO RUN OUT THAT WAY...

AND WHEN I SAY "GO"...

--YOU RUN IN THE OPPOSITE DIRECTION.

...

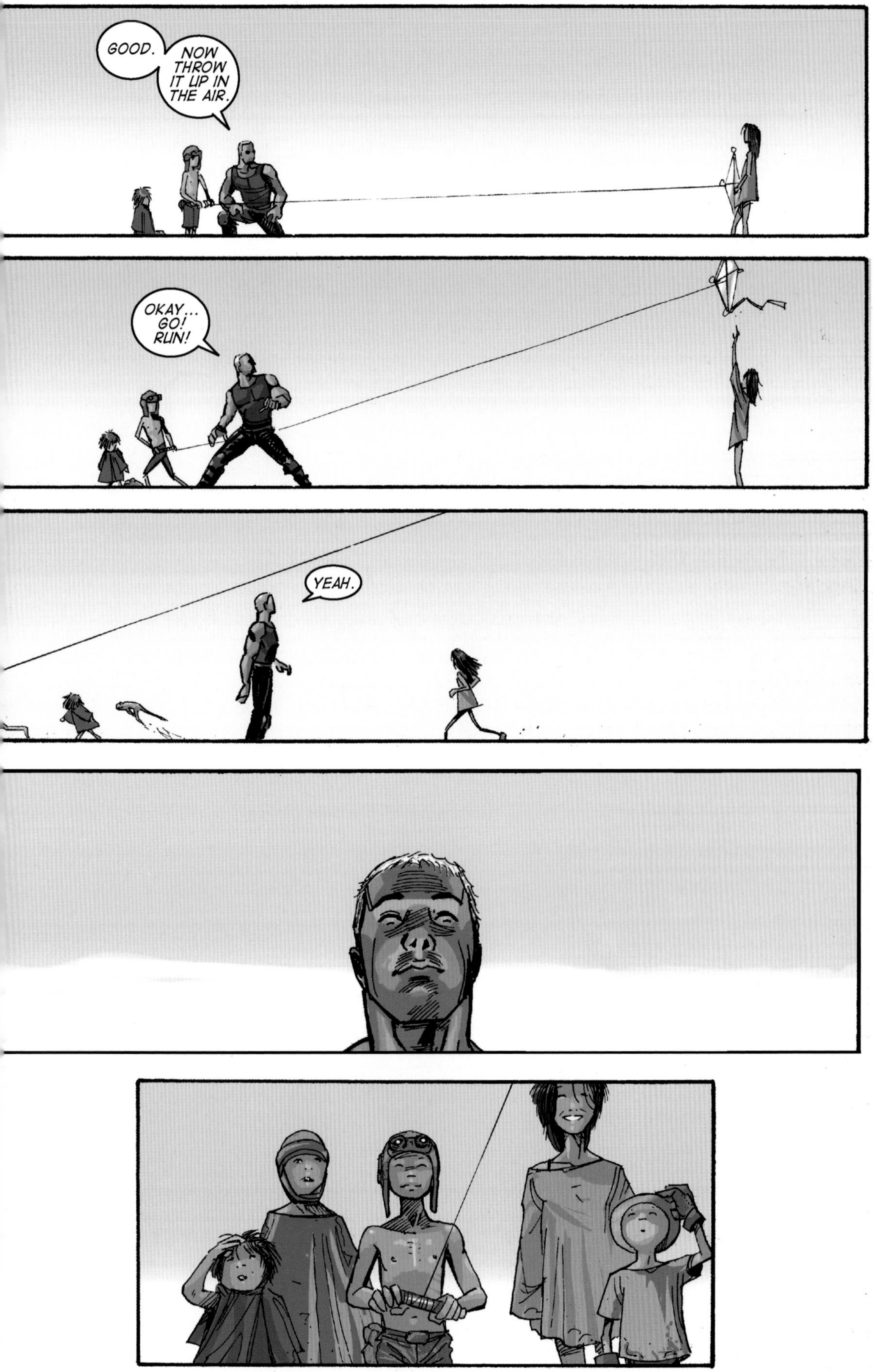
GOOD.
NOW THROW IT UP IN THE AIR.
OKAY... GO! RUN!
YEAH.

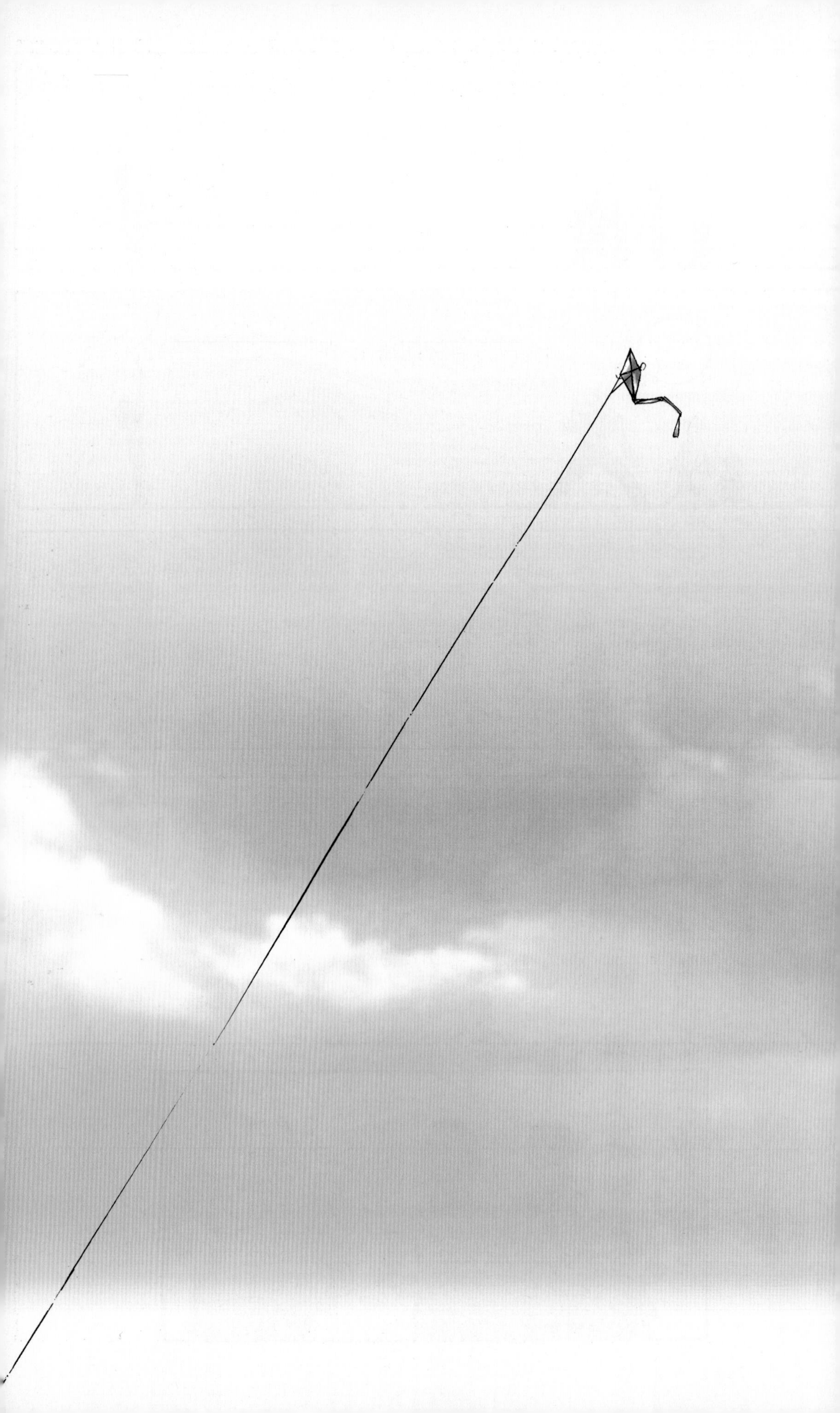

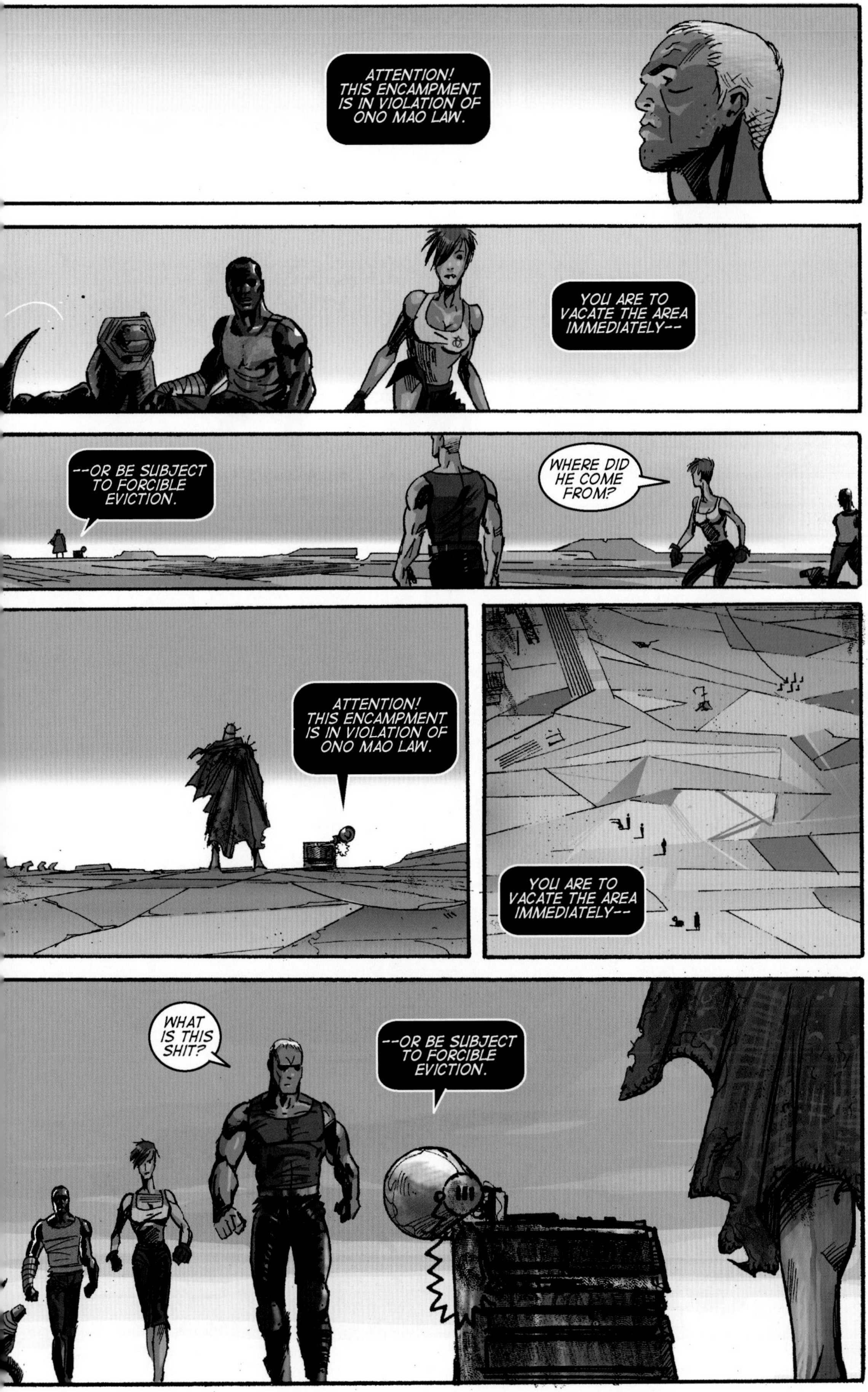
ATTENTION! THIS ENCAMPMENT IS IN VIOLATION OF ONO MAO LAW.
YOU ARE TO VACATE THE AREA IMMEDIATELY--
--OR BE SUBJECT TO FORCIBLE EVICTION.
WHERE DID HE COME FROM?
ATTENTION! THIS ENCAMPMENT IS IN VIOLATION OF ONO MAO LAW.
YOU ARE TO VACATE THE AREA IMMEDIATELY--
WHAT IS THIS SHIT?
--OR BE SUBJECT TO FORCIBLE EVICTION.

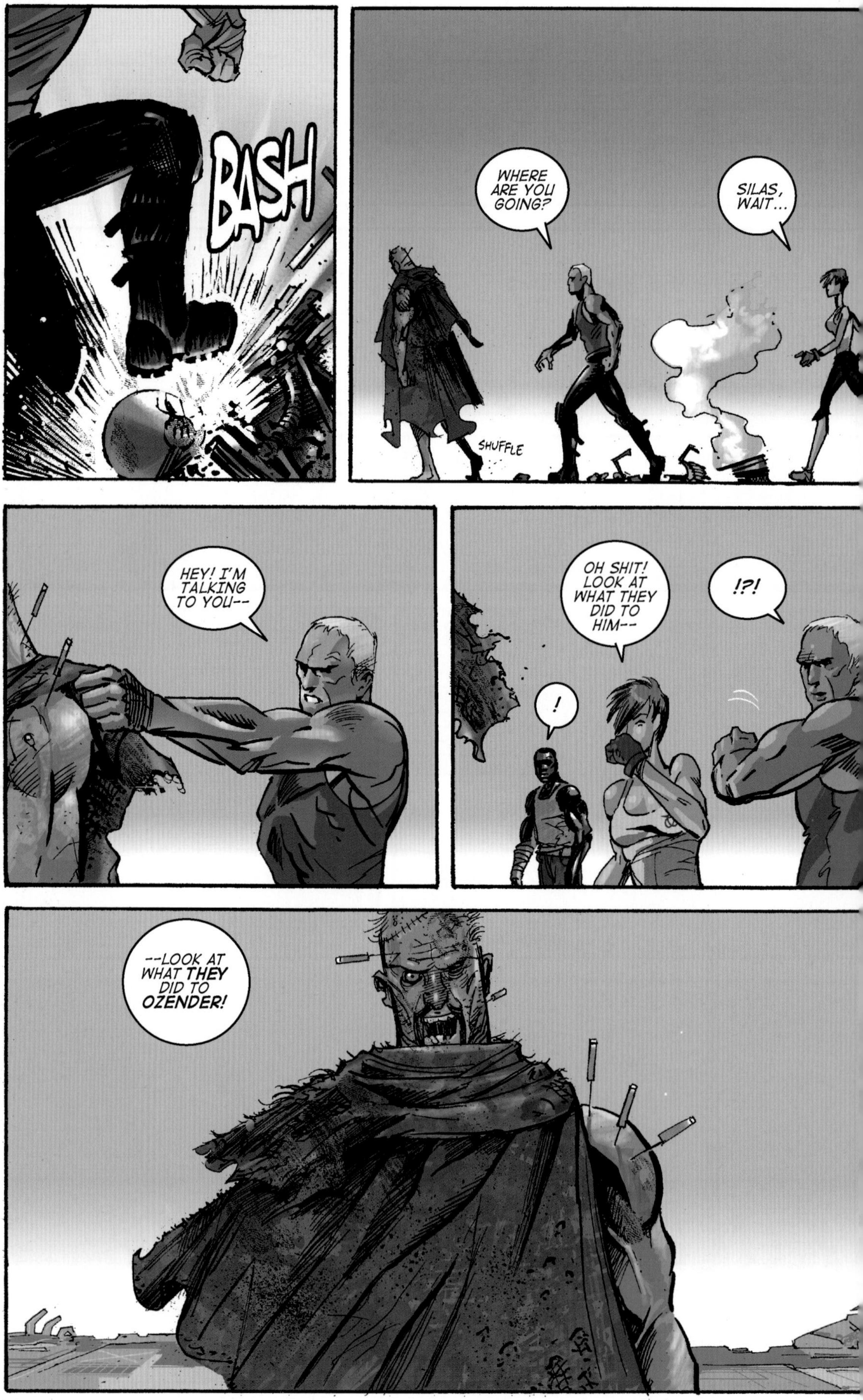
BASH
WHERE ARE YOU GOING?
SILAS, WAIT...
SHUFFLE
HEY! I'M TALKING TO YOU--
OH SHIT! LOOK AT WHAT THEY DID TO HIM--
!?!
!
--LOOK AT WHAT THEY DID TO OZENDER!

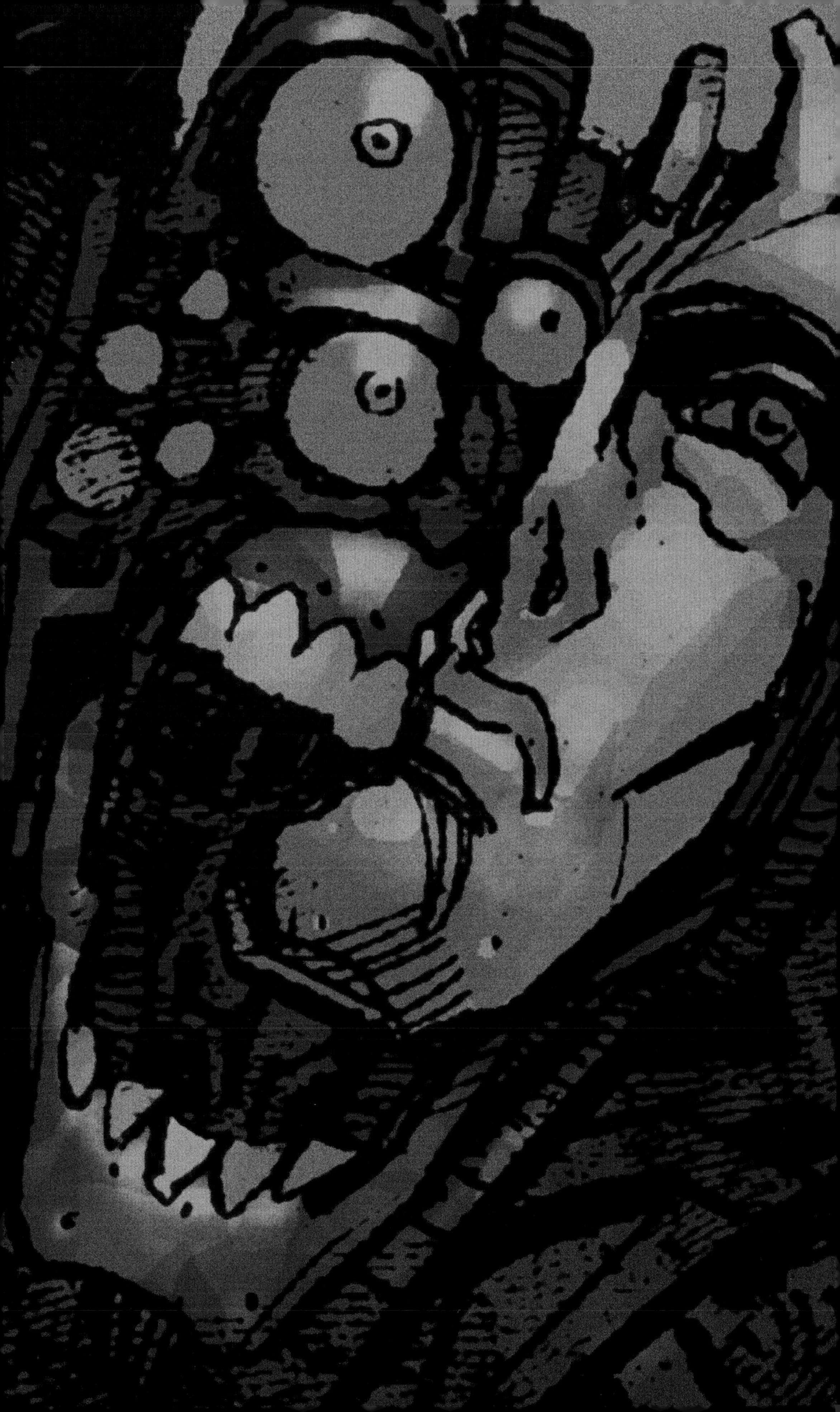

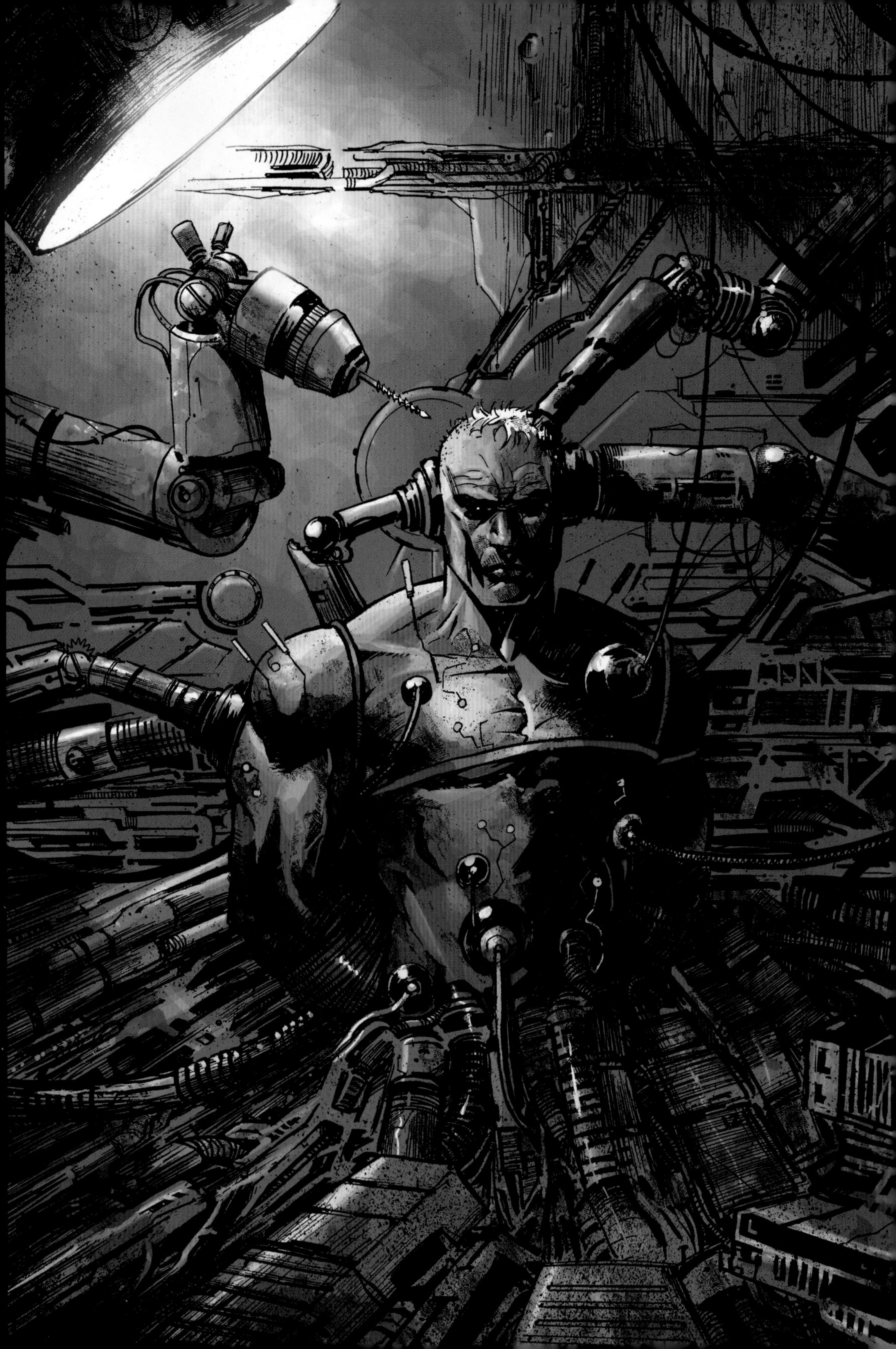

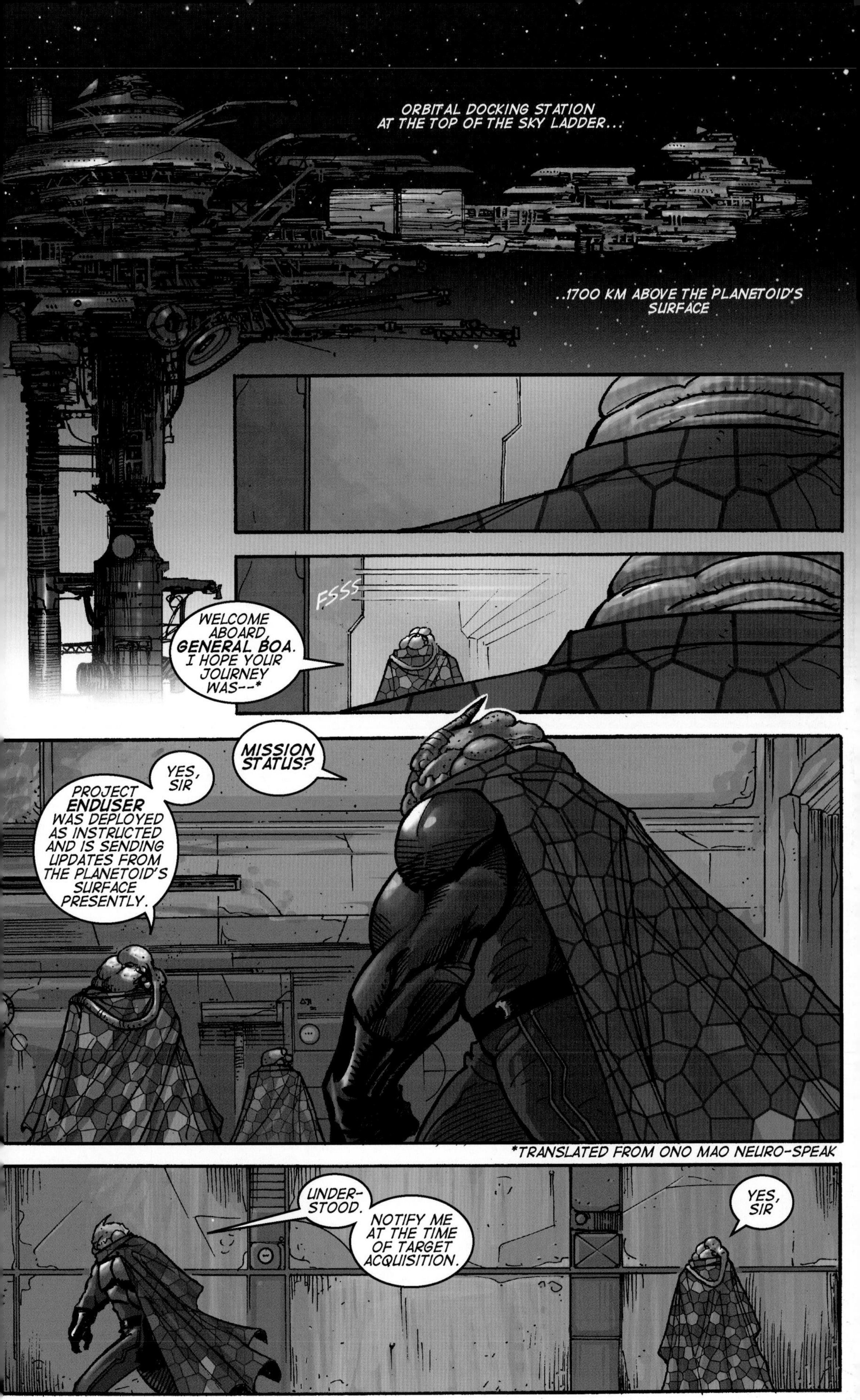
ORBITAL DOCKING STATION AT THE TOP OF THE SKY LADDER...
..1700 KM ABOVE THE PLANETOID'S SURFACE
FSSS
WELCOME ABOARD, GENERAL BOA. I HOPE YOUR JOURNEY WAS--*
MISSION STATUS?
YES, SIR
PROJECT ENDUSER WAS DEPLOYED AS INSTRUCTED AND IS SENDING UPDATES FROM THE PLANETOID'S SURFACE PRESENTLY.
*TRANSLATED FROM ONO MAO NEURO-SPEAK
UNDER-STOOD.
NOTIFY ME AT THE TIME OF TARGET ACQUISITION.
YES, SIR

RICTER, TRY TO REROUTE THE FEED.

REROUTING ... ...

SYSTEM UNRESPONSIVE.

DAMN... ANY OTHER IDEAS?

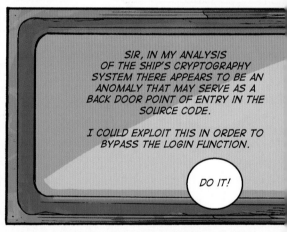

SIR, IN MY ANALYSIS OF THE SHIP'S CRYPTOGRAPHY SYSTEM THERE APPEARS TO BE AN ANOMALY THAT MAY SERVE AS A BACK DOOR POINT OF ENTRY IN THE SOURCE CODE.

I COULD EXPLOIT THIS IN ORDER TO BYPASS THE LOGIN FUNCTION.

DO IT!

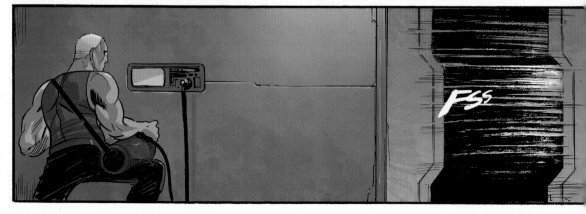

WHAT... IS... THIS...?

SCANNING SERIAL RFID*...

*RADIO-FREQUENCY IDENTIFICATION

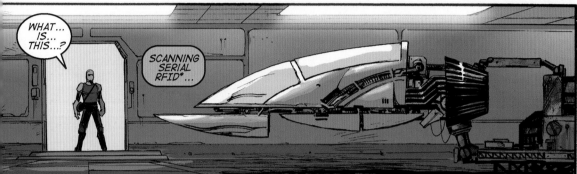

THIS SPACECRAFT IS AOKI MOTOR'S ENTRY INTO THE ANNUAL TRANS-STELLAR LUXURY RACING EXPO.

WHAT KIND OF ENGINE DOES THIS THING HAVE?

THIS CRAFT HAS A HADRON FUEL CELL ENGINE CAPABLE OF FULL WARP.

A HADRON FUEL CELL!

RICTER, IS THIS THING CAPABLE OF GETTING OUT OF THE PLANETOID'S STRATOSPHERE AND INTO SPACE?

YES, THEORETICALLY THIS CRAFT IS CAPABLE OF DOING SO.

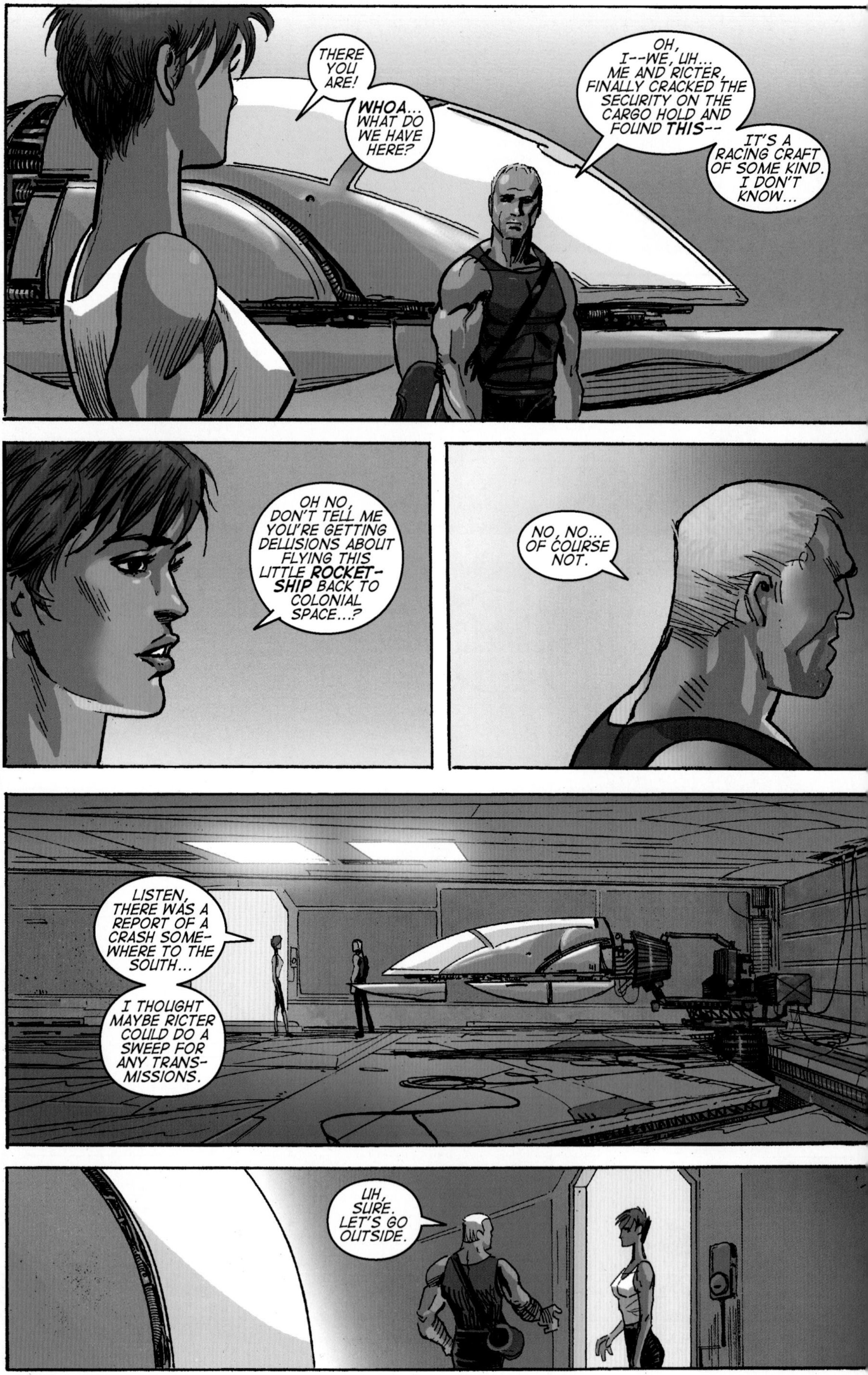

THERE YOU ARE!
WHOA... WHAT DO WE HAVE HERE?
OH, I--WE, UH... ME AND RICTER, FINALLY CRACKED THE SECURITY ON THE CARGO HOLD AND FOUND THIS--
IT'S A RACING CRAFT OF SOME KIND. I DON'T KNOW...
OH NO, DON'T TELL ME YOU'RE GETTING DELUSIONS ABOUT FLYING THIS LITTLE ROCKET-SHIP BACK TO COLONIAL SPACE...?
NO, NO... OF COURSE NOT.
LISTEN, THERE WAS A REPORT OF A CRASH SOME-WHERE TO THE SOUTH...
I THOUGHT MAYBE RICTER COULD DO A SWEEP FOR ANY TRANS-MISSIONS.
UH, SURE. LET'S GO OUTSIDE.

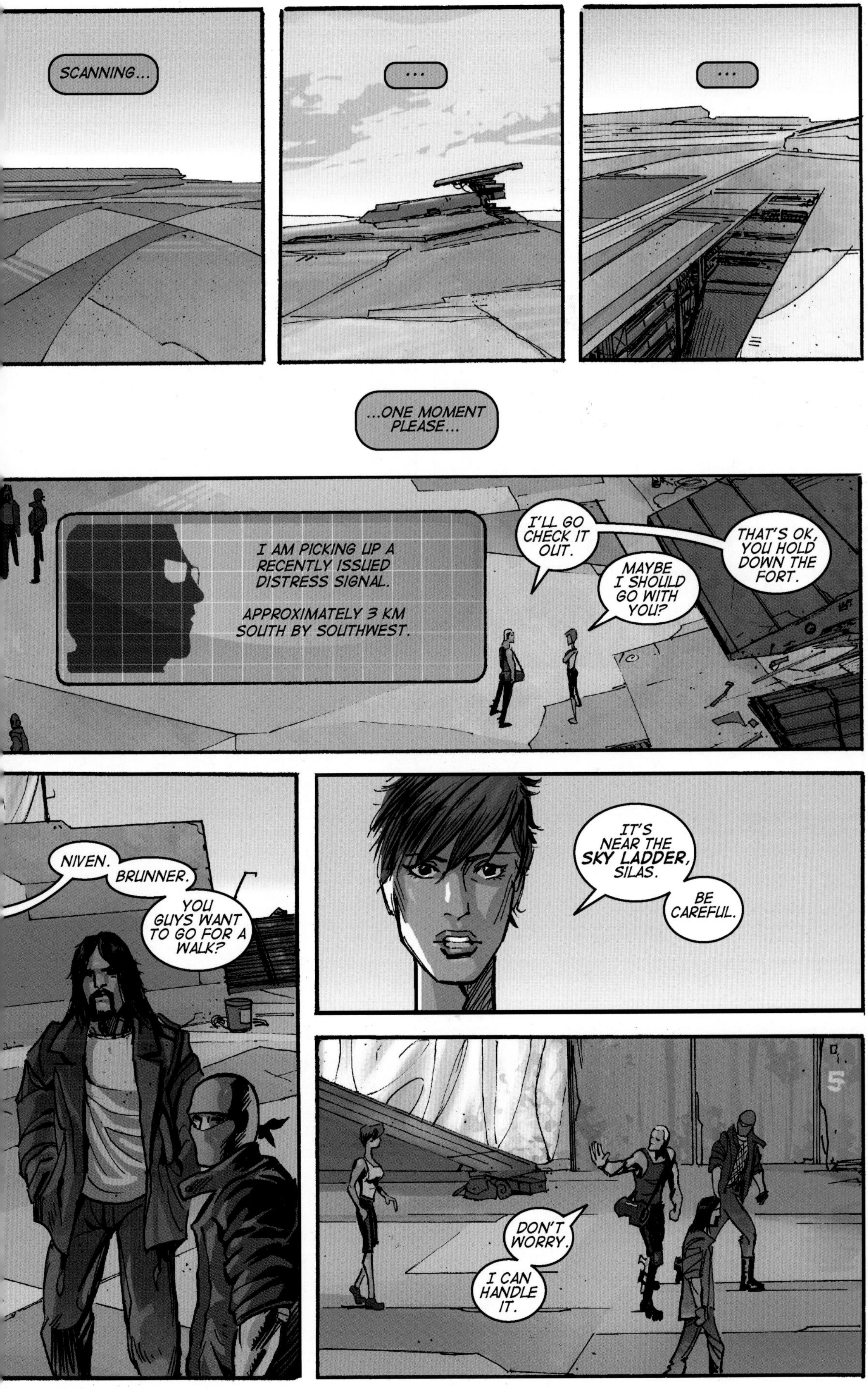
SCANNING...
...
...
...ONE MOMENT PLEASE...
I AM PICKING UP A RECENTLY ISSUED DISTRESS SIGNAL.
APPROXIMATELY 3 KM SOUTH BY SOUTHWEST.
I'LL GO CHECK IT OUT.
MAYBE I SHOULD GO WITH YOU?
THAT'S OK, YOU HOLD DOWN THE FORT.
NIVEN.
BRUNNER.
YOU GUYS WANT TO GO FOR A WALK?
IT'S NEAR THE SKY LADDER, SILAS.
BE CAREFUL.
DON'T WORRY.
I CAN HANDLE IT.

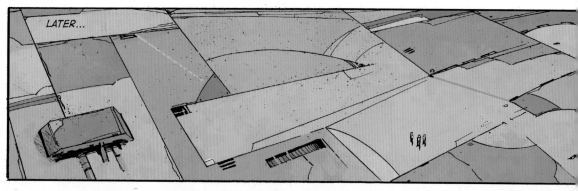

LATER...

IT'S GETTING KIND OF COLD OUT HERE...

YEAH, IT LOOKS LIKE A STORM IS COMING.

IT TENDS TO RAIN A LOT THIS TIME OF YEAR.

ATTENTION: APPROACHING CRASH SITE.

I DON'T GET IT.

...IT'S JUST A BUNCH OF JUNK.

OVER THERE.

...LOOKS LIKE AN ESCAPE POD.

 WHAT'VE WE GOT?

 UH... IT'S EMPTY.

 THAT'S WEIRD.

MAYBE THEY WALKED OFF SOME-WHERE...?

 RICTER, DO A LOCAL SCAN FOR SIGNS OF HUMAN LIFE.

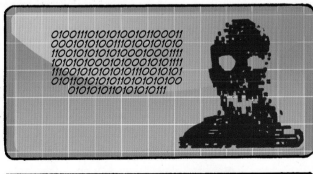 0100111010101001011000011
0001010100111010010101010
1100101010101100010000111
1010101000101000101011111
1110010101010101110010101
0101010101011010101010100
0101010110101010111

 !?!

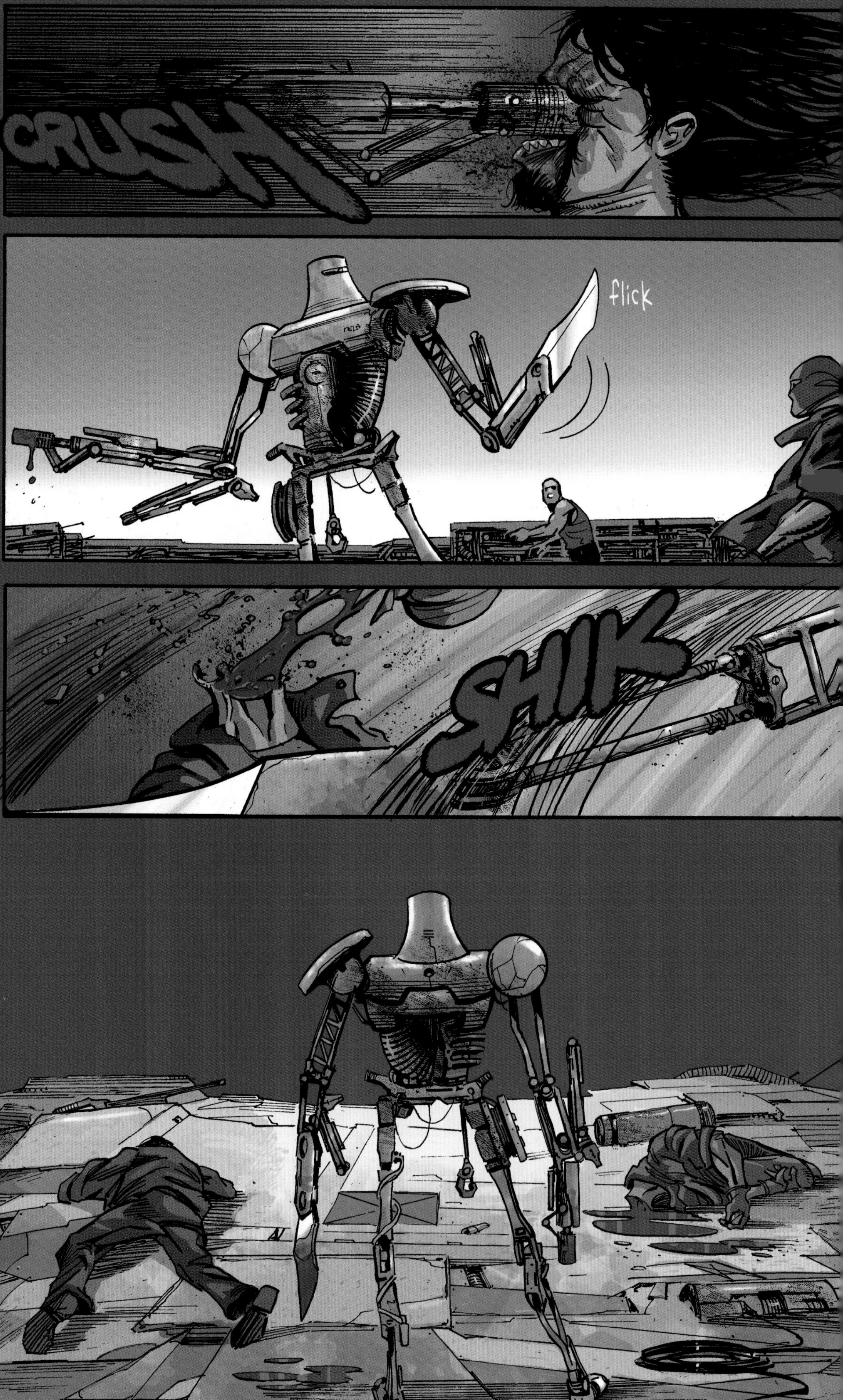
CRUSH
flick
SHIK

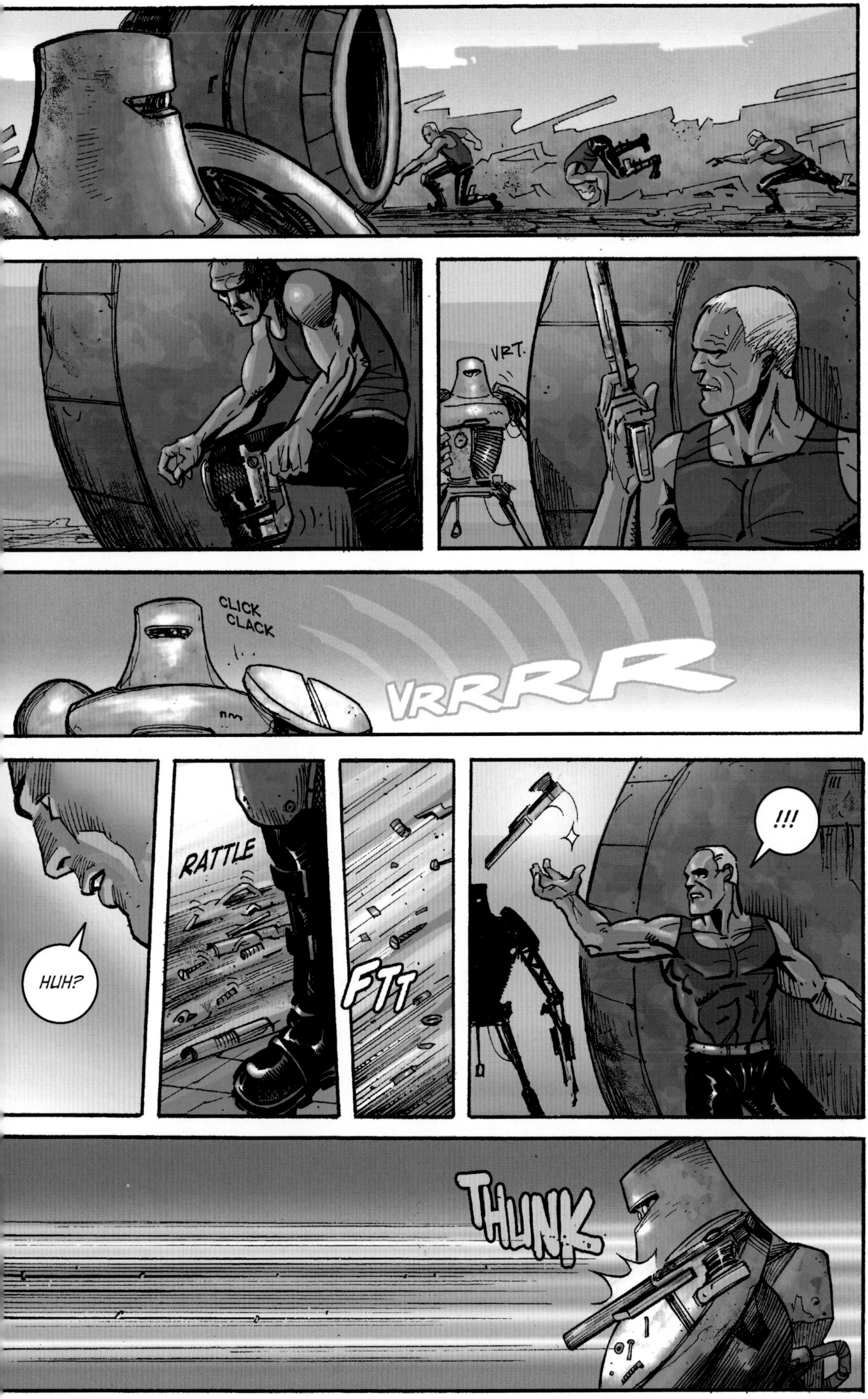
VRT.
CLICK
CLACK
VRRRR
HUH?
RATTLE
FTT
!!!
THUNK

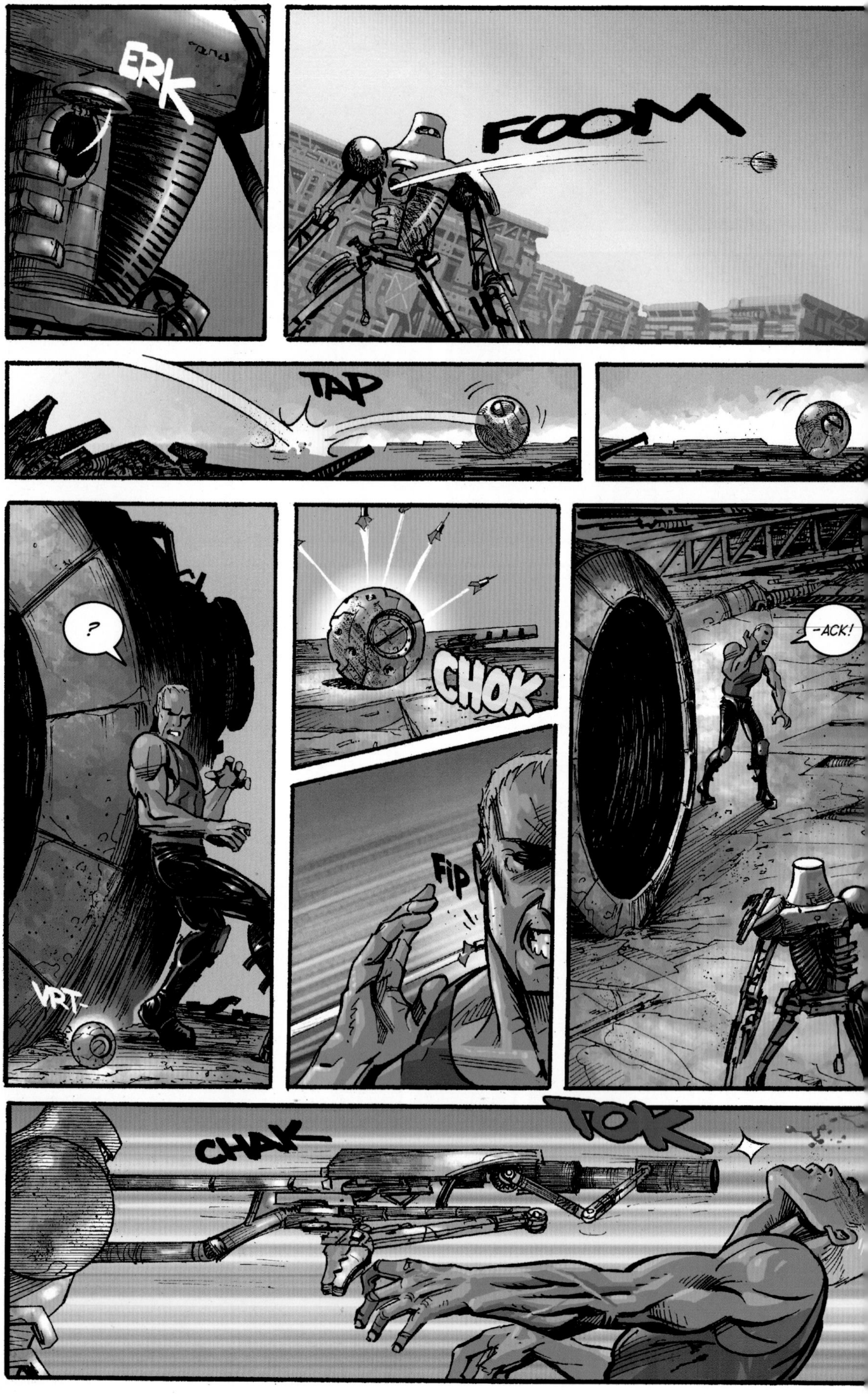
ERK
FOOM
TAP
?
VRT-
CHOK
FiP
-ACK!
CHAK
TOK

THUD

CLACK

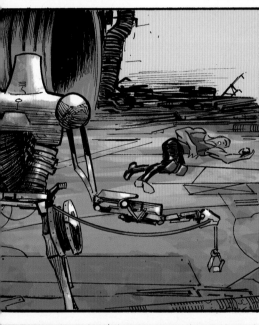

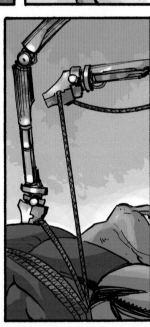

SHFF

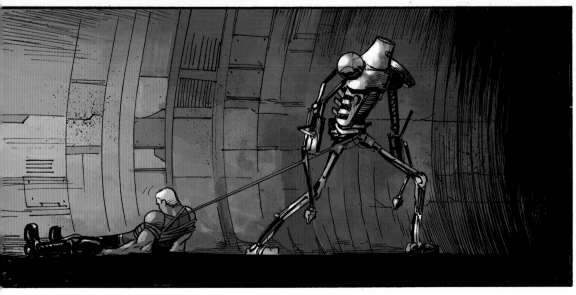

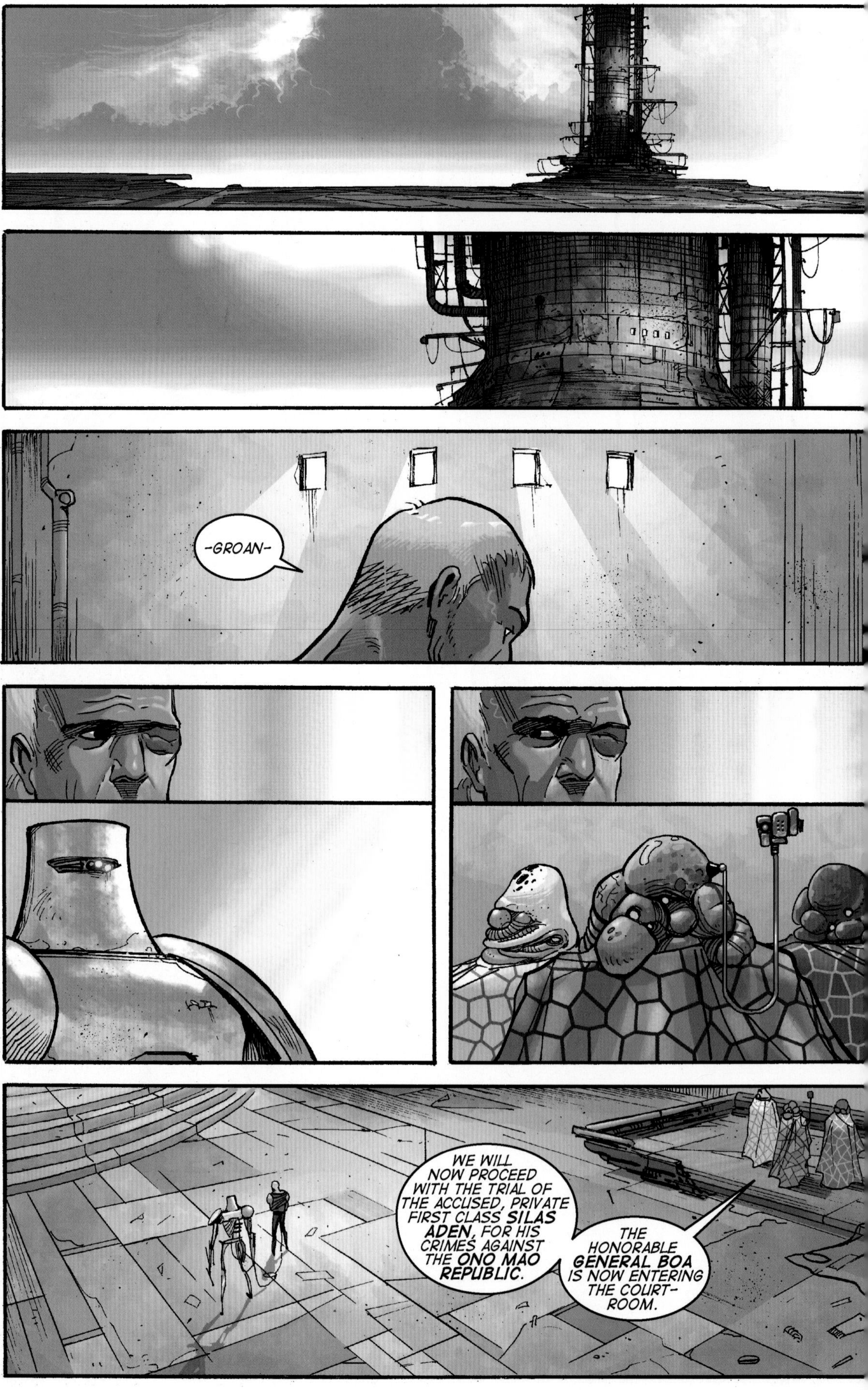
-GROAN-
WE WILL NOW PROCEED WITH THE TRIAL OF THE ACCUSED, PRIVATE FIRST CLASS SILAS ADEN, FOR HIS CRIMES AGAINST THE ONO MAO REPUBLIC.
THE HONORABLE GENERAL BOA IS NOW ENTERING THE COURT-ROOM.

VUMP

PRIVATE FIRST CLASS SILAS ADEN, YOU STAND ACCUSED OF THE FOLLOWING CRIMES:

TRESPASSING ON THE TERRITORIAL SPACE OF THE ONO MAO...

FORCILBY BOARDING AN ONO MAO VESSEL...

MULTIPLE VIOLATIONS OF TRAFFIC AND SAFETY ORDINANCES WHILE OPERATING A STARCRAFT...

THEFT, PIRACY, EVADING ARREST...

DESTRUCTION OF PROPERTY, TERRORISM, AND PUBLIC URINATION.

HOW DO YOU PLEAD TO THESE CHARGES?

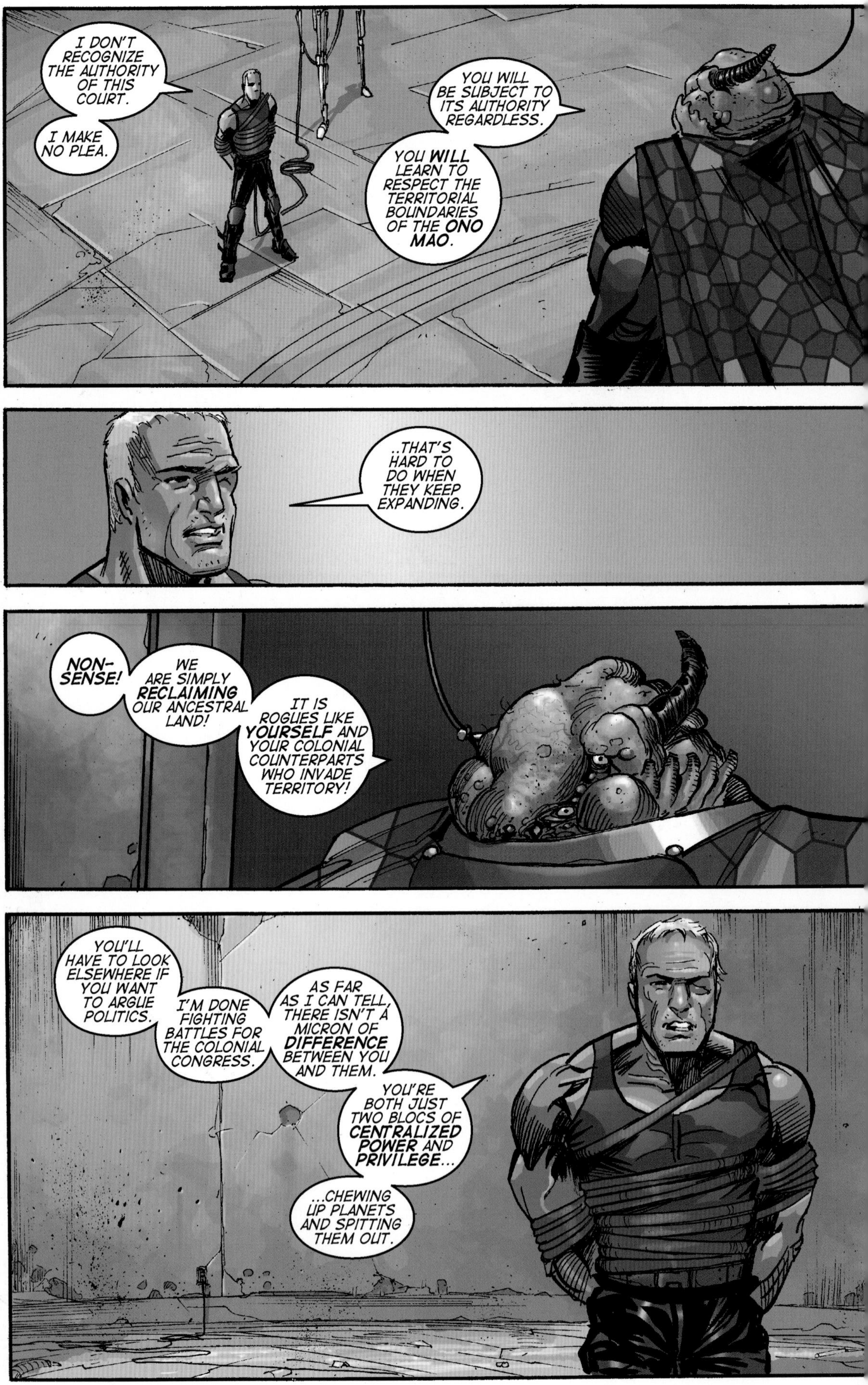

I DON'T RECOGNIZE THE AUTHORITY OF THIS COURT.
I MAKE NO PLEA.
YOU WILL BE SUBJECT TO ITS AUTHORITY REGARDLESS.
YOU **WILL** LEARN TO RESPECT THE TERRITORIAL BOUNDARIES OF THE **ONO MAO**.
..THAT'S HARD TO DO WHEN THEY KEEP EXPANDING.
NON-SENSE!
WE ARE SIMPLY **RECLAIMING** OUR ANCESTRAL LAND!
IT IS ROGUES LIKE **YOURSELF** AND YOUR COLONIAL COUNTERPARTS WHO INVADE TERRITORY!
YOU'LL HAVE TO LOOK ELSEWHERE IF YOU WANT TO ARGUE POLITICS.
I'M DONE FIGHTING BATTLES FOR THE COLONIAL CONGRESS.
AS FAR AS I CAN TELL, THERE ISN'T A MICRON OF **DIFFERENCE** BETWEEN YOU AND THEM.
YOU'RE BOTH JUST TWO BLOCS OF **CENTRALIZED POWER** AND **PRIVILEGE**...
...CHEWING UP PLANETS AND SPITTING THEM OUT.

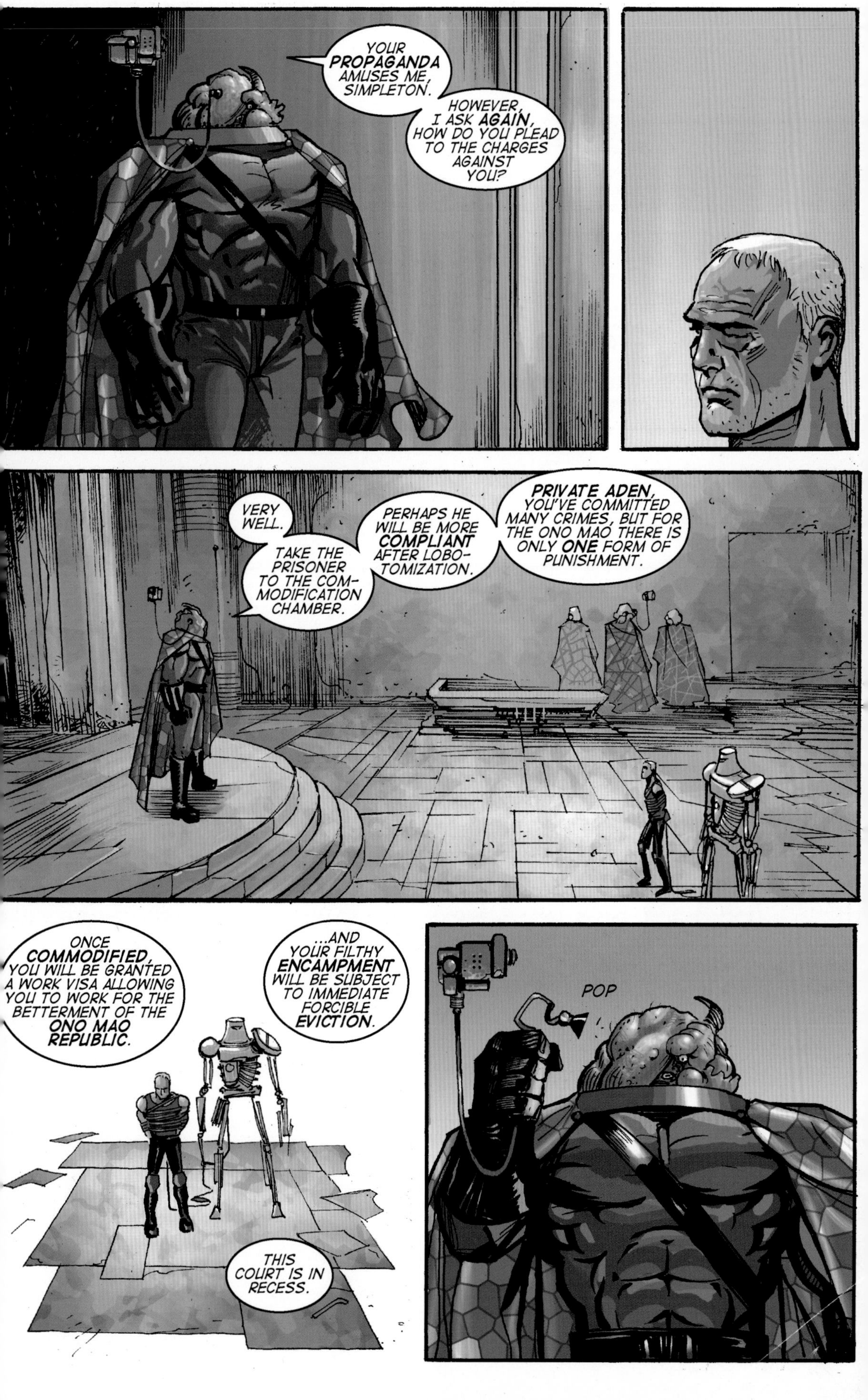
YOUR PROPAGANDA AMUSES ME, SIMPLETON.
HOWEVER, I ASK AGAIN, HOW DO YOU PLEAD TO THE CHARGES AGAINST YOU?
VERY WELL.
TAKE THE PRISONER TO THE COMMODIFICATION CHAMBER.
PERHAPS HE WILL BE MORE COMPLIANT AFTER LOBOTOMIZATION.
PRIVATE ADEN, YOU'VE COMMITTED MANY CRIMES, BUT FOR THE ONO MAO THERE IS ONLY ONE FORM OF PUNISHMENT.
ONCE COMMODIFIED, YOU WILL BE GRANTED A WORK VISA ALLOWING YOU TO WORK FOR THE BETTERMENT OF THE ONO MAO REPUBLIC.
...AND YOUR FILTHY ENCAMPMENT WILL BE SUBJECT TO IMMEDIATE FORCIBLE EVICTION.
THIS COURT IS IN RECESS.
POP

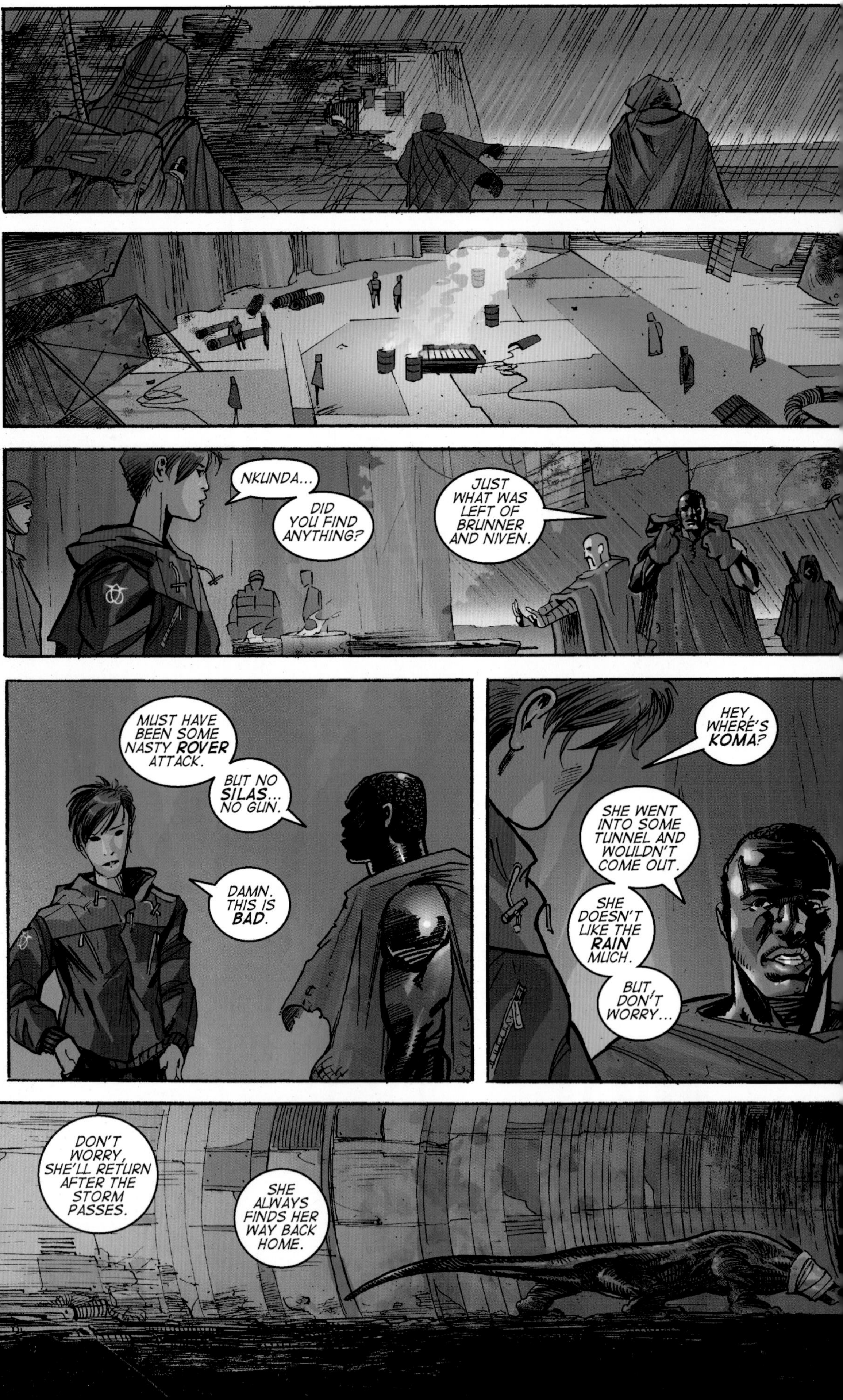
NKUNDA...
DID YOU FIND ANYTHING?
JUST WHAT WAS LEFT OF BRUNNER AND NIVEN.
MUST HAVE BEEN SOME NASTY ROVER ATTACK.
BUT NO SILAS... NO GUN.
DAMN. THIS IS BAD.
HEY, WHERE'S KOMA?
SHE WENT INTO SOME TUNNEL AND WOULDN'T COME OUT.
SHE DOESN'T LIKE THE RAIN MUCH.
BUT, DON'T WORRY...
DON'T WORRY, SHE'LL RETURN AFTER THE STORM PASSES.
SHE ALWAYS FINDS HER WAY BACK HOME.

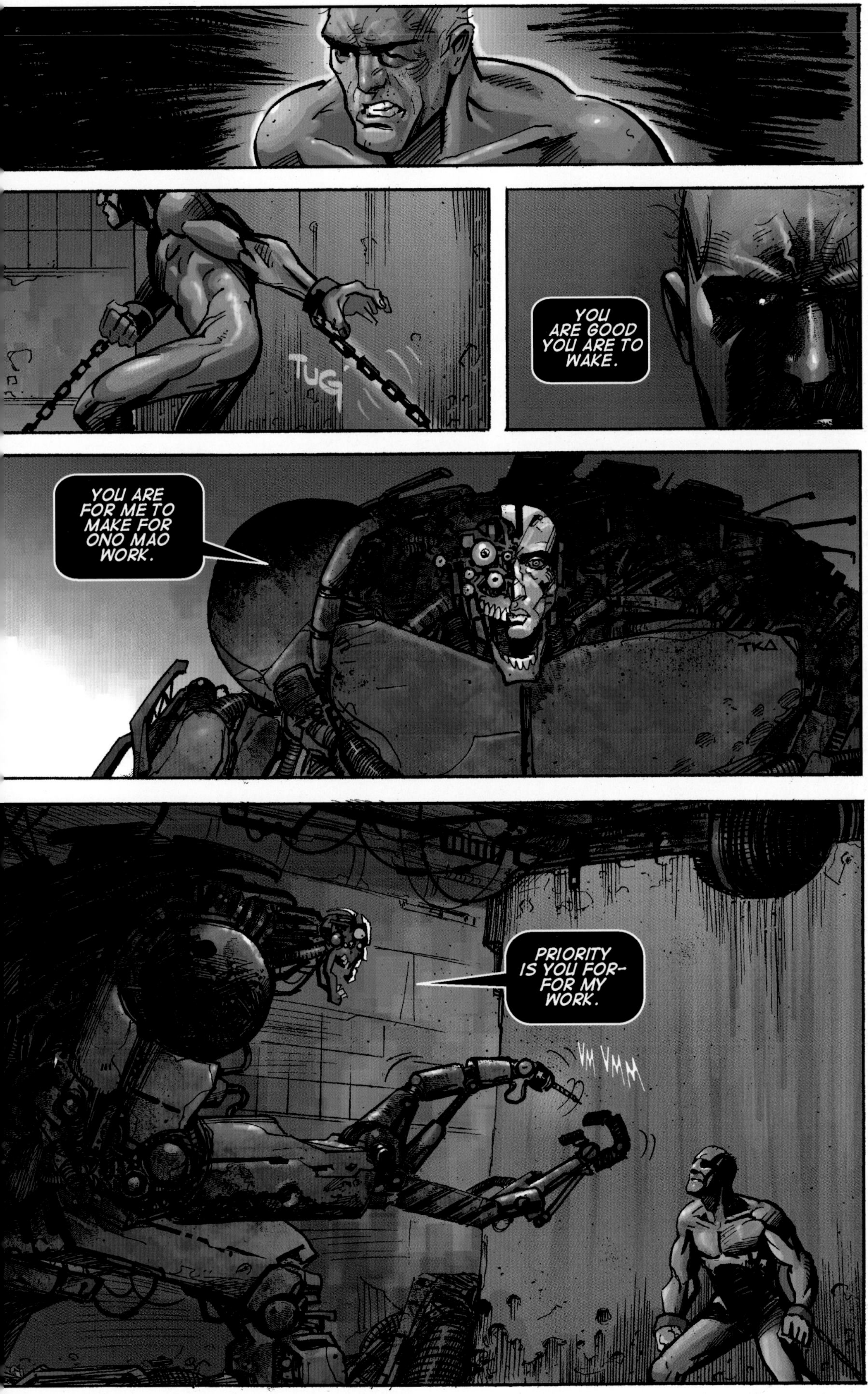
TUG
YOU ARE GOOD YOU ARE TO WAKE.
YOU ARE FOR ME TO MAKE FOR ONO MAO WORK.
PRIORITY IS YOU FOR-FOR MY WORK.
VM VMM

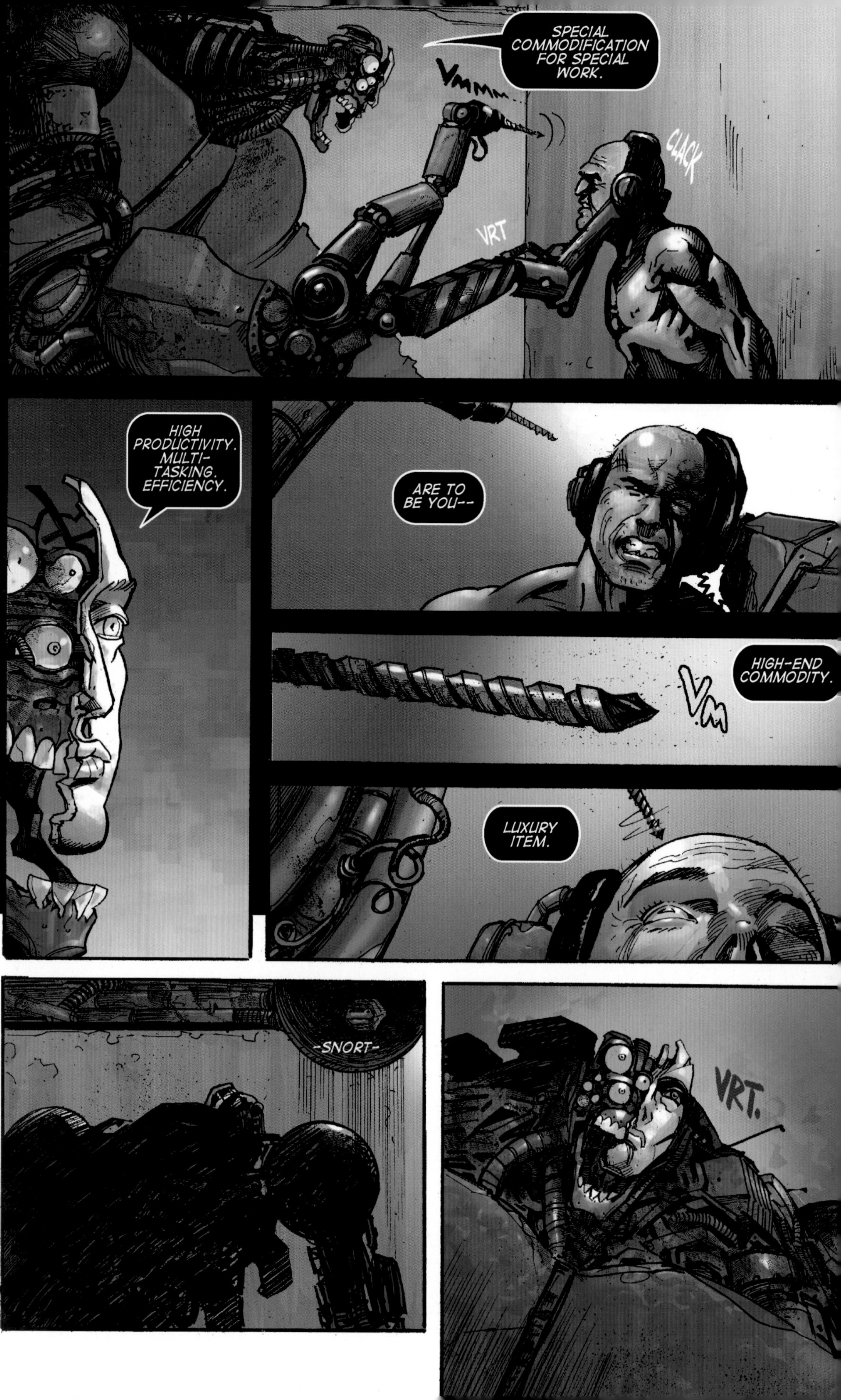
SPECIAL COMMODIFICATION FOR SPECIAL WORK.
VMMMM
CLACK
VRT
HIGH PRODUCTIVITY. MULTI-TASKING. EFFICIENCY.
ARE TO BE YOU--
HIGH-END COMMODITY.
VM
LUXURY ITEM.
-SNORT-
VRT.

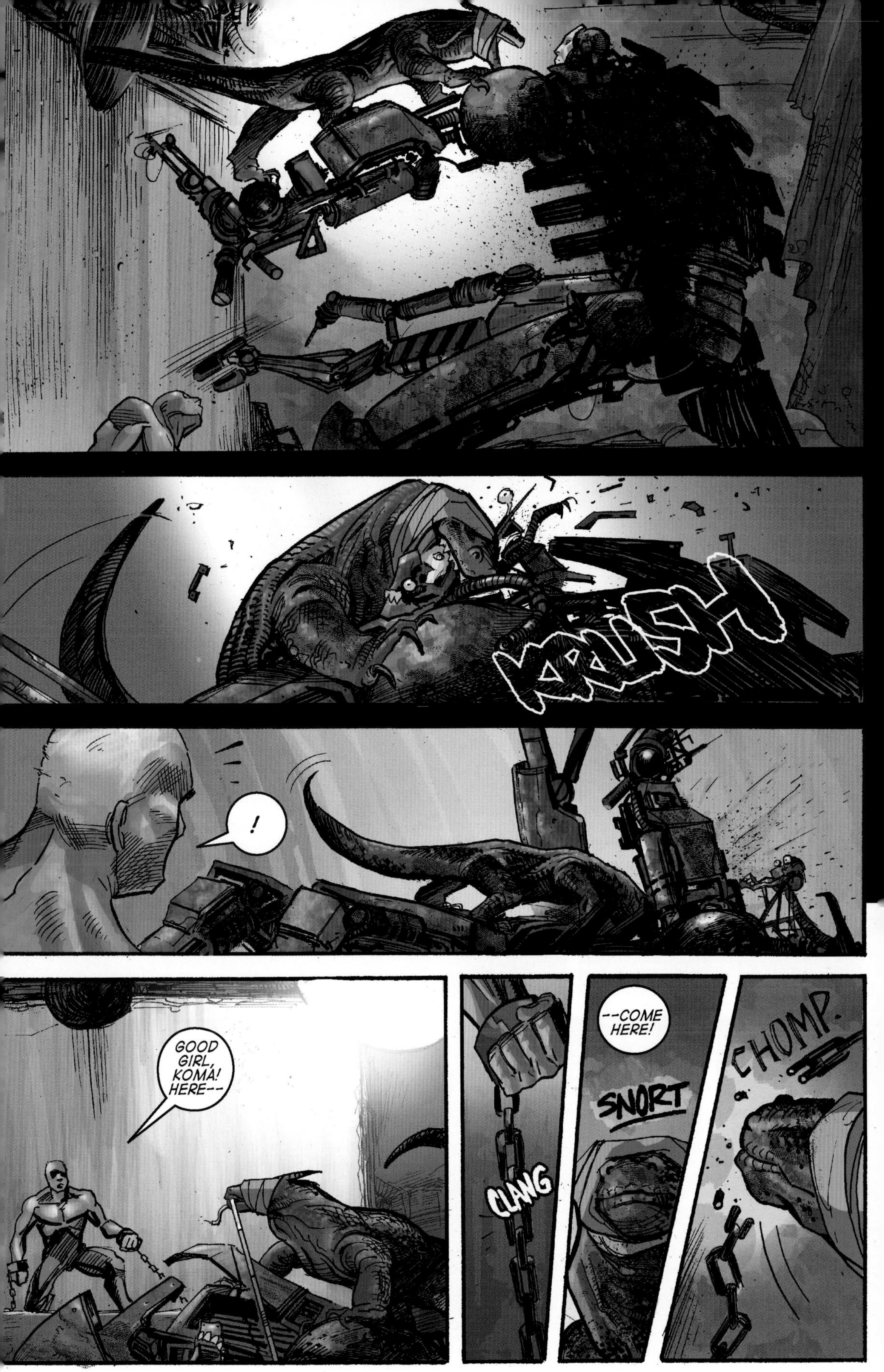
KRUSH
!
GOOD GIRL, KOMÁ! HERE--
CLANG
--COME HERE!
SNORT
CHOMP.

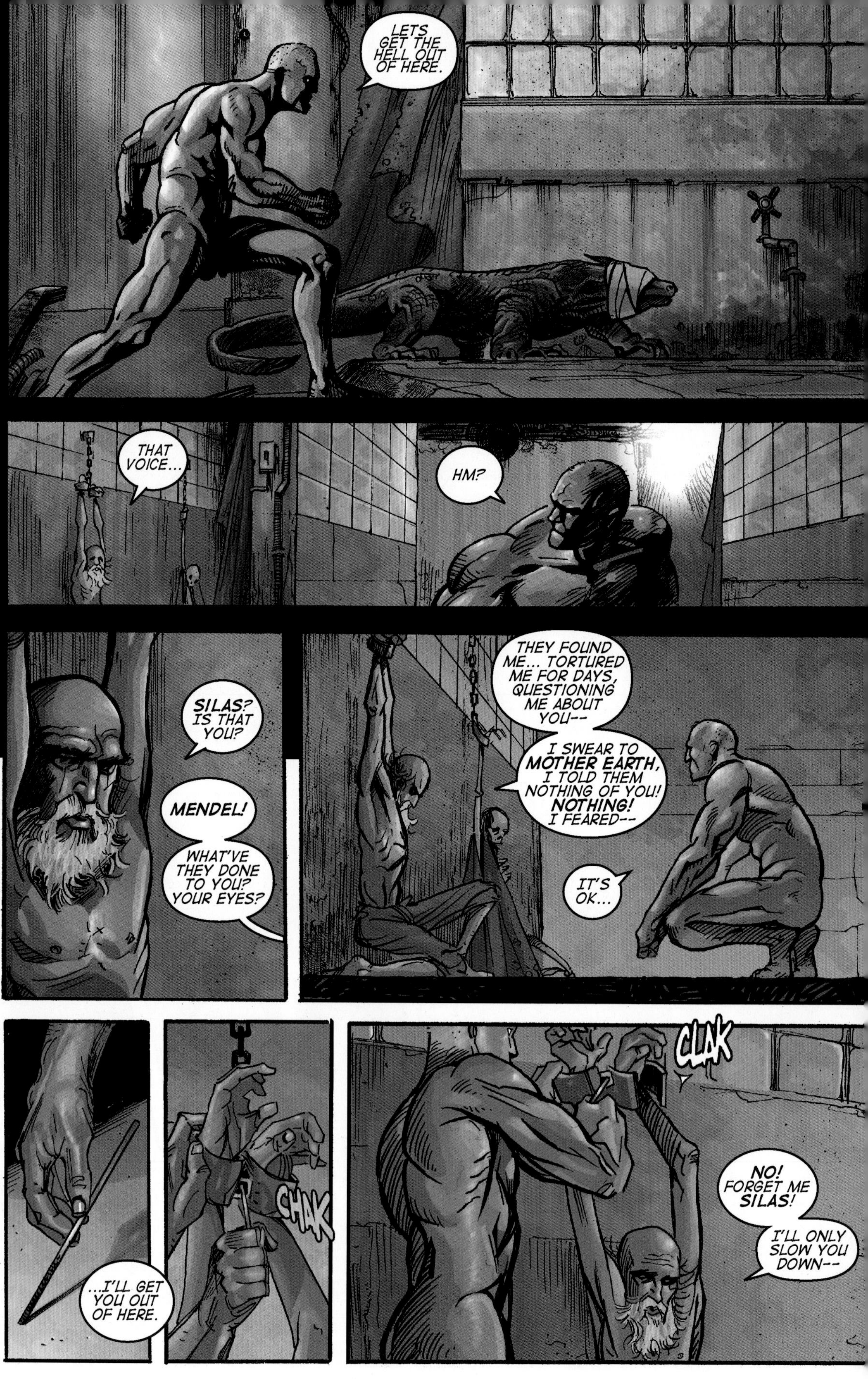
LETS GET THE HELL OUT OF HERE.
THAT VOICE...
HM?
SILAS? IS THAT YOU?
MENDEL!
WHAT'VE THEY DONE TO YOU? YOUR EYES?
THEY FOUND ME... TORTURED ME FOR DAYS, QUESTIONING ME ABOUT YOU--
I SWEAR TO MOTHER EARTH, I TOLD THEM NOTHING OF YOU! NOTHING! I FEARED--
IT'S OK...
...I'LL GET YOU OUT OF HERE.
CHAK
CLAK
NO! FORGET ME SILAS!
I'LL ONLY SLOW YOU DOWN--

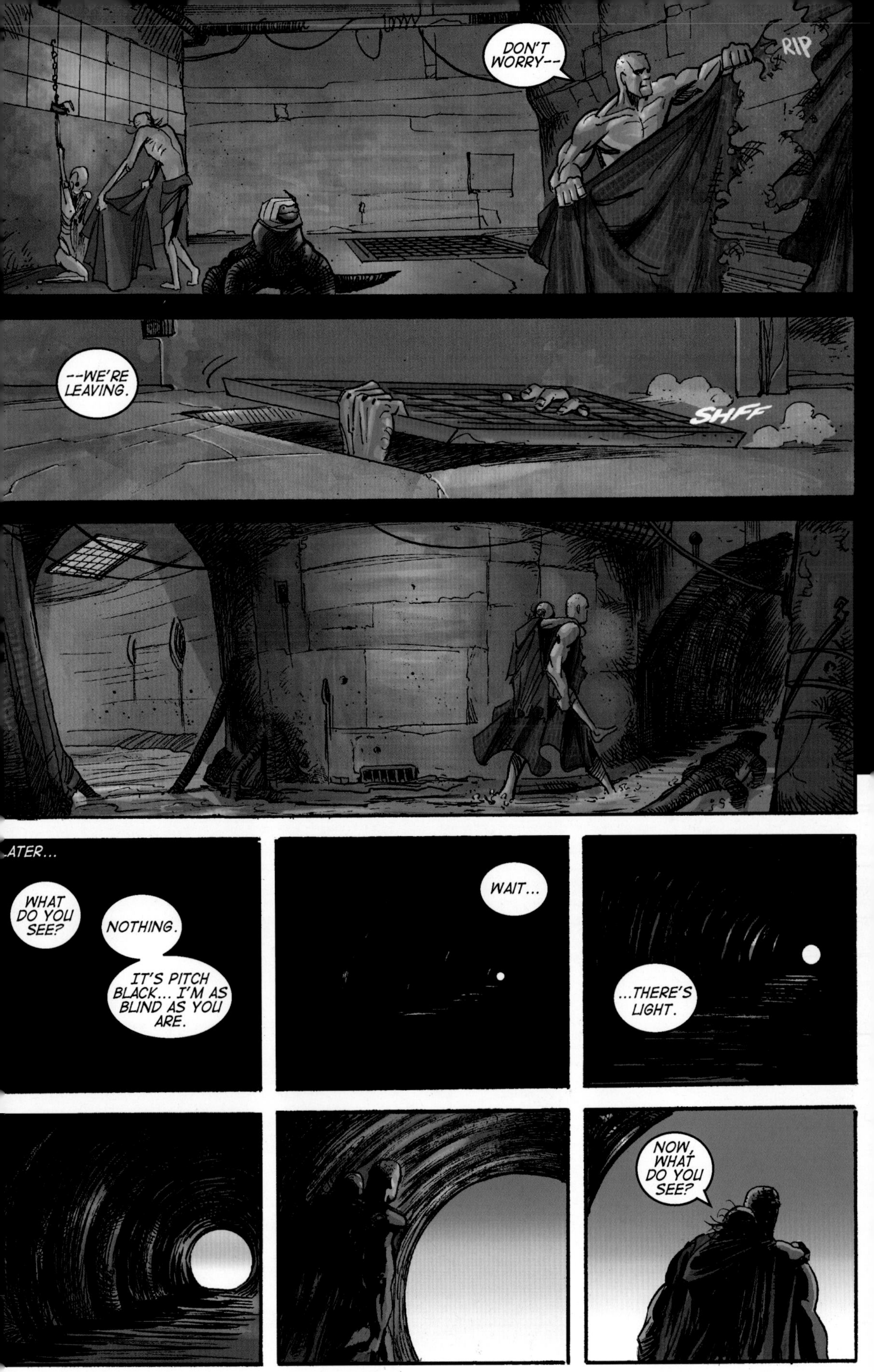

DON'T WORRY--
RIP
--WE'RE LEAVING.
SHFF
LATER...
WHAT DO YOU SEE?
NOTHING.
IT'S PITCH BLACK... I'M AS BLIND AS YOU ARE.
WAIT...
...THERE'S LIGHT.
NOW, WHAT DO YOU SEE?

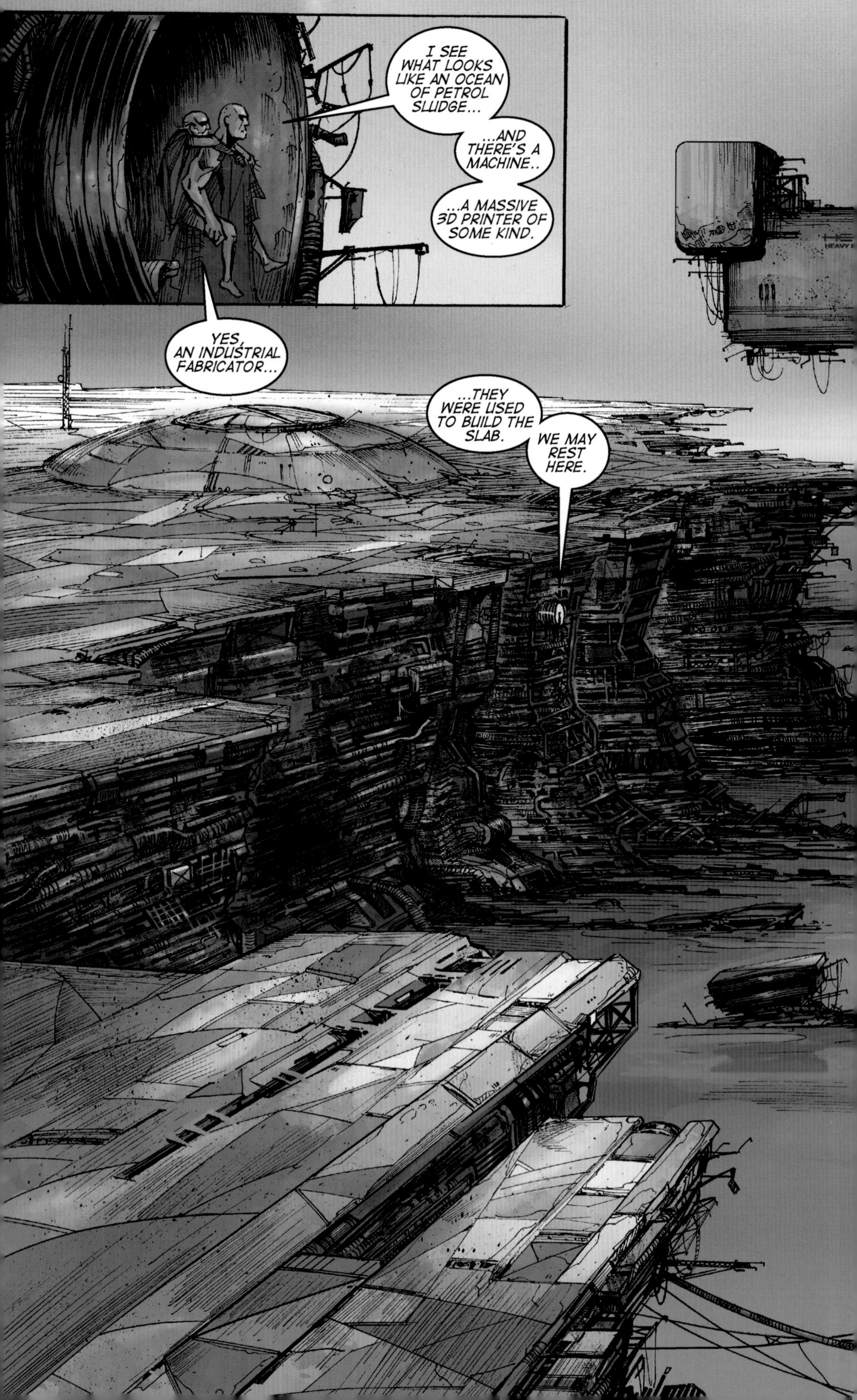
I SEE WHAT LOOKS LIKE AN OCEAN OF PETROL SLUDGE...
...AND THERE'S A MACHINE..
...A MASSIVE 3D PRINTER OF SOME KIND.
YES, AN INDUSTRIAL FABRICATOR...
...THEY WERE USED TO BUILD THE SLAB.
WE MAY REST HERE.

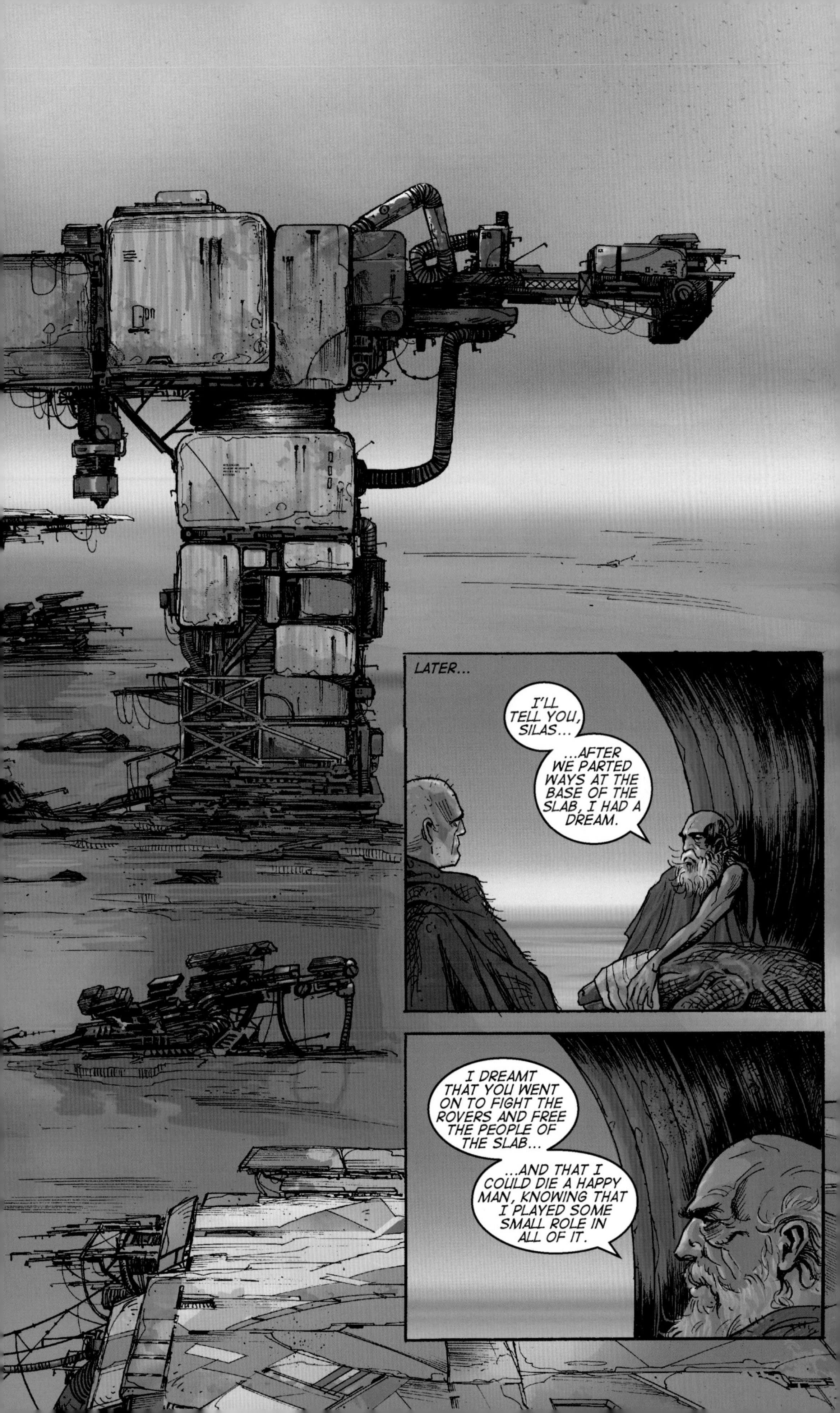
LATER...
I'LL TELL YOU, SILAS...
...AFTER WE PARTED WAYS AT THE BASE OF THE SLAB, I HAD A DREAM.
I DREAMT THAT YOU WENT ON TO FIGHT THE ROVERS AND FREE THE PEOPLE OF THE SLAB...
...AND THAT I COULD DIE A HAPPY MAN, KNOWING THAT I PLAYED SOME SMALL ROLE IN ALL OF IT.

HM... FOR A TIME THAT MAY HAVE BEEN POSSIBLE.

BUT NOW THE *ROVERS* WILL COME AND DESTROY ALL WE BUILT.

ALL BECAUSE I FUCKED UP AND LOST THAT GUN!

DON'T DESPAIR.

PERHAPS THE SETTLERS CAN ESCAPE AND RE-GROUP.

YOU'VE HELPED THOSE PEOPLE A GREAT DEAL. YOU'RE A *GOOD* MAN.

NO, I'M NOT.

IN SOME WAYS I'M NO BETTER THAN THE ONO MAO. I...

GO ON, SON...

I'VE... *EXPLOITED* PEOPLE... ENSLAVED THEM FOR PROFIT.

I TOLD YOU I WAS A SMUGGLER, BUT I SAID NO-THING OF MY *CARGO.*

SOMETIMES IT WAS ARMS OR STOLEN GOODS.

BUT SOMETIMES IT WAS *EBOTAK*...

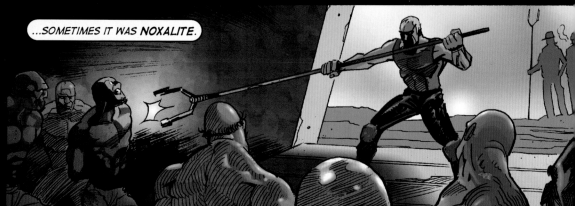

...SOMETIMES IT WAS *NOXALITE.*

WE CRAMMED THEM INTO CARGO CON- TAINERS, WE--

-SOB-

I'M SO ASHAMED.

THERE, MY BOY.

THIS WORLD MAKES MONSTERS OF MEN.

YOU AREN'T THE ONLY ONE WITH A BURDEN TO BEAR.

YOU SPOKE OF THE NOXALITES, RUGGED MOUN- TAIN PEOPLE AS I UNDERSTAND IT.

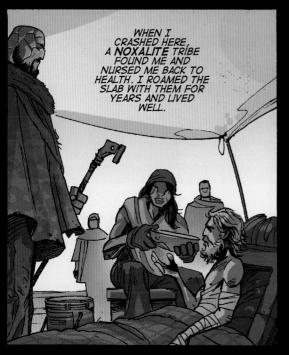

WHEN I CRASHED HERE, A NOXALITE TRIBE FOUND ME AND NURSED ME BACK TO HEALTH. I ROAMED THE SLAB WITH THEM FOR YEARS AND LIVED WELL.

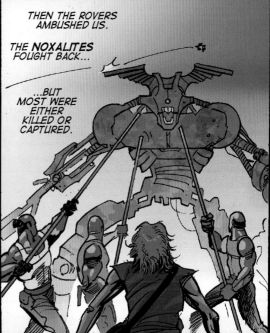

THEN THE ROVERS AMBUSHED US.

THE NOXALITES FOUGHT BACK...

...BUT MOST WERE EITHER KILLED OR CAPTURED.

AND ME?

I RAN.

I RAN AWAY AND DIDN'T LOOK BACK.

IN SHAME, I EXILED MYSELF TO THE SCRAPLANDS.

--BUT YOU WOULD'VE BEEN KILLED OR CAPTURED *YOURSELF* IF YOU HAD STAYED AND FOUGHT.

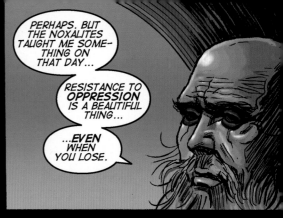

PERHAPS. BUT THE NOXALITES TAUGHT ME SOMETHING ON THAT DAY...

RESISTANCE TO *OPPRESSION* IS A BEAUTIFUL THING...

...*EVEN* WHEN YOU LOSE.

SO WHEN YOU RETURN TO YOUR SETTLEMENT, AND THE ROVERS COME...

YOU TOO, WILL HAVE TO ASK YOURSELF IF YOU HAVE SOMETHING WORTH *FIGHTING* FOR.

...NOW LET AN OLD MAN GET SOME REST.

THE NEXT MORNING...

MENDEL...

MENDEL!?!

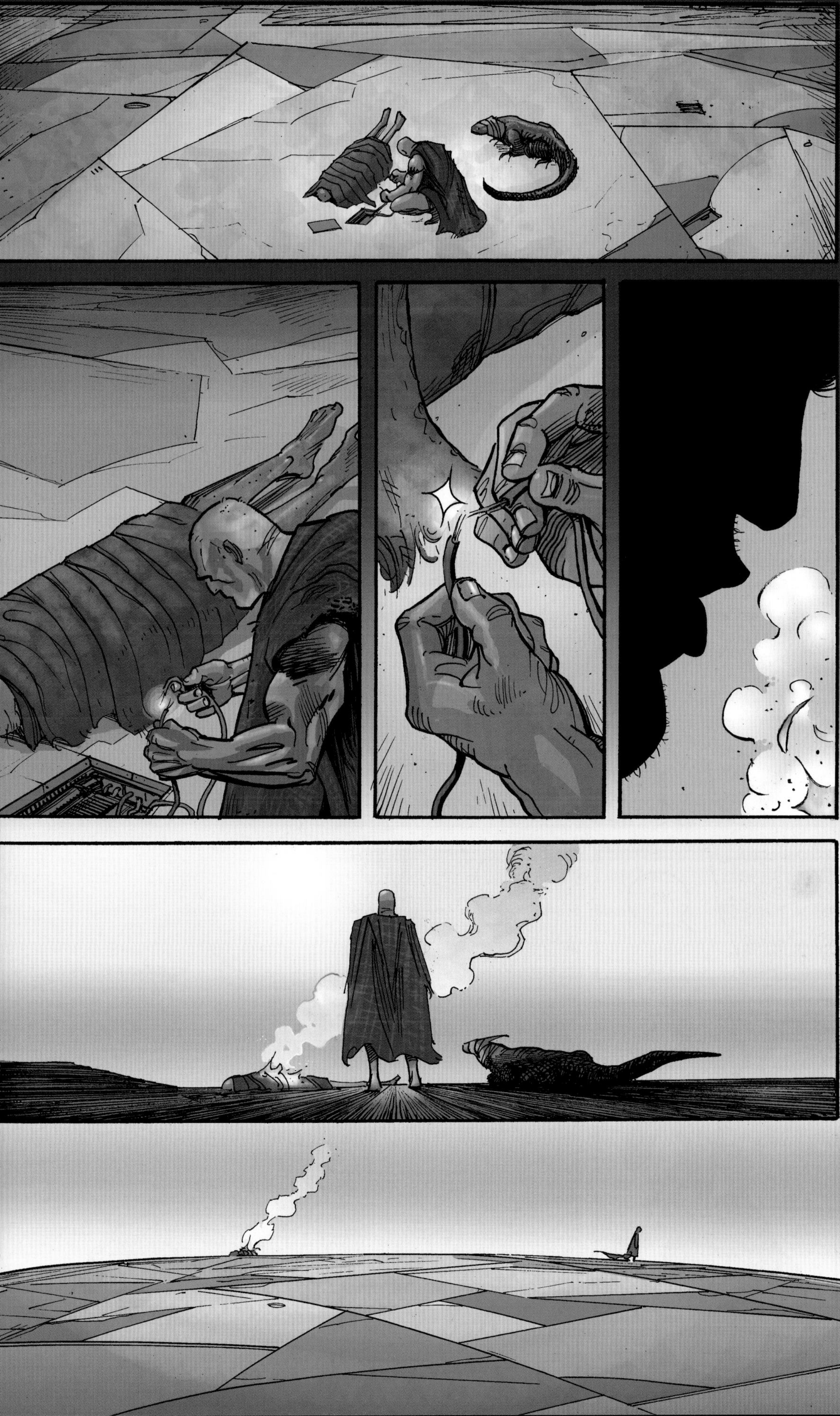

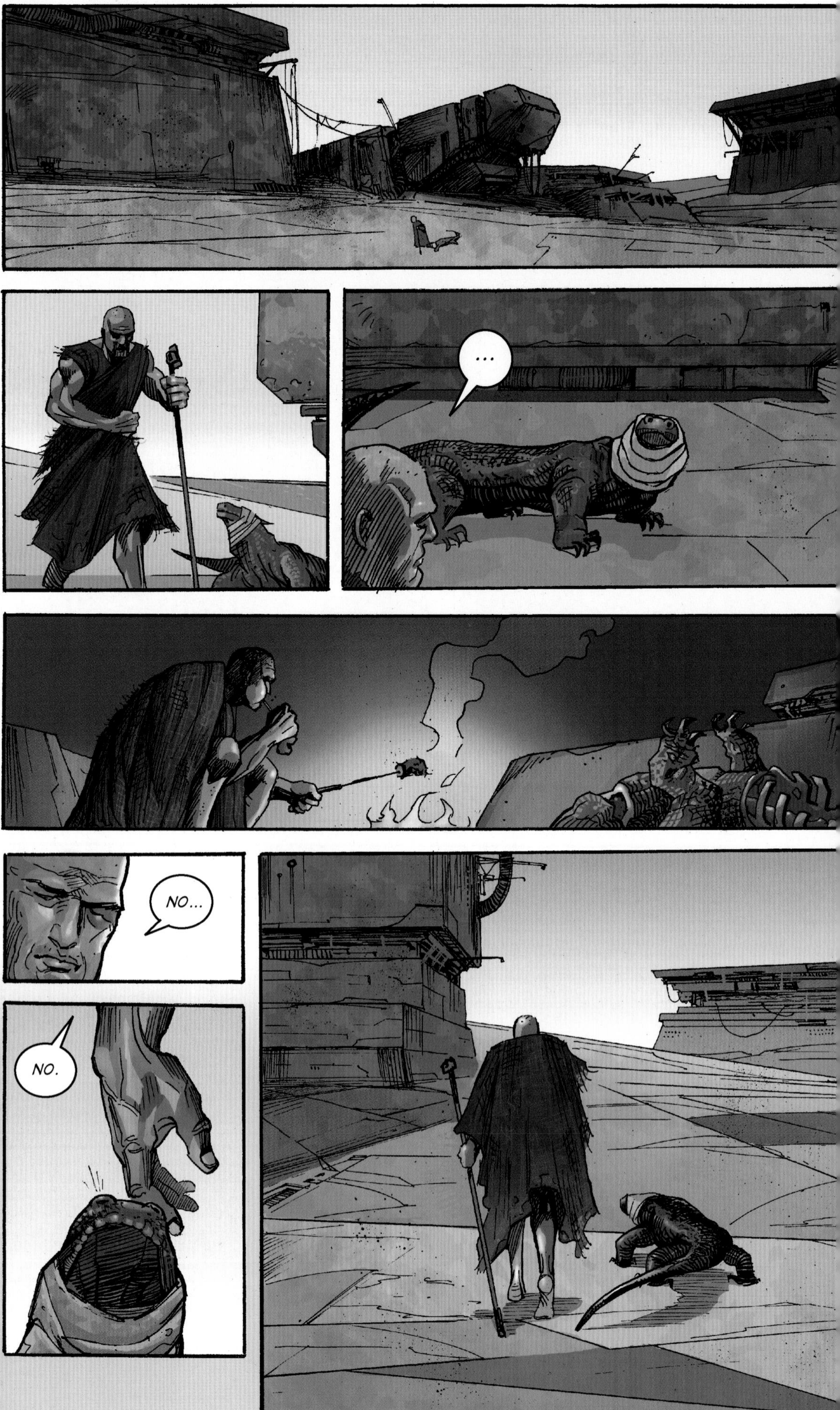
...
NO...
NO.

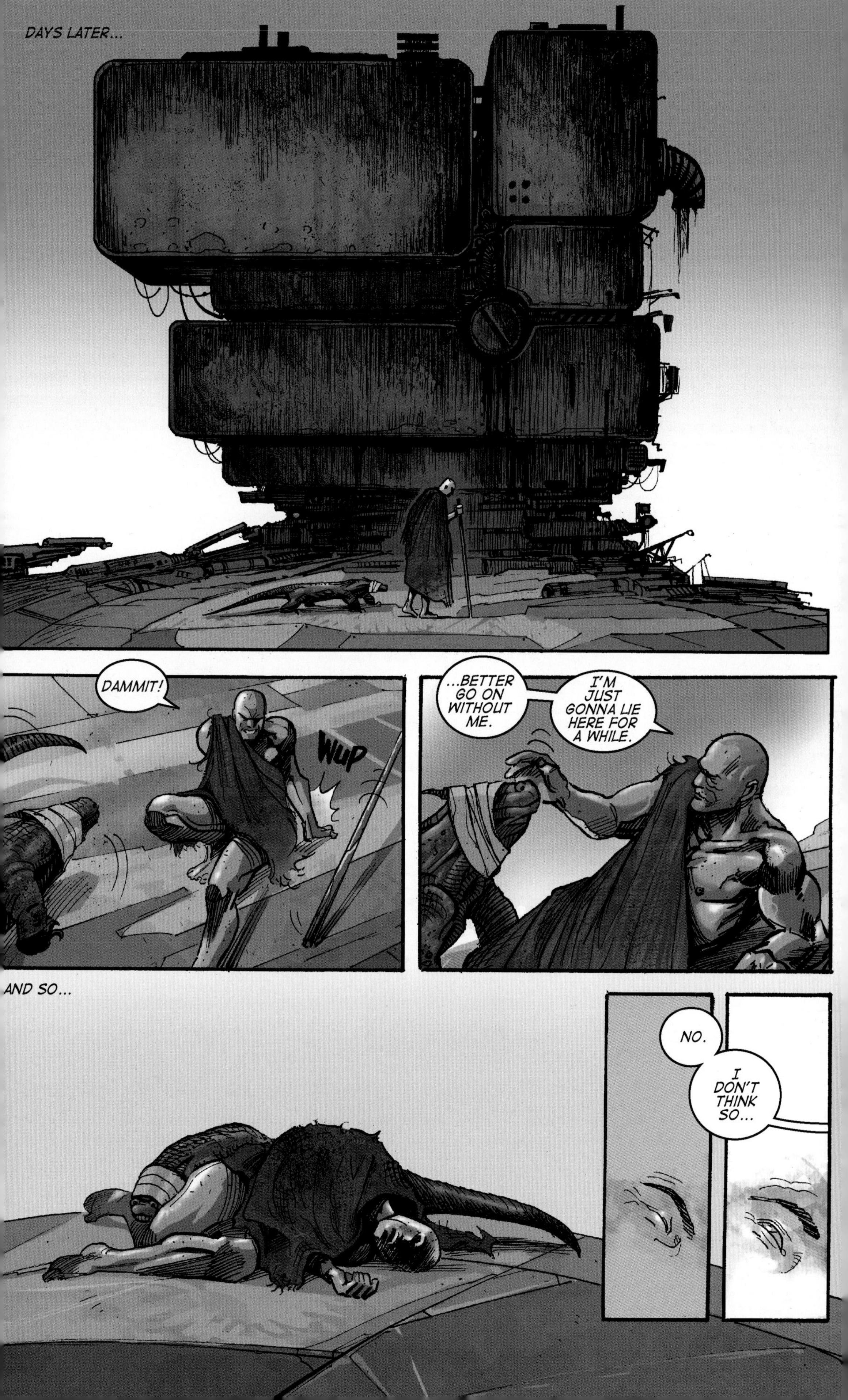
DAYS LATER...
DAMMIT!
WUP
...BETTER GO ON WITHOUT ME.
I'M JUST GONNA LIE HERE FOR A WHILE.
AND SO...
NO.
I DON'T THINK SO...

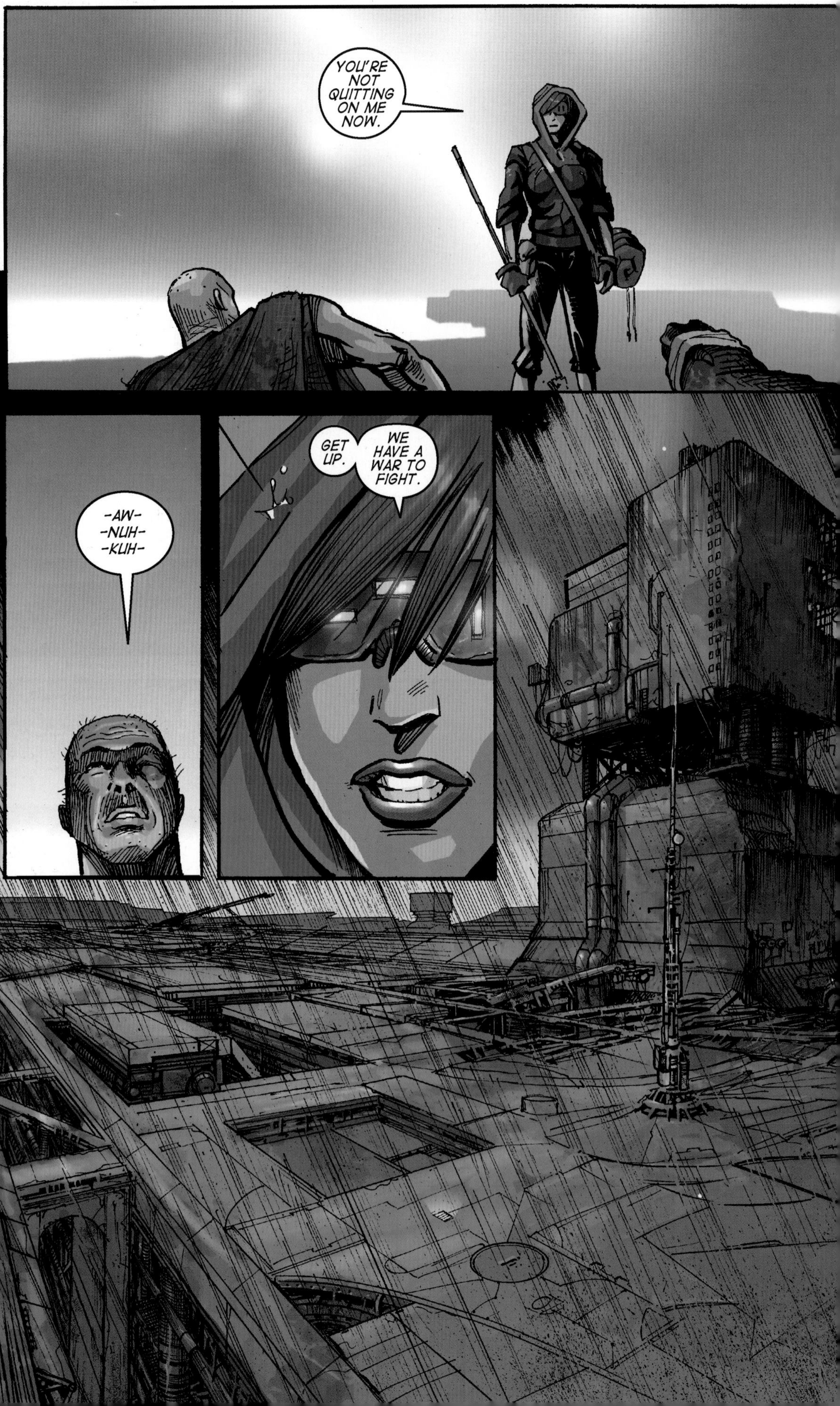
YOU'RE NOT QUITTING ON ME NOW.
-AW- -NUH- -KUH-
GET UP.
WE HAVE A WAR TO FIGHT.

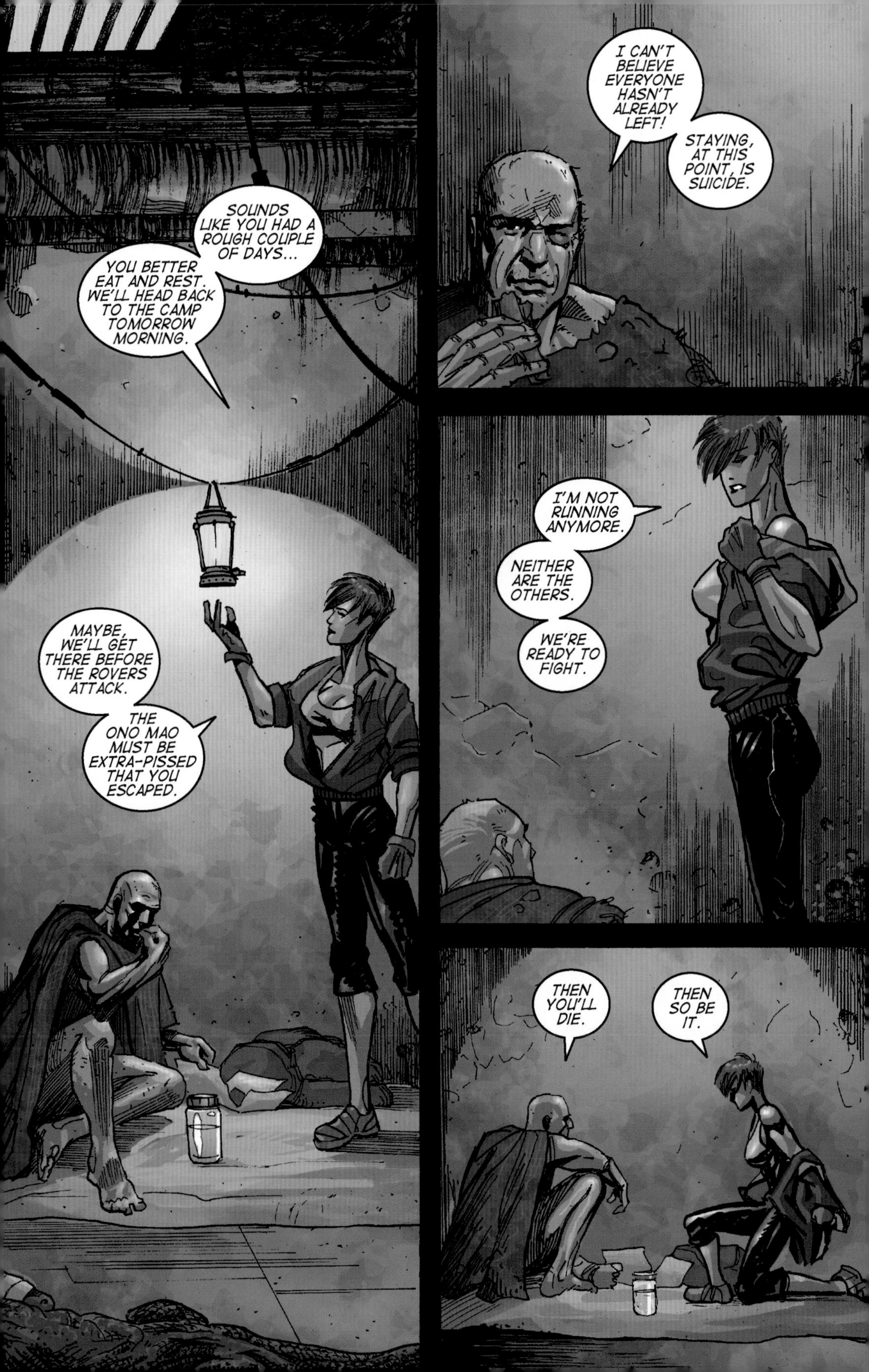
SOUNDS LIKE YOU HAD A ROUGH COUPLE OF DAYS...
YOU BETTER EAT AND REST. WE'LL HEAD BACK TO THE CAMP TOMORROW MORNING.
MAYBE, WE'LL GET THERE BEFORE THE ROVERS ATTACK.
THE ONO MAO MUST BE EXTRA-PISSED THAT YOU ESCAPED.
I CAN'T BELIEVE EVERYONE HASN'T ALREADY LEFT!
STAYING, AT THIS POINT, IS SUICIDE.
I'M NOT RUNNING ANYMORE.
NEITHER ARE THE OTHERS.
WE'RE READY TO FIGHT.
THEN YOU'LL DIE.
THEN SO BE IT.

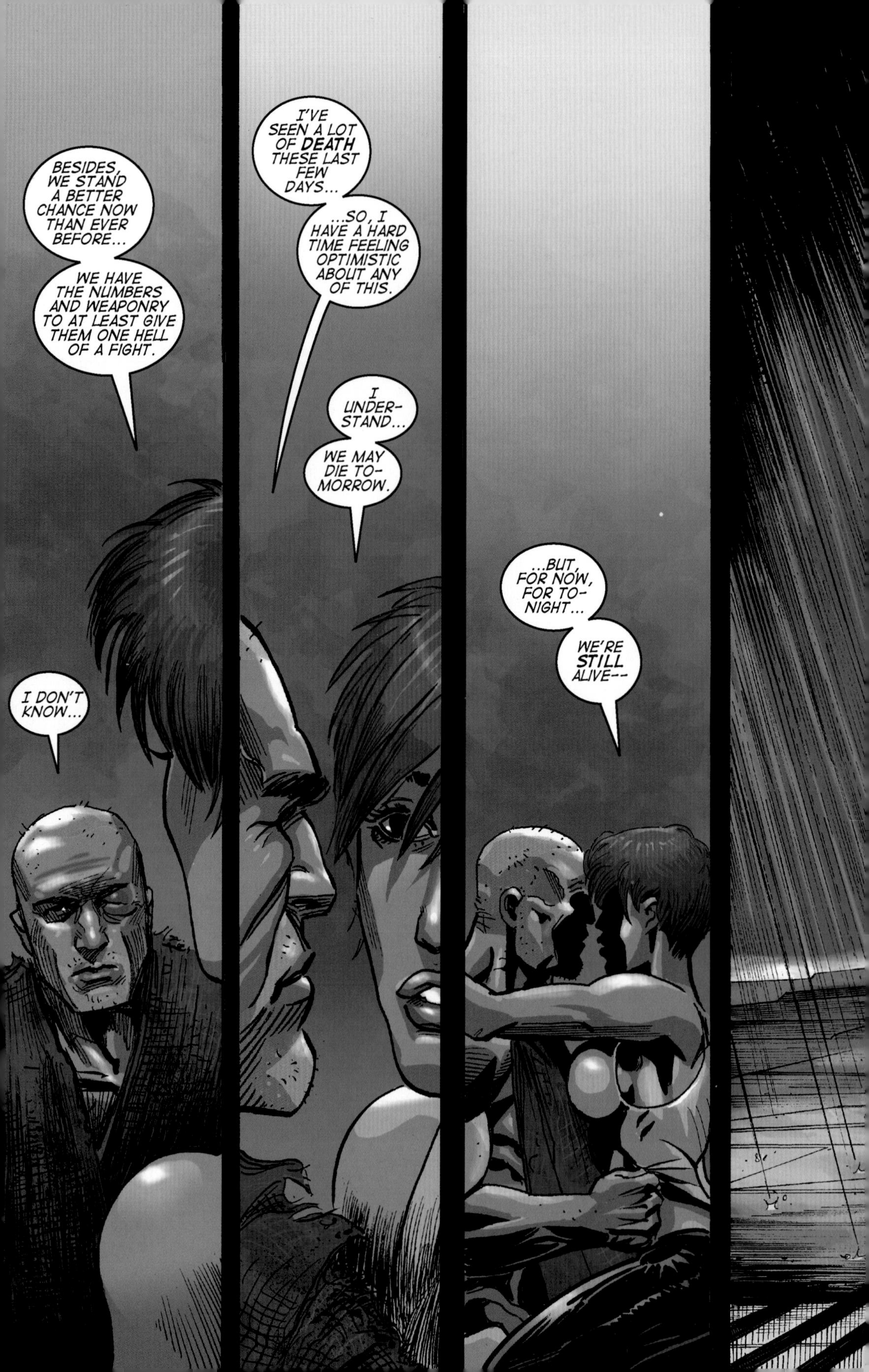
BESIDES, WE STAND A BETTER CHANCE NOW THAN EVER BEFORE...
WE HAVE THE NUMBERS AND WEAPONRY TO AT LEAST GIVE THEM ONE HELL OF A FIGHT.
I DON'T KNOW...
I'VE SEEN A LOT OF DEATH THESE LAST FEW DAYS...
...SO, I HAVE A HARD TIME FEELING OPTIMISTIC ABOUT ANY OF THIS.
I UNDER-STAND...
WE MAY DIE TO-MORROW.
...BUT, FOR NOW, FOR TO-NIGHT...
WE'RE STILL ALIVE--

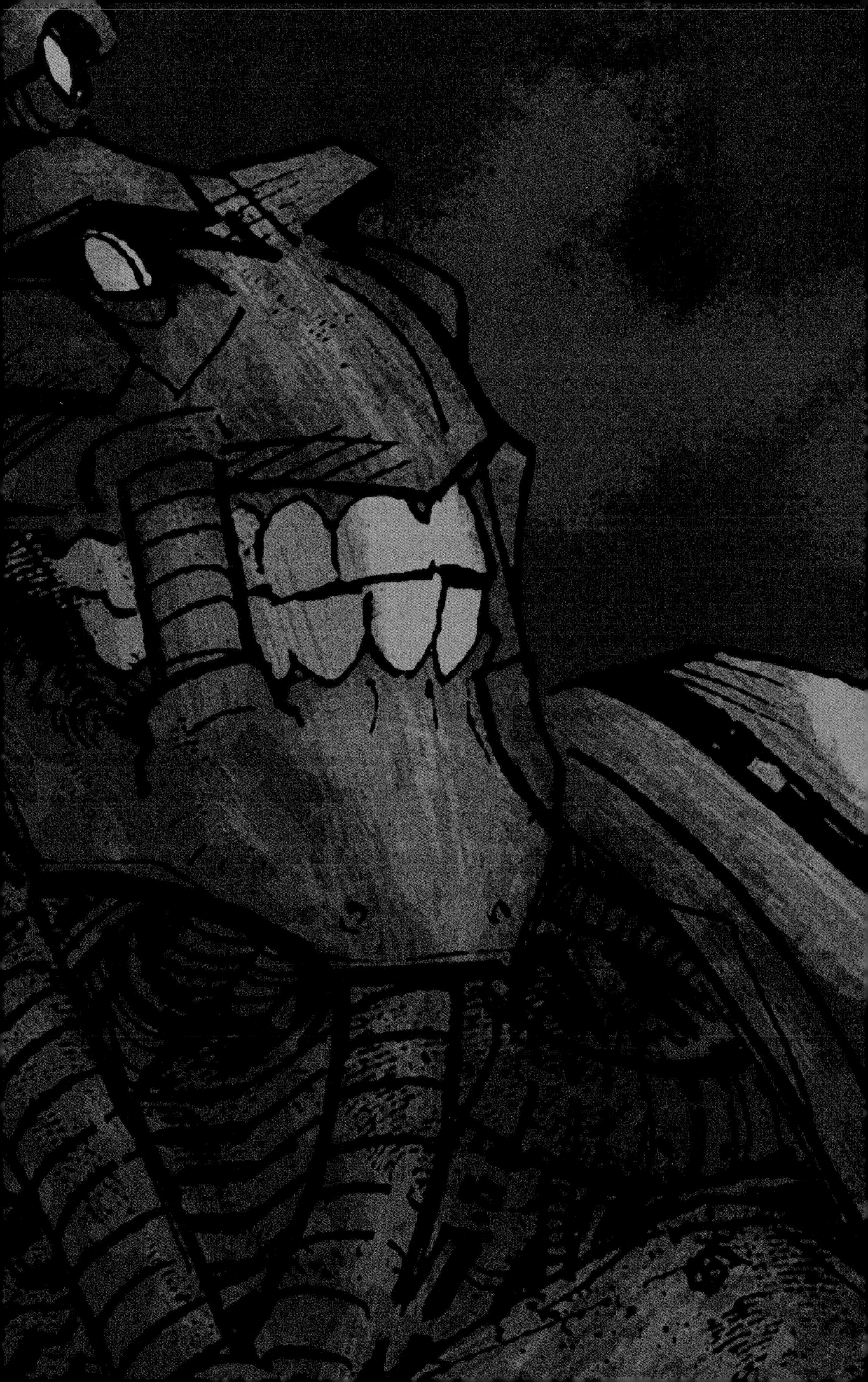

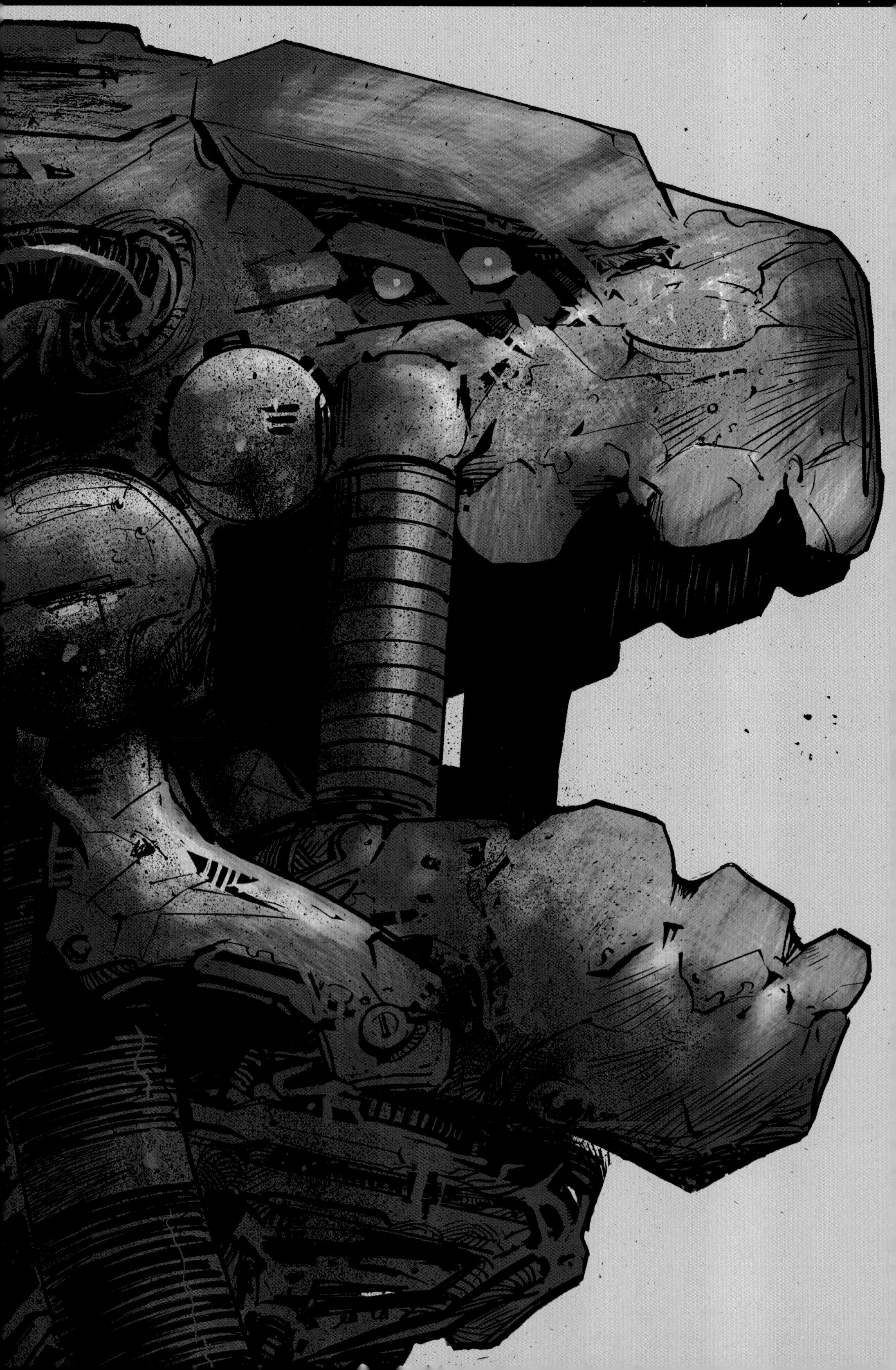

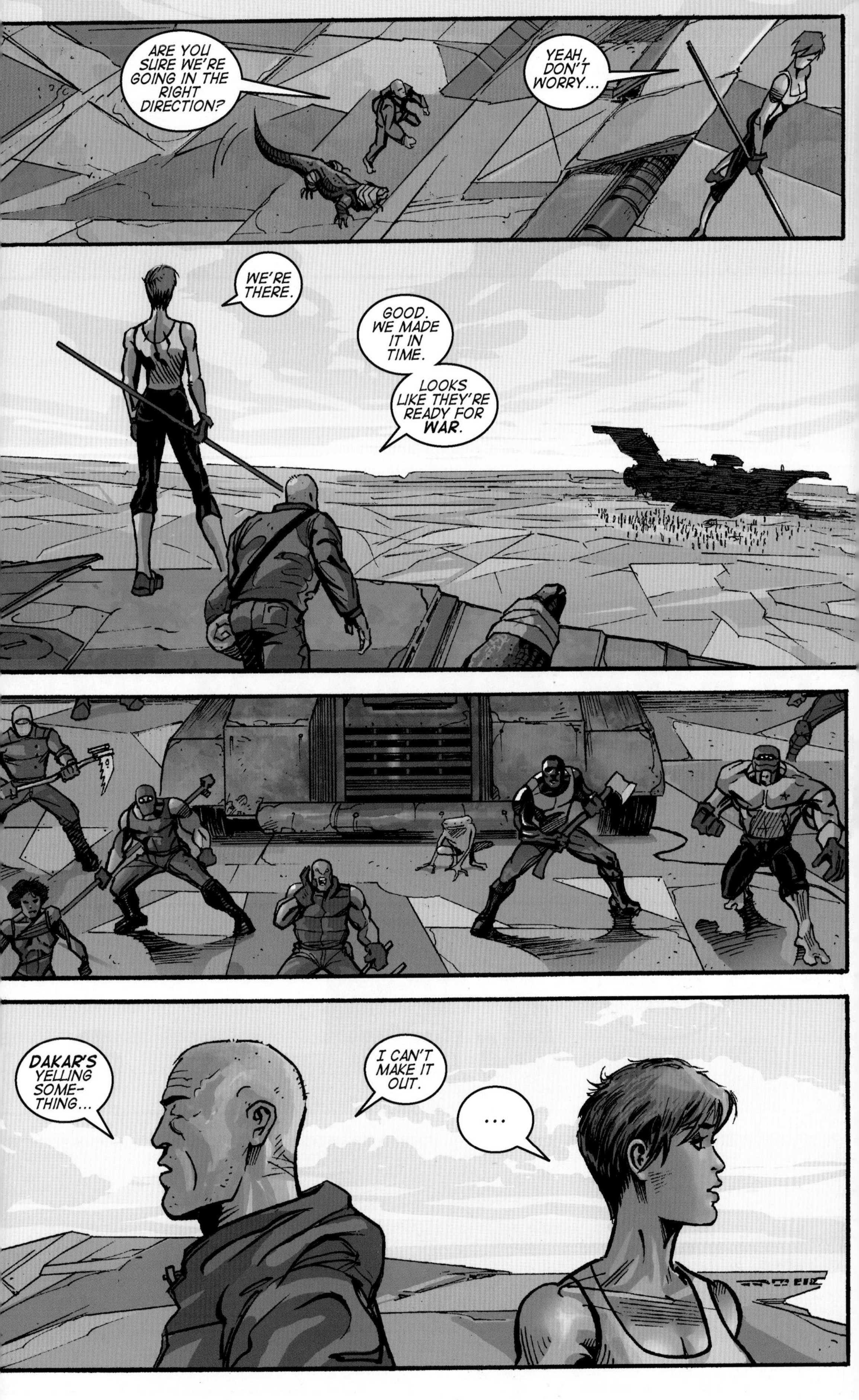
ARE YOU SURE WE'RE GOING IN THE RIGHT DIRECTION?
YEAH, DON'T WORRY...
WE'RE THERE.
GOOD. WE MADE IT IN TIME.
LOOKS LIKE THEY'RE READY FOR WAR.
DAKAR'S YELLING SOME-THING...
I CAN'T MAKE IT OUT.
...

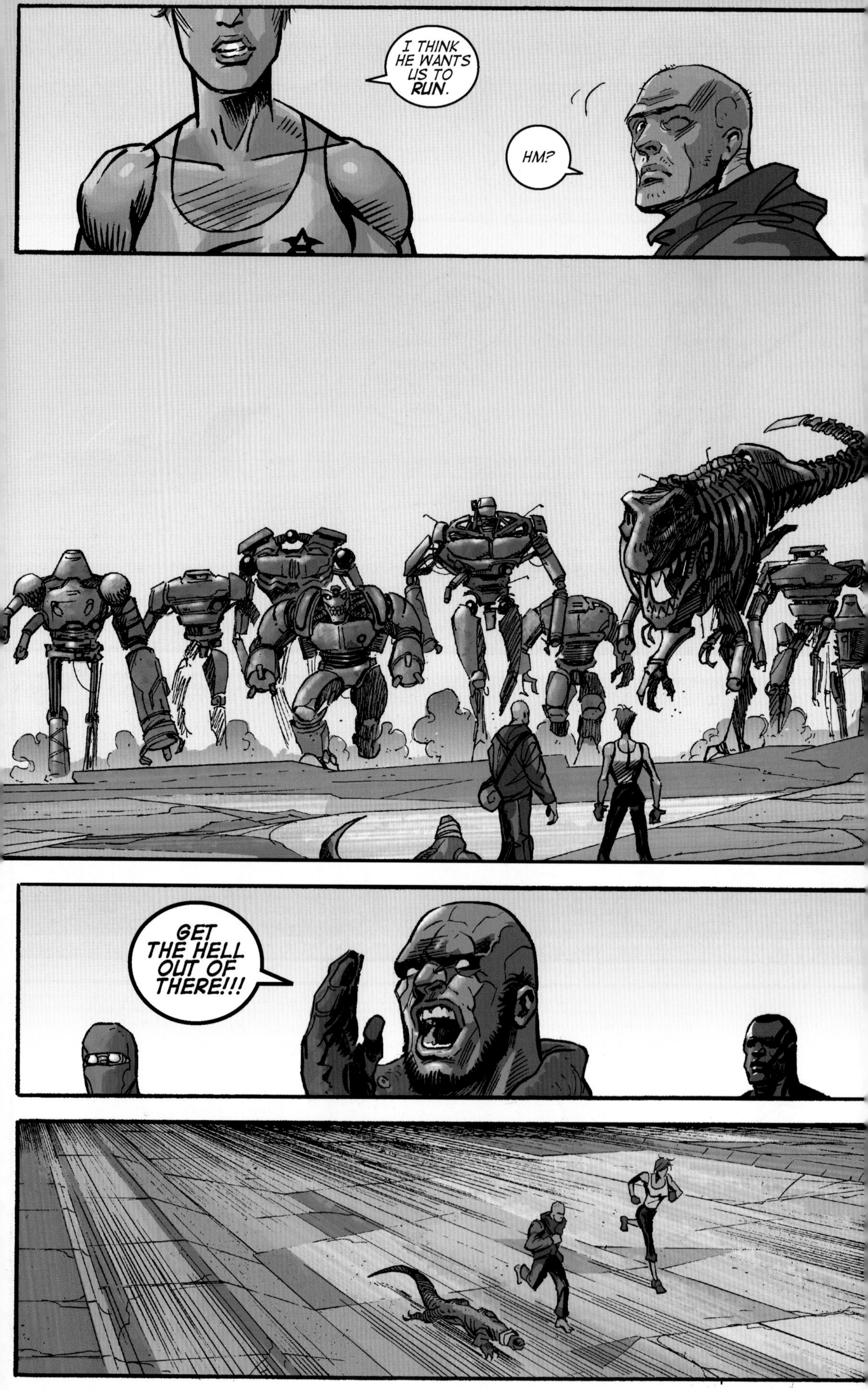
I THINK HE WANTS US TO RUN.
HM?
GET THE HELL OUT OF THERE!!!

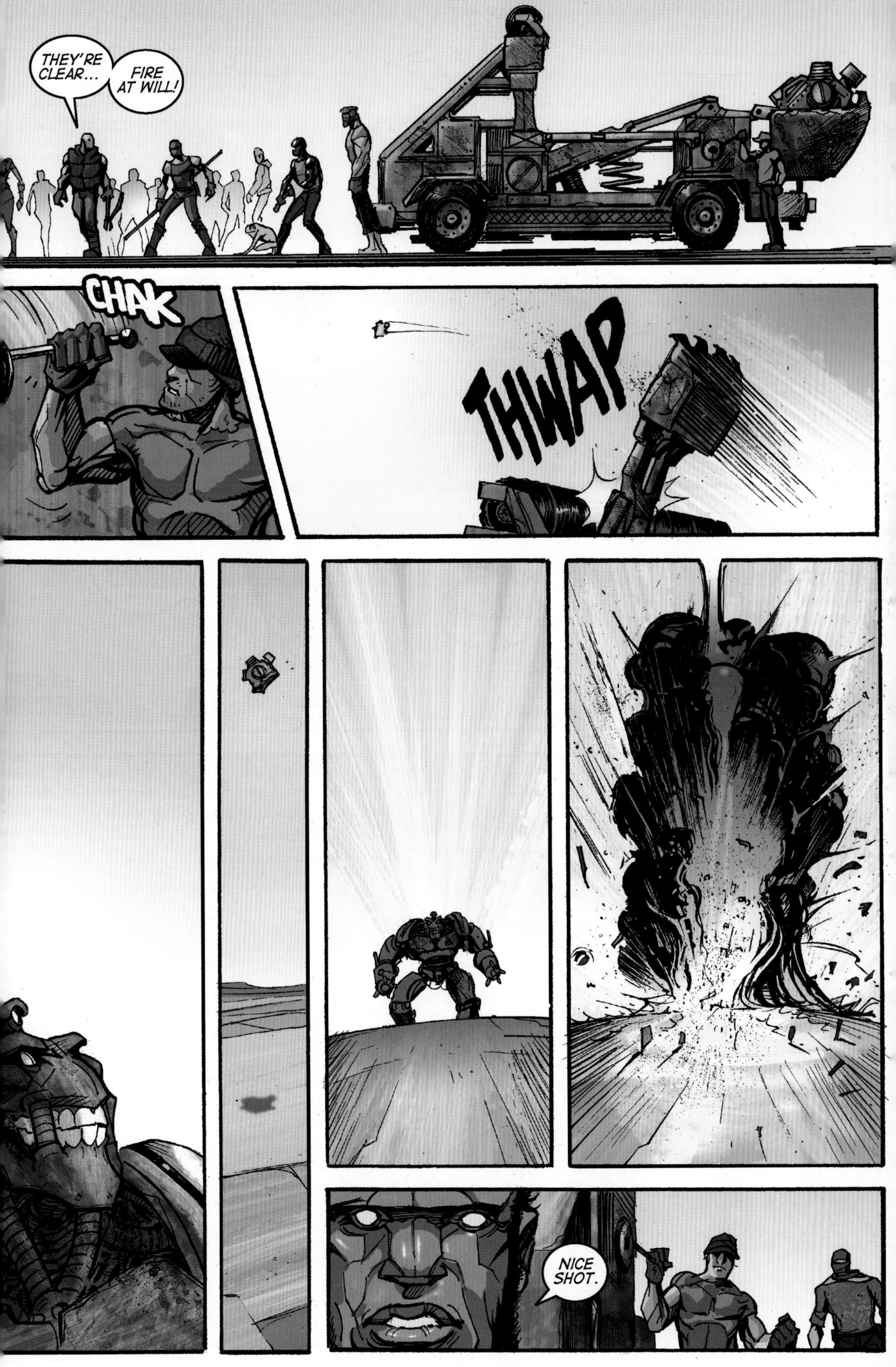
THEY'RE CLEAR...
FIRE AT WILL!
CHAK
THWAP
NICE SHOT.

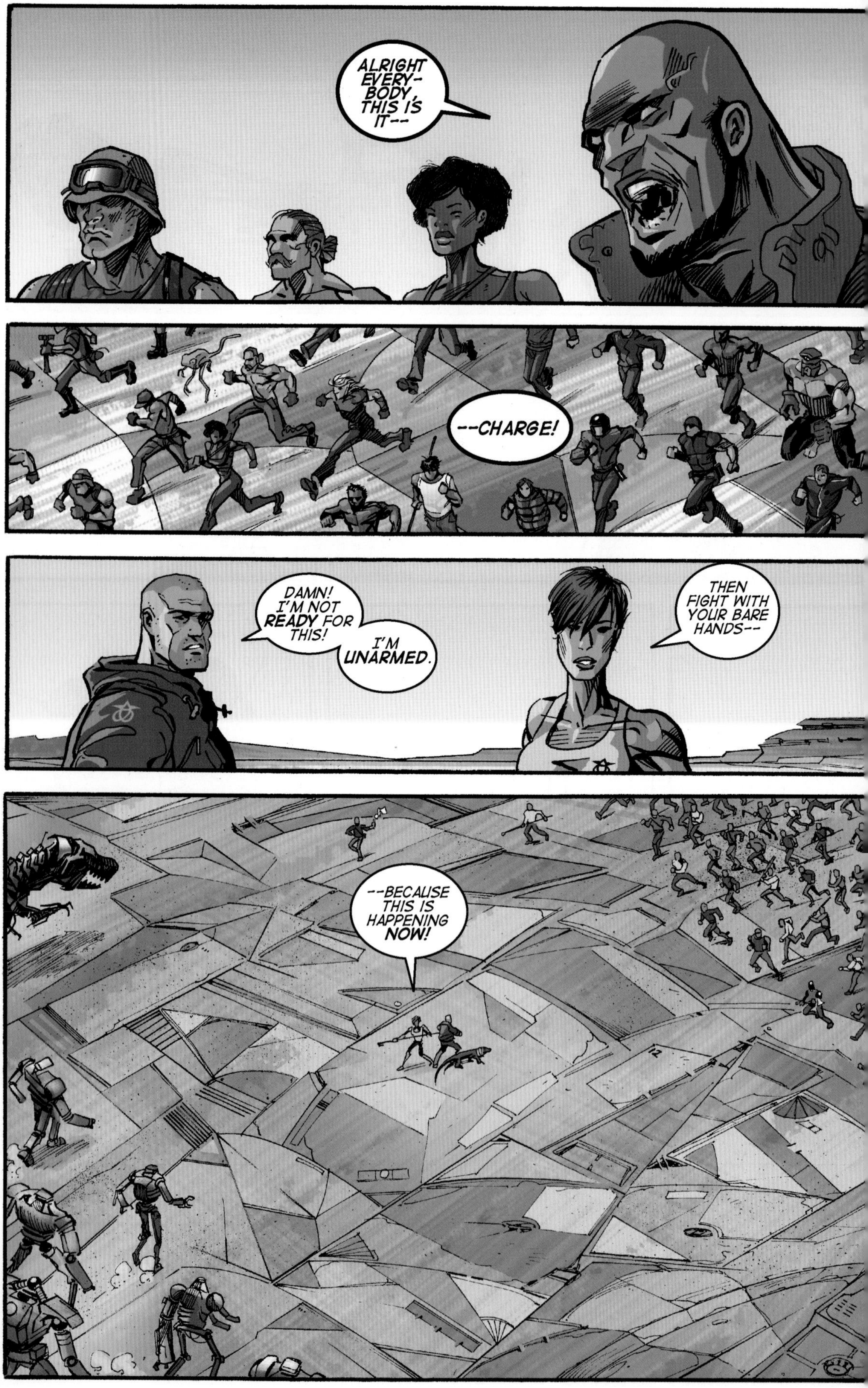
ALRIGHT EVERY-BODY, THIS IS IT--
--CHARGE!
DAMN! I'M NOT READY FOR THIS!
I'M UNARMED.
THEN FIGHT WITH YOUR BARE HANDS--
--BECAUSE THIS IS HAPPENING NOW!

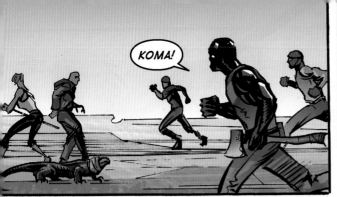

CHAPTER FIVE

KOMA!

THANKS FOR TAKING CARE OF HER.

-HMPH- SHE TOOK CARE OF ME.

HERE, SILAS--

--TAKE THIS.

THANKS NKUNDA.

WELCOME BACK.

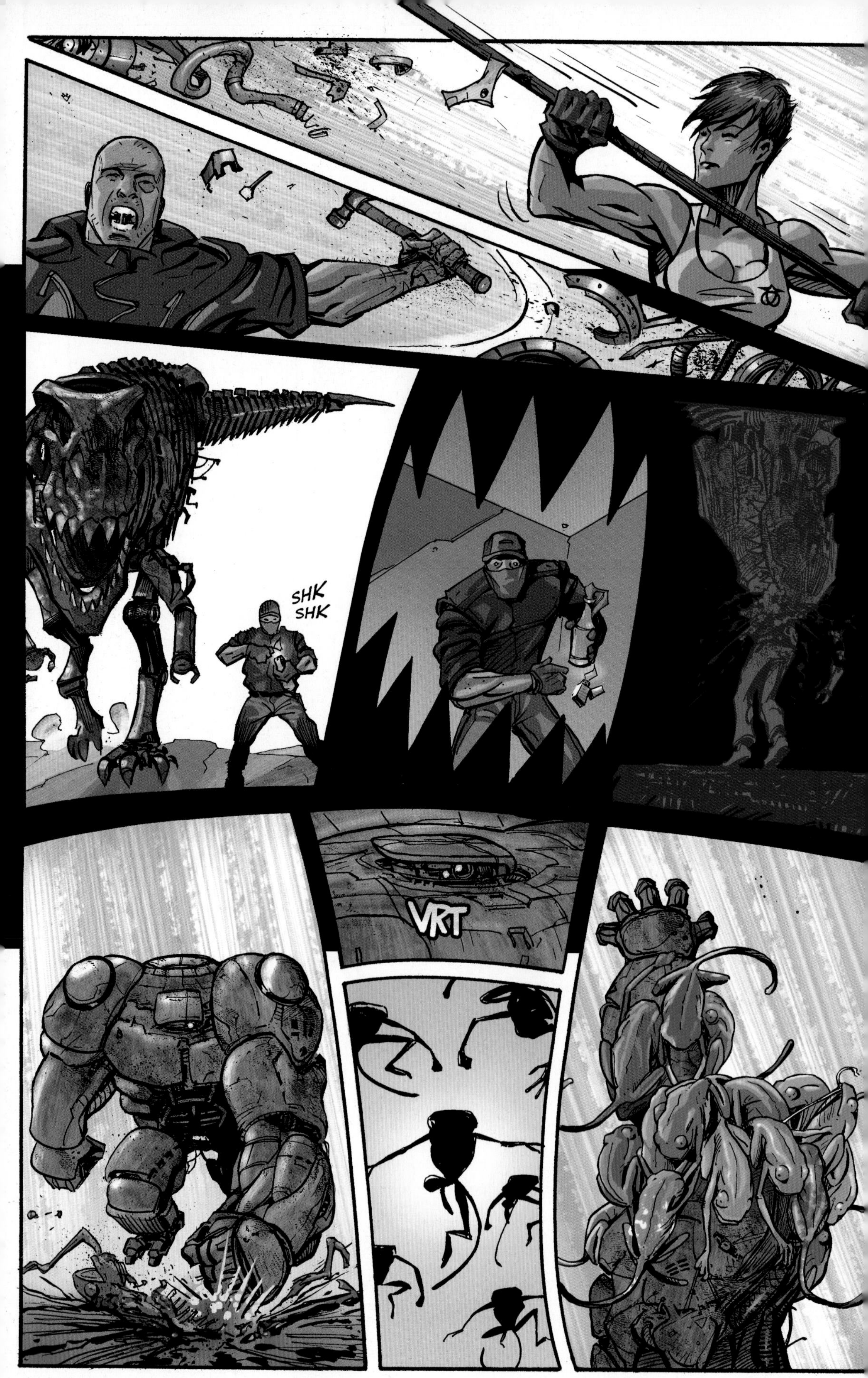
SHK
SHK
VRT

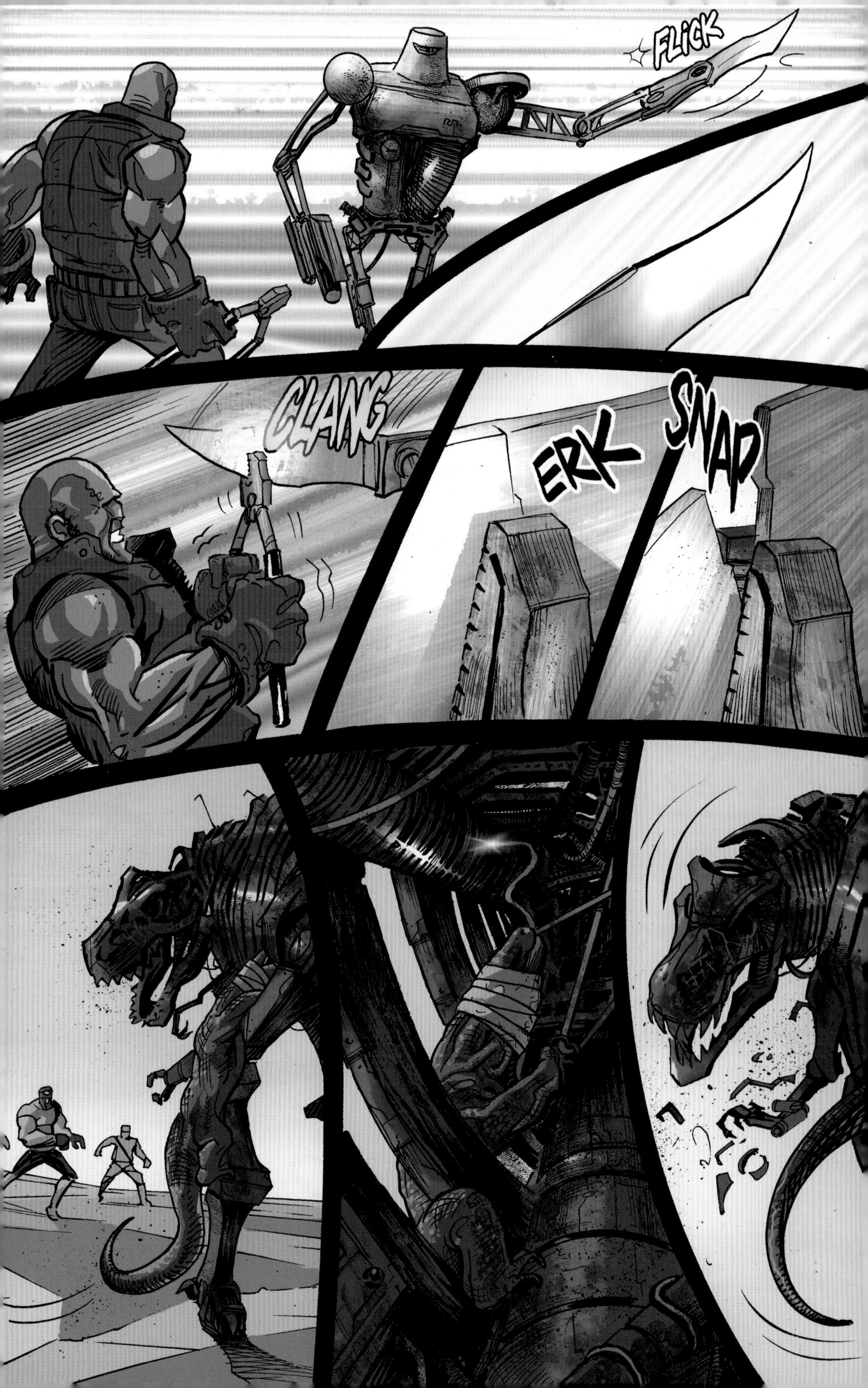
FLICK
CLANG
ERK
SNAP

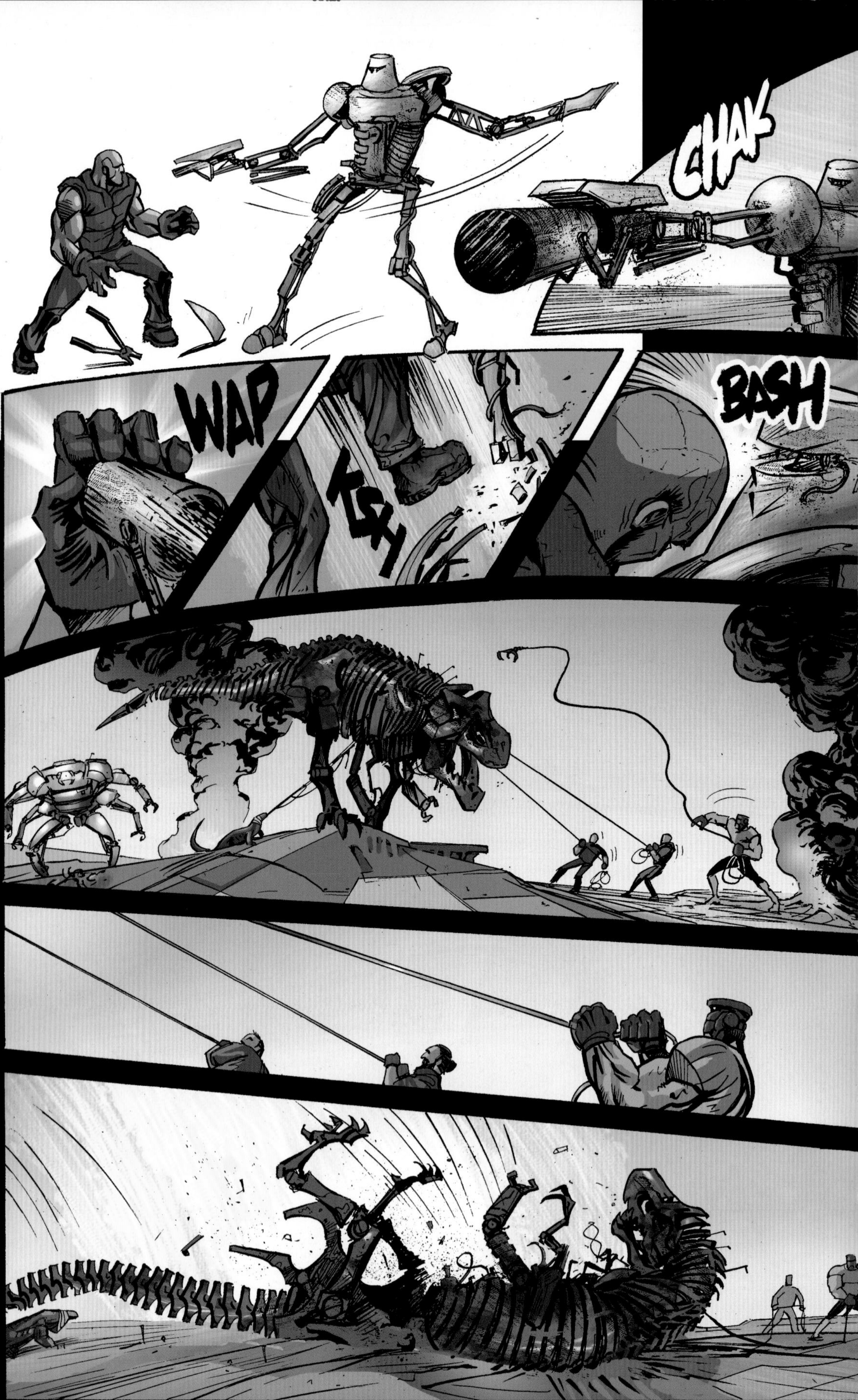
CHAK
WAP
KSH
BASH

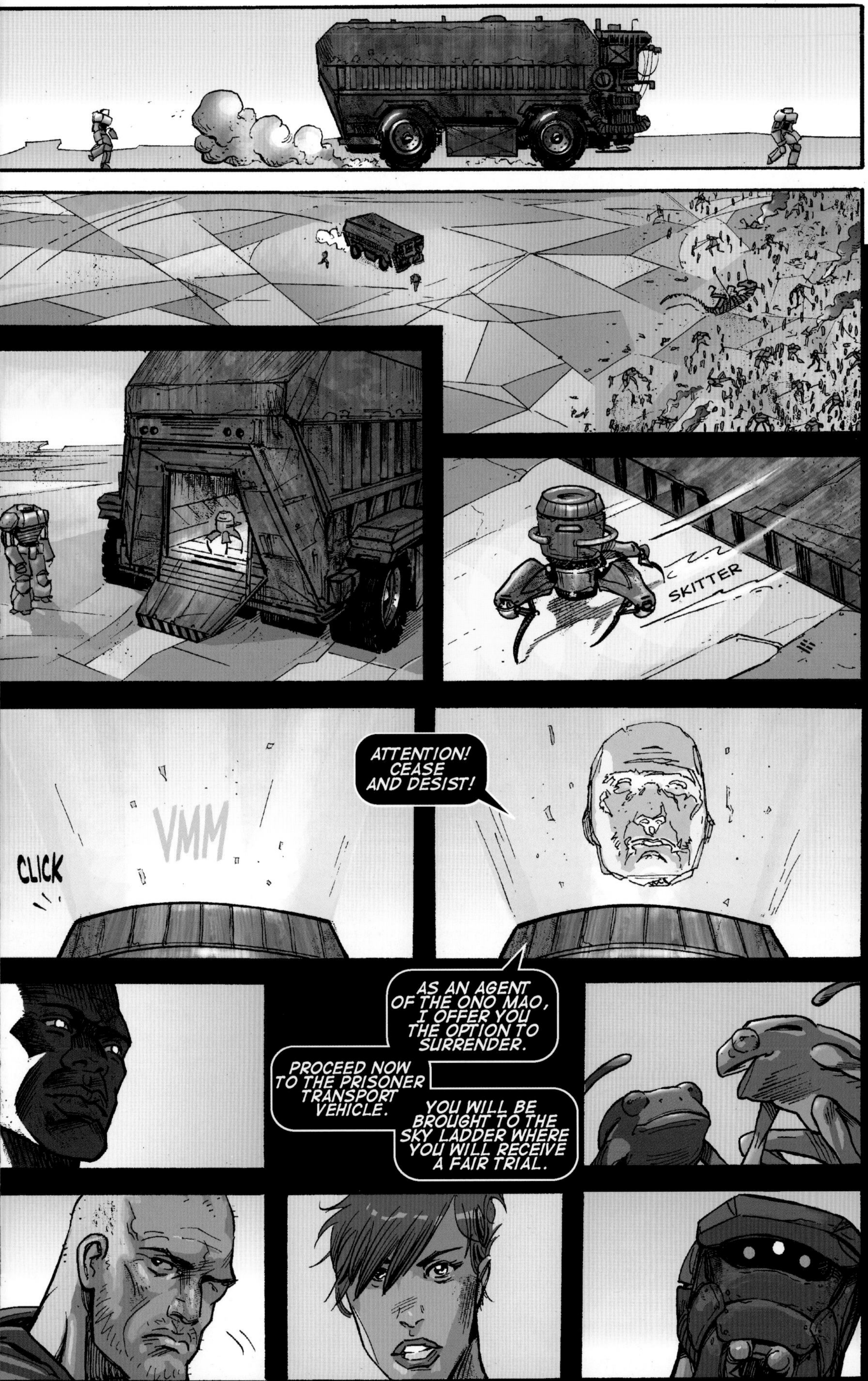
SKITTER
VMM
CLICK
ATTENTION! CEASE AND DESIST!
AS AN AGENT OF THE ONO MAO, I OFFER YOU THE OPTION TO SURRENDER.
PROCEED NOW TO THE PRISONER TRANSPORT VEHICLE.
YOU WILL BE BROUGHT TO THE SKY LADDER WHERE YOU WILL RECEIVE A FAIR TRIAL.

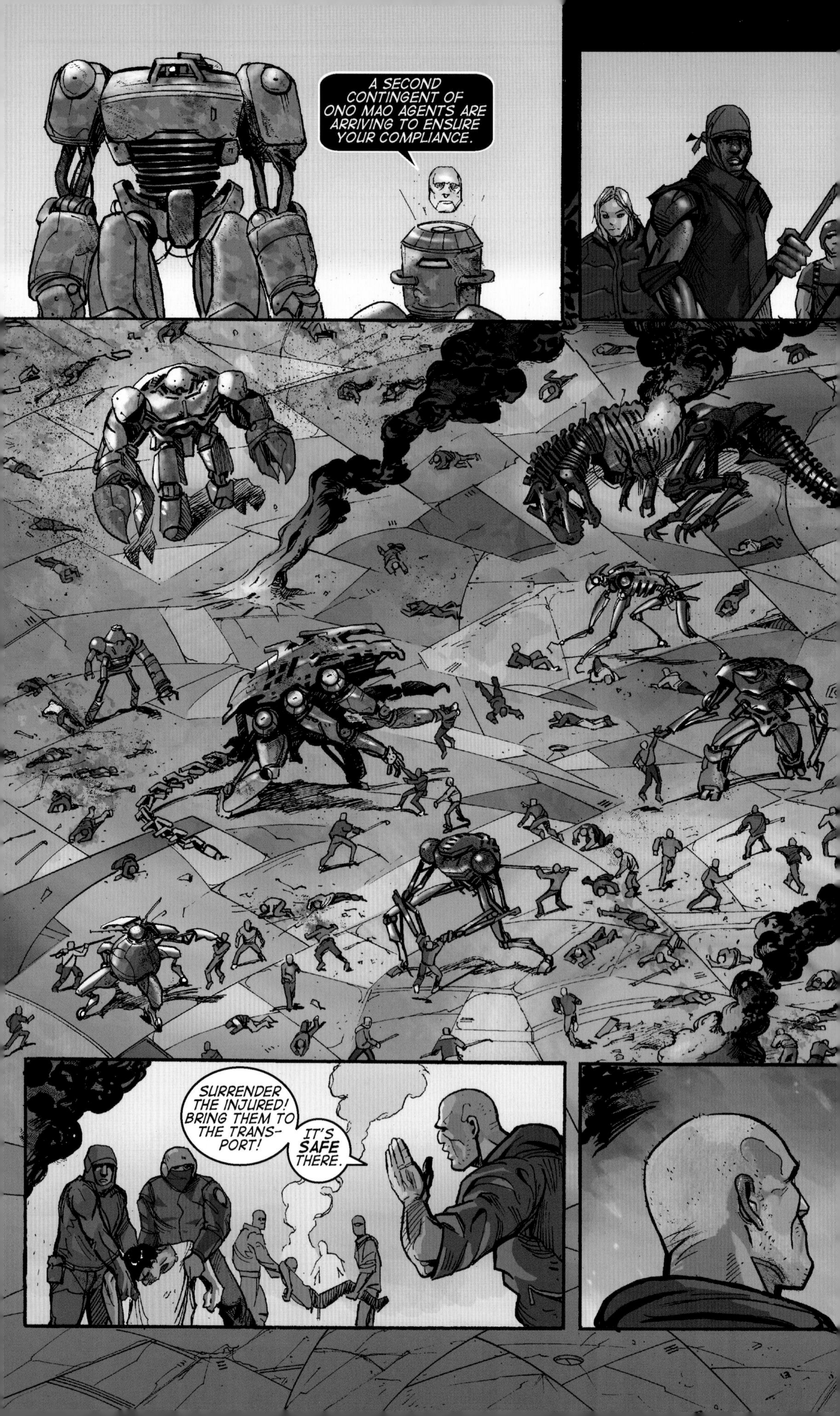
A SECOND CONTINGENT OF ONO MAO AGENTS ARE ARRIVING TO ENSURE YOUR COMPLIANCE.
SURRENDER THE INJURED! BRING THEM TO THE TRANS-PORT!
IT'S SAFE THERE.

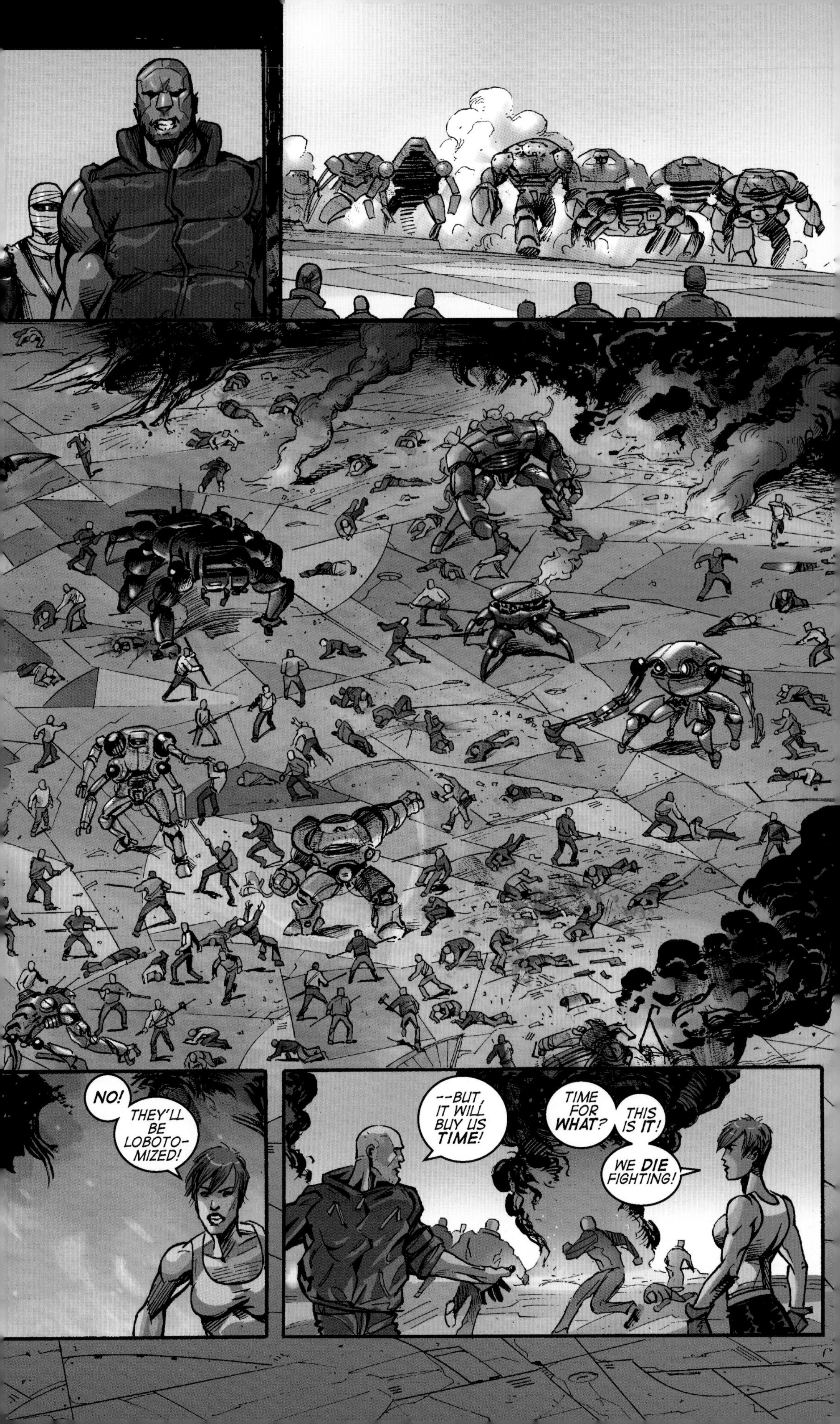
NO!
THEY'LL BE LOBOTO-MIZED!
--BUT, IT WILL BUY US TIME!
TIME FOR WHAT?
THIS IS IT!
WE DIE FIGHTING!

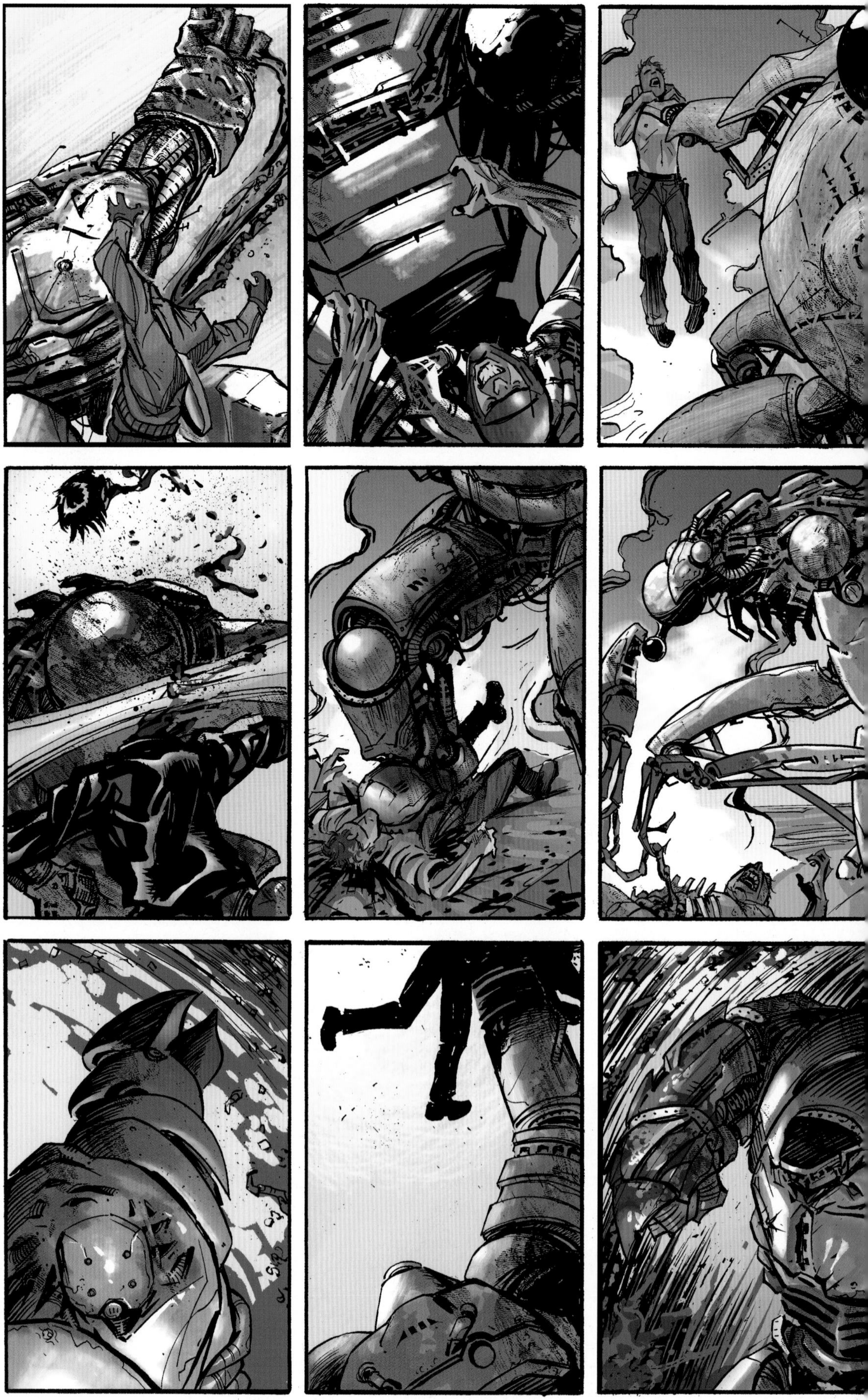

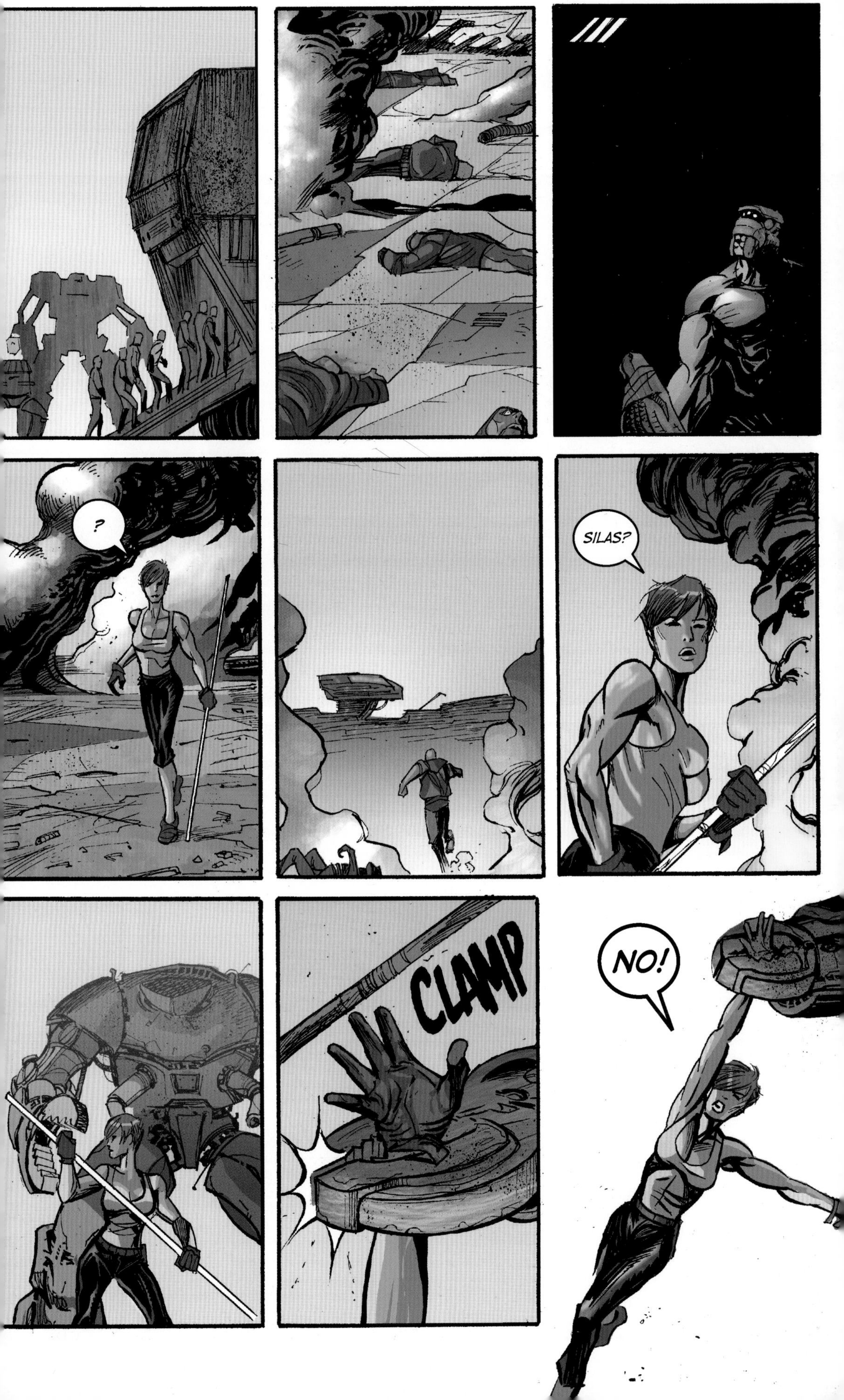
///
?
SILAS?
CLAMP
NO!

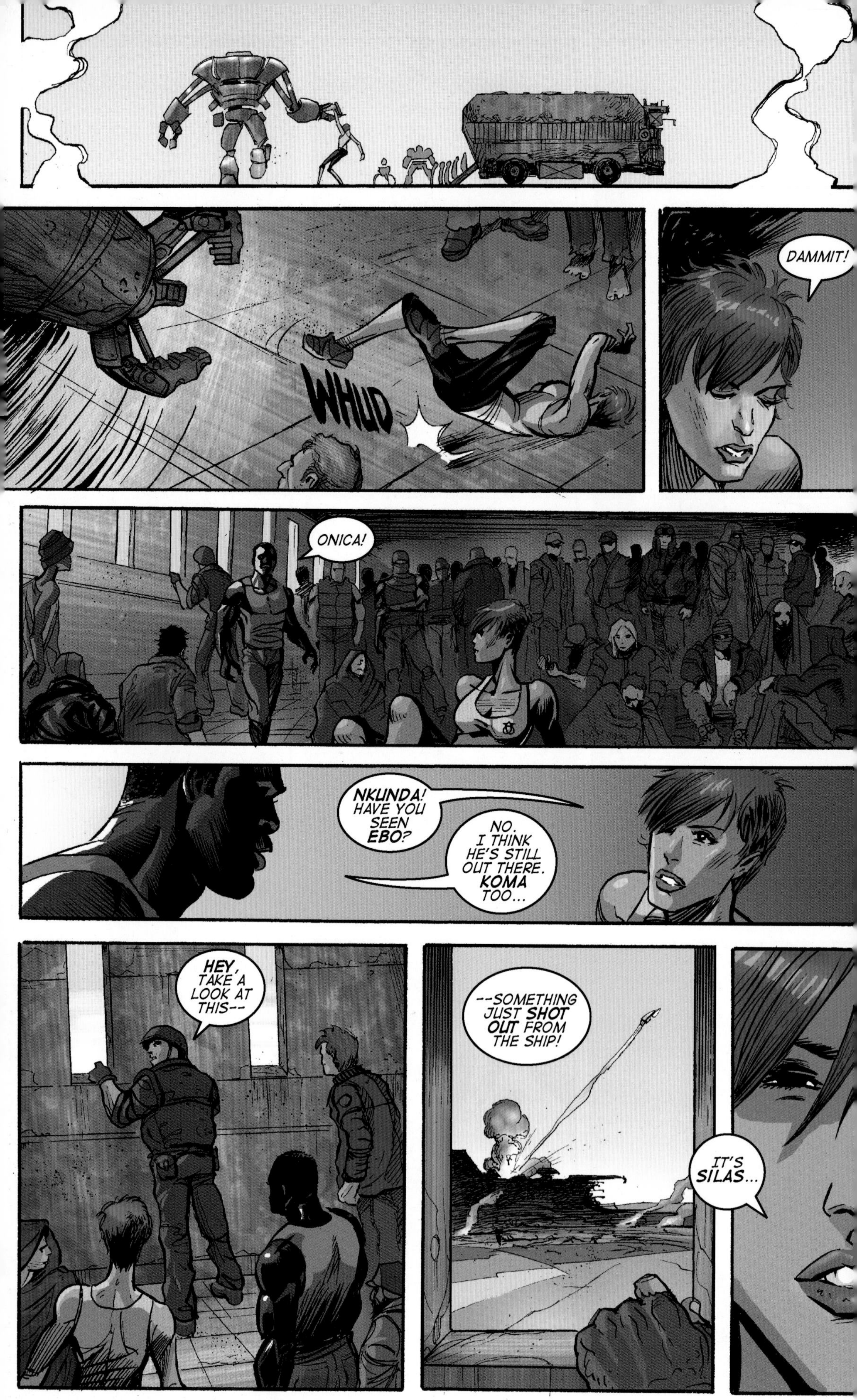
WHUD
DAMMIT!
ONICA!
NKUNDA! HAVE YOU SEEN EBO?
NO. I THINK HE'S STILL OUT THERE. KOMA TOO...
HEY, TAKE A LOOK AT THIS--
--SOMETHING JUST SHOT OUT FROM THE SHIP!
IT'S SILAS...

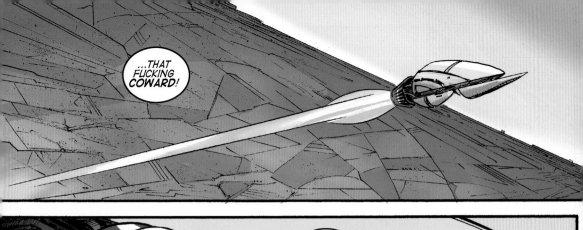

...THAT FUCKING COWARD!

DAMN. I HAVE NO IDEA HOW TO FLY THIS THING. COMPUTER, ACTIVATE PROGRAM: RICTER.

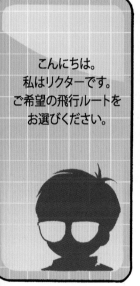

こんにちは。
私はリクターです。
ご希望の飛行ルートを
お選びください。

OH, UH...

CALIBRATE LANGUAGE.

GREETINGS.

I AM RICTER, YOUR INTERACTIVE ANALYTICAL ASSISTANT.

PLEASE VOCALIZE YOUR DESIRED FLIGHT PATH.

ONE SECOND...

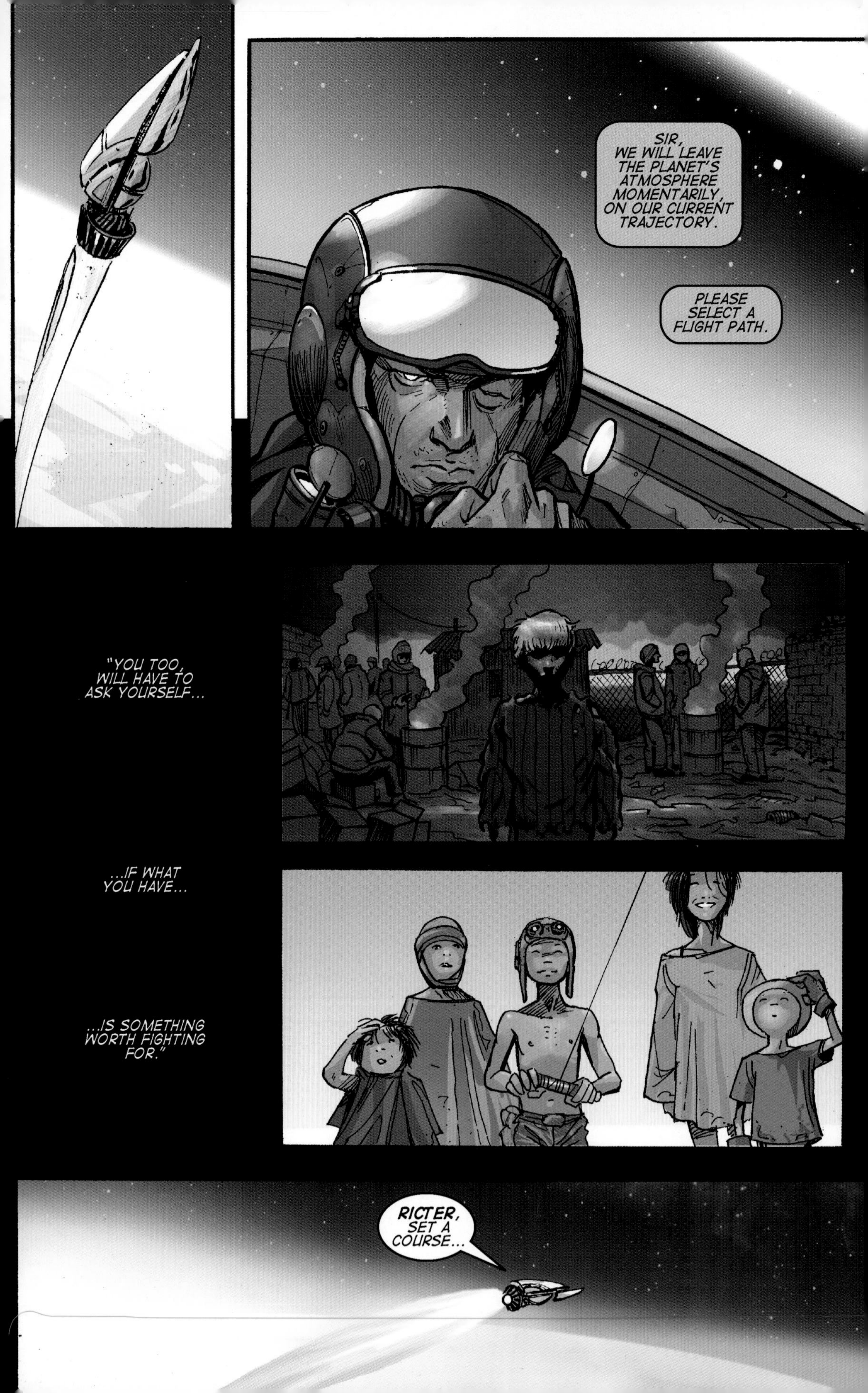
SIR, WE WILL LEAVE THE PLANET'S ATMOSPHERE MOMENTARILY, ON OUR CURRENT TRAJECTORY.
PLEASE SELECT A FLIGHT PATH.
"YOU TOO, WILL HAVE TO ASK YOURSELF...
...IF WHAT YOU HAVE...
...IS SOMETHING WORTH FIGHTING FOR."
RICTER, SET A COURSE...

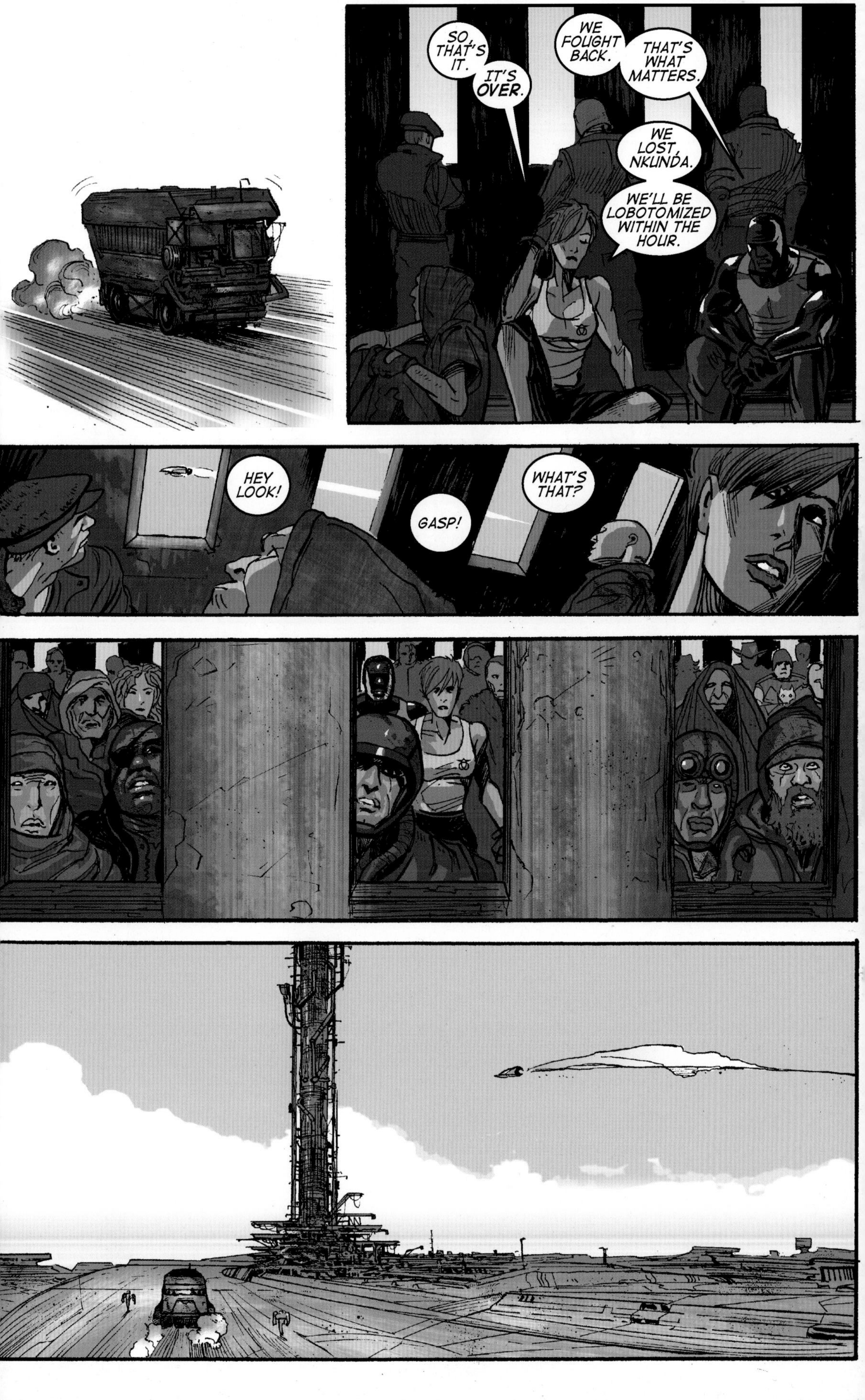
SO, THAT'S IT.
IT'S OVER.
WE FOUGHT BACK.
THAT'S WHAT MATTERS.
WE LOST, NKUNDA.
WE'LL BE LOBOTOMIZED WITHIN THE HOUR.
HEY LOOK!
GASP!
WHAT'S THAT?

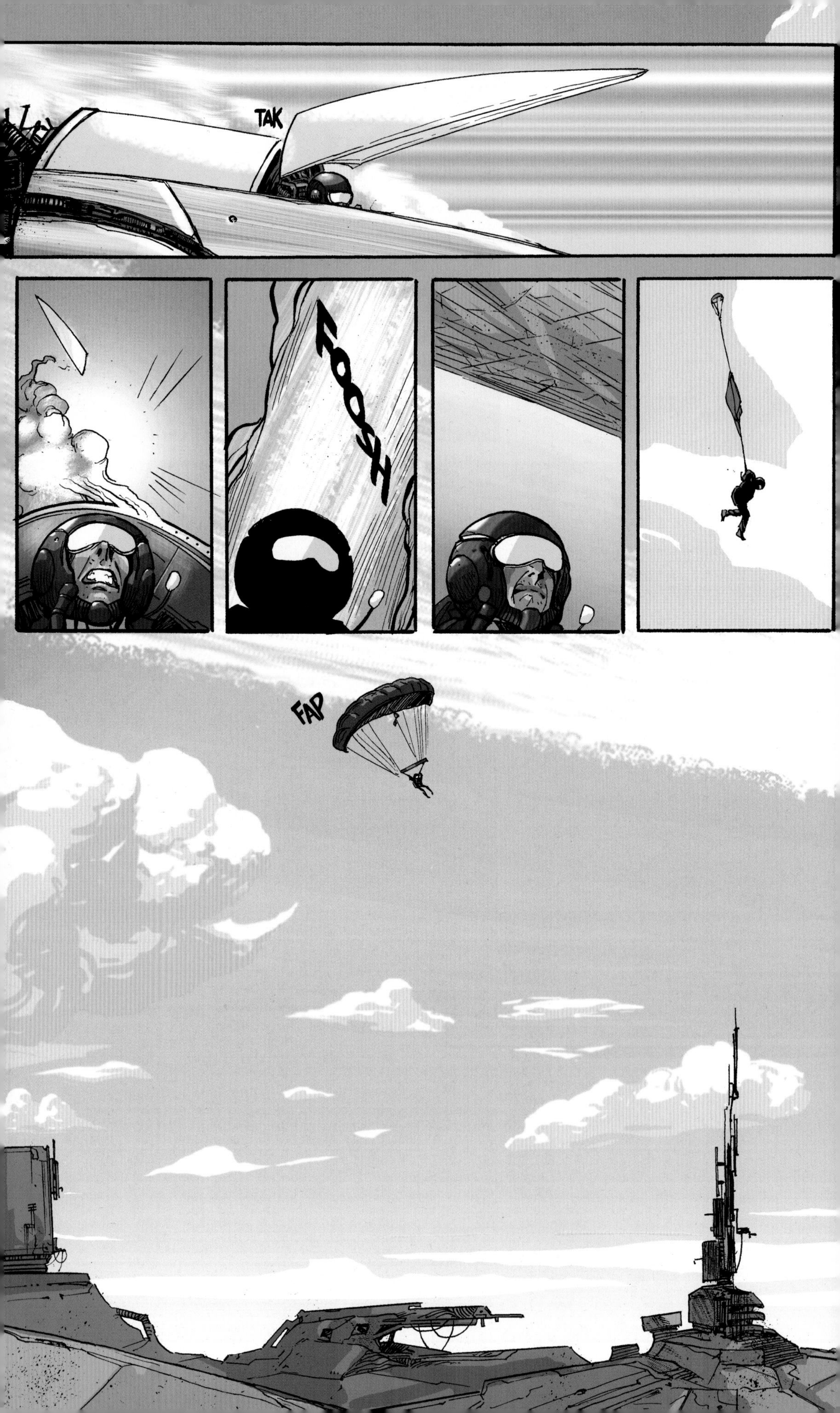
TAK
FOOSH
FAP

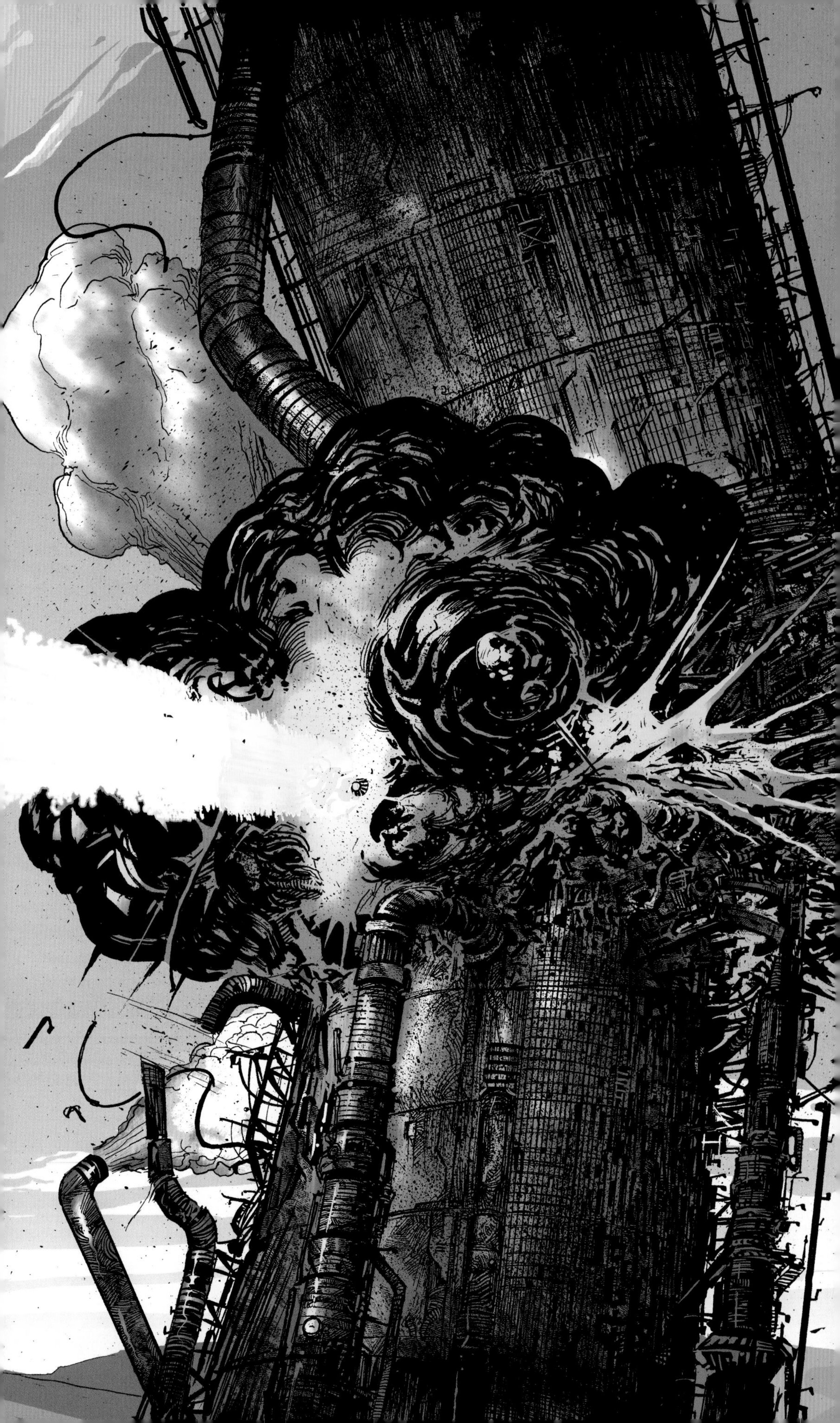

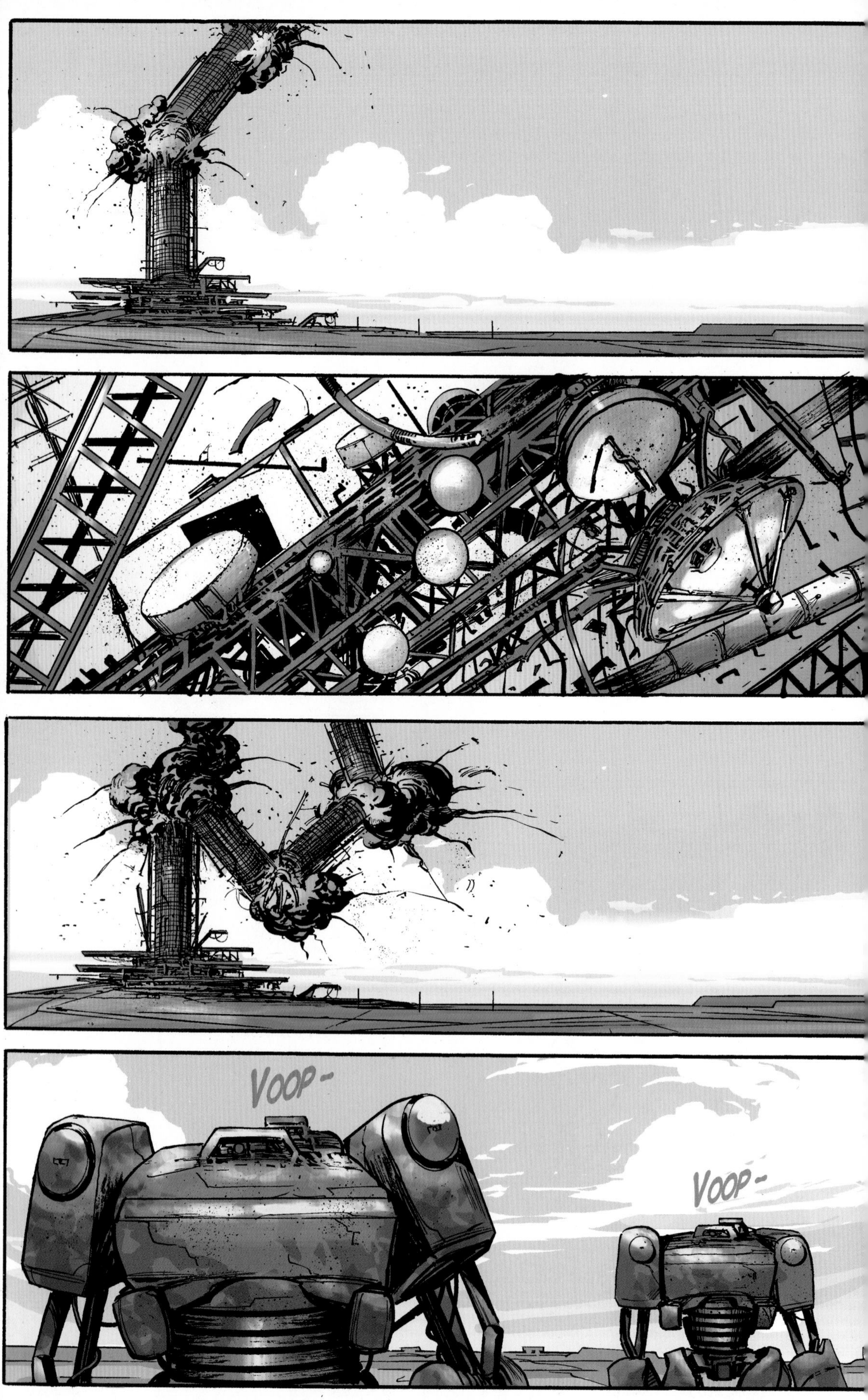
VOOP-
VOOP-

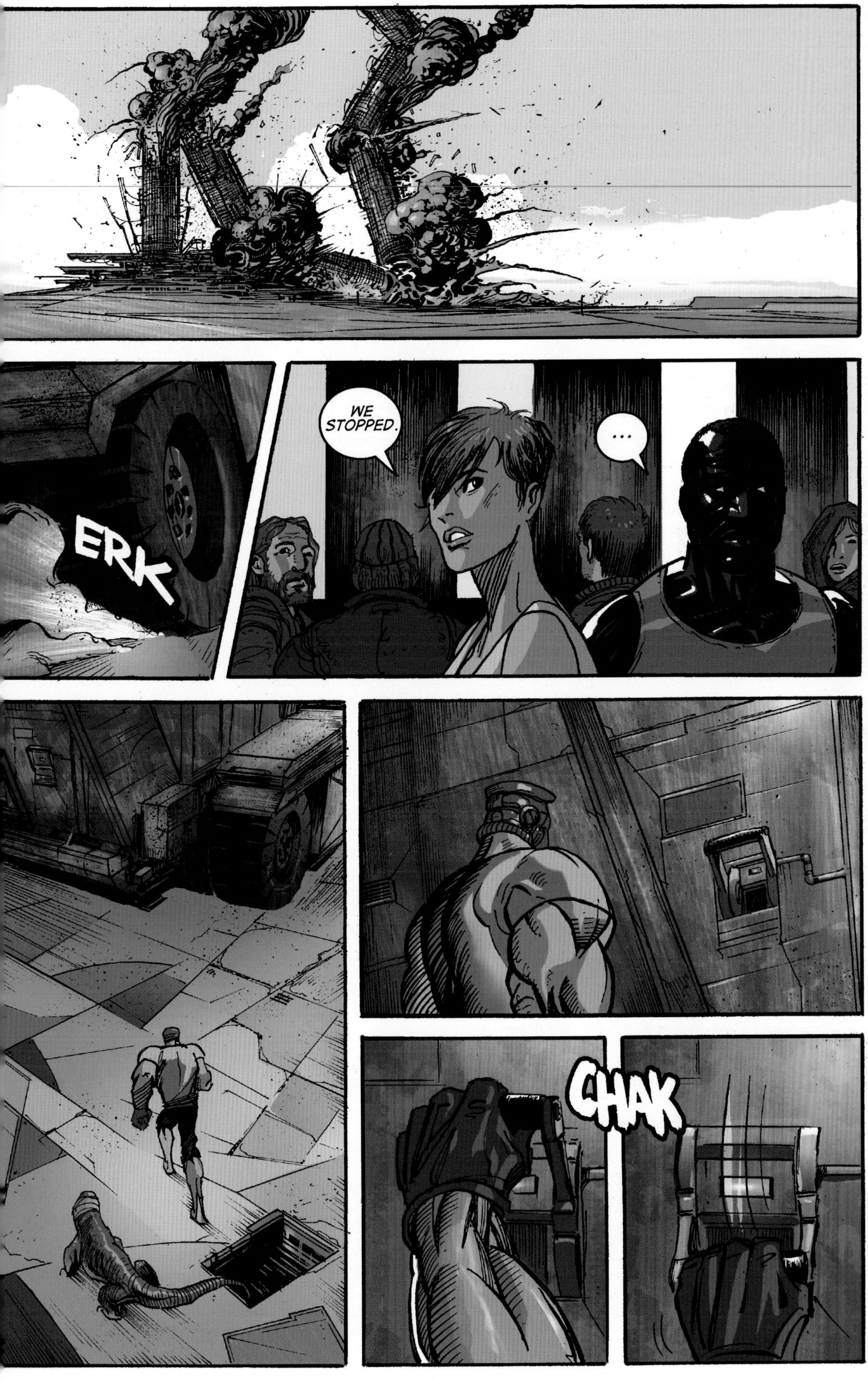
ERK
WE STOPPED.
...
CHAK

*ENSIGN! WHAT THE **HELL** IS GOING ON DOWN THERE?

SIR, THE **SKY LADDER** HAS SUSTAINED SOME SORT OF **IMPACT!**

THE STATION IS IN RAPID **DESCENT!**

QUICKLY, BEGIN **EMERGENCY** EVACUATION PROCEDURES!

NO TIME, SIR!

WE'RE GOING **DOWN!**

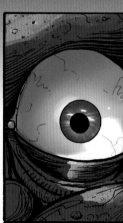

*TRANSLATED FROM ONO MAO NEURO-SPEAK

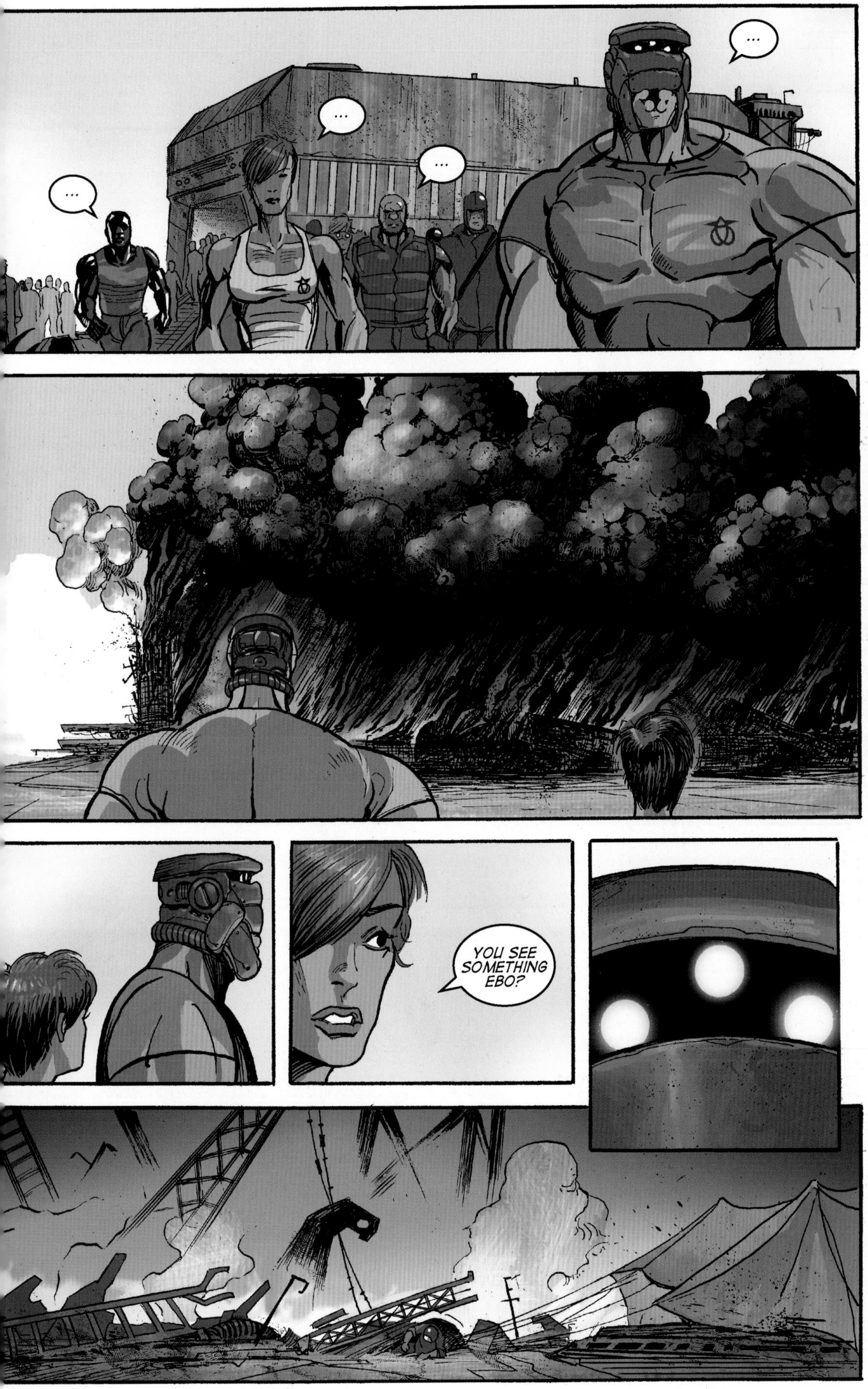
...
...
...
...
YOU SEE SOMETHING EBO?

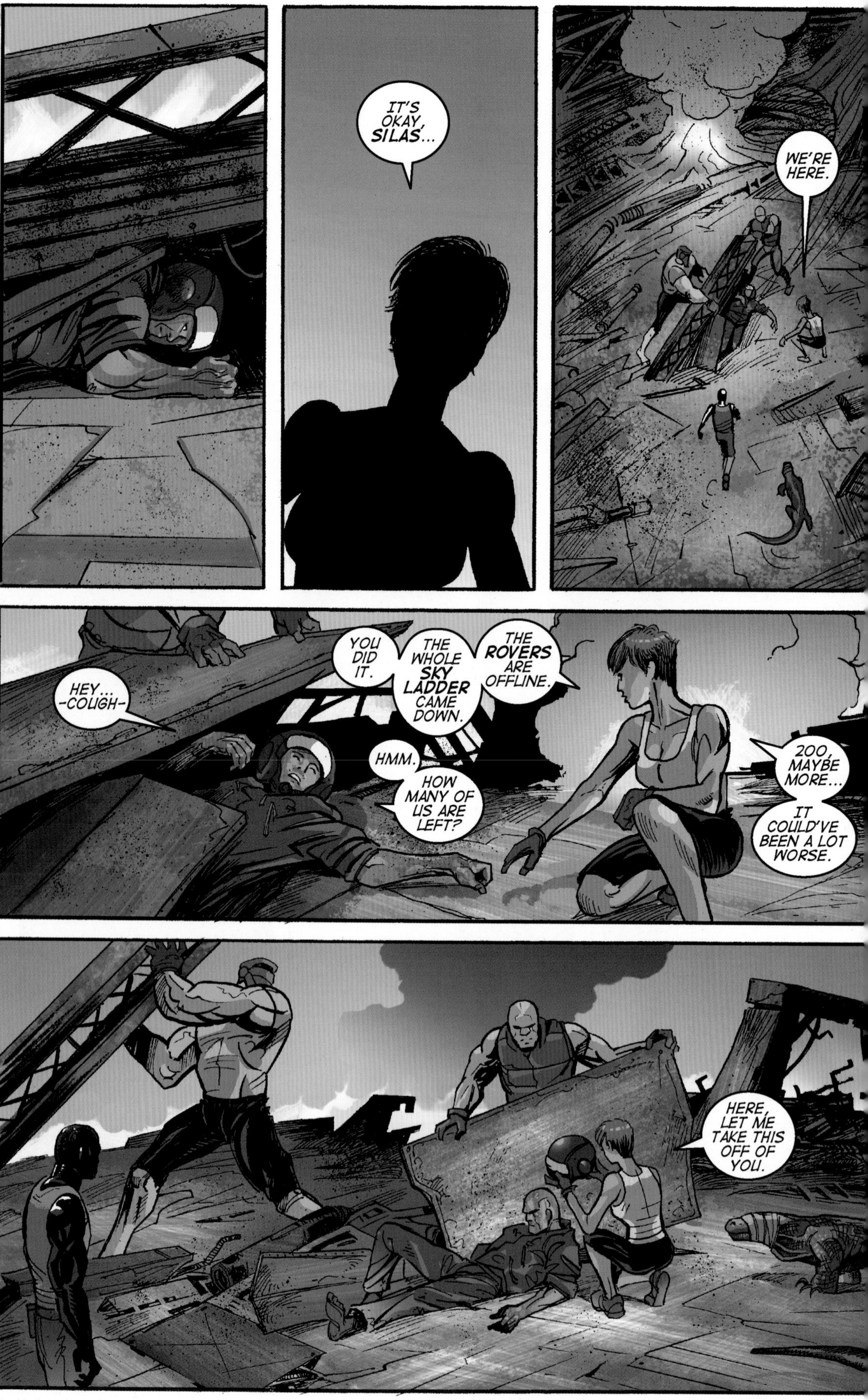
IT'S OKAY, SILAS...
WE'RE HERE.
HEY... -COUGH-
YOU DID IT.
THE WHOLE SKY LADDER CAME DOWN.
THE ROVERS ARE OFFLINE.
HMM. HOW MANY OF US ARE LEFT?
200, MAYBE MORE...
IT COULD'VE BEEN A LOT WORSE.
HERE, LET ME TAKE THIS OFF OF YOU.

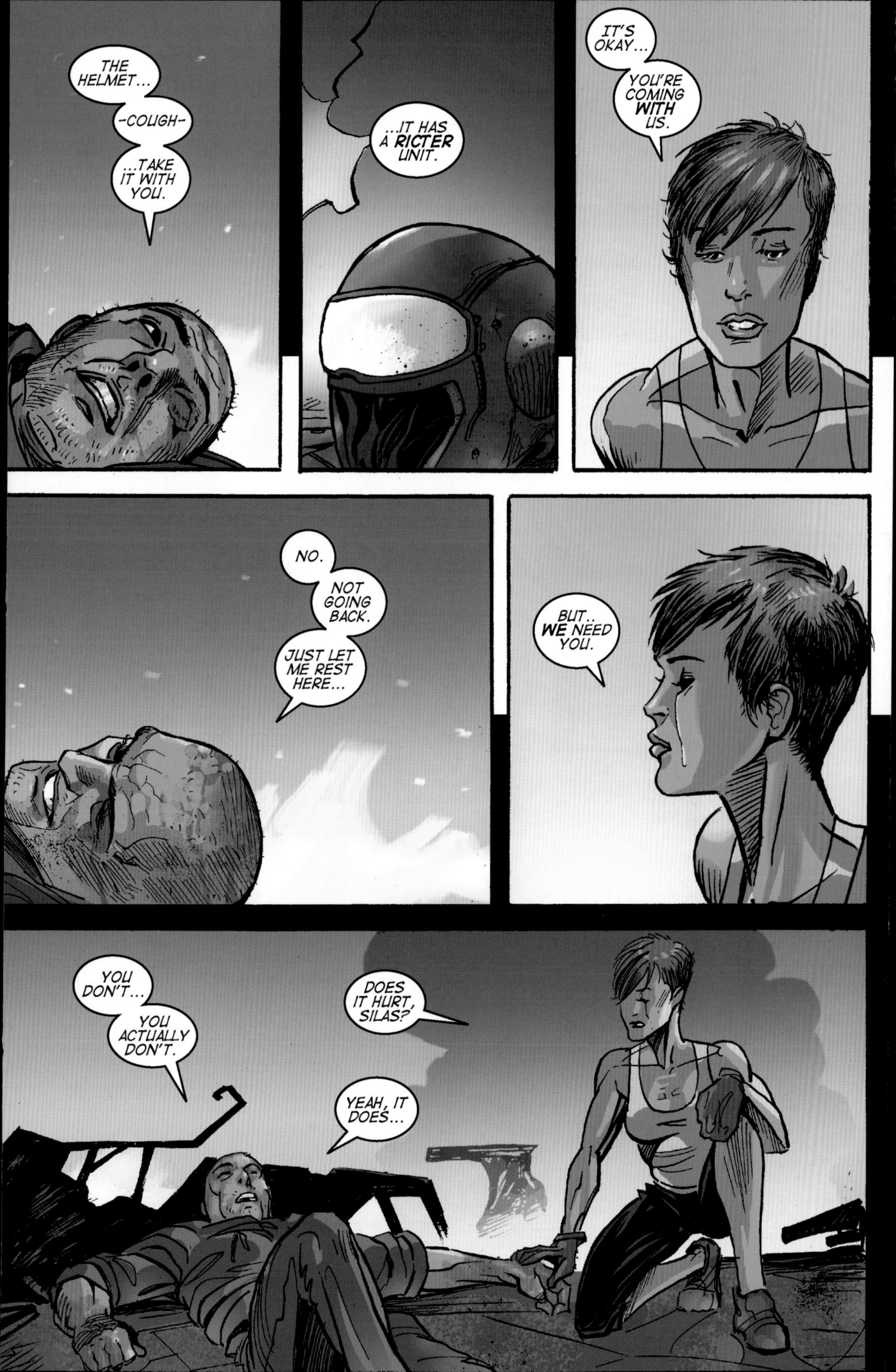
THE HELMET...
-COUGH-
...TAKE IT WITH YOU.
...IT HAS A RICTER UNIT.
IT'S OKAY...
YOU'RE COMING WITH US.
NO.
NOT GOING BACK.
JUST LET ME REST HERE...
BUT.. WE NEED YOU.
YOU DON'T...
YOU ACTUALLY DON'T.
DOES IT HURT, SILAS?
YEAH, IT DOES...

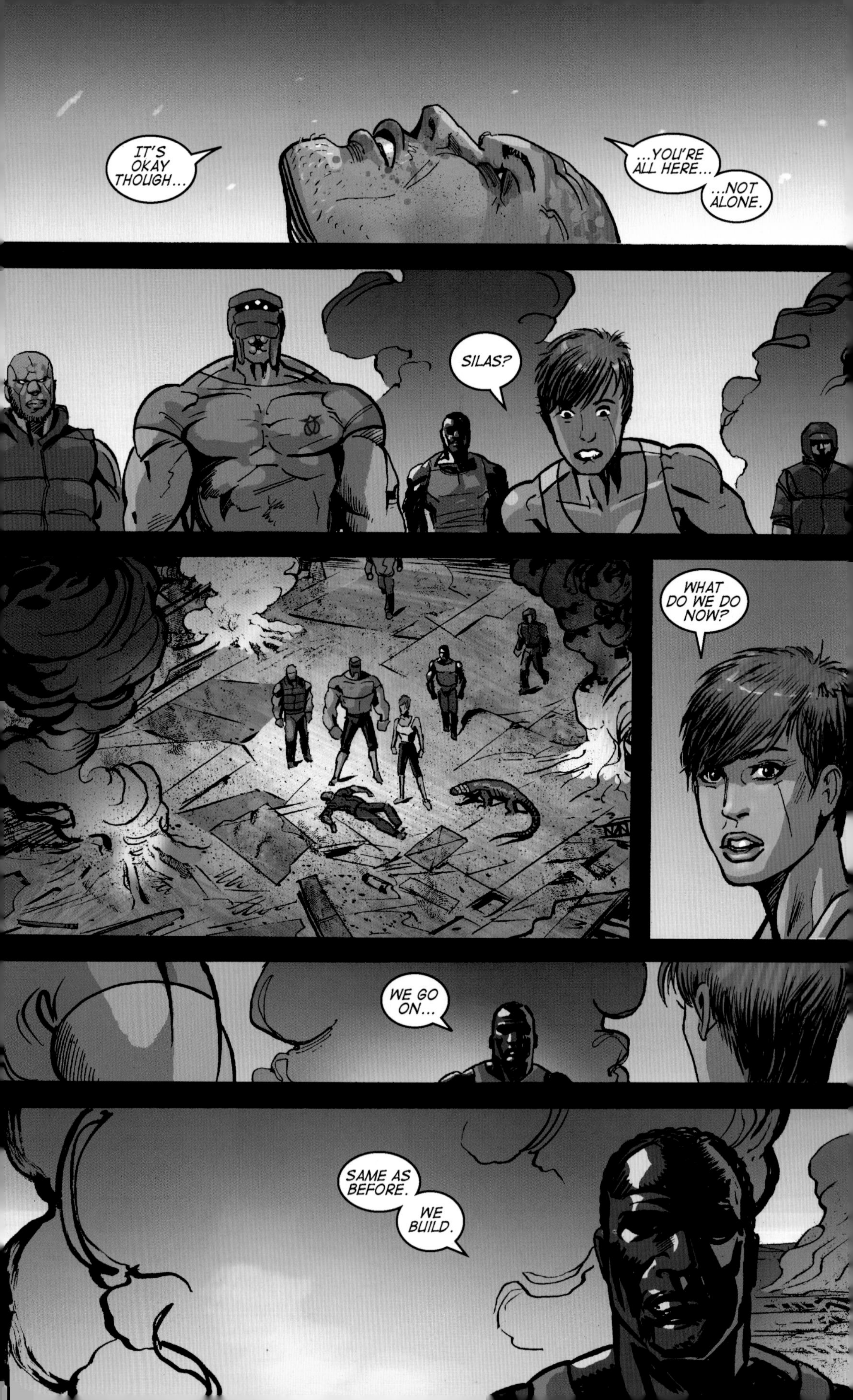
IT'S OKAY THOUGH...
...YOU'RE ALL HERE...
...NOT ALONE.
SILAS?
WHAT DO WE DO NOW?
WE GO ON...
SAME AS BEFORE.
WE BUILD.

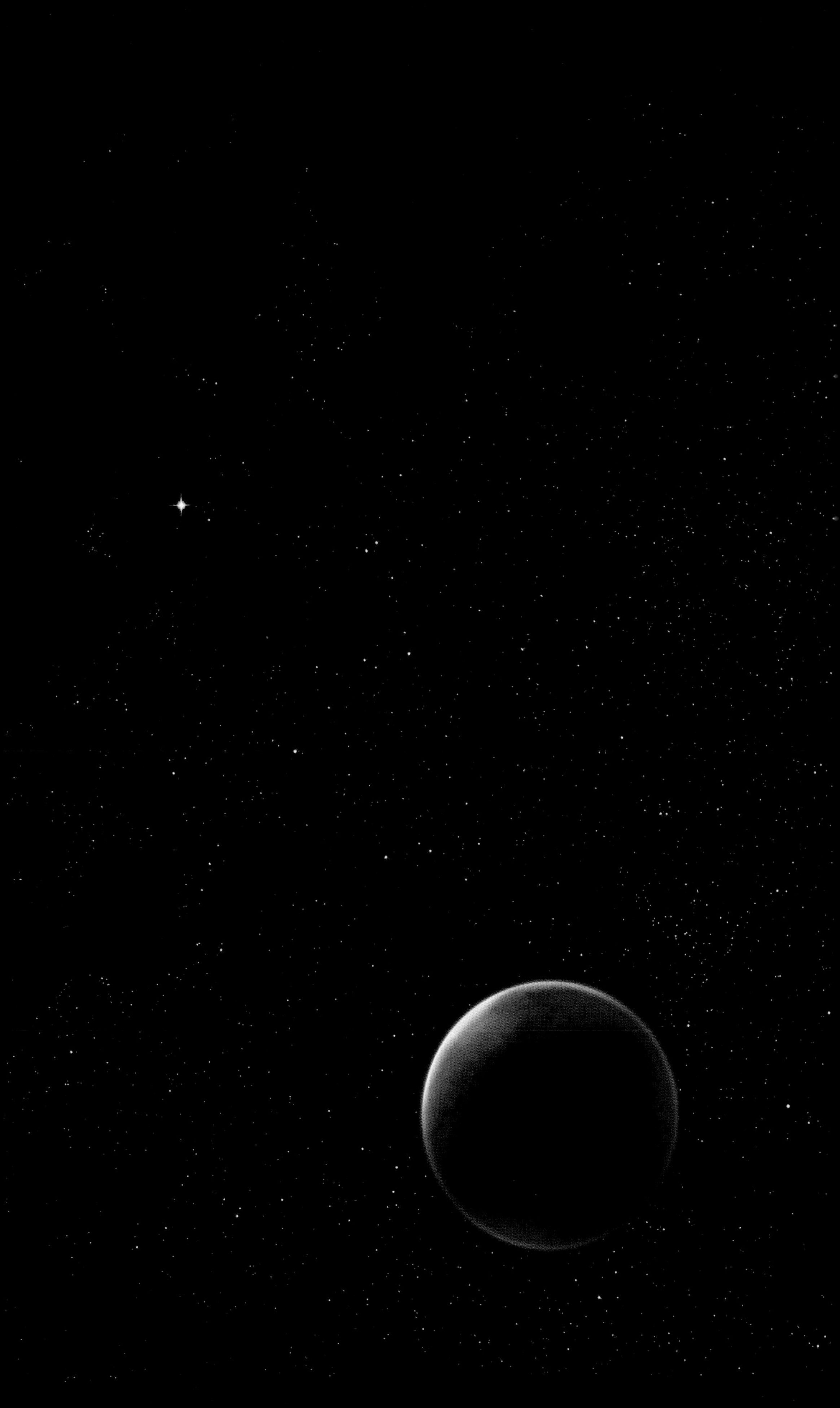

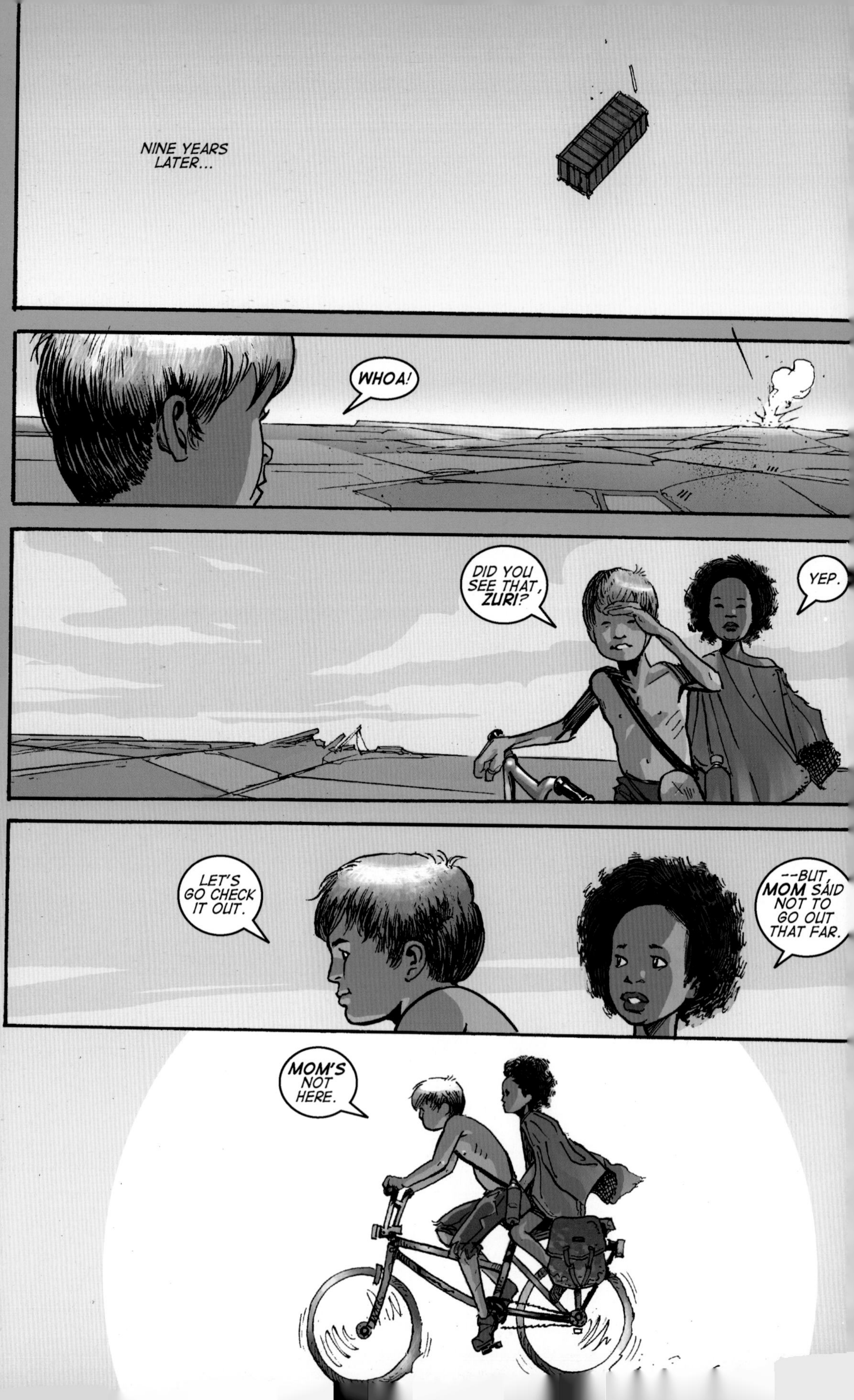
NINE YEARS LATER...
WHOA!
DID YOU SEE THAT, ZURI?
YEP.
LET'S GO CHECK IT OUT.
--BUT, MOM SAID NOT TO GO OUT THAT FAR.
MOM'S NOT HERE.

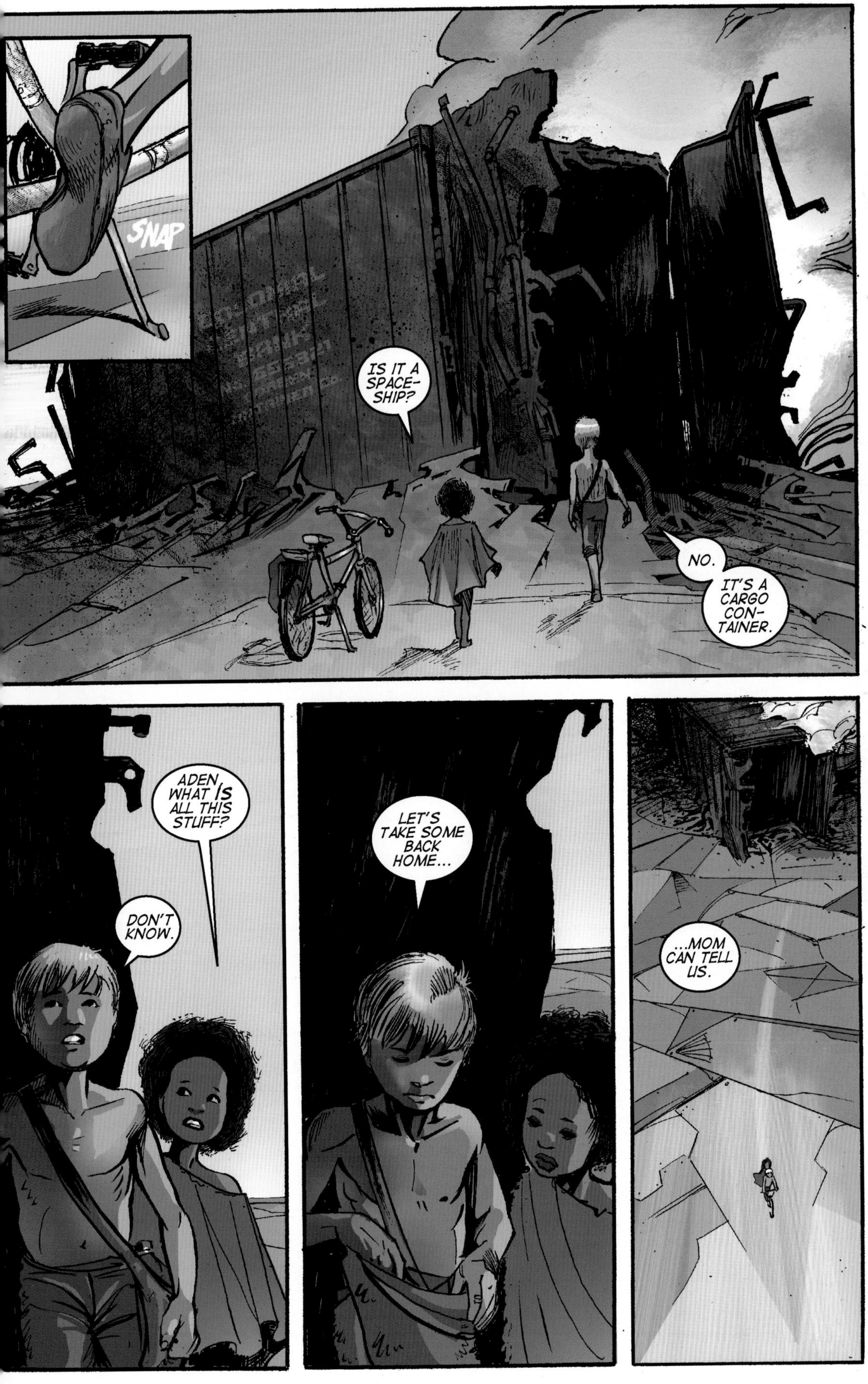

SNAP
IS IT A SPACE-SHIP?
NO.
IT'S A CARGO CON-TAINER.
ADEN WHAT IS ALL THIS STUFF?
DON'T KNOW.
LET'S TAKE SOME BACK HOME...
...MOM CAN TELL US.

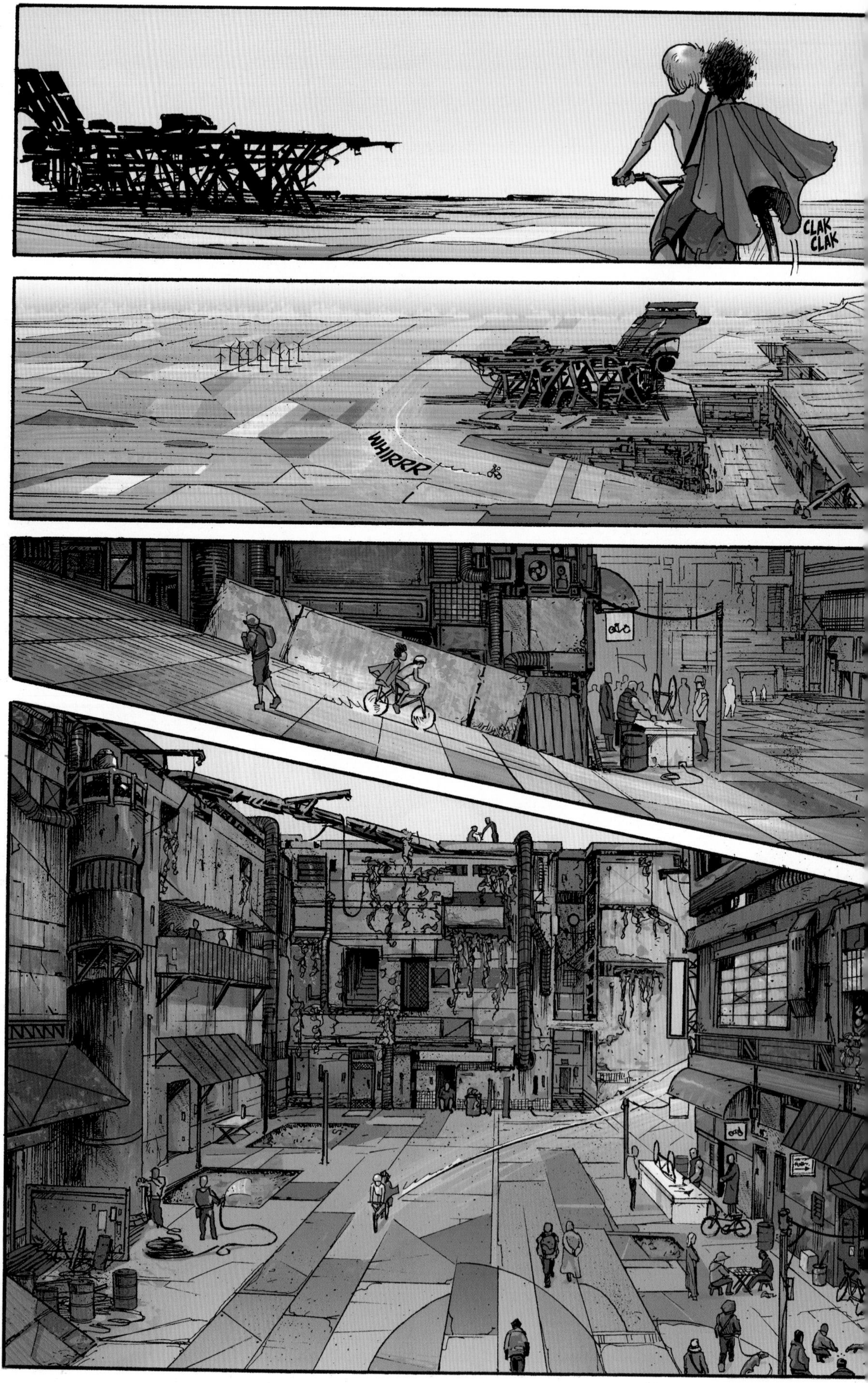
CLAK
CLAK
WHIRRR

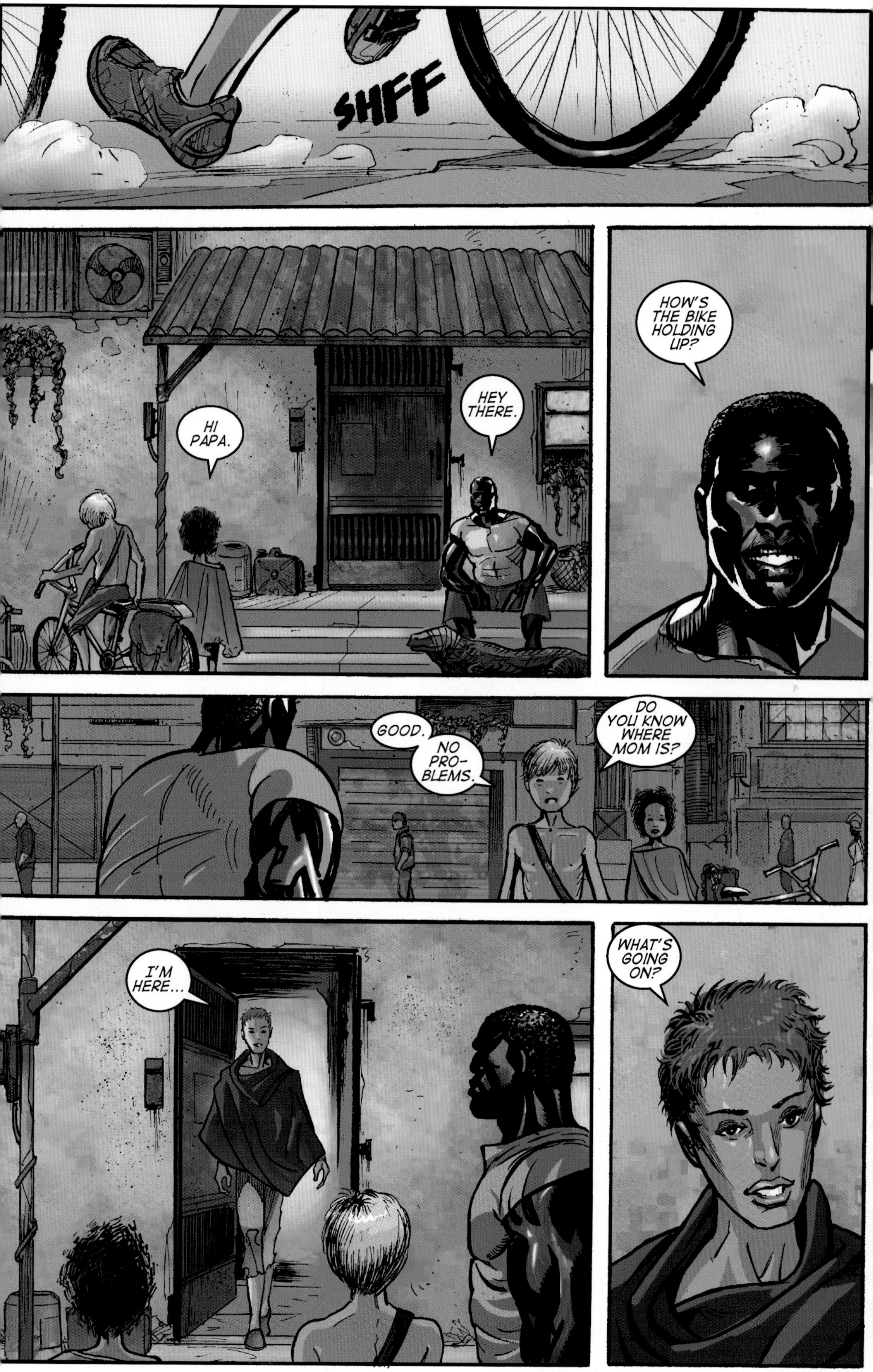
SHFF
HI PAPA.
HEY THERE.
HOW'S THE BIKE HOLDING UP?
GOOD.
NO PRO-BLEMS.
DO YOU KNOW WHERE MOM IS?
I'M HERE...
WHAT'S GOING ON?

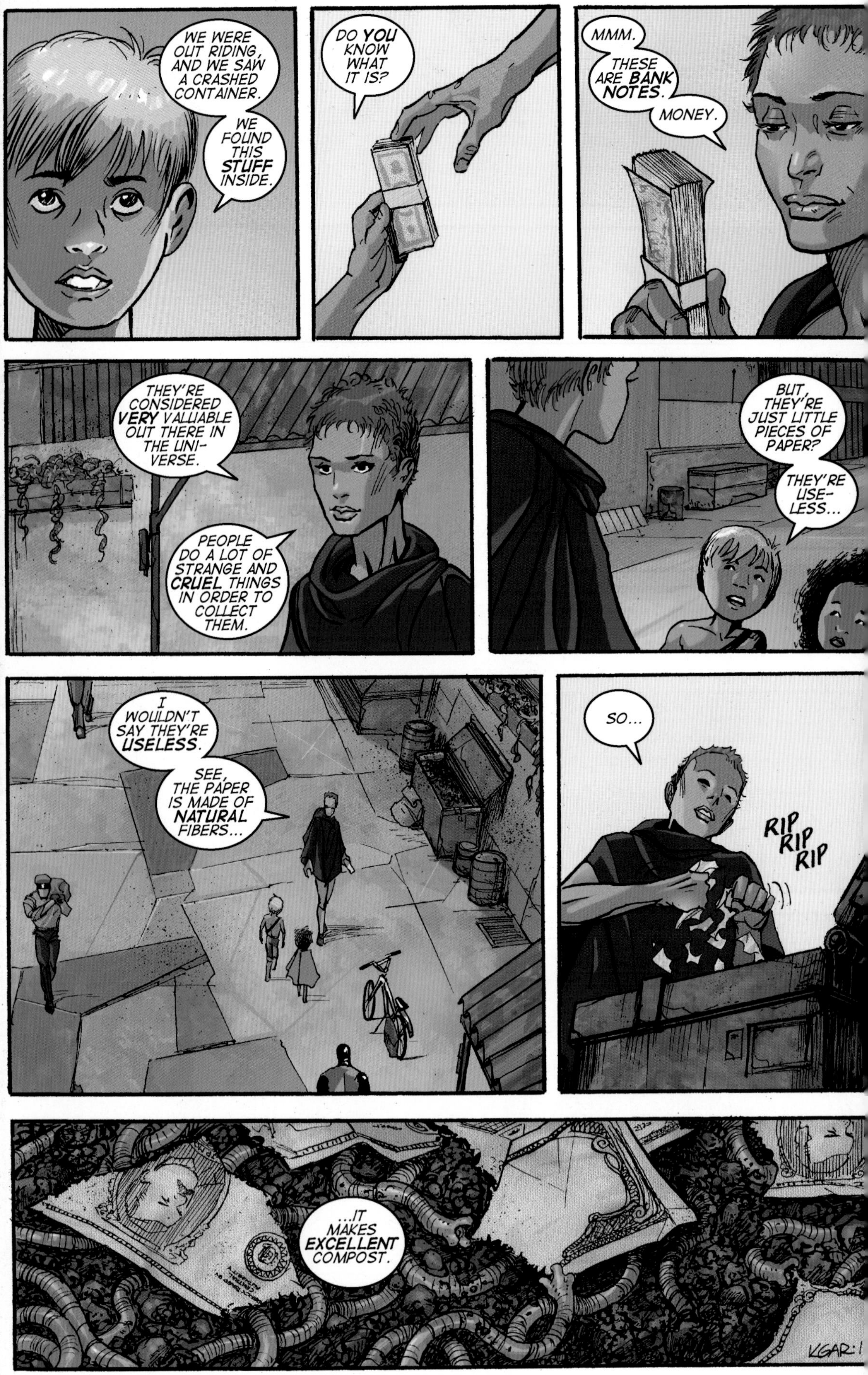
WE WERE OUT RIDING, AND WE SAW A CRASHED CONTAINER.
WE FOUND THIS **STUFF** INSIDE.
DO **YOU** KNOW WHAT IT IS?
MMM.
THESE ARE **BANK NOTES**.
MONEY.
THEY'RE CONSIDERED **VERY** VALUABLE OUT THERE IN THE UNI-VERSE.
PEOPLE DO A LOT OF STRANGE AND **CRUEL** THINGS IN ORDER TO COLLECT THEM.
BUT, THEY'RE JUST LITTLE PIECES OF PAPER?
THEY'RE USE-LESS...
I WOULDN'T SAY THEY'RE **USELESS**.
SEE, THE PAPER IS MADE OF **NATURAL** FIBERS...
SO...
RIP RIP RIP
...IT MAKES **EXCELLENT** COMPOST.
KGAR:1

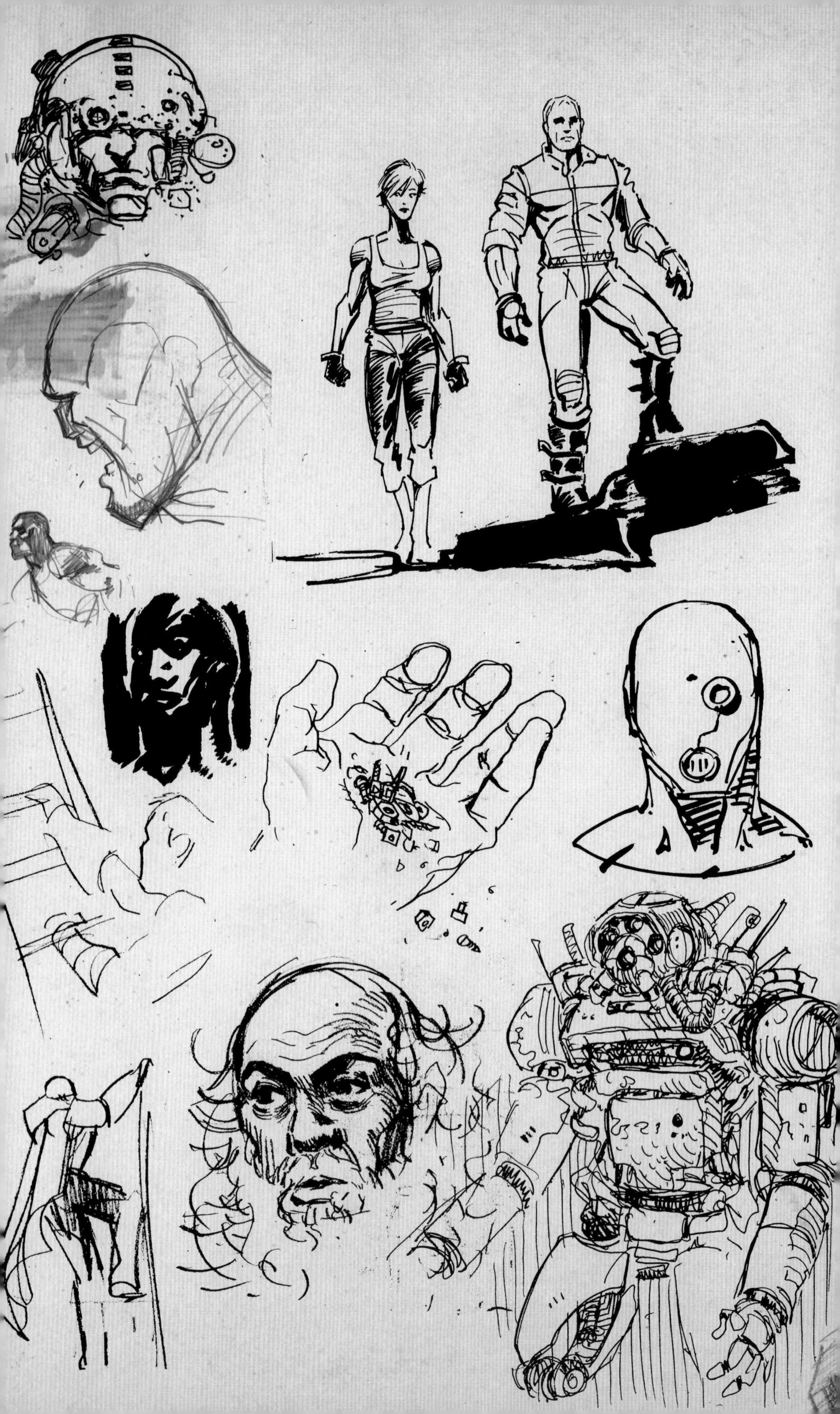

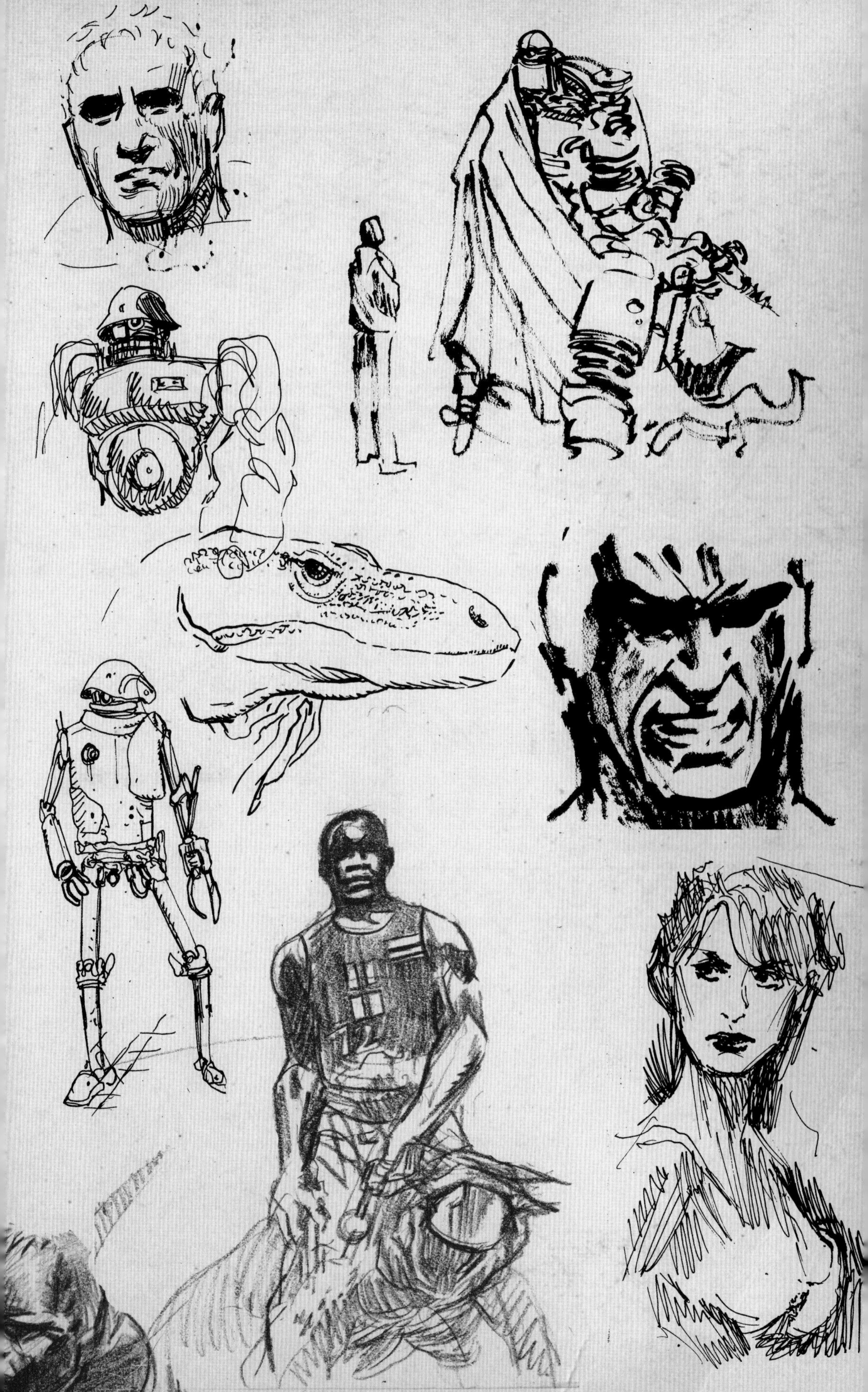

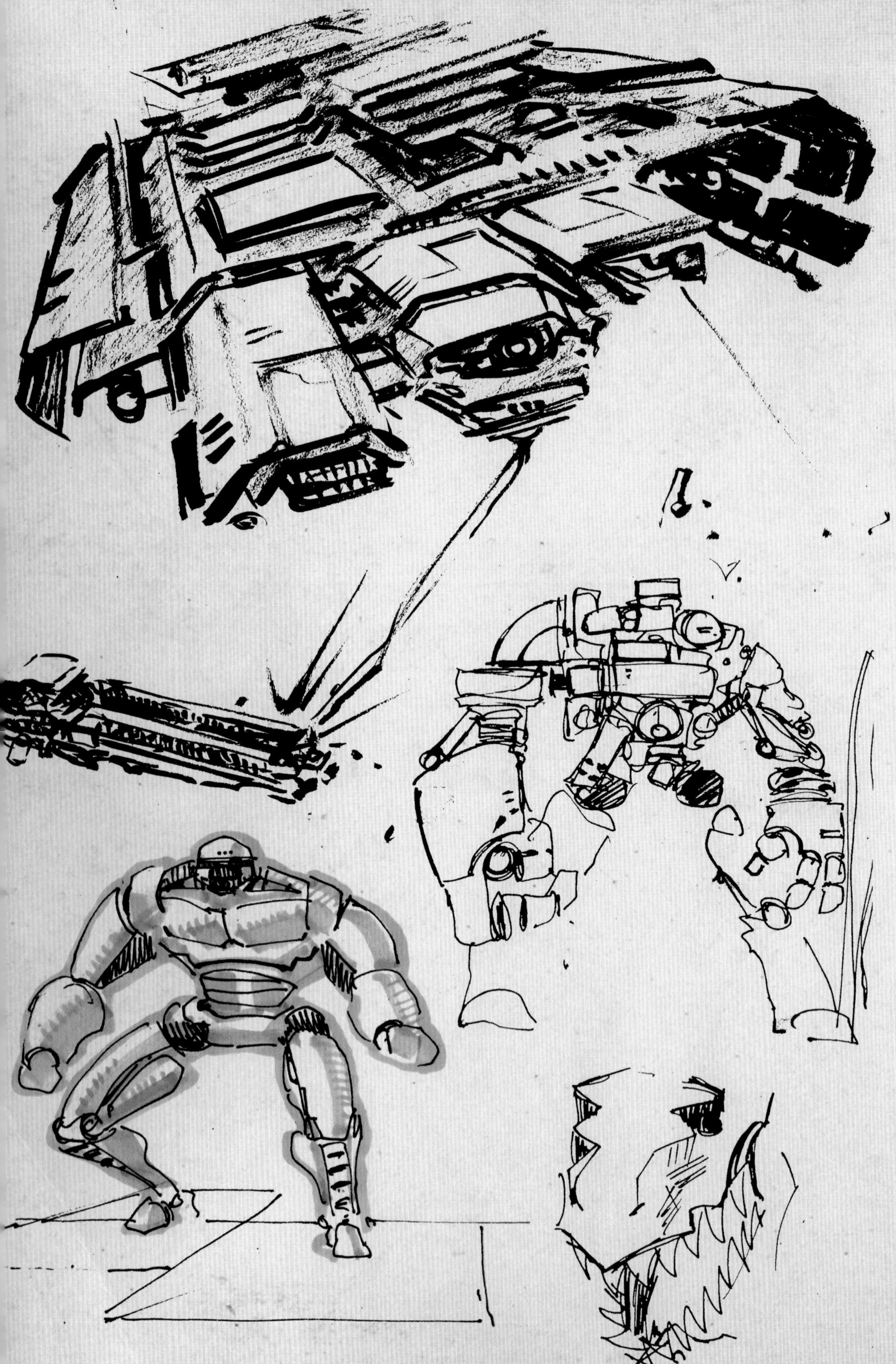

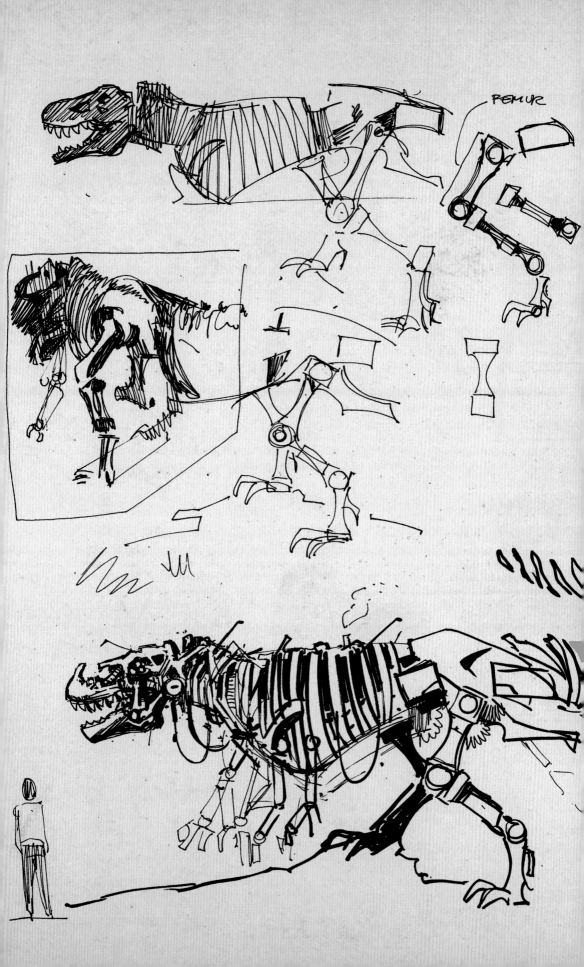

FEMUR

The creation of Planetoid has at least one commonality with the story itself, which is that very little in life is accomplished without the help and support of others. So, it is my pleasure to acknowledge and thank some of the great people who have helped me in getting this story out of my head and into your hands.

This book is dedicated to my parents who have never wavered in their love and support of me and my pursuit of a career comics. I must thank the hardworking team at Image Comics. Major thanks to Eric Stephenson who took a chance on this comic and showed great patience with its gaffe-prone creator. Also at Image, I want to thank the very talented Drew Gill who designed the Planetoid logo and inside covers, in addition to walking me through the technical aspects of comic book production. Thanks, Drew! And, of course, I'm in great debt to Ron Richards for championing this work and bringing it to Image in the first place.

I want to thank all of the comics community, and specifically the readers and retailers who supported this comic. Along the way I have been fortunate to have received words of encouragement from creators like: Erik Larsen, Nate Simpson, Brandon Graham, Sean Murphy, Joe Keatinge and Michael Moreci. I owe a particular debt to Paul Montgomery of iFanboy and Rob Patey from AICN for shining a spotlight on this comic early on.

And last but not least — in fact, most — I want to thank the lovely Yuka Kawakami who lived and breathed Planetoid for over a year with me.

› Ken Garing

9